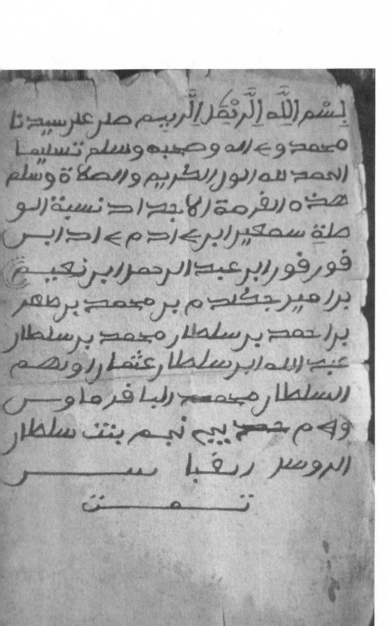

بِسْمِ اللَّهِ الرَّحْمَنِ الرَّحِيمِ صَلَّ عَلَى سَيِّدِنَا
مُحَمَّد وَ عَلَى اللَّه وَصَحْبِهِ وَسَلَّمَ تَسْلِيمًا
الحَمْدُ لِلَّهِ النُّورِ الكَرِيمِ وَالصَّلَاةِ وَسَلَّمَ
هَذِهِ الفُرْصَة الأَبْجَدِ انَّ نِسْبَة الوُ
صْلَة سَمَكِير ابْرَكَدَم بَرَدَ ابْس
فُورِ فُورِ ابْرِ عَبْدِ الرَّحْمَن ابْرِ نَعِيم
بَرَ مِيرِ جَكَدَم بَرِ مُحَمَّد بَرِ طَغَر
بَرَ حَمَد بَرِ سُلْطَان مُحَمَّد بَرِ سُلْطَان
عُبَيد اللَّه ابْرِ سُلْطَان عُثْمَان رَاوَنَصَم
السُّلْطَان مُحَمَّد الباَ فِرْ مَاوَس
وَهُم حُمَد يَجِي نُجُم بِنْت سُلْطَان
الروسر رِيقَبا سِسُ
تَمَّت

di *nasaliya*, or genealogy

Dar al-Kuti and the Last
of the Trans-Saharan
Slave Trade

Dar al-Kuti and the Last Years of the Trans-Saharan Slave Trade

Dennis D. Cordell

The University of Wisconsin Press

Published 1985

The University of Wisconsin Press
114 North Murray Street
Madison, Wisconsin 53715

The University of Wisconsin Press, Ltd.
1 Gower Street
London WC1E 6HA, England

First printing

Printed in the United States of America

Library of Congress Cataloging in Publication Data
Cordell, Dennis D., 1947–
    Dar al-Kuti and the last years of the trans-Saharan slave trade.
    Bibliography: pp. 246–268.
    Includes index.
    1. Dar-al-Kuti (Central African Republic)—History.
2. Slave-trade—Central African Republic—Dar-al-Kuti.
I. Title.
DT546.39.D37C67   1984   967'.41   84-40147
ISBN 0-299-09520-7

For Joel and Ron

Contents

Maps

Figures

Acknowledgments

It is a pleasant duty to offer at long last my appreciation to all who have provided me guidance, encouragement, and assistance over the course of this project. First mention must go to the people of Dar al-Kuti who welcomed me into their homes and shared their knowledge of the past with me. Most of those who gave their time so willingly are listed in the bibliography, but special thanks are due Abakar Tidjani, a grandson of Muhammad al-Sanusi and municipal leader in Ndele, who took an active concern in recording the history of the sultanate and introduced me to many people in Ndele. In addition, the advice and aid of Muhammad Abakar, my research assistant, were very much appreciated.

An expression of gratitude is also due numerous Central African governmental officials, in both Bangui and Ndele. Iddi Lala, former director of the Ecole Nationale d'Administration, and his family graciously invited me to share their home for several weeks during my first stay in Bangui, and their hospitality and continuing friendship are much appreciated. I would also like to thank Messieurs Yessi and Licky of the Musée Boganda, the institution in charge of overseeing research in the Central African Republic, for their help and advice. In Ndele local officials were very conscious of the need to record the past of the region and helped me whenever possible, and I would like to thank Zoumande David, former Préfet du Bamingui-Bangoran, Madame Zoumande, and Akem David for their efforts on my behalf.

Other individuals in the Central African Republic, France, and Chad contributed much to this study. Joe Kimmins, a former director of the Peace Corps in the Central African Republic, was a constant source of practical assistance and encouragement. His perceptive comments concerning the problems facing the country and its people displayed a concern for the individual African that is all too rare among members of the international assistance establishment. Scott Stephens and Amalia Barbieri, Peace Corps volunteers in Bangassou and Bouar, provided great encouragement, and their arduous rainy-season trek to visit me in Ndele is an event that I have long remembered. In addition, resident French scholars and clergy welcomed me and shared their extensive experience of the country and its people with me. Among them, Professor Dampierre (Bangassou), Professor Vidal (Bouar), R. P. Oliver (Bangui), and R. P. DeMoustier

(Ndele and Miamane) deserve special thanks. In Paris I was fortunate to have the occasion to discuss issues of North Central African history with Professor Pierre Kalck, former resident of the Central African Republic and author of several seminal works on the history of the region, while in Chad I was warmly received by the director and staff of the Institut tchadien des sciences humaines (INTSH), who arranged access to the archives during my brief stay in Ndjaména.

Fellowships from the Social Science Research Council financed my research abroad as well as several months of further work after my return, and a grant from the American Council of Learned Societies enabled me to revise the initial manuscript for publication. Finally, generous awards from the University Lecture Series Fund for Faculty Excellence of Dedman College, at Southern Methodist University, and from Stephen and Fannie Kahn helped finance the publication of this book. I would like to express my gratitude to all of these organizations, institutions, and individuals, while assuming responsibilities for the judgments and conclusions embodied in this work.

Others have been of invaluable assistance during the course of this study. Very special thanks are due my former advisor, Jan Vansina, who has been a constant source of insight, enthusiasm, and inspiration since I first decided to venture into the almost uncharted field of North Central African history. To Steven Feierman I express appreciation for introducing me to the theories of social anthropology which proved central to my research in history. I am grateful to Philip D. Curtin, also a former advisor, for his helpful letters to me in the field and for making me aware of the great excitement and value of cultivating a broad comparative approach to historical investigation. I wish to thank Humphrey J. Fisher, whose lengthy comments on the entire manuscript, and those sections dealing with Islam in particular, greatly improved the final product. I also want to express appreciation to Stephen and Jane Baier for detailed and penetrating criticism of early drafts of this manuscript.

I am also grateful to friends and colleagues at Southern Methodist University. James Early, R. Hal Williams, and David Weber all offered support in their own ways. And for their conscientious work in typing and composing the final version of this manuscript I wish to thank Mona Wildman of the Department of History, and Barbara Huckaby and Peggy Lynn Smith formerly of the Department of History, along with Kathleen Triplett and Sheryl St. Germain of the Office of Word Processing. And I want to express appreciation to June Schelling of the Dedman Graphics Lab who composed the final copy.

Members of my family not only persevered, but offered steady encouragement throughout the long duration of this project. My mother and grandmother were unswerving in their support. Ronald Fiscus has been a source of much appreciated advice and concern since I first considered doing African history when we were Peace Corps volunteers in Chad. Last but by no means least, my lover Joel Gregory has been a constant source of affection, concern, and intellectual stimulation over the past six years. His attention to matters of epistemology and analysis in general, and his comments on economic aspects of this study in particular, have contributed to a much improved book.

List of Abbreviations

Archives

ANF-SOM (Paris)	Archives Nationales de France, Section d'Outre-Mer, Paris
ANF-AE (Paris)	Archives Nationales de France, Ministère des Affaires Etrangères, Paris
AAV (Vincennes)	Archives Nationales de France, Ministère d'Etat chargé de la Défense Nationale, Service historique de l'Armée, Château de Vincennes
ANF-SOM (Aix)	Archives Nationales de France, Section d'Outre-Mer, Dépôt à Aix-en-Provence
PRO (London)	Public Record Office, London
ANT	Archives Nationales du Tchad, Ndjaména
AMBB	Archives du Musée Boganda, Bangui
BENA	Bibliothèque de l'Ecole Nationale d'Administration, Bangui
APBB	Archives de la Préfecture du Bamingui-Bangoran, Ndele
ASPN	Archives de la Sous-Préfecture de Ndele, Ndele
CC	Collection Cabaille, Bangui

Journals

BSRC	*Bulletin de la société des recherches congolaises*
AF	*Afrique Française*
AF-RC	*Afrique Française: renseignements coloniaux*
JAH	*Journal of African History*

Interviews

OA	Oral Accounts, available at the Archives of Traditional Music, Indiana University, Bloomington; and the Memorial Library, University of Wisconsin, Madison

Introduction

In 1750 northern Ubangi-Shari remained quite isolated. Ties between this area and the Zaire region were few, and connections with the Muslim north were intermittent at best. The region thus lay between the two commercial systems that linked North Central Africa with the outer world. To the south and southwest, the Zaire basin trading network drained slaves and ivory to the West African coast and the Atlantic economy, while to the north, caravans took the same exports across the Sahara to the Mediterranean and the Middle East.

Northern Ubangi-Shari lay just south of the Islamic frontier, a zone that roughly coincided with the southern limits of the Muslim sultanates of Wadai, Bagirmi, and Dar Fur. In this area, as in other parts of Sahelian Africa, the Muslim states near the desert edge acted as the major intermediaries between areas farther south and the wider world north of the Sahara. Although the links between the sultanates and northern Ubangi-Shari were tenuous in the eighteenth century, they heralded the integration of the region into the emerging international economy. Beginning in the sixteenth century, the regional economy of the Mediterranean basin and northwestern Europe became increasingly global, and by the late eighteenth century its peripheries included the Americas, East and South Asia, and the coasts of Africa.[1] While Europe ultimately became the core of this expanding economy, the Islamic world lay on its nearest periphery and progressively became a part of it. And via the expansion of the Muslim economies, other more distant regions were drawn into the world economy. Such was certainly the case with Africa just south of the Sahara in general, and the societies of Ubangi-Shari in particular. These societies had always altered in response to internal needs and external pressures, but the growth of contact with the global economy brought greater and more rapid change—at first by way of the expanding Muslim economies to the north, and then through European penetration from the south. This was the dominant theme in the history of northern Ubangi-Shari for the next hundred and fifty years. Many other changes were related to it.

The primary aim of this study is to examine the expansion of contact between Muslims and non-Muslims along the Islamic frontier in North Central Africa in the nineteenth and early twentieth centuries. The study focuses on the Muslim sultanate of Dar al-Kuti but also explores broader historical themes. The inquiry thus proceeds on two levels, an approach that recommends itself for two reasons. First, very few local historical studies exist for this part of Africa, and Dar al-Kuti was of sufficient importance to merit this kind of attention. In the early 1800s Dar al-Kuti was simply a geographical expression appended to a stretch of the Islamic frontier on the southwestern fringes of the Muslim state of Wadai. During the course of the century, however, Muslim influence became more pronounced, and the area became a province of the Wadaian client state of Dar Runga. Then in the 1890s it emerged as a nearly autonomous entity with its own sphere of influence encompassing north-central and eastern Ubangi-Shari all the way to the present border between the Central African Republic and the Sudan. Its economy was based on slave-raiding, slave-trading, agriculture, and the exchange of captives for northern trade goods. These activities brought profound changes to non-Muslim societies throughout the area.

But to write about Dar al-Kuti without any reference to the regional context would result in a study of restricted value. If specific studies are few, general histories of this part of Africa—today's Central African Republic, Chad, southern Libya, and western and southern Sudan—are virtually non-existent.[2] It thus seems both wise and useful to place the history of Dar al-Kuti in the context of the history of the surrounding area.

In fact, Dar al-Kuti serves quite well as a touchstone for a regional study. The themes of the sultanate's history may to a large degree be viewed as local manifestations of general trends. Such pairing is apparent in part 1. The first chapter presents the broad history of relations between Muslims and non-Muslims in North Central Africa, while the following two chapters detail the nature and development of such contacts in Dar al-Kuti. The overview is based largely on printed sources, while the local history grows out of oral traditions and archival research. This complementary approach, in both scope and source materials, is meant to provide a local study while going some of the way toward presenting a broader history.

The three chapters of part 2 focus on Ndele, a settlement founded in the late 1890s as the capital of Dar al-Kuti, and the area immediately around it. Chapter 4 is a study of the organization of the city, based in large part on exploration of the extensive ruins of the town that are still visible today. Chapters 5 and 6 deal with political economy—slavery, the slave trade, agriculture, and long-distance trade. These chapters thus comprise a micro-history of precolonial Ndele. But at the same time they, too, have wider significance. Ndele was probably the most important slave-raiding and slave-trading capital in North Central Africa, but it was by no means the only one. There were similar settlements throughout the area: Dem Zubayr, Dem Idris, and Dem Genawi in the Bahr al-Ghazal; Mbele, Saᶜid Baldas, and Zemongo in eastern Ubangi-Shari; Zemio, Rafai, and Bangassou along the Mbomu River in southern Ubangi-Shari; and small centers scattered through Banda country. With the exception of Bangassou, the subject of an ethnohistorical study by Dampierre,[3] little research has been done on these towns; yet fragmentary evidence collected during the course of research on Dar al-Kuti suggests many parallels between these slave-raiding centers and Ndele.

This book is based on fieldwork conducted in the former sultanate of Dar al-Kuti, today part of the Préfecture du Bamingui-Bangoran in the northern Central African Republic. Research in the field consisted of two main tasks. The first, largely unanticipated, was the measurement and mapping of the ruins of precolonial Ndele. Limitations of time, personnel, and funds, along with the large area of the site, precluded a more ambitious archaeological survey.[4] The second major project consisted of locating and interviewing individuals who were old enough to recall events in the precolonial period themselves or whose parents had told them about the early history of Dar al-Kuti. Because slave-raiding continued into the second decade of this century, I went to Ndele hoping to collect oral traditions on this topic. I made a concerted effort to obtain a mix of informants that accurately reflected the heterogeneous population of the precolonial sultanate. Those interviewed included both Muslims and non-Muslims, as well as individuals belonging to the major ethnic groups (and subgroups) of the region. Some informants were and are relatively affluent and influential; others were not and are not (see bibliography). I paid particular attention to balance the testimonies of Ndele residents with those of informants in outlying villages. As a result of slave-raiding, French resettlement and forced labor schemes, and flight from both, rural populations have tended to be more permanent than those in Ndele and the immediate environs. Hence much of the information concerning the earliest history of the sultanate came from rural informants. Interviews were conducted in Chadic Arabic without a translator in all cases but two, when the informants spoke Sango and Banda. The extensive use of Chadic Arabic does not reflect bias in favor of Muslims, for older non-Muslims also speak the language. In the early part of the century Chadic Arabic was the language of trade and the ruling class of Dar al-Kuti; consequently, many non-Muslims learned it.

During all the sessions, a research assistant was present to answer questions about matters such as non-Arabic loan words, local geography, specialized crafts vocabulary, and plant terminology. In all cases, informants' testimonies were compared with each other, and all other available information, to reconstruct as accurate a picture of the precolonial history of Dar al-Kuti as possible. To this end, archival research in 1973 and 1975 in Chad (Ndjaména), France (Paris and Aix-en-Provence), Great Britain

(London), and the Central African Republic (Ndele and Bangui) complemented the field inquiry.

For reasons related to the current economic crisis in the publishing
industry, this volume has taken some time to see the light of day. Since I
completed field research, the preoccupations and approaches of African
historical studies have changed substantially. Various theoretical concerns
have come and gone, and more data have become available about the
continent generally. In the wake of both, African history has become
conceptually and methodologically more sophisticated. The present text
has been revised to reflect the evolution of the discipline—without
burdening the data with more theoretical weight than they can bear. The
Dar al-Kuti "story" nonetheless merits telling, particularly since the
passage of time and the recent upheavals in the Central African Republic
and Chad have undoubtedly thinned the ranks of informants, disturbed the
terrain, and further disrupted the regional political economy.

Part 1
NORTH CENTRAL AFRICA AND THE INTERNATIONAL ECONOMY: THE RISE OF DAR AL-KUTI

Chapter 1
An Overview: The Lake Chad–Nile Region and Ubangi-Shari, 1750–1900

Physical Setting

North Central Africa includes parts of three major watersheds: the eastern Chad basin, the western Nile system, and the valleys of the northern affluents of the Zaire River. The Zaire region is often called Ubangi-Shari because it lies between the Ubangi River in the south and the Shari River (actually part of the Chad basin) in the north. These three immense watersheds come together in an extensive highland zone that roughly coincides with contemporary political boundaries in the region. In the north, a chain of hills and plateaux running from north to south just west of the Chad-Sudan border separates the Nile and Chad basins. In the south, within the boundaries of today's Central African Republic, the range splits into two branches; one extends southeast dividing the Nile and Zaire watersheds immediately west of the Central African Republic–Sudan frontier, while the other stretches just south of the Central African Republic–Chad border, defining the limit between the Chad and Zaire systems. From the Chad-Nile-Zaire divide, the terrain gradually descends in all directions.

In this part of Africa, the amount of annual rainfall increases from north to south, and the year is divided into a rainy season and a dry season whose lengths vary with the latitude. In the northern reaches of the Chad and Nile basins, which extend far into the Sahara, there is almost no rain at all, but in the less dry Sahelian and savanna regions to the south, a March-October rainy season alternates with an October-March dry period. As for the northern Zaire area, it is the most southern and hence the wettest of the three basins.

Each basin has its own geographic and hydrographic characteristics.[1] The Chad basin consists of open plains broken only by a few rock

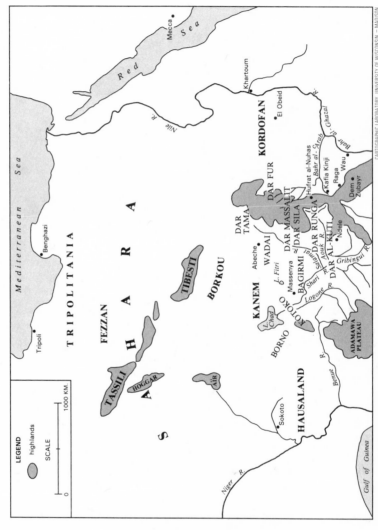

Map 1. The Lake Chad–Nile Region and North Central Africa

8

outcroppings, most of which are westward extensions of the highlands along the watershed's eastern limits. With the exception of the Shari, which in any case collects most of its water from tributaries rising in the south, rivers flow only seasonally, during and shortly after the rains. But even seasonal rains inhibit movement in areas such as the Salamat, a lowland area in the southeastern part of the basin that becomes a huge marsh between June and November each year.

The Saharan and Sahelian portions of the western Nile watershed resemble the Chad terrain. The plains of eastern Dar Fur and Kordofan descend towards the Nile, interrupted by a few highland areas such as the Nuba Mountains. Streambeds in this northern region are similarly dry most of the year. But further south the western Nile watershed is quite different. Again, the land slopes to the east, but it is cut by many streams and swampy areas that come together to form the Bahr al-ᶜArab and the Bahr al-Ghazal, important tributaries of the White Nile. During the rainy season, many of these watercourses overflow their banks, creating vast marshes that make travel impossible. This area is roughly aligned with the marshy Salamat area in the southeastern Chad basin, so that together, the Salamat and Bahr al-Ghazal areas create an east-west barrier of lowlands stretching for nearly a thousand kilometers.

The Zaire basin lies entirely south of the Sahelian zone. From the highlands along the Central African Republic–Chad and –Sudan borders, the land descends to the south and southwest. The area is lightly wooded and cut by numerous streams, most of which contain water throughout the year. Although there are no vast swamps like those in the Salamat and Bahr al-Ghazal, high waters during the rainy season severely limit travel. Farther south, the tropical forest begins just north of the Ubangi and Mbomu rivers.

The most striking geographical characteristics of the basin are the numerous abrupt rock outcroppings that stud the terrain.[2] In the northern part of the watershed they are associated with the highlands separating the Chad and Zaire basins. Farther south, they take the shape of isolated peaks or huge piles of boulders jutting skyward for several hundred meters and surrounded by open plains. Such formations are also found in the southern Chad basin as western extensions of the highlands along the Central African Republic–Sudan border and eastern projections of the Adamawa highlands of Cameroon. Some are barren and dry; others are covered with brush and have their own water supply. Many are perforated by caves, hollows, and underground passageways; others are smooth and provide no shelter. Called *kagas* by the Banda peoples, these outcroppings have played an important role in the recent history of the region—the names of individual peaks turn up frequently as points of reference in oral traditions. During the period of intense Muslim slave-raiding in the late nineteenth and

early twentieth centuries, kagas sheltered refugee populations and at times
served as rallying points for non-Muslim resistance. They also provided
secure stopping places along trade routes in the region. Perhaps because of
their bizarre physical aspect, they were also associated with place spirits
and myth by many peoples.

As everywhere, rainfall and environment had a major influence on the
historical development of societies in the three basins. Moisture was
sufficient to permit economies based on agriculture in all but the northern
portions of the Chad and Nile basins. Nearly everywhere, sorghums and
millets constituted the major crops; only along the Ubangi in the southwest
did root crops such as yams and manioc prevail before the end of the
nineteenth century. In the Chad and northern Nile regions, adjacent to the
Sahara and Sahel, Africans also raised animals. Camels and cattle were the
prestige products, although goats and sheep were also important. Farther
south in the Zaire and southwestern Nile basins, sleeping sickness ruled out
animal husbandry on a large scale, and this had much to do with the
flourishing regional commerce in livestock between north and south in the
late nineteenth century.[3]

Geography, and proximity in particular, likewise channeled the evolution of African societies. Being farther north, the central Chad and Nile
basins were the first to be drawn into the expanding Muslim economies of
the Sahara and Nile valley. Partly for this reason, it was there that the
earliest states arose. Institutions of centralized power also evolved among
societies along the Ubangi River headwaters in the extreme south—for
reasons undoubtedly related to the ecological gradient of wooded savanna
and forest, as well as the incorporation of the area into the expanding Zaire
River commerce.

African societies in both the north and the south imported increasing
quantities of long-distance trade goods as they became part of growing
regional economies. In the north more than in the south, slaves and ivory
were exported in exchange for these goods. Such commerce encouraged
violence, which by the late nineteenth century altered basic features of life
such as agriculture and population distribution. As is recounted in the
following pages, root crops spread at the expense of grain, and settlements
became larger and more concentrated.[4] All of this altered the larger political
economy.

Political Landscape

The political geography of the Chad, western Nile, and northern Zaire
basins included both states and stateless societies in the nineteenth century.

In the Chad basin the major Muslim states were Borno, near Lake Chad; Bagirmi, located along the Shari River southeast of Borno; and Wadai, whose nucleus lay in the highlands along the eastern border of the watershed. Lesser Muslim polities, such as the Kotoko "principalities" on the lower Shari and Logone Rivers between Borno and Bagirmi,[5] and a cluster of small sultanates stretching south from Wadai to the Salamat, became clients of these major states.

The sultanates included Dar Massalit and Dar Tama immediately adjacent to Wadai, and Dar Sila and Dar Runga farther south. All of these states followed a pattern of development similar to that of Wadai: a single ethnic group came to dominate interethnic politics in the core area, and then the sultanate expanded by incorporating other peoples. These small units are of direct relevance to this study for two reasons: first, it was through them that Wadai expanded its influence in the Islamic border regions and non-Muslim areas to the south; second, it was Dar Runga, the southernmost of the sultanates, that founded Dar al-Kuti as its own Muslim client colony still further south—in the border region between the Shari (Chad basin) and Ubangi (Zaire basin) watersheds.[6]

The most numerous group of non-Muslims in the Chad basin are the Sara peoples living in the south. They are divided into many subgroups speaking related languages. They never formed a centralized state and, despite their linguistic ties, had no sense of common identity. Most Sara lived in small settlements and most groups made war among themselves. Limited centralized authority existed only among the Majingay in the northern Sara lands, where, by the late nineteenth century, a dozen chiefs combined the roles of initiation leader and earth chief.[7]

In the western Nile watershed Dar Fur was the major Muslim state in the early 1800s. It bordered Wadai, but lay east of the Chad-Nile divide. Like its neighbor, Dar Fur had expanded from a mountainous core area inhabited by a small number of related peoples to a large state with a sphere of influence extending beyond the Islamic frontier in the south. But unlike Wadai, whose power grew during the century, the Fur state suffered reversals at the hands of powerful rivals on all sides. In fact, some of the southern sultanates mentioned above, such as Dar Sila and Dar Runga, began the century as satellites of Dar Fur and only later slipped into the Wadai orbit.

In the southern part of the basin, there were no large states in the early part of the century. The non-Muslim Banda, Kresh, and related peoples who lived there were organized into numerous small social units resembling those of the Sara.[8] Following the Egyptian annexation of the Sudan, however, Muslim merchants in pursuit of slaves and ivory began to establish fortified commercial centers among the southern peoples. They armed their followers, and their settlements became small, centralized states.

A neat and stable geopolitical chart cannot serve as a guide to the history of the northern Zaire basin during the nineteenth century. No large state existed throughout the century, although several, including Dar al-Kuti, emerged in this period. Most of the peoples in the region were recent arrivals. Their oral traditions indicate that their most extensive social unit—like that of their non-Muslim neighbors in the Nile and Chad zones— was the extended residential unit held together by the ideology of lineage. Even these small groups moved repeatedly during this time. Ethnic and linguistic maps such as those found in the colonial reports, or in studies such as Murdock's *Africa: Its Peoples and Their Culture History*, and Greenberg's *Languages of Africa*, show where people lived at the time the Pax Gallica was imposed on Ubangi-Shari around World War I.[9] As Prioul observes, such charts do not document the turmoil which preceded campaigns of "pacification."[10]

The upheavals before World War I, and those that followed during the French colonial occupation, make it exceedingly difficult to reconstruct a detailed history of this part of North Central Africa. To this problem must be added the gaps in information stemming from the lack of basic historical research. This study attempts to overcome these problems by building bridges across time and space—looking at similar historical developments in other parts of the continent, be they contemporary or not. Allusions to such other places appear in the notes with some frequency. The gaps have also been minimized by interpreting sparse extant data with reference to broader analytical frameworks. One of the most useful of these constructs is the frontier hypothesis.

Dar al-Kuti and the Frontier

From its conception, this study has proceeded on the assumption that the history of Dar al-Kuti is the history of a frontier society. The frontier as an explanatory concept, first articulated by Frederick Jackson Turner in 1893, has been widely applied by historians of American expansion; other scholars have since used frontier theory to understand historical evolution in other parts of the world. These efforts have produced increasingly sophisticated comparative analyses. Among these studies, that of Thompson and Lamar has been particularly helpful in comprehending relations between Muslims and non-Muslims in Dar al-Kuti.[11]

Thompson and Lamar's definition of a frontier is of particular importance. It is both spatial and temporal:

> We regard a frontier not as a boundary or line, but as a territory or zone of interpenetration between two previously distinct societies. Usually, one of the societies is indigenous to the region, or at least has occupied it for many generations; the other is intrusive. The frontier "opens" in a given zone when the first representatives of the intrusive society arrive; it "closes" when a single political authority has established hegemony over the zone.[12]

The southern Chad, far northern Zaire, and southwestern Nile basins constituted a frontier zone where Muslims from farther north interacted with local non-Muslim peoples. But the Islamic frontier—like most—was more complex than the model, since it was the stage for interaction among many more than two societies. "Non-Muslim" is a very loose category which masks important distinctions among the Sara, Banda, Kresh, Manza, Nduka, and other peoples living within the zone. The Muslims were similarly diverse, and it is important not to exaggerate the unity of the Islamic community (*cumma*). Ethnic cleavages remained important as different Muslim groups competed for wealth and power.

The frontier model has a temporal element as well. The frontier era in Dar al-Kuti dates from the 1820s to the French colonial conquest of 1900–1911. Over this time the "frontier process" did indeed tend to group and fuse the earlier diverse groups into only two—Muslims and non-Muslims.[13] Muslims enjoyed a stronger corporate identity because they were the "strangers" and the minority. They also shared the common ideology of Islam. But as time passed, non-Muslim peoples—once dispersed in small family settlements—concentrated in larger villages to defend themselves more effectively against slave-raiders. These changes and others created a broader sense of identity.

Cross-cutting cleavages, another feature of the frontier model, also developed in Dar al-Kuti, first when Muslim traders aligned with Nduka earth chiefs, and later when Muslim raiders and non-Muslim clients fought alongside each other. It was at this time that the technological and organizational gap, cited by Thompson and Lamar as another feature of the frontier process, assumed major importance.[14] Muslim access to the products of long-distance commerce meant access to firearms and ammunition, and this shifted the balance of power in the frontier zone decidedly in their favor.

While the frontier perspective has proved useful for interpreting the history of Dar al-Kuti, its prism distorts historical vision in one major way: it is deterministic. Perhaps because the "frontier" as an analytical construct was conceived just after the closing of the American West and was used to explain what many believed to be the "Manifest Destiny" of the United

States, the frontier approach implicitly assumes the eventual triumph of one society over the other(s). Thompson and Lamar write that frontiers "open" and "close." Such a view threatens to reduce the history of Dar al-Kuti to a tale of Muslim conquest. Nothing is farther from fact or from my intent. The Islamic frontier opened, to be sure; it never closed, but was transformed. Moreover, even at the height of Muslim power, when Muslims directed affairs of state, the land was hardly part of the supposedly peaceful and homogeneous "Dar al-Islam" ("Land of Islam"); rather, it belonged to the non-Muslim "Dar al-Harb" ("Land of War") where Muslims and non-Muslims were in conflict. The ruler's inability to impose Islam completely on all of his subjects is reflected in his attention to rites associated with the traditional religions of the Banda and Nduka.[15] Furthermore, as might be expected in a settlement distant from the intellectual centers of the Islamic world and whose economy by 1900 depended essentially on violence, few of the institutions associated with Islamic learning existed in Ndele. Those that did affected only a small proportion of its inhabitants. This situation was not peculiar to North Central Africa, but was and is common along the Islamic frontier throughout Sahelian Africa. Hence Dar al-Kuti might be viewed as another case study of acculturation to Islam on the desert fringe. To judge from the medieval histories or *tarikhs*, other regions once on the Islamic frontier certainly now lie completely within the Dar al-Islam. But Dar al-Kuti did not share this fate. Although Grech wrote that the great variety of belief systems in the land just after the turn of the century was yielding to the advance of Islam, the French conquest in 1911 brought this frontier process to an end.[16]

Thus, while the frontier perspective has proved useful in organizing and interpreting the scattered information on the history of North Central Africa, this study rejects its teleological bias. But putting aside questions of whether, if, or how the frontier closed in Dar al-Kuti, it clearly opened not with conquest but with contact.

Expanding Muslim Presence in the
Non-Muslim South, 1750–1850:
A Muslim Perspective

Before the early nineteenth century, northern Muslims had only vague notions about the geography and peoples of northern Ubangi-Shari. This ignorance is indicated in the very sketchy descriptions of the area included in the Muslim-European travel literature—Muslim testimonies transmitted or published by Europeans. Authors readily identify the Muslim states of the desert fringe, but lands and populations farther south are usually lumped together and labeled simply as non-Muslims.[17] When al-Tunisi visited Wadai and Dar Fur in the first decade of the nineteenth century, the inhabitants of the sultanates referred to the non-Muslim lands in the south as Dar Jenakherah and Dar Fertit. These terms may have designated specific ethnic groups at one time, but by 1800 they were more often employed as general geographic labels. M. Seetzen noted this usage among pilgrims from the Chad area interviewed in Cairo in the early nineteenth century.[18] Judging from al-Tunisi's accounts, the northerners did have individual names for some non-Muslim peoples, but most of these lived near their frontiers.[19]

Ignorance about regions farther south stemmed from the lack of sustained and intense contact. In the years after 1750 and perhaps even before, border populations had occasionally fallen prey to Muslim raiders who inaded during the dry season in search of ivory and slaves for delivery to the Sahel. By the time of al-Tunisi's visit, Bagirmi, Wadai, and Dar Fur had each carved out spheres of influence and raiding zones south of their borders.[20] But claims to these territories, like later European claims to the African interior, did not issue from familiarity. In the case of Ubangi-Shari, for example, incursions were few, shallow, and irregular, since most of the demands for captives could be met by raiding non-Muslim peoples remaining within the Muslim states themselves or in immediately adjacent areas such as the Salamat, Dar Runga, Dar Sila, and the lands of the Sara. Wider-ranging expeditions were so rare that in response to al-Tunisi's inquiries in Dar Fur, people still cited as a major source of information a Furian mission that had traveled south for five months in the late eighteenth century.[21]

The relative isolation of the southern regions did not last. Contact expanded throughout the nineteenth century. Examined from year to year, the change appears to have been gradual, although punctuated by a few abrupt transitions. Ties developed in two ways: through the southward movement of the Muslim slave-raiding frontier, and through the appearance of Muslim peddlers and religious teachers and counselors (*faqih/fuqaha'* or *faqir/fuqara'* [Arabic]). Although the violence associated with slave-raiding and the large bodies of men it required made raiding the more visible of the two kinds of interaction, the slower infiltration of petty traders such as the Jallaba from the Nile area, faqihs, and Muslims combining the roles of peddler and teacher probably made a greater contribution to the creation of permanent bonds with the north.[22]

These different modes of interaction did not stem from divergent economic preferences. Both raiders and traders wanted slaves and ivory to export northward. But whereas the raiders were outsiders who attacked non-Muslim settlements, killing or carrying off the inhabitants, the traders and occasional faqihs established themselves in southern villages, offering imported goods for ivory and captives usually taken from neighboring peoples. For the area as a whole, of course, the result was the same— warfare and depopulation. Yet on the local level, the second kind of contact meant that some Muslims were able to settle peacefully and permanently beyond the Islamic frontier. In so doing, they extended the boundaries of the Muslim world and founded southern outlets for the commercial networks that spanned the Sahel and Sahara.

Overall, Muslim awareness of the lands and peoples to the south increased in the decades just after 1800, but the raiding and trading frontier advanced only slowly and irregularly. Contacts were largely the result of individual initiative and expanded in some areas more quickly than in others. Places like Dar Runga and Dar Goula, which seemed very distant and almost unreal to Muslims at the beginning of the century, by mid-century were treated simply as neighboring lands (although as late as 1836, the Jallaba traders reporting to French traveler Edmond de Cadalvene described the rhinos of Dar Runga in terms that make the animal sound like a mythical creature).[23] After mid-century, the "distant and almost unreal" lands beyond the fringe retreated farther and farther south, finally ceasing to exist by around 1890 with the incorporation of the whole of North Central Africa into the "known world" of the Muslims.

The writings themselves best document the progress of communication between the Muslim north and the non-Muslim south between 1800 and 1850. During his visit to Dar Fur in the 1790s William Browne noted that slaves came from the following sources: "Dar Kulla," or the land of the Goula, who, in the late nineteenth century at least, lived near Lake Iro in the Salamat and Lake Mamoun in northern Ubangi-Shari; Dar Runga, the small sultanate in the southern Salamat just north of the Aouk River; and "Gnum Gnum," probably a reference to the Azande peoples whose expansion from homelands near the equatorial forest had carried them north of the Mbomu River by this time.[24]

Fifteen years later, al-Tunisi's acquaintances also identified Dar Goula as a source of captives, but in addition they mentioned other peoples such as the Binga, Shala, Banda, and Farah, all east of the Goula and south of the frontiers of Wadai and Dar Fur. At roughly the same time, one of Seetzen's Bornoan informants in Cairo reported having seen Banda slaves in Dar Fur. On the basis of information collected in Shendi on the Nile, John Burckhardt, a British merchant and explorer, wrote that captives sold in Kordofan and Dar Fur came from Banda lands as well as other regions called Baadja and Fetigo located somewhere in Dar Fertit.[25]

One of German traveler Heinrich Barth's informants, a faqih who at one time had lived in Dar Fur, told him of two Furian expeditions that had gone south in 1823 and 1825 until they came to a river called the Kubanda. This story may well be an updated version of that recorded by al-Tunisi in the eighteenth century, although Barth included a detailed itinerary in his brief mention of the missions.[26] Finally, in the late 1840s, a Runga pilgrim in Jiddah told Fulgence Fresnel, French consul in Arabia, that Muslim traders and raiders had penetrated as far as the Wamba River, said to be south of Dar Runga and west of the Banda—possibly a reference to the Ouham River south of the lands of the Sara.[27] But despite this evidence of long-distance contact, most raids in the first half of the century still took place in areas near the Muslim states; Ignatius Pallme noted that captives sold in Kordofan came predominantly from the borderlands.[28]

Dar Fur, the Khartoumers,
and the Non-Muslim South

The political history of Dar Fur during this period also suggests that the southern lands were being increasingly integrated into the desert network. In the early nineteenth century, rulers of the state attempted to consolidate and routinize administration in the heartlands of their domain. The success of these policies partially depended on expanding and controlling long-distance commerce with the Mediterranean basin. Merchants dealing with the area were mainly interested in acquiring ivory and slaves, exports that came from the non-Muslim south; as a result, the sultanate sought greater control over these regions. These attempts eventually failed. Internal political difficulties repeatedly put a brake on expansion, while the state faced growing external competition from other Muslim states and trading organizations. In the end, Dar Fur even lost its own independence.

The efforts of the sultans to increase power at the center translated into greater reliance on slave officials and a standing corps of slave soldiers, groups whose primary loyalties bound them to the ruler rather than to a particular lineage. Up until the late eighteenth century, the sultan had been dependent on levies of fighters raised by the leaders of various Fur lineages to serve for a limited time. External events further encouraged the change in recruitment. In 1821 Dar Fur lost the eastern tributary state of Kordofan to the slave troops of Egyptian sultan Muhammad ᶜAli, and the Egyptians threatened Dar Fur's eastern borders for the next fifty years. Muhammad ᶜAli's troops were part of a standing army, a product of his much larger scheme to modernize the Egyptian state following a period of French occupation, and in Dar Fur the loss of Kordofan was in part attributed to the lack of such a force.

Competition from other Muslims in the southern regions also encouraged the change in traditional military practice. Beginning in the 1840s, merchants of diverse nationalities who had their headquarters at Khartoum on the Nile expanded their ivory and slave-raiding operations into the southern and southwestern Sudan. Known as the "Khartoumers," these traders soon threatened the commercial position of Dar Fur in the south. In the years that followed, they diverted much of the flow of ivory and slaves away from Dar Fur. Their success stemmed from a variety of tactics, including alliances with local leaders and the creation of permanent armed camps in the south beyond the Islamic frontier. And like Muhammad ᶜAli, but on a smaller scale, the Khartoumers maintained standing forces of captives. To Dar Fur the message was clear, and in an effort to outflank his adversaries, the Fur sultan adopted their military tactics. He began building his own standing detachment of *bazingirs* (slave troops [Chadic Arabic]).[29] This new recruitment policy almost certainly increased the demand for slaves in Dar Fur, which in turn led to more frequent and extensive raiding among the non-Muslim peoples in the south.

During the remainder of the century, Fur fortunes continued to be closely linked with commercial hegemony over non-Muslim lands in the south. The disposition of control over the trade routes and transport illustrates the vital character of this southern connection. The rulers of Dar Fur had tradition-ally guaranteed access to the south by concluding transport and toll agreements with the Rizayqat Arabs, cattle nomads who lived southeast of the Fur highlands and controlled the commercial routes between the sultanate the non-Muslim territories beyond the Bahr al-Ghazal. But at about the time the Khartoumers and Jallaba (lesser Muslim traders from the Nile frequently associated with the larger merchants) began trading in the south, relations between Dar Fur and the Rizayqat deteriorated and eventually led to armed conflict. Although Gustav Nachtigal, a German traveler and physician, cited the theft of a horse as the cause of these hostilities, the source of disagreement was obviously much more deep-seated, because the Fur sultan Muhammad al-Husayn launched eighteen military campaigns against the Rizayqat between 1840 and 1856.[30]

The Khartoumers and Jallaba continued to encroach on Dar Fur's sphere of influence in the south, and the Rizayqat abetted these efforts. Their participation became explicit in 1866 when Rahma Mansur al-Zubayr, the major Khartoumer in the Bahr al-Ghazal, made an agreement with the Rizayqat allowing him direct access to Kordofan and permitting the Arabs to collect tolls on the route. The accord was mainly designed to provide al-Zubayr with an outlet to the north that avoided the Nile region where the Turko-Egyptian authorities had banned the slave trade, but it also brought an influx of North African merchants to the Bahr al-Ghazal. They further undermined the Fur middleman position by dealing directly with countrymen residing in Kordofan.[31] The decline of trade between Dar Fur and the south had a severe effect on the economy of the sultanate, and when Nachtigal visited there in 1873, he noted that "the prosperity of the country was declining more and more."[32]

The diminished supply of slaves and ivory arriving in Dar Fur from the non-Muslim south made it difficult for the sultan and other political figures to obtain the trans-Saharan goods necessary to assure the loyalty of followers and appease rivals. This situation produced discontent and encouraged domestic turmoil. In 1874, a final opportunity to restore prosperity presented itself when efforts of the Turko-Egyptian administration to stem the slave trade in Kordofan compelled al-Zubayr and other Khartoumers to shift their commercial routes to the west. Had the sultan and prominent Fur leaders been powerful enough, they might have finally forced al-Zubayr to acknowledge their middle position in long-distance trade with the north. But internal discord prevented a united front. Instead of reasserting Fur influence in the south, the sultan was defeated in battle by al-Zubayr and his army of bazingirs and Muslim traders from beyond the Islamic frontier. Only the intervention of the Turko-Egyptian authorities prevented al-Zubayr from proclaiming himself governor of Dar Fur. Following the defeat of the sultan, many Fur retreated to their traditional highland homelands, where they resisted the incorporation of Dar Fur into the Turko-Egyptian Sudan.[33] In 1881 the Turko-Egyptian administration fell victim to a popular Islamic revolt led by a leader who proclaimed himself the Mahdi, and his state came to be called the Mahdiya. Between 1881 and 1898 the Mahdists attempted to conquer all of the Sudan, including Dar Fur. But the Fur rejected Mahdist suzerainty. During this period traffic on the routes between Dar Fur and the southern regions stopped almost completely.[34] Other factors influenced the events mentioned above; nonetheless, it is quite clear that for Dar Fur, the integration of the non-Muslim southern lands into the desert network during the nineteenth century was essential to the well-being of the state. When integration failed, the state contracted to its core Fur region.

Wadai and the Non-Muslim South

In Wadai, events after 1800 also led to increased intervention in lands to the south, although these areas were not permanently incorporated into the state until the second half of the century. Wadaian history between 1800 and 1850 oscillated between expansion and isolation prompted by internal strife. The power of the sultanate in the south expanded and contracted in accordance with events in the northern heartlands. Furthermore, the assertion of Wadaian control in the south during this period was invariably accompanied by efforts to open or renew commercial relations with North Africa. These developments reinforced each other. To obtain North African products, Wadai had to supply slaves and ivory; both came from the non-Muslim south.

The reigns of the two most important Wadaian sultans in the first half of the century, Sultan Sabun (1803–13, or 1805–15) and Sultan Muhammad al-Sharif (1834– or 1835–58), illustrate the dual nature of this foreign policy.[35] Their activities also signaled the closer integration of the south into the Saharan system. Around 1810, Sabun sponsored the opening of the first direct caravan link with the Mediterranean, which stimulated the growth of long-distance commerce and fostered communities of foreign traders in the sultanate. Bouts of xenophobia in Wadai and desert raiding stopped all caravans for years at a time during his reign, but the overall result was a great increase in commercial exchange by mid-century.[36] At the same time, the sultan launched a remarkable series of campaigns on the southern fringes of Wadai, first invading Bagirmi, then subduing Dar Tama, and finally reducing Dar Sila and Dar Runga to tributary status. He also attacked regions west of the Wadaian heartland and was in the midst of preparations for a campaign against Borno when he died.[37]

While in most cases local events and conflicts provided the justification for these military actions, it seems unlikely that Sabun, said to be one of the wisest and most far-sighted Wadaian rulers, was unaware of their commercial advantages. The campaigns did not always result in the permanent incorporation of new territories into the sultanate, but fighting and tribute brought captives for settlement as well as for export.[38] In addition, the submission of these partially Muslimized border states provided Wadai with a base for sending raiding expeditions farther south later in the century—to Dar al-Kuti and other parts of northern Ubangi-Shari.[39]

Sultan Muhammad al-Sharif assumed power in the 1830s. In the years following the death of Sabun, internal crises tore Wadai; six sultans rose and fell.[40] The upheavals disrupted long-distance trade and encouraged the southern regions to reassert their independence. To all appearances, Wadai even lost its own autonomy when an army from Dar Fur put Sabun's brother, Muhammad al-Sharif, on the throne. The new ruler paid tribute to his eastern neighbor for a year, but stopped shortly thereafter, declaring Wadai to be once again independent. During the early part of his reign, he, too, turned his attention to the south and initiated campaigns against Dar Tama, Bagirmi, and Dar Runga; he also invaded Borno and Kanem.[41] And al-Sharif also coupled these undertakings with a renewal of desert trade.[42] But in later years of his rule, the sultan's expansive foreign policy, like those of his predecessors, succumbed to domestic difficulties. Campaigns in the borderlands became less frequent, and trade with the north stopped once again. Foreign merchants were persecuted, and many fled the country.[43] Wadai again failed to establish permanent control over the northern caravan routes and the lands to the south.

Wadaian political and economic fortunes improved greatly during the decades following al-Sharif's death in 1858. Between this time and 1898, only two rulers came to the throne, and their reigns were marked by internal peace and the expansion of trans-Saharan trade. As in the past, the growth of long-distance commerce across the desert was accompanied by Wadaian efforts to expand control in the south. This time, the Wadaian rulers were more successful in creating lasting ties in both north and south.

After al-Sharif died, his eldest son ᶜAli ruled Wadai for eighteen years. It was during his reign (1858–76) that the Wadai-Benghazi caravan route inaugurated by Sultan Sabun became a major avenue of trans-Saharan commerce. ᶜAli reversed many of the xenophobic policies of his father and encouraged the return of foreign traders and pilgrims. He also maintained close ties with the Sanusiya Muslim brotherhood, whose desert lodges lay along the trade route in Libya and the northern Chad basin.[44] On the domestic front, the new ruler possessed a remarkable ability to assuage dissident groups within the sultanate.[45] These policies and attributes produced a climate of security that stimulated commerce within Wadai as well as trade with North Africa. In addition, the Wadai-Benghazi corridor probably attracted traffic from the eastern routes through Dar Fur and Kordofan, where the conflicts among the Fur sultans, the Khartoumers, and the Turko-Egyptian authorities had disrupted long-distance exchange.

Under ᶜAli, Wadai reestablished and then tightened control over the satellite sultanates in the southeastern Chad basin. Between 1858 and 1861, Dar Runga and areas of the southern Salamat acknowledged Wadai's supremacy. And in 1871, the sultan made war on Bagirmi, reportedly taking between 20,000 and 30,000 Muslim and non-Muslim captives, many of whom were resettled in rural Wadai.[46] All of these regions had been conquered before, only to reassert their independence. But it is perhaps a sign of increased Wadaian interest in the southern borderlands that this round of conquests was definitive. With the exception of the decade of the 1880s, when Rabih b. Fadlallah, a Sudanese slave raider formerly associated with al-Zubayr, invaded Dar Runga and took over the sultanate along with its southern client state of Dar al-Kuti, Wadai maintained its hegemony over these lands until the early colonial era. Even then the sultanate ceded these territories to the French only after a period of stiff resistance lasting more than ten years.[47]

During ᶜAli's reign and afterward, the ᶜaqid al-Salamat, the Wadaian governor traditionally charged with overseeing southern affairs, became one of the state's most powerful officials. By the time Nachtigal visited Wadai, annual tribute from the Salamat Arabs amounted to 100 slaves, between 500 and 600 oxen, 1,000 pieces of cloth (*takaki* [Arabic], strips of locally produced cloth employed as currency), and as much ivory, honey, rhino horn, and other products as the ᶜagid could collect. About 4,000 slaves taken from non-Muslim populations in the south arrived in Abeche every third year, although it is hard to tell what percentage were sent as tribute freely paid and what part were taken in raiding by the ᶜaqid.[48]

Wadai remained politically stable and continued to prosper during the reign of ᶜAli's brother Yusuf, who succeeded him in 1876. Yusuf maintained good relations with the Sanusiya order, which by this time had lodges in many parts of the Chad basin and had become the de facto government of the Libyan interior.[49] Following his brother's example, Yusuf encouraged Hausa pilgrims and peddlers to come to Wadai and traded with Sultan ᶜAliya of Sokoto.[50] Such an extended period of peace probably attracted trade and traders from Dar Fur and the Nile region, where the turmoil that accompanied the rise and rule of the Mahdiya after 1881 had further undermined long-distance commerce.

In the last quarter of the nineteenth century, the territories south of Wadai continued to be a major source of the slaves and ivory necessary for trans-Saharan commerce in the eastern Sudan. With the closing of the Nile basin between the non-Muslim lands and North Africa, much of the southwestern Sudan became part of the commercial hinterland of Wadai.[51] Some traders and raiders from the Bahr al-Ghazal shifted their operations westward into the Ubangi-Shari area. Others who remained in the Sudan directed their exports toward Wadai, and at least one major Hausa merchant in Abeche had agents in Wau, Raga, and Kafia Kinji—all collection points for slaves and ivory in the southwestern Sudan.[52]

In the 1880s, and even more so in the 1890s, Muslim traders from Wadai and the satellite states also became more numerous in the non-Muslim lands directly south of the sultanate. In the mid-1890s, Wadaian merchants began to trade directly with the rulers of Bangassou, Rafai, and Zemio on the Mbomu River in the far south.[53] Rafai, for example, agreed to buy Wadaian donkeys, cattle, and horses.[54] At the end of Yusuf's reign, then, it is safe to say that the non-Muslim lands of Ubangi-Shari were more completely integrated into the economic life of Wadai and the desert network beyond than at any previous time in their history. For non-Muslim peoples, such integration translated into slave-raiding and slave-trading on an unprecedented scale.

Contact between Muslims and Non-Muslims
in the Nineteenth Century:
A Non-Muslim Perspective

The historical record of the southern non-Muslim peoples confirms the general trends reported in the Muslim sources for the years before 1850. At the moment, this record consists largely of oral traditions which yield neither names of individual leaders nor specific policies pursued towards the north. Yet the sources do indicate a general southern reaction to closer involvement with the Muslims of the desert fringe: the oldest historical traditions among peoples in region after region along this stretch of the Islamic frontier tell of southward migration to escape the Muslim slave-raiders. While in many instances early African historiography succumbed to the temptation to invent great migratory tales to explain historical changes not otherwise easily understood, the migration traditions among peoples of the Islamic borderlands south of Wadai and Dar Fur do not serve this purpose. They do not explain the borrowing of an institution or the appearance of a ruling lineage. They are straightforward and simple: the Muslim raiders attacked, and the survivors either paid tribute or fled. Although these traditions have no obvious etiological *raison d'être* their general accuracy is supported by linguistic evidence as well as the later historical record. A brief survey of the area shows the drift of the information collected thus far, while more extensive commentary is included on the Banda and the Kresh—peoples that played an important role in the history of Dar al-Kuti (map 2).

Beginning with the Dar Fur borderlands, Binga traditions report that they once lived in the neighborhood of Shala, a location confirmed by al-Tunisi early in the nineteenth century. To the southwest lived the Yulu, people who spoke a language closely related to Binga. Shortly after 1800, they paid tribute to Dar Fur. But the growing frequency of *ghazzias* (slave-raids [Arabic]) pushed them farther south in the following decades. Traditions of the Kara, whose language resembles Binga and Yulu, suggest that they also once lived farther north and migrated southward to avoid Muslim raiders.[55]

To the west, the Goula of Lake Mamoun and Lake Iro also suffered Muslim attacks that prompted migration. Traditions of the Goula of Lake Mamoun suggest that around 1750, when they resided near Jabal Marra in southern Dar Fur, Muslim raiding and intermarriage with the Kara led them, too, to move southward.[56] As for the Goula of Lake Iro, Browne and al-Tunisi reported that they were raided by the Furians as well as the Wadaians, leading Modat, the French resident in Ndele in 1910, to theorize that this caused some of them to migrate to the southwest.[57] Those who re-mained reacted either by retreating into the swamps at the edge of Lake Iro

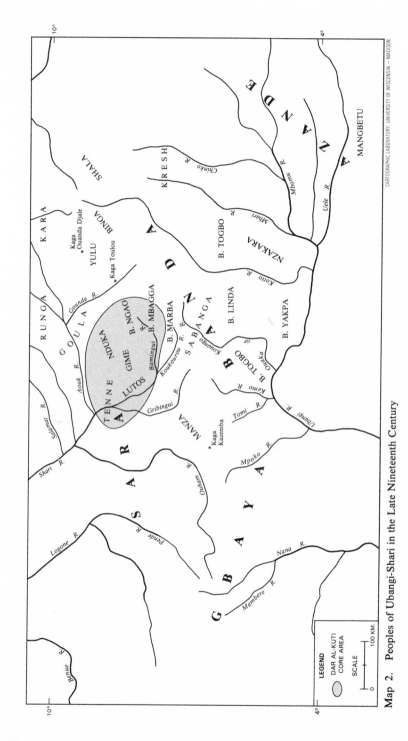

Map 2. Peoples of Ubangi-Shari in the Late Nineteenth Century

GBAYA

SARA

RUNGA

KARA

SHALA

YULU

BINGA

KRESH

GOULA

TENNE

NDUKA

GIME

LUTOS

B. NGAO

B. MBAGGA

B. MARBA

SABANGA

MANZA

B. TOGBO

B. LINDA

B. TOGBO

B. YAKPA

NZAKARA

ZANDE

MANGBETU

*Kaga
Ouanda Djale

*Kaga Toulou

*Kaga
Kazemba

Salamat R.

Shari R.

Logone R.

Benue R.

Pende R.

Mambere R.

Nana R.

Ouham R.

Mpoko R.

Ubangi R.

Tomi R.

Kemo R.

Ouaka R.

Kouango R.

Koukourou R.

Bamingui R.

Gribingui R.

Aouk R.

Gounda R.

Kotto R.

Mbari R.

Mbomu R.

Chinko R.

Uele R.

LEGEND

DAR AL-KUTI
CORE AREA

SCALE

100 KM.

10°

4°

10°

4°

CARTOGRAPHIC LABORATORY, UNIVERSITY OF WISCONSIN – MADISON

24

where Muslim horsemen could not follow, or by agreeing to pay tribute. Barth wrote that the Goula paid an annual tribute in slaves to Wadai, while Fresnel reported that the Goula of Iro purchased their safety by furnishing both Dar Fur and Wadai with 1,000 captives annually.[58]

The early history of the Sara peoples, the westernmost groups to be considered here, is similar. As with the Binga, Yulu, Kara, and Goula, the Sara probably once lived north or northeast of their present location; they, too, migrated south or southwest to the Shari River region to escape Muslim ghazzias.[59] Although these peoples migrated away from the traditional slave-raiding states of Wadai and Dar Fur, their movements took them closer to Dar al-Kuti, destined to become one of the region's major slave-exporting states in the late nineteenth and early twentieth centuries.

Shifting east, to the Nile-Shari-Zaire watershed that marks today's frontier between the Sudan and the Central African Republic, the traditions of the Kresh peoples describe a by-now-familiar response to the increasing involvement of Muslims in southern affairs in the early nineteenth century.[60] The Kresh, like the Sara and Banda peoples, are a congeries of peoples sharing similar languages (or dialects of the same language). Up until recently, however, they do not seem to have had a sense of political or cultural unity; in fact, the term *Kresh* (with its variants *Kreich*, *Krech*, *Kredj*) was applied by foreigners, possibly by Muslim traders and raiders from the north.[61]

Early traditions, references in al-Tunisi, and linguistic affinities between Kresh and Binga, Yulu, Kara, Goula, and Sara have led most writers on the Kresh to conclude that they once lived in the northern part of the Nile-Shari-Zaire watershed near the Dar Fur borderlands.[62] Threatened by Furian raiding expeditions, they began moving south and southwest probably around 1800, though remaining in the general area of the divide. Victimized by further Muslim raiding in the middle part of the century—this time from the Khartoumers—they migrated westward in the 1870s, 1880s, and 1890s. There they posed a major threat to the growth of Dar al-Kuti near the end of the century, which led the sultanate's ruler, Muhammad al-Sanusi, to send out bands of his bazingirs to attack Kresh settlements. In response, many Kresh fled back to the east; others were captured and sold, or incorporated into the population of Ndele, the new capital of Dar al-Kuti founded by al-Sanusi in the 1890s.[63]

The Banda

The Banda peoples also have a history of flight, migrating in hopes of escaping or perhaps controlling increased intercourse with the expanding zone of Muslim influence in North Central Africa in the late eighteenth and early nineteenth centuries. The Banda number about 440,000 today, and are a major people in the Central African Republic. They are divided into a myriad of subgroups scattered throughout the central and eastern parts of the country, but primarily concentrated in the southern Ubangi basin, north of the Mbomu and Ubangi rivers. Smaller, refugee populations live east and west of this area of concentration, in the southwestern Sudan and southwestern Central African Republic.

The general pattern of early Banda history resembles the historical experience of the other non-Muslim peoples. Like them, the Banda probably lived further north in the late eighteenth century. Al-Tunisi placed them nearer the Muslim states of the Sahel, although the exact location of their homelands has been a subject of speculation.[64] The Banda apparently also faced increased Muslim raiding in the early nineteenth century and responded to this threat in the same manner as their non-Muslim neighbors. They headed south, probably following river valleys such as the Kotto and Kouango which flowed towards the Mbomu and Ubangi.

The history of the Banda after 1850 is also a tale of raiding and forced migration. The greater source material available for the period—mainly oral traditions collected during the colonial era—shows a complex interplay of several themes which were probably important in earlier times.

In the 1840s and 1850s, the greatest threat to the Banda groups still came from the Muslim raiders of Wadai and Dar Fur. The major population drift consequently continued to be towards the south, probably intensifying with the establishment of the permanent Wadaian client group south of the Aouk River in Dar al-Kuti. Pierre Kalck agrees with Modat in suggesting that the Banda slowly moved down the river valleys toward the Ubangi River during this period, and goes on to theorize that the present concentration of population in the lower Kotto River region, just north of its confluence with the Ubangi, dates from this time.[65] Banda groups also followed other river valleys to the south. Traditions of the Yakpa, for example, indicate that they moved south along the Kouango, while the Togbo made their way along the Tomi River after leaving the Kotto.[66]

Beginning in the 1870s and continuing through the 1880s, slave-raiding from the east also threatened the Banda. Ghazzias launched by the Khartoumers from armed camps in the southwestern Sudan reached some Banda groups. Others were attacked by Kresh peoples pushing west either to escape the Khartoumers or to capture neighboring Banda to trade with them. Although there were roughly a dozen important Khartoumer merchants in the southwestern Sudan at this time, the slave-raiding parties of al-Zubayr seem to have penetrated most deeply into Banda country.[67] These expeditions were motivated partly by personal ambition, but the

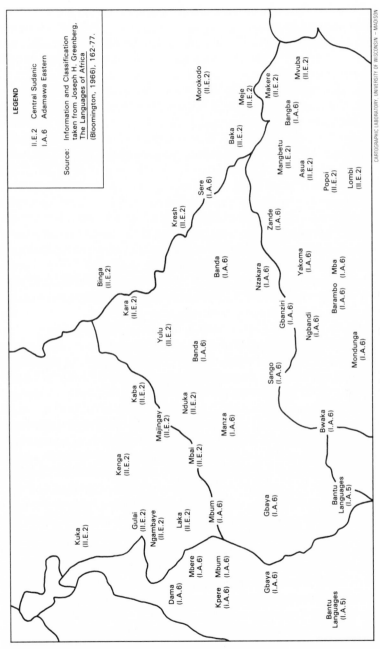

Map 3. The Distribution of the Central Sudanic and Adamawa Eastern Languages

LEGEND

II.E.2   Central Sudanic
I.A.6   Adamawa Eastern

Source: Information and Classification
taken from Joseph H. Greenberg.
The Languages of Africa
(Bloomington, 1966), 162-77.

CARTOGRAPHIC LABORATORY, UNIVERSITY OF WISCONSIN - MADISON

Morokodo (II.E.2)
Mvuba (II.E.2)
Bangba (I.A.6)
Makere (II.E.2)
Meje (II.E.2)
Baka (II.E.2)
Mangbetu (II.E.2)
Asua (II.E.2)
Popoi (II.E.2)
Lombi (II.E.2)
Sere (I.A.6)
Kresh (II.E.2)
Zande (I.A.6)
Banda (I.A.6)
Binga (II.E.2)
Kara (II.E.2)
Nzakara (I.A.6)
Yakoma (I.A.6)
Mba (I.A.6)
Barambo (I.A.6)
Gbanziri (I.A.6)
Ngbandi (I.A.6)
Mondunga (I.A.6)
Yulu (II.E.2)
Banda (I.A.6)
Kaba (II.E.2)
Nduka (II.E.2)
Majingay (II.E.2)
Manza (I.A.6)
Sango (I.A.6)
Bwaka (I.A.6)
Kenga (II.E.2)
Mbai (II.E.2)
Bantu Languages (I.A.5)
Gulai (II.E.2)
Kuka (II.E.2)
Ngambaye (II.E.2)
Laka (II.E.2)
Mbum (I.A.6)
Gbaya (I.A.6)
Mbere (I.A.6)
Dama (I.A.6)
Mbum (I.A.6)
Kpere (I.A.6)
Gbaya (I.A.6)
Bantu Languages (I.A.5)

27

decision by the Egyptian government in 1865 to curtail the slave traffic on the Nile may well have ultimately resulted in a greater demand for captives farther west. In any case, the treaty that al-Zubayr negotiated in 1866 with the Rizayqat Arabs suggests that exporting slaves by way of Khartoum had become impossible.[68]

In the 1870s al-Zubayr's lieutenants Ma ᶜAli and Kheir Allah raided far western Banda groups such as the Mbagga, the Ngao, and the Tombaggo. They also devastated nearby Dar al-Kuti during this campaign. About the same time, before his invasion of Wadaian territory, Rabih b. Fadlallah set up camp near the Chinko River and preyed upon Banda groups living north of the Mbomu, as well as the nearby Azande, Nzakara, and Kresh. These depredations continued even after the Egyptian authorities forcibly detained al-Zubayr in Cairo in 1875.[69] The merchant's son Sulayman directed the campaigns until his death in 1879.

The Khartoumer ghazzias changed the dominant direction of the Banda migrations. Whereas up to the 1860s the major Muslim threat lay north of the Banda, and encouraged them to head south, the Khartoumers pressured them to move southwest. And in fact, the oral traditions of many Banda groups indicate that they migrated southwest from river valley to river valley. A few examples will serve to illustrate this pattern of movement.[70]

Among the Banda Ngura of the Bamba River region in central Ubangi-Shari, the elders told colonial officials in 1906 that sixty years previously the group had lived in the vicinity of the Kotto. Several decades later, they fled west to the Kouango, hoping to find shelter from Muslim raiding and attacks by other Banda groups. But the Banda Linda and Banda Tombaggo already living in the area attacked the newcomers, causing them to migrate farther west to the shores of the Bamba.[71] The Banda Marba migrated in the same fashion, abandoning the Ippy River valley for areas to the southwest.[72] Traditions of the Banda Ngao collected in Ndele in 1974 suggest a similar stepwise westward migration from the Kotto area in the time of al-Zubayr.[73]

From 1880 to 1911, the violence that had previously forced the Banda and other non-Muslim peoples south and then southwest caught up with them. Threatened by the Turko-Egyptian authorities following Sulayman's death in 1879, Rabih and his bazingirs soon moved west themselves and began raiding Banda lands for captives to incorporate into their military units or exchange for arms. The response of the Banda peoples was familiar. They sought to move out of harm's way. But this time they could not move west, since other peoples, the Gbaya and Manza, inhabited those lands. As a result, groups fled in diverse directions, sometimes remaining together and sometimes splitting into smaller bands. The history of the Banda during this period is one of irregular movement in response to Rabih's own erratic peregrinations.

Before leaving Ubangi-Shari for points northwest in 1890, Rabih set in motion events that would pose a greater menace to the Banda and other non-Muslim peoples than any earlier danger. He installed Muhammad al-Sanusi as sultan of Dar al-Kuti. Armed with firearms initially acquired in 1891 through the massacre of the first French expedition to reach the sultanate, al-Sanusi and his followers began intensive raiding among the Banda, Kresh, Yulu, Binga, Kara, Goula, and Sara. The violence continued and even increased for the next twenty years over an ever-expanding zone that eventually extended to today's Central African Republic-Sudan border region in the east and almost to the Mbomu and Ubangi rivers in the south.

As a sometime vassal of Wadai based in an area traditionally within the commercial sphere of that sultanate, al-Sanusi took advantage of established links with the desert trade routes to exchange slaves, ivory, and other exports for cloth, arms, and other goods from the north. As the heir of Rabih and the Khartoumer tradition of al-Zubayr, he founded an armed camp in northern Ubangi-Shari and employed technological advantages copied from his Sudanese mentor to inflict great losses on the non-Muslim peoples south and east of his domains. His detachments carried off, killed, or chased eastward nearly all the Kresh. The Goula were forced to leave Lake Mamoun, while the Kara, Sara, and Yulu also suffered from raiding. It is no exaggeration to say that many Banda peoples see their history during these decades, at least until al-Sanusi caught them and incorporated them into his following, as a tale of continual flight and disorder. To many Banda, this period is known simply as the "Time of War."[74]

As the preceding overview indicates, rising demands for slaves, ivory, and other African imports in North Africa, the Middle East, and Europe between 1750 and 1900 brought increased interaction between Muslims and non-Muslims along the Islamic frontier. As the economic hinterland of the Saharan trading network expanded in the south, its demands were increasingly felt by peoples who were previously only marginally affected by it or not affected by it at all. Among non-Muslims who populated these areas, expanded contact with the north initially translated into the appearance of small numbers of Muslim traders and faqihs in their midst, along with occasional bands of Muslim slave-raiders. The Islamic frontier moved progressively southward.

In the Muslim states of the desert edge such as Wadai and Dar Fur (and Bagirmi and Borno), expanded trade with the Muslim north and the non-Muslim south between 1750 and 1900 brought rulers greater wealth and power. Northern imports judiciously distributed, and slaves from the south incorporated into their military forces, became important means of assuring personal loyalty and building a power base independent of lineage ties. But as the history of both Wadai and Dar Fur shows, too great an economic dependence on the trans-Saharan network could also contribute to internal disorder when the flow of goods from the north, and slaves and ivory from the south, was interrupted.

After 1850, and particularly after 1870, the trans-Saharan system had an increasingly adverse impact on the non-Muslim peoples south of the desert. Greater demand in the north for slaves and ivory brought many more raiders and ghazzias. The higher level of violence prompted many groups of non-Muslim peoples to flee farther south. Eventually they could put no more distance between themselves and the raiders, and Muslim marauders established extensive raiding operations in non-Muslim zones. Entire peoples nearly disappeared. A few raiders and traders, most notably al-Zubayr, Rabih, and al-Sanusi of Dar al-Kuti, built new, multiethnic political units in the south by surrounding themselves with non-Muslim captives who acquiesced in the hope of at last finding peace, and perhaps acquiring northern goods. Most of these new states only endured a short time, since their power was based on a precarious superiority in firearms and tactics. Rival centers of power invariably developed to challenge them.

Chapter 2
Dar al-Kuti: Early Muslim Settlement, Commerce, and Islam

The history of Dar al-Kuti in the nineteenth and early twentieth-centuries can be divided into two periods based on the degree of Muslim commercial penetration, Islamic influence, and centralized political power.[1] The first era encompasses the years from the establishment of Muslim settlements in the 1820s to the 1870s and early 1880s, when the Khartoumer marauders arrived in the region. Their raids marked the beginning of a second period characterized by a great expansion of slave-raiding, as well as an increased level of violence generally. The French conquest of Dar al-Kuti in 1911 brought this era to a close.

The following pages focus primarily on the first period, when colonies of Muslims from the north came to flourish among the non-Muslim populations of Dar al-Kuti. In addition, the chapter documents—mainly through reference to oral traditions—the emergence of a lineage of faqih-traders with political, economic, and religious ties to the northern Muslim states of Dar Runga, Wadai, and Bagirmi. These individuals laid the foundations on which al-Sanusi was later to build his sultanate. But discussion of these developments is best prefaced by an overview of the land and peoples of Dar al-Kuti.

Physical Setting

The earliest direct references to Kuti identify it as that portion of the southeastern Chad basin immediately south of the Aouk River and east of the lands of the Sara.[2] This usage has not changed significantly; the inhabitants of the northern Central African Republic still refer to the Aouk flood plain north and west of Ndele as Dar al-Kuti.[3] Members of the French scientific and military missions that began to frequent the area in the late 1890s altered the scope of the term in their reports, broadening it to include Banda lands in the northern Zaire watershed,[4] a shift of meaning readily explained by the balance of power then prevailing in northern Ubangi-

Shari. Al-Sanusi was the most prominent local ruler in the area when the French arrived, and they consequently identified Dar al-Kuti with his domains, which by that time encompassed Banda territories to the south and southeast.[5] In this chapter, "Dar al-Kuti" will be used in its earlier and more restricted sense to refer to the Aouk plain, whereas the much larger area conquered by al-Sanusi will be called the sultanate of Dar al-Kuti. This usage also reflects the distinction made by many informants between the time of al-Sanusi and all earlier leaders; the changes he wrought were so great that they count him as the first "sultan" in the region.[6]

The area of Dar al-Kuti forms an irregular triangle with northwestern, eastern, and southern boundaries (see map 4). The northwestern frontier is marked by the Aouk River, a stream that flows southwest for about 230 kilometers from its origin at the point where the Aoukale and Kameur Rivers come together, to the place where it converges with the Bamingui to form the Shari. From the Aouk, the lands of Kuti stretch away to less well-defined borders in the east and south. The eastern limit follows the Tete (or Manovo) and Koumbala (or Massaberta), streams running north to the Aouk from the slopes of highlands east of Ndele; the southern frontier runs west from Ndele to the Bangoran River and on to the confluence of the Bamingui and Aouk.

Northern and western Dar al-Kuti consists primarily of plains—either permanent marshes, or lowlands subject to flooding during the rains. In the southeast near Ndele, however, the westernmost projections of the high-lands along the Central African Republic-Sudan border break up the terrain, but at this point, they are steep hills divided by rocky valleys rather than separate plateaux. Throughout Dar al-Kuti there are numerous streams. The larger ones flow throughout the year, while the smaller ones dry up in the dry season. Some, such as the Jangara, run northward to the Aouk, and others, such as the Miangoulou and the Jamssinda, head south to the Bangoran. This environment supports the vegetation characteristic of the African savanna: tall grasses blanket the plains, broken here and there by trees. Dense gallery forests line many of the watercourses where greater moisture and humidity permit more luxuriant plant growth.[7]

These gallery forests are such a distinguishing feature of the terrain that they may well have given the region its name. Asked about the derivation of the word *kuti*, informants immediately responded by saying that it was used by the Nduka—the people with the longest history of residence in the area— to refer to a very close thicket of trees and underbrush. Most informants emphasized the density of such a forest: "you do not see your brother at all, when you enter this place you do not see your brother at all"; or, "there are many trees, and when you enter, it is dark and you get very confused . . . you lose your way."[8]

This interpretation may be nothing more than a simple folk etymology, but the history of slave-raiding in the region suggests that it merits some consideration. Before al-Sanusi secured the region, and even afterwards, Wadaian horsemen occasionally came south during the dry season to take captives. Because the plains afforded little shelter from attacks, the Nduka sought protection by either building their villages in the dense gallery forests along major streams or fleeing to these areas. In the southeast, they also safeguarded themselves by locating their settlements on or near the rocky hills which were separated by wooded valleys. This was probably the most common mode of day-to-day defense. The forests were (and are) frequently infested with tse-tse flies, which would have made permanent residence there very uncomfortable; at the same time, however, the insects made the thickets more attractive as places for temporary refuge because they threatened the health of the Wadaian horses.[9]

The Nduka

All sources suggest that the Nduka are the oldest remaining inhabitants of Dar al-Kuti.[10] They live in the eastern two-thirds of the region adjacent to the related Sara. In between the Sara and the Nduka are smaller groups of people, such as the Lutos (perhaps also called the Routou, Aretou, and Leto), the Gime (Djemmi), and the Tenne (Tane).[11] Prioul suggests that these populations lived farther east in the mid-nineteenth century, moving west in the 1880s to escape slave-raiding. In any case, the French expeditions of the following decade came into contact with all of them except the Lutos.[12] These peoples share similar styles of life and speak related languages.[13] In descriptions and linguistic classifications composed early in the colonial period and since, the authors shuffle and reshuffle these peoples and their languages into different groups.[14] But in the absence of extensive linguistic research it is impossible to choose one scheme over the others. It suffices to note that the data indicate the existence of a cluster of eastern Sara and Sara-related languages, spoken by peoples whose cultures are also similar. The Nduka of Dar al-Kuti are the easternmost representatives of this group.[15]

The Nduka divide themselves into as many as eight subgroups.[16] Like their Sara neighbors to the west, they apparently never formed part of a larger state. Each small group had its own homeland, and political organization was decentralized.[17] Leadership roles were limited. Authority within each subgroup was vested in two ritual figures, the *ngarje* or earth chief and the leader of the *sumali* or boys' initiation rite. On occasion, these positions were held by the same individual, who as a result, enjoyed

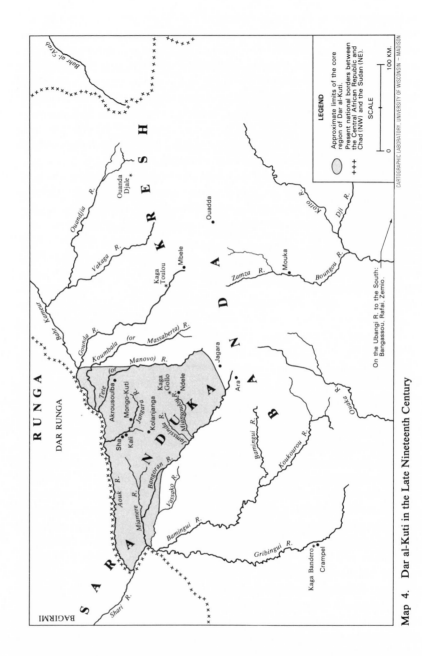

Map 4. Dar al-Kuti in the Late Nineteenth Century

LEGEND

Approximate limits of the core
region of Dar al-Kuti.

+++ Present national borders between
the Central African Republic and
Chad (NW) and the Sudan (NE).

SCALE

0   100 KM.

CARTOGRAPHIC LABORATORY, UNIVERSITY OF WISCONSIN – MADISON

On the Ubangi R. to the South:
Bangassou, Rafaï, Zemio.

BAGIRMI

S A R A

R U N G A

DAR RUNGA

K R E S H

N D U K A

B A N D A

Bahr al-'Arab

Ouandjia R.

Vakaga R.

Bahr Kameur

Gounda R.

Ouanda
Djalé

Mbele

Kaga
Toulou

Ouadda

Zamza R.

Mouka

Boungou R.

Kotto R.

Dji R.

Koumbala (or Massaberta) R.

Manovo R.

Tete (or

Jagara

Akrousoulba

Mongo-Kuti

Jangara R.

Kolanjanga

Kaga
Gollo

Ndele

Ara

Ouaka R.

Sha

Kali

Miangoulou R.

Tomi R.

Aouk R.

Miamere R.

Bangoran R.

Vassako R.

Bamingui R.

Koukourou R.

Bamingui R.

Shari R.

Gribingui R.

Kaga Bandero

Crampel

34

increased prestige. The ngarje presided over planting and harvest rituals, offered libations at the locations where important place spirits were believed to reside, and performed other rites necessary to bring good fortune in hunting, fishing, and gathering activities. In short, he was responsible for the fertility and well-being of the land; and in return, he had a right to a certain portion of all that came from his domains. The duties of the sumali leader were more restricted, being limited to the conduct of ceremonies connected with boys' initiation and manhood training. Such rituals only occurred every several years, but the leader remained influential in the community during the hiatus between ceremonies.[18]

The small-scale societies of the Nduka resembled others in the region. Among the Sara, Jaulin's analysis of the boys' initiation and wider patterns of political and social organization offers a guide to understanding parallel aspects of Nduka culture—particularly since the Sara and Nduka are closely related.[19] Southwest of Dar al-Kuti, among the Gbaya of the Ouham River valley, the traditional *wan*, or earth chief, occupied a position resembling that of the Nduka ngarje; in fact, among the Gbaya he was also known as an ngarage.[20]

The Runga

The Runga also played an important role in the history of Dar al-Kuti. Unlike the Nduka, the Runga were not an autochthonous population, but were migrants who began moving south from their homelands across the Aouk in Dar Runga in the early nineteenth century. Also unlike the early Nduka, the Runga professed Islam. In fact, they were probably the first Muslim population to settle in Dar al-Kuti in large numbers; today the region is one of the very few in the Central African Republic where villages of Muslim cultivators are found in the countryside.

Writers on the Central African Republic have theorized that the Runga are a mixed Sara-Banda population. Given the proximity of the Runga to these peoples, this conclusion is not surprising, but the linguistic and cultural data suggest otherwise.[21] The Runga possess their own language and culture, and both appear to be more closely related to those of Wadaian populations to the north than to the southern Sara and Banda. Map 3 (chapter 1) indicates that the Banda and Sara belong to two different language groups (Greenberg's I.A.6 and II.E.2, respectively). Were the Runga only a product of Banda and Sara intermarriage, one would expect their language to resemble those spoken by their forebears. But this is not the case. Greenberg apparently had no data on Runga, but he classes Tama and Dagu (Dajo), languages spoken farther north and similar to Runga, in an Eastern Sudanic group (II.E.1) distinct from both Sara and Banda. Runga word lists collected in Wadai and Dar Fur and published by Browne (1806) and Jomard (1845) support this classification. Gaudefroy-Demombynes also placed these languages in different groups based on vocabularies assembled around 1900.[22] And finally, the Runga of Dar al-Kuti today say that their language more closely resembles those spoken in Wadai than Sara or Banda.[23]

Linguistic clues also suggest that pre-Islamic Runga religion shared some features with the traditional religions of the Zaghawa peoples in northern Wadai. Both the Runga and Zaghawa, for example, use the term *kunus* to describe similar pre-Islamic rituals that took place outside the village and involved sacrifices to the ancestors, or offerings to the mountains and trees where important place spirits resided. The word *kunus* is thus more than a simple loan word; its use by the Runga and the peoples of northern Wadai indicates that they shared a basic ritual. Neither the Banda nor the Sara use the term.[24]

Like the Nduka, the Runga divide themselves into smaller subgroups, which fall into two divisions: those who migrated south to Dar al-Kuti, and those who remained in Dar Runga.[25] The southern Runga sometimes call themselves Runga-Kuti, a reference to their ties with the Nduka as well as to their geographical location. Despite this designation, they minimize the distinction between themselves and the northern Runga, a viewpoint in keeping with the proximity of Dar Runga and Dar al-Kuti and continued contact between them. Many families in the south have close relatives living in the north, and Runga traders frequently travel from one area to the other.[26] Because this study focuses on Dar al-Kuti, the term Runga will be used alone to refer to the southern Runga (Runga-Kuti) unless otherwise specified. As for the subgroups, only the Runga-Bagrim, who played a special role in the establishment of early Muslim communities in Dar al-Kuti and later rise of the sultanate, will be given individual consideration.

The Runga of Dar Runga and Dar al-Kuti are primarily an agricultural people who earn their livelihood by growing millets, sorghums, and beans.[27] In the south, they also have raised manioc as an insurance crop since the early part of the century. Despite the emphasis on cultivation, however, many individuals engage in fishing and commerce either part-time or for part of their lives. In the north, a few people own cattle as well; the Runga have no great equestrian tradition, and horses are not common among them. Crafts include the weaving of grass mats, baskets, and platters, and up until recently, they also grew, spun, and wove cotton into cloth for wear and exchange.

Most of the Runga in both north and south are Muslims, and in Dar al-

Kuti they count themselves followers of the Tijaniya brotherhood. Political authority in a Runga village is usually vested in a Muslim chief who governs largely by consensus, whereas ritual powers are in the hands of Muslim religious leaders—teachers and healers usually called faqihs, and prominent members of the Tijaniya. The Runga in the south, in addition, acknowledge the powers and responsibilities of the Nduka ritual leaders over the land. In turn, some Nduka ritual leaders have converted to Islam while continuing to perform their traditional duties.

Broader authority in the north was traditionally wielded by the sultans of Dar Runga, whose state dates from at least the eighteenth century. In the south, the creation of broader bases of power occurred concurrently with the development of the sultanate of Dar al-Kuti.

The Beginnings: Early Muslim Infiltration and the Runga-Bagrim

Muslim infiltration into Dar al-Kuti can be seen as part of the overall southward shift of the Islamic frontier in North Central Africa in the nineteenth century. However, this phenomenon took a shape adapted to local conditions. Muslims probably began arriving in the first several decades of the nineteenth century, when the first references to the region appear in the Muslim-European travel literature.[28] The newcomers were not part of a mass migration; instead, they came to Dar al-Kuti in small groups to trade the goods of regional commerce—most notably the homespun cotton cloth produced on narrow looms in the Sahel just to the north, rather than the broader cloth that later poured in through trans-Saharan exchange to become the mainstay of long-distance commerce. Some settled in the area, taking wives from the Nduka and establishing permanent ties with prominent local figures; others came to trade only during the dry season, when travel was easier, returning north before the rains. This latter pattern accommodated itself well to the agricultural calendar of the peoples of Dar al-Kuti, who spent much of the dry season hunting elephants for ivory which they then gave to the northerners in payment for their goods. Slaves were not the major export of Dar al-Kuti at this time, although slave-raiding parties from Wadai sometimes passed through the region.[29]

Some of the products and general patterns of this regional commerce are known. First, crafts specialization has provided a basis for exchange for a long time. The Nduka, the Sara, and the Bagirmi are producers of excellent pottery. The Nduka, in particular, are famed for making large (1.5m × 1m) jars called *dabanga*, that are desired items of local exchange. The Runga, on the other hand, have long been noted weavers, and have traded the products of their handiwork. Iron goods were also important in regional trade, and these items—hoes, *sagaies* (daggers), spears, and throwing knives—came from Banda, Sara, and Nduka blacksmiths; the Runga do not enjoy a reputation for ironworking, and even when they lived in Dar Runga before migrating south, they relied on neighboring peoples for their iron goods. In addition to these products, narrow, homespun cloth from the Muslim zones to the north was a major trade item, although the Runga continued to produce cloth after their move to Dar al-Kuti.[30]

Local environmental differences afforded a second basis for regional exchange. In Dar al-Kuti, fishing provided the Runga communities along the Aouk with a product in demand in other locales. Villages near the river—notably Bilkinya and Akrousoulba—have a long history of trading dried fish to settlements not located on water.[31] Copper from Hufrat al-Nuhas in the southwestern Sudan may also have stimulated regional and long-distance commerce in northern Ubangi-Shari. In the nineteenth century, European travelers in Muslim zones farther north noted that copper from these mines made its way to markets in Hausaland, Dar Fur, Kordofan, and the Nile area. It is likely that the metal was traded in adjacent portions of Ubangi-Shari as well. Banda informants maintain that a "very long time" ago, bridewealth was partially paid in *mbala*, large copper anklets similar to those described by Browne and Pallme. According to the Banda, these ornaments came from far away. How the metal was marketed and transported is unclear, but Nachtigal's informants suggested that a trade route linked the mines with Banda country farther west.[32] Recent mineralogical surveys in the Central African Republic conclude that, despite traces of copper near Ouanda-Djale in the northeast, no other deposits exist in the eastern part of the country that could have been worked before the invention of modern techniques.[33]

The Muslims who went to Dar al-Kuti during these early years were predominantly from Dar Runga and Bagirmi. Informants invariably cite these two peoples as the first migrant groups, which is not surprising, since both states lay nearby—Dar Runga just north of the Aouk, and Bagirmi several hundred kilometers downstream along the Middle Shari.[34] By the 1830s, the Runga south of the Aouk had become numerous enough to prompt the Runga sultan to appoint a regional governor. As for Bagirmi, it was farther from the area, but the Shari River provided a natural access route, and the inhabitants of the state have a long history of river navigation.[35] Moreover, drought and persecution of Muslim teachers in Bagirmi in the early decades of the nineteenth century prompted many individuals to emigrate east and southeast. Bagirmi also came into indirect contact with Dar al-Kuti through western Sara groups such as the Majingay and Kaba, whose territories lay within the Bagirmi sphere of influence, but who also had dealings with the eastern Sara and the Nduka. The clearest evidence for the existence of links between Bagirmi and Dar al-Kuti is provided by Barth. During his stay in the capital at Massenya in 1852, the explorer collected information on the Sara lands and Dar al-Kuti. Using terminology probably employed in Bagirmi, he called the Nduka homeland Kutingara, which means "Kuti chiefs" in the Sara, Barma (Bagirmi), and Nduka languages.[36]

It is impossible to separate the dual currents of Muslim influence from Dar Runga and Bagirmi in the early nineteenth century. First, itinerant traders and migrants from both states appeared south of the Aouk about the same time. Second, a mixed group of people called the Runga-Bagrim emerged during this period. This group has provided the political, economic, and religious leadership of Dar al-Kuti from the time the Runga sultan first appointed a governor to the present day. The name Runga-Bagrim suggests that these people were the descendants of direct Runga-Bagirmi intermarriage in Dar al-Kuti, but the pattern of migration indicates that such was not the case. Oral traditions claim that the newcomers from Dar Runga and Bagirmi were mainly men who settled and then intermarried with the Nduka. If this is so, then the Runga-Bagrim must have issued from the incorporation of some of these men into the same Nduka lineages and were therefore a mixed Runga-Bagirmi-Nduka group. It seems reasonable to suspect, too, that the early Runga and arrivals from Bagirmi sought close ties with the Nduka, given the special regard that later Muslim migrants had for them as the principal inhabitants of Dar al-Kuti, and their practice of taking Nduka wives.[37]

An alternative explanation, and one which also has some basis in oral tradition, suggests that the the Runga-Bagrim are the products of a two-step migration. One important informant insisted that they were descendants of Bagirmi migrants who first settled in Dar Runga and intermarried with the Runga. Later, they or their descendants reportedly came into conflict with their Runga countrymen, and moved south of the Aouk where they married Nduka women.[38]

In any case, the data for Dar al-Kuti remain inconclusive, and both Dar Runga and Bagirmi await serious historical inquiry.[39] Given the proximity of all three regions, it is quite possible that both patterns of movement and incorporation occurred at one time or another. What is very clear is that the Runga-Bagrim do have close ties with the Nduka. Today among both the Nduka and the Runga, traditions recalling close ties with Bagirmi are common, even though everyone agrees that by the time of al-Sanusi in the 1890s there were few purely Bagirmi residents or traders in Dar al-Kuti. These claims are confirmed by the absence of references to the Bagirmi in

Banda traditions, an understandable omission because extensive Banda settlement in Dar al-Kuti came only with the beginning of intensive raiding and the forced relocation of Banda captives by Rabih and al-Sanusi in the late 1880s, 1890s, and early 1900s. By that time, the early Bagirmi population would have disappeared.[40]

The Bagirmi Factor

The reconstruction of the history of the Runga-Bagrim forms part of a larger effort to explain what might well be termed the "Bagirmi factor" in the history of North Central Africa. Throughout the first half of the nineteenth century, and perhaps even before, Bagirmi was an important center of crafts and commerce in the Sahel and savanna regions east of Borno; it also possessed a sphere of religious and political influence that extended beyond its boundaries. Although exports of locally manufactured and dyed cloth, non-Muslim slaves from lands to the south, and eunuchs were partially responsible for Bagirmi's commercial prominence, its influence seems to have stemmed primarily from the migration of large numbers of people from the core area to other parts of North Central Africa. Paradoxically, this emigration came from an area that, in the colonial period at least, suffered from a chronically low birthrate that alarmed European authorities.[41] The question, therefore, is how and why these movements occurred, and what effects they had on surrounding areas.

Some elements of an eventual explanation are already obvious. First, it is clear that much mobility was involuntary. The Wadaian sultans Sabun and ^cAli, for example, both took many craftsmen back to Wadai after campaigns in Bagirmi in 1816–17 and 1871. Groups of refugees also left Bagirmi following internal succession crises, conflicts which were common in the state's history. These forced migrations were in part responsible for a proliferation of Bagirmi settlements throughout the region. Nachtigal noted the existence of ten Bagirmi villages in southern Wadai in the early 1870s, and when he visited Dar Fur, the explorer reported that Bagirmi communities were found everywhere in the state as a result of migrations which began in the previous century.[42]

Commercial motivations also prompted some Bagirmi to leave their homeland. In neighboring lands to the east, Bagirmi crafts products were as popular as Bagirmi craftsmen. Cloth woven and dyed in Bagirmi was in demand among the Sara, as well as among the peoples of Wadai and southern vassal states such as Dar al-Kuti. Bagirmi's preeminent position in this realm largely resulted from the contacts that the state enjoyed with Borno and Hausaland. Both were important centers of cloth manufacture and dyeing, and the eastward diaspora of Hausa and Bornoan traders and pilgrims brought techniques associated with these activities to Bagirmi. From there, the cloth and the techniques spread farther east. Bagirmi traders were important agents of this diffusion, although increasing numbers of Hausa and Bornoan peddlers joined them during the nineteenth century. Itinerant Bagirmi traders were common in the lands of the Sara, which is to be expected, since many Sara chiefs were Bagirmi clients. The emergence of the Runga-Bagrim in Dar al-Kuti shows that these traders also ventured beyond the sphere of Bagirmi political authority. The presence of additional Bagirmi communities in Wadai and Dar Fur suggests that a Bagirmi commercial network linked all these regions with the homeland.[43]

Bagirmi also enjoyed considerable religious and political influence in North Central Africa. Three important elements of that influence may be discerned. The first of these was Fulani clerics, who played a singularly important role in the religious history of Bagirmi. This is true both in the early spread of the faith along the Middle Shari and in attempts at Islamic reform in the nineteenth century. This latter phase of Islamization stemmed in large measure from connections with Hausaland and Borno, where the Fulani-led *jihads* (holy wars) of Usuman dan Fodio, religious teacher and founder of the Sokoto Caliphate, made a definition of and adherence to orthodox Islam an important political issue.

In the second half of the nineteenth century, several long-established and influential Islamic centers existed in Bagirmi. The most notable was Bidri, a village located just east of the capital at Massenya; AbuGhern, just to the north, was another. A Fulani settlement, Bidri had long supplied religious advisors to the court of the Bagirmi sultan.[44] It is not known when the village was founded, but Nachtigal theorized that the Fulani arrived in the area east of Lake Chad in the fifteenth century, citing as evidence their involvement with the Bulala of Lake Fitri, the dominant people in the region at the time. His judgment is in accord with Barth, who linked Bidri with the building of Massenya in the late sixteenth century.[45] Over time, intermarriage with local women produced a Fulani-Bagirmi religious class which continued the tradition of learning and preaching. The central role of Fulani-Bagirmi clerics becomes clearer in the state's later history. They fostered Islamization in Bagirmi and regions to the east; in addition, they were, and remain, important in lands to the west—the Fulani emirates of the Logone and even Borno itself.

But as the Bagirmi state took shape, clashes occurred when Fulani-Bagirmi clerics joined with more recently arrived Muslims to condemn the rulers (*mbangs*) at Massenya for trying to reconcile the demands of orthodox Islam with the traditional beliefs of many of their subjects. These conflicts erupted in periodic purges of Fulani religious leaders in Bagirmi. As a result, many returned to their homelands farther west. Others, however, migrated eastward to Wadai and northern Ubangi-Shari, where they propagated the faith. People in these areas, places like Dar al-Kuti, remember Bagirmi as the provenance of these men of piety.[46]

Apart from the general eastward drift of the Fulani which brought these herders and their religious leaders to Bagirmi, two other external factors encouraged Islamization along the Middle Shari, Muslim emigration, and the image of Bagirmi as a center of Islam. There was, as already noted, the pilgrimage. Although Bagirmi was not a Muslim land of long standing, it lay between West Africa and the Hijaz. The deeper penetration of Islamic influence in the west which came with the Fulani jihads stimulated greater numbers of the faithful to make the *hajj*. And, as Works, al-Naqar, and Birks have shown, this more or less coincided with increased use of the sub-Saharan pilgrimage route which ran directly east through the Sahel to the holy places of Arabia.[47]

In the early 1800s, when Islamic revivalism was at its peak in lands to the west, pilgrims probably represented the segment of society most deeply committed to practicing what they considered to be proper or orthodox Islam; hence their sacrifices to make the pilgrimage. In Bagirmi and elsewhere along the hajj route, conflicts frequently pitted these travelers against local authorities. Some pilgrims traveled alone or only with their immediate families, but others, notably Muslim teachers with wide reputations, moved with large entourages and attracted other followers along the way. They had a double impact on Bagirmi. They inspired respect for the faith among local peoples, but they also posed a threat to the Bagirmi rulers. And not only did they criticize the syncretic Islam of the mbangs, but they were a drain on food supplies in the regions they crossed. They also urged people to abandon their villages and join their parties, thus menacing the demographic foundations of the state.

Faqih Sharif al-Din was a case in point. A Fulani teacher from the Niger region, he arrived at the borders of Bagirmi in 1856. During his trip from the west, he had amassed a large following. Austere and reported to possess powers of prophecy, Sharif al-Din called himself *mahadi*, a variant of *Mahdi*, the name given to the expected harbinger of the end of the world in Islamic eschatology. Mai ᶜUmar of Borno (1837–53; 1854–71) was reluctant to allow him into his realm, but eventually did so, and many of his subjects joined the faqih's entourage. By the time Sharif al-Din reached Bagirmi, his party numbered several thousand, including a fighting force. The mbang ᶜAbd al-Qadir refused to authorize entry to his lands, maintained that he could not afford to lose any more of his people, and suggested that the faqih skirt Bagirmi territory to the south. Sharif al-Din refused and marched to Bugoman near the Bagirmi capital. Nachtigal later reported that many Fulani, Arabs, and Bagirmi joined him, "leaving their domestic hearths in order to win Paradise in the train of holy war." The mbang decided to meet the challenge with armed force. In the ensuing clash, he and several of his important military leaders were killed, while Sharif al-Din and his followers moved up the Shari. But the faqih soon lost control of the party. Numerous people deserted to return home, only to be killed by Mohammedu, the new mbang. The entire undertaking fell apart soon after when non-Muslims southeast of Bagirmi killed the faqih. Some of his party fled north to Wadai, others tried to return home, and still others settled in neighboring regions.[48] Some of these individuals may well have made their way to nearby Dar Runga and Dar al-Kuti.

The increased flow of pilgrims from West Africa grew out of a third set of events—the jihads of Usuman dan Fodio and associated efforts to establish Islamic orthodoxy in Hausaland and Borno. The link was quite direct. Part of Usuman dan Fodio's prophecy concerned the imminent appearance of a Mahdi who was to be preceded by a mass migration of Muslims to the east, towards the Nile and Mecca beyond. This meant that the way had to be prepared. Dan Fodio is said to have designated a cousin, Muhammadu Lamiinu (also called Muhammad al-Hajj al-Amin or Aahi Buulo), to conquer Bagirmi in 1815, and bring it into the Sokoto Caliphate. Such a campaign seemed critical because the Bagirmi rulers had already begun persecuting Fulani in their lands in an effort to forestall a jihad.[49]

Muhammadu Lamiinu and his forces arrived in Bagirmi in 1820; however, they were opposed by the established religious communities, which had long provided advisors to the Bagirmi court and were presumably implicated in the practice of syncretic Islam. The mbang also resisted outside interference. A confrontation ensued, and the Bagirmi forces were victorious. Most of the followers of Lamiinu dispersed westward, crossed the Logone River, and eventually founded the Fulani state of Kalfu, which was linked closely with Sokoto.[50]

In Bagirmi the persecution that accompanied this conflict brought an exodus of the Fulani. Once again clerics moved into the lands east and south of the Shari. This diaspora was further encouraged by a long drought which hit Bagirmi sometime during the reign of Mbang Bourgomanda II (1807–46, Nachtigal chronology), bringing with it a great famine.[51] These events roughly coincide with testimonies collected in Dar al-Kuti claiming that drought and "conflict in the north" resulted in a wave of Muslim immigration at this time.[52] Thus the infiltration of Muslims into Dar al-Kuti appears to be at least indirectly tied to the jihads in Hausaland and Borno.

For all of these reasons, then, peoples to the east viewed Bagirmi as a source of Islamic influence. During the first Wadaian campaign against

Bagirmi, for example, sultan Sabun took great care to pay proper respect to the *ulama'* (religious scholars) of each village in his path; he also left pious offerings at the tombs of local saints. While his motivations were undoubtedly as much political as religious, they still indicate a special regard for Bagirmi as a cradle of the faith.[53]

The tapestry intertwining these threads remains to be woven, but what is apparent beyond question is that the Bagirmi factor greatly influenced the history of the lands bordering the state in the east—lands such as Dar al-Kuti. Claims to possess religious and political ties with Bagirmi came to be a source of legitimacy in lands that never formed part of the Bagirmi state. This reputation for piety lives on today in Dar al-Kuti, where the Runga-Bagrim provide religious leaders for other Runga and Muslim Nduka communities.[54]

The Earliest Muslim Ruler of Dar al-Kuti

In the 1830s, after some years of Runga and Bagirmi infiltration into Dar al-Kuti, the sultan of Dar Runga formalized Runga claims to the area with the appointment of a governor (*ᶜaqid*). By this time, Dar Runga was a tribute-paying client of Wadai, and Dar al-Kuti consequently found itself indirectly incorporated into the greater Wadaian sphere, a position that it would occupy for most of the period up to the French conquest. Annexation does not seem to have brought any great or immediate changes in its wake. It did stimulate immigration, but there was no flood of migrants, and most newcomers still arrived in small groups, attracted by the prospects of small-scale regional commerce. These Muslims, like their predecessors, settled among the indigenous Nduka, marrying and trading with them. They were weak numerically and militarily, and the pillaging and slave-raiding among the neighboring Banda and Kresh that passed for commerce later in the century had not yet begun.[55]

All of the sources on the history of Dar al-Kuti identify the earliest governor as a Bagirmi or Runga-Bagrim migrant, a pilgrim *achevé* or *manqué*, who married the daughter of the Runga sultan, and then settled south of the Aouk to administer the area on behalf of his father-in-law. At least five partial or complete lists of rulers link him with the flesh-and-blood figures who governed later in the century (see appendix 2). Without exception, these later rulers, including Muhammad al-Sanusi and his descendants, who continue to hold positions of authority, claim close kinship affiliation with this first ᶜaqid.[56]

Most writings on the first ᶜaqid, from the turn of the century to the present, reproduce traditions collected by Emile Julien, the first French resident in Dar al-Kuti, who served as a de facto ambassador to the court of al-Sanusi in 1902.[57] Julien gives the ruler the name ᶜUmar Jugultum al-Bagirmai and suggests that he was a son of the Bagirmi sultan, Bourgomanda, who fled his homeland during a succession crisis following his father's death in 1826. He then reportedly went to Mecca, returned to Dar Runga where he married the sultan's daughter, and migrated south to administer Dar al-Kuti in 1830. He ruled until his death forty years later, whereupon Kobur replaced him. More specific information about this early figure is not available today, and judging from Julien's account it was not available at the turn of the century either. The salient features of his career, as narrated in oral traditions recorded by Julien, conform to an Islamic archetype in the Lake Chad-Nile region: A Muslim religious figure appears, in this case from Bagirmi, but more commonly from the Nile area or Dar Fur. Usually he is said to be a faqih or an *al-hajj*, one who has completed the pilgrimage. The local ruler, sometimes a Muslim himself, encourages the holy man to settle and offers to give him his daughter in marriage, generally without exacting bridewealth. The migrant accepts, and usually succeeds his father-in-law.[58]

Very likely this sequence of events did unfold in the Lake Chad-Nile region, maybe even several times; pilgrimage routes crossed the region, and pilgrims frequently enjoyed a special regard among the peoples whose lands they traversed. The point is not that such an event could not have occurred in Dar al-Kuti, but rather that it is not certain that it did. Until research on Bagirmi and Dar Runga or further work in Dar al-Kuti provides more solid data, the narrative describing the arrival of the first ᶜaqid can only be accepted as a stylized version of this event.

Besides failing to distinguish the individual ruler from the generalized narrative, the few details provided by Julien raise questions. According to Nachtigal, the best source for the history of Bagirmi, and the one accepted by both Gaden and Devallée (who did research in the area), the Bagirmi sultan Bourgomanda did not die in 1826, but ruled until 1846. Barth described a long period of domestic turmoil and resistance to foreign intervention in Bagirmi following the invasion by Sultan Sabun of Wadai in 1816–17, but included no information on royal exiles who emigrated to the east. At the very least, then, Julien's dates are probably wrong.[59]

These dates pose a second problem as well. Jugultum's forty-year reign seems too long, particularly in light of the much shorter periods during which Kobur and al-Sanusi ruled Dar al-Kuti, and the lengths of reigns in neighboring states such as Wadai, Dar Fur, and Bagirmi.[60] The neatness of the reign's beginning and end (1830–70) also arouses suspicion.

A final question centers on the name Jugultum (or Djougoultoum, French transliteration). The name is probably of Bagirmi or Sara origin, which would support the traditions claiming a connection with these areas.[61] However, it also closely resembles the name Jugeldu (or Djougueldou, French transliteration), belonging to one of twelve mythical brothers said to have founded the Bagirmi state.[62] Hence the appearance of the name in the Dar al-Kuti list may simply be a case of "genealogical parasitism," the grafting of all or parts of one kinglist onto that of a nearby state of greater antiquity—a practice aimed at creating an aura of legitimacy.[63]

After these objections are taken into consideration, Dar al-Kuti is left with an early ruler possessing a purported Bagirmi pedigree and a reputation for piety. The dates of his reign are indefinite, although the Muslim-European travel literature and Nachtigal suggest that Dar al-Kuti was incorporated into Dar Runga and Wadai in the 1830s. This is all that can be said of the first ^{c}aqid of Dar al-Kuti. To claim more would be to replace historical probability with wishful thinking. Yet even this small bit of information is useful, for it provides a basis for discussing Kobur, the first definitely historical figure to rule Dar al-Kuti.

Kobur, Faqih and Trader

Kobur became the Muslim governor of Dar al-Kuti in the late 1860s or early 1870s, and ruled until 1890 when Muhammad al-Sanusi, his nephew and a client of Rabih, succeeded him. He died two years later, the year following the arrival and massacre of the Mission Crampel, the first European expedition to reach the area.

Kobur's reign was a watershed in the history of Dar al-Kuti. When he came to power, the Muslim population south of the Aouk was still small, consisting of first- or later-generation Runga and Bagirmi, along with a few recently arrived Hausa and Bornoan trader-pilgrims. While limited slave-trading took place, intense raiding had not yet begun. But several hundred kilometers southeast of Dar al-Kuti, among the Banda, Sudanese traders were already building *zaribas* (armed camps [Arabic]) which served as headquarters for raiding parties. Closer to home, a group of al-Zubayr's bazingirs from southern Dar Fur ravaged Kobur's own village in 1876; in the same decade, Rabih appeared in Ubangi-Shari, first pillaging Banda lands and then invading Dar al-Kuti and Dar Runga. In addition to these Muslim raiders, Ngono, a nearby Banda Ngao war leader with military and commercial ties to the Muslim merchants of the Bahr al-Ghazal, also attacked Kobur and his followers in 1874, and again in 1877 or 1878—the second time on the heels of the ruler's encounter with al-Zubayr's forces.[64] Although this catalog of conflict makes it appear that Kobur was menaced from all sides, it exhausts the list of major challenges to his rule. They affected him only intermittently, but they were harbingers of change.

The circumstances surrounding Kobur's rise to power are unknown, although he is purported to have been the son of his predecessor (see appendix 2). Like his forebears, he is said to have been of Bagirmi origin, and enjoyed a reputation for piety. Unlike his forebears, however, most of the traditions about him are vivid. They repeatedly emphasize his role as a faqih, indeed a great faqih, who inspired followers by his example. A story still told in Dar al-Kuti suggests that Kobur even impressed Rabih with his holiness and renown: After deposing Kobur in favor of al-Sanusi, Rabih supposedly had the former ruler placed in chains and guarded; at nightfall when it came time to pray, Kobur stood up and the chains fell from his feet. The guard, fearing that harm would surely come to anyone who imprisoned such a holy man, reported the matter to Rabih, who ordered Kobur's release.[65]

Kobur's reputation did not bring him a return to power, but he was numbered among al-Sanusi's advisors until his death in 1892. His direct descendants carried on this religious tradition. He had ten sons, some of whom lived into the 1920s, and all of whom were respected faqihs in Dar al-Kuti.[66] Reckoning with Kobur's position as a faqih is fundamental to understanding his leadership role in Dar al-Kuti. His power stemmed from his prestige and reputation, along with his commercial activities. He never possessed the absolute military strength that al-Sanusi would have, nor was his trading operation as extensive as that of his successor. Differences in both style and scale set the two leaders apart, and all the oral sources on Dar al-Kuti recognize these distinctions. They emphasize that while Kobur was a revered faqih, al-Sanusi was the first sultan. Kobur was special, but his position was in keeping with the role of a traditional faqih and Muslim village chief. Al-Sanusi, on the other hand, was a new kind of figure.[67]

As for Kobur's commercial undertakings, they were modest alongside those of al-Sanusi, but apparently considerable by prevailing standards. He exchanged ivory, slaves, and lesser exports for imported beads and cloth. How he collected slaves and ivory, and how he distributed the goods received in return for them, is not evident, but it seems that an extensive network of direct commercial dealings, marriage alliances, blood partnership pacts, tribute payments, and gift exchange similar to that which underlay al-Sanusi's state was also an important feature of Kobur's operations (see chapters 5 and 6). In addition, his position as a faqih also enabled him to mediate trade between the increasing numbers of foreign Muslim traders—a few Jallaba had by now joined the growing group of Hausa and Bornoans—and the local Runga (Runga-Nduka) and Nduka.[68]

Unlike his predecessors and his successor, Kobur did not expand the

Islamic frontier, but the first decade of his rule was significant because apart from his own dealings, he established Dar al-Kuti as an important Muslim commercial outpost. Cognizant that peaceful relations with the north encouraged traders to come south with their goods, he remained a faithful client of the sultan of Runga; probably as a further aid to communication and commerce, he multiplied his marriage alliances with the northern Runga and the other Wadaian satellite states. He also acknowledged the ultimate authority of Wadai, the major power in the eastern Chad basin in the 1870s, by regularly offering tribute. Within Dar al-Kuti, he ruled wisely. Julien's sources described Kobur as a leader who maintained harmony between the Muslims and non-Muslims in his domains, a sensitivity that undoubtedly grew out of the fact that he was born in this frontier zone himself and was of mixed Runga-Bagirmi-Nduka ancestry.[69]

These policies had commercial rewards. Apart from attacks by al-Zubayr's forces and the Banda Ngao, the trade routes linking Dar al-Kuti with the savanna and Sahel were safe in the 1870s, and the country prospered from long-distance commerce. Increasing numbers of northern Muslim merchants appeared, and many new Runga settlers migrated south from their homeland. It is said, too, that increasing quantities of ivory flowed into Dar al-Kuti from Banda territories farther south, suggesting that secure trade routes and regularized patterns of exchange joined these areas and Kobur's domains.[70] Slaves were traded in addition to ivory, but they had not yet become the dominant commodity of long-distance exchange. This transformation came in the 1880s with Rabih's campaigns in northern Ubangi-Shari and the southeastern Chad basin.

The Settlements at Kali, Sha, and Mongo-Kuti on the Eve of Rabih's Invasion

Only for the 1870s, on the eve of Rabih's invasion, is information sufficient to reconstruct a detailed and reliable picture of the major Muslim and non-Muslim settlements in Dar al-Kuti. Even this late in the nineteenth century, the region south of the Aouk remained a remote corner of the Wadaian empire. It was an important source of ivory and captives, but not as crucial a supply area as parts of the Salamat, which were farther north and more accessible from the heartlands of the state.

Nachtigal's informants told him that the whole of Dar al-Kuti comprised only fourteen villages, and that the land could be crossed from east to west in two days' march.[71] This description may well include only the large villages visited by northern Muslim traders, and may overlook the smaller settlements scattered in the bush and gallery forests. But it still serves to underscore the limited extent of Kobur's domains, making it easy to see why he was careful to maintain cordial relations with the larger, more populated Muslim zones to the north, as well as with his non-Muslim Nduka neighbors. It explains, too, why none of the sources looking back from a post-Rabih and al-Sanusi perspective regard Kobur as a sultan possessing great military clout.

Kali, Sha, and Mongo-Kuti were three of the most important settlements south of the Aouk in Kobur's time, and remained so until al-Sanusi founded Ndele in 1896. The villages lay very near one another in central Dar al-Kuti, Kali and Sha near the Jangara River separated only by a small secondary stream and Mongo-Kuti about ten kilometers distant. In terms of population and function, Kali and Sha were quite distinct from Mongo-Kuti. The population of Kali and Sha was made up of Runga, assimilated Runga-Nduka, and foreign Muslim traders, whereas Mongo-Kuti was inhabited almost exclusively by Nduka Kutikovo led by their earth chief Wuda. No foreign merchants resided there. This situation remained much the same nearly twenty years later in 1891; French administrator Albert Dolisie's report on the Mission Crampel—based on papers and witnesses that survived the massacre—noted the existence of two villages in Dar al-Kuti located three hours' march apart, one populated by indigenous peoples and the other inhabited by Muslims. His witnesses made no distinction between Sha and Kali, an understandable error since they probably looked like a single village.[72]

Kali was Kobur's village, and he or his father is said to have been its founder. The most cosmopolitan center in the area, its people included the Runga-Bagrim, other Runga-Nduka, and newly arrived Runga, along with Bagirmi, Hausa, Bornoans, and a few Jallaba traders who came to live there mainly during the dry season. The houses in Kali, including that of Kobur, were made of woven straw, and there was a small mosque of the same construction; the village had no market, and most important transactions took place either in merchants' homes or Kobur's compound.[73]

Considering the history of Runga and Bagirmi settlement and inter-marriage with the Nduka in Dar al-Kuti earlier in the century, it seems reasonable to suspect that Kali began as a village of foreign Muslim traders who lived apart from the indigenous non-Muslim population in a manner similar to that of Muslim merchants in other, better known parts of sub-Saharan Africa. Over time, as a result of marriages with local Nduka women and virilocal residence, Kali lost its completely foreign character. But it retained its Muslim identity, since the offspring of Runga-Nduka unions were raised as Muslims, and new Muslim migrants continued to join the settlement.

Yet this explanation does not account for Kali's special religious character. This trait clearly distinguished it from Sha and other precolonial Runga villages south of the Aouk, and continues to distinguish its successor community at Koundi from neighboring Runga settlements. Without doubt, this aspect of Kali's history is linked to the position of Kobur as a faqih. Beyond that, the Bagirmi heritage of the inhabitants must be of some importance, since almost all of the Runga-Bagrim in Dar al-Kuti lived in Kali.

Al-Sanusi was one of the Runga-Bagrim who did not reside in Kali. He lived on the other side of the stream at Sha.[74] This is Sha's main claim to fame; little else is known about it. The village was much smaller than Kali, and like its neighbor, its population consisted mainly of Runga and Runga-Nduka, although only a few Runga-Bagrim lived there. Foreign merchants were not numerous in Sha until the late 1880s, when al-Sanusi became a major trader and invited them to settle near him. But even in Kobur's time, the people of Sha had access to imported goods because they were free to trade in nearby Kali. All in all, Sha in the 1870s and early 1880s was little more than a satellite settlement of Kobur's center, becoming important in its own right only after al-Sanusi's rise to prominence. At that time, it took the name Sha-Guegar (political post or headquarters [Chadic Arabic]). But even with this linguistic enhancement, it never had the distinctive identity of Kali or Mongo-Kuti.[75]

Mongo-Kuti was a large settlement whose population consisted mainly of Nduka and Runga-Nduka. The Runga today refer to the village as Karnak, a Chadic Arabic word meaning fortress, an allusion to its location in or near one of the nearly impenetrable gallery forest thickets (*kuti* [Nduka]).[76] The most famous earth chief of Mongo-Kuti was Wuda, described variously as a Nduka or a Runga-Nduka, and a Muslim or a non-Muslim. He maintained close ties with the Muslim settlements at Kali and Sha, and participated in Islamic observances while continuing to perform traditional Nduka rites associated with the land. He presented both Kobur and al-Sanusi with offerings of grain and other products, and in return received imported goods from them. These bonds continued to be of importance long after Kobur died and al-Sanusi moved to Ndele. Many of the people from Mongo-Kuti joined the sultan in his new capital, and even though Wuda remained in his village, he frequently visited al-Sanusi. And at the height of his career as a slave raider and slave-trader, the sultan never attacked the Nduka of Dar al-Kuti.[77]

There were other important settlements in Dar al-Kuti in Kobur's time. Nduka villages included Uio, Kakaba, Ngara, and Voko; Runga also lived at Kolanjanga and Bringel.[78] Today little information remains regarding these communities, and their existence was not recorded in the early colonial documents. In part, this absence of data is a result of resettlement

policies followed by al-Sanusi and later French authorities. After founding
Ndele, the sultan relocated most of the population of Dar al-Kuti in his
capital. When he was assassinated in 1911, many people returned to rebuild their villages at their former sites, only to be uprooted again a decade
and a half later when the French regrouped all settlements along two major
roads.[79] These upheavals scattered the population of smaller villages to
such a degree that violence associated with Rabih and al-Sanusi's raiding
campaigns and state-building have also effaced much of the detail from
earlier traditions dealing with Kobur and his years as faqih-ruler of lands
south of the Aouk.

Chapter 3
Dar al-Kuti: The Formation of the Sultanate

Between the 1880s and 1911, Dar al-Kuti emerged as an important economic, political, and military force in North Central Africa. The state became a major transit zone linking the northern Zaire and eastern Chad basins, while its new capital at Ndele developed into the largest and most influential commercial center along the Islamic frontier in this part of Africa. In 1901, the French observer Emile Julien suggested that the sultanate and its trade routes might become the heart and arteries of a vast commercial system which would promote the circulation of merchants, products, and slaves in the lands between the Shari and the Nile.[1] In fact, by 1901 many traders from the Nile basin had already made their way to Dar al-Kuti, and the flow continued in the following decade, although the state's sphere of influence never extended as far east as the Nile. To the west, the Upper Shari had fallen under the sway of the sultanate, and slave-raiding on a large scale in this area, as well as in regions south and southeast of Dar al-Kuti, had already begun to produce a steady stream of captives for sale in Ndele. The stream swelled between 1901 and 1911. Summing up the economic role of the capital during this period, another more recent French writer has termed the city the keystone of the region,[2] and indeed it was, for it received caravans of people and goods from most points of the compass, and redirected them.

In the late nineteenth and early twentieth centuries, Dar al-Kuti became a periphery of a periphery of the expanding capitalist economy, with significant local repercussions: the tremendous growth of slave-raiding and slave-trading in northern Ubangi-Shari; the diffusion of new arms, military techniques, and training into the region from neighboring Muslim zones; the appearance of European goods in increasing quantities; and the later deep involvement of the French in local affairs. This chapter describes this transformation and suggests how it came about; it attempts to explain why Dar al-Kuti developed from a remote district of the Wadaian empire informally ruled by a revered faqih into a sultanate so important that its capital is still found on most continental maps of Africa and globes of the world. These developments are best understood by way of a chronological presentation of the history of the sultanate from the time of Kobur to the death of Muhammad al-Sanusi in 1911, which heralded the colonial era.

Dar al-Kuti, Rabih, and
Secondary Empire

Rabih first arrived in the Dar al-Kuti area in about 1878 after leaving southern Dar Fur, where he had split with his colleague Sulayman, son of his former employer al-Zubayr. He spent the next fifteen years in the northern Zaire and southeastern Chad basins, a sojourn crucial to his later conquests of Bagirmi and Borno. During this time he pressured surrounding Muslim states such as Wadai, probing for political or military weaknesses, and looking for commercial outlets and sources of arms. He also built an army. When Rabih left Dar Fur he had a following of only several hundred men, but by 1889, a year before leaving Dar al-Kuti definitively, the Sudanese leader commanded a force of more than ten thousand. This transformation and others that stemmed from it brought important demographic, economic, military, and political changes to Dar al-Kuti and nearby lands.[3]

Between 1878 and 1891, Rabih's presence affected the entire region, although few sources agree exactly on when he raided or camped in any particular locale. He moved his headquarters only a few times during these years, whereas his bands roamed widely every dry season, pillaging as far south as the Nzakara sultanate of Bangassou on at least one occasion, and as far north as the Salamat region of Wadai. But to appreciate Rabih's overall impact, it is not necessary to distinguish his peregrinations from those of his men; it is important to know where he *or* his bands carried out ghazzias or set up camp during this time.

Informants today do not recall the specific dates of Rabih's raids, but their testimonies verify the general accuracy of figure 1: the Sudanese war leader raided for several years among the Banda before attacking the Sara; he devastated Dar Runga on several occasions; his men clashed with the Nzakara southeast of Dar al-Kuti. Overall, people clearly separate Rabih's ghazzias from those of al-Sanusi. This distinction partly grows out of the fact that Rabih killed or took many Muslim Runga into slavery, and not surprisingly, the present Runga of Dar al-Kuti judge this practice to have been morally reprehensible, since good Muslims would not enslave coreligionists.[4] A less subjective interpretation of events has perhaps also led people to separate the raids of Rabih and al-Sanusi. In Dar al-Kuti Rabih is seen as the first figure to unleash widespread violence—the marauder who introduced a "Thirty Years' War" of ghazzias. Even while

Figure 1

Peoples and Areas Raided by Rabih or his Bands
1879–1891

Approximate Dates	People	Homelands	Location Relative to Dar al-Kuti
a) 1879	Banda, Kresh	Gounda R. Valley	E
b) 1880	Runga	Dar Runga	N
c) 1882–1885	Runga	Dar Runga	N
	B. Mbagga, B. Ngao	Koukourou R. area	SE
	B. Marba, B. Tombaggo	Kagas	SW
	B. Ngura, B. Ndi	Poungoubou, Dje, and Balidja	NE
d) 1883–1884	Runga, Hemat Arabs	Dar Runga, Salamat	SE
e) 1883–1884	Nzakara and SE Banda	Bari R. area in Bangassou (Bali) sultanate	SW
f) 1885	Manza	Kaga Kazemba	N
g) 1885	Sara	Lake Iro	W and NW
h) 1886	Sara and Nduka	Middle Shari and W. Dar al-Kuti	NW
i) 1887–1888	Sara	Denze near Kyabe	NW
j) 1887	S. Tunia and Tomak	Middle Shari (Neillim and Gundi)	NW
	Sara	Sara lands	N
k) 1888	Runga	Dar Runga	SE
	Banda	Ouaka R. region	NW
l) 1889	Somrai	near Damraou	NW
m) 1890	Sara	Middle Shari	NW
n) 1889–1891	Sara	Sara lands	N
o) 1890	Runga	Kouga in Dar Runga	SW
p) 1891	B. Ngao	Bala R. Valley	N
	Runga	Dar Runga	E
	Kresh, Goula	Gounda R. area, Lake Mamoun	E

B = Banda   K = Kresh   S = Sara

Figure 1 (Continued)

Peoples and Areas Raided by Rabih or his Bands
1879–1891

Sources:

a) Julien, "Mohamed-es-Senoussi" (1925), 108–9.

b) Adeleye, "Rabih b. Fadlallah, 1879–1893," 229.

c) ANF-SOM (Paris), Papiers Julien, 6P.A., ctn. 1, "Rapport du Cap^ne Julien sur sa reconnaissance du Ba-Mingui, du Koukourou, et de la Koddo du 21 mars au 6 avril 1901," Fort-Crampel, 17 April 1901; Fernand Gaud, *Les Mandja (Congo-Français)* (Brussels, 1911), 105.

d) Hallam, "The Itinerary," 173; Modat, "Une tournée," 228; Bruel, *La France équatoriale africaine*, 281.

e) Modat, "Une tournée," 229.

f) Gaud, *Les Mandja*, 95–96; A. M. Vergiat, *Moeurs et coutumes des Mandja* (Paris, 1937), 28.

g) Modat, "Une tournée," 229–30; Hallam, "The Itinerary," 174–76.

h) Ibid.

i) Ibid.

j) PRO (London), FO2/118, XJ6230, Wingate (Director of Military Intelligence), "Memo on the Western Sudan," Cairo, 5 March 1893.

k) Kalck, "Histoire," 2:308–9.

l) Modat, "Une tournée," 230.

m) Adeleye, "Rabih b. Fadlallah, 1879–1893," based on archival materials, 230–31 and 231n1.

n) Arbab Djama Babikir, *L'Empire de Rabeh* (Paris, 1950), 31–32; Hallam, "The Itinerary," 177.

o) ANT, W53.9, "Documents et études historiques sur le Salamat, réunis par Y. Merot: Note du sujet de Rabah au Salamat," Am-Timan, 1950; ANT, W53.9, "Documents et études historiques sur le Salamat, réunis par Y. Merot: Rabah et Senoussi au Dar Rounga," Mangueigne, 1950.

p) Kalck, "Histoire," 2:307; Gaud, *Les Mandja*, 99–100; Modat, "Une tournée," 195, 230–31.

55

al-Sanusi still ruled, the residents of Ndele condemned his mentor. Al-Hajj Abdu, al-Sanusi's advisor, told Chevalier that Rabih had "eaten all the land . . . where he passed, he took all"; Modat noted that among Muslims a popular cradle song went as follows: *Rabi jo, razassa dugo* ("Rabih came, the bullets fell").[5] Today the Sudanese invader is called the "bearer of war" or the "master of fighting";[6] informants search their imaginations for images that convey a sense of the size and strength of his army: "When they moved down the road and came to a tree, they went right over it and it disappeared, they were as numerous as a [swarm of] flying termites."[7] "When they crossed a river, they splashed so much water on the banks that the level of the stream plummeted."[8] The inhabitants of Dar al-Kuti assess Rabih's significance on the basis of what they know about their immediate region, but their judgment is accurate from a broader perspective. Rabih's sojourn near the Aouk is one of the earliest instances of the far westward shift of the southern Sudanese slave-raiding and slave-trading network. In the 1860s the efforts of the Turko-Egyptian administration to control the slave trade in the Nile region had led al-Zubayr to seek commercial outlets through Dar Fur, and in the following decade the government's successful attempts to take over Dar Fur and subdue al-Zubayr prompted Rabih to move still farther west to Ubangi-Shari. After 1881, Rabih was suspicious of the Mahdiya, and this attitude along with the turmoil that accompanied the Mahdist revolution led him to remain in the west. Other less successful and lesser-known Sudanese war leaders, such as the Kresh chief Sa°id Baldas and the Azande sultan Zemio, followed his example.[9]

Rabih's migration and the great westward expansion of slave-raiding and slave-trading in the late nineteenth century were also regional manifestations of "secondary empire."[10] During the century, societies in widely separated parts of Africa gained short-lived strategic advantages over their neighbors by being the first groups in their regions to borrow new weapons and notions of military organization. Although in some cases—notably that of the Mfecane in southern Africa—these innovations were completely African in character, in most instances they were of European origin. Europe at this time was making rapid advances in firearms technology, and the major powers re-equipped their armies as each new generation of weapons made its appearance. Obsolete older generations of guns were then sold in other parts of the world, and these successive waves of almost up-to-date arms provided any group that could acquire them a temporary edge over its neighbors. Such superiority was fragile, because nearby people had only to locate their own source of weapons to redress the balance, or even shift the advantage to themselves.[11]

The Egyptian conquest of the Sudan is the most obvious example of secondary empire in the Lake Chad–Nile region, and the Sudanese raiders' invasion of lands farther west is directly related to it. Muhammad ᶜAli's (1805–48) drive to modernize Egypt beginning in the 1820s led to the purchase of European firearms and the recruitment of European mercenaries to train his troops. In short order, the Egyptian leader turned his army into a force capable of overwhelming African states to the south. By 1879, following ᶜAli's campaigns and those of his successors, Egypt formally controlled the whole of today's Sudan along with portions of Eritrea, northern Uganda, and northeastern Zaire.[12]

The consolidation of Egyptian rule over this vast area proved more difficult than the initial conquests. Individuals such as Rabih, Saᶜid Baldas, and Zemio on the western frontiers of the conquered territory used the Egyptian presence to acquire advanced arms and training. But they then moved farther west beyond the sphere of Egyptian control, to set up their own preserves. Starting with small, well-armed forces that accompanied them from the Sudan, they became warlords with their own armies created through the Turko-Egyptian practice of slave recruitment. Unlike the Egyptians, however, these leaders did not usually purchase slave recruits. Because they were operating in non-Muslim zones among small-scale societies, their arms and organization gave them a tremendous military advantage. They raided for slaves, integrating boys and young men into their detachments, taking girls and young women into their followings, and giving the others to northern traders in exchange for additional arms, powder, and the standard goods of long-distance trade.[13]

Rabih employed these recruitment policies and military advantages very effectively in northern Ubangi-Shari and Dar al-Kuti after 1878. When he first headed west, he was already a seasoned soldier. Arbab Djama Babikir, a son of one of Rabih's lieutenants, claimed that Rabih began his military career with a stint in the Khedival army in Egypt, where he learned to ride and to use firearms; he later served at least ten years with the forces of al-Zubayr in the southwestern Sudan and Dar Fur. Many of the men who migrated with him had similar backgrounds.[14]

The Sudanese leader arrived in the west with his forces already organized into military detachments of about 125 men, each headed by a banner commander and other officers. Although there were some mounted troops, most were foot soldiers, and both groups had a mix of weapons ranging from flintlocks to breechloaders of varying sophistication.[15] As his men took captives, first among the eastern Banda and Kresh and later among the western Banda and Sara (see figure 1), Rabih enrolled the prisoners in newly created detachments. Many of the new unit commanders came from the same ethnic groups. Following their incorporation, Rabih and his Sudanese lieutenants drilled the recruits and trained them in the use of firearms. Rabih steadily increased his forces in this manner. Between 1882 and 1885 he integrated many Banda Mbagga, Marba, Tombaggo, and Ndi into his army; by 1885 these fighters were already deployed in the campaigns against the Manza.[16]

Banda, Kresh, and Sara troops formed a large part of Rabih's forces by the time of the great offensives against Bagirmi, Borno, and the French after 1891. A Bornoan informant in Ndele who was an adolescent in Rabih's capital in Borno in the 1890s remembered many Banda, Kresh, and Sara soldiers. The Bornoans did not know where these troops were from, but nonetheless became familiar with their names and could tell them apart. The first census of Fort-Lamy (1911), a post settled by veterans of Rabih's forces after his defeat by the French in 1900, gives some indication of the composition of his army. Of a total population of 3,148, there were 952 Sara, 307 Banda, and 21 Kresh. The Sara were the most numerous, while the Banda ranked fourth. But these totals by no means represent the total force of Rabih's army. Many Banda, Sara, and Kresh returned home after 1900 and once there, many joined the forces of Muhammad al-Sanusi.[17]

Rabih's presence in Ubangi-Shari and the Chad basin between 1878 and 1891 had dramatic demographic effects. In many districts, virtually everyone disappeared. When he first arrived in Dar al-Kuti, for example, many Banda moved to the south and southwest to lands between Ndele and Mbres—a 200-kilometer stretch of territory. By the time he left for points west, even much of this zone had been deserted; al-Sanusi's depredations completed the process. Rabih's ghazzias also uprooted Banda living southeast of the state along the route to the Upper Kotto, but the effect was less severe.[18]

Ironically, however, Rabih's campaigns weighed much more heavily on the Muslim Runga of Dar Runga than on the non-Muslims to the south. In the early 1880s, the mid-1880s, and again in 1890, the Sudanese warlord devastated the sultanate. In the early 1880s Chevalier's informants described Dar Runga as a very populous state; the Runga sultan exercised real power over Kobur and the Muslims of Dar al-Kuti.[19] Rabih's raids scattered the population. Many Runga fled south to join the Runga of Dar al-Kuti, while others were killed or captured and sold into slavery; Rabih incorporated only a few Runga into his army. Following Rabih's departure, Dar Runga never regained its former power and population; today it remains an "empty quarter."[20]

Rabih's sojourn also prompted greater Wadaian interest and armed intervention in the area. Sultan Yusuf of Wadai did not accept the presence of a large and growing military force on his southern borders with equanimity. Rabih first approached the Wadaian ruler submissively, seeking to be his client and requesting that trading parties from the north with guns and powder be allowed to cross Wadaian territory to reach him.

This tack failed, as Yusuf cut off the flow of commerce altogether. Rabih then turned to violence. He attacked the Wadaian vassal state of Dar Runga, and in 1883 and 1887 his forces also clashed with those of the Wadaian governor of the Salamat. Rabih's men won the first encounter, while the second was a draw. But the Wadaian blockade continued, leading Rabih to raid farther west among the Sara of the Middle Shari, an area outside Wadai's sphere of influence, between 1887 and 1890. Yusuf finally permitted caravans to proceed to Rabih's camps, but maintained an embargo on arms and munitions. He also launched punitive expeditions against the Runga, who had failed to pay tribute during Rabih's campaigns. The Sudanese intruder was by now receiving a limited supply of weapons through Bagirmi and Borno. But the quantities were insufficient to meet the needs of his growing army, and the search for arms and commercial outlets eventually led him west to Bagirmi and Borno. But before leaving, he reaffirmed his hold over Dar al-Kuti and Dar Runga, returning there in 1890.[21]

The Fall of Kobur and
the Rise of Al-Sanusi

During most of Rabih's thirteen years in Ubangi-Shari, Kobur continued to rule at Kali-Sha. The two men were not close allies, although, for reasons probably related to caravan commerce, the invader never ravaged the major settlements of Dar al-Kuti. Kobur regarded Rabih as a bandit, and avoided showing him any special deference despite his greater power. It is also true that because Kobur was a vassal of Dar Runga and Wadai, Rabih's presence put him in a difficult position—particularly after the raids among the Runga and skirmishes with Wadai. In general, Kobur survived the decade by acceding whenever possible to Rabih's demands as well as to those of Wadaian representatives in the area.[22]

But Kobur only barely outlasted the 1880s. In late 1890, three years after shifting his camp west to raid among the Sara and trade with Bagirmi and Borno, Rabih abruptly returned to Kali-Sha and deposed the revered faqih. The immediate cause of Rabih's action is apparent: between 1887 and 1890 Kobur openly received emissaries from Wadai and continued to pay tribute to the sultan in Abeche.[23] Apart from this obvious provocation, other long-range considerations probably led Rabih to act as he did. Theories about his motivations cluster around the notion that Rabih saw Dar al-Kuti, and northern Ubangi-Shari generally, as his bridge to the Sudan and the Mahdiya. Some commentaries suggest that the Sudanese leader realized that he would have to conquer Bagirmi to secure supply routes with the lands further west, and a faithful client in Dar al-Kuti would assure an escape route to the east in the event of defeat. A different opinion maintains that Rabih had already conceived of the conquest of Borno, and simply wanted to establish dependable lines of communication between the far west and the Sudan by setting up vassals in Dar al-Kuti and Bagirmi. The escape route hypothesis never came to the test, since Rabih vanquished Bagirmi. As for the other interpretation, Rabih did not espouse the Mahdist cause in the 1880s, but he did send messages to the Sudan by way of Bagirmi and Dar al-Kuti in the early 1890s. Once he had moved even farther west beyond the reach of its military forces, he became a very vocal proponent of the Mahdiya.[24]

Before departing, Rabih installed al-Sanusi as ruler of Dar al-Kuti, and set about securing his client's position. He first annexed the devastated plains of Dar Runga, declaring that al-Sanusi would administer both areas. Then, in early 1891, he set out with the new ruler on an extended raiding expedition to eliminate any immediate threats to the new land; they hit Dar Runga in the north, Kresh and Goula settlements to the east, and Banda Ngao villages to the southwest. Rabih also provided the sultan with a small military detachment, a few firearms, a limited supply of munitions, and even a harem. Finally an exchange of kin affirmed the political ties that bound the two men together. Rabih gave al-Sanusi one of his wives, who in turn gave his eldest daughter in marriage to Rabih's son Fadlallah. And when the Sudanese warrior left Dar al-Kuti in March 1891, he took two of al-Sanusi's Runga relatives with him as hostages.[25]

Al-Sanusi's background and earlier dealings with Rabih suggest that the Sudanese raider's decision to place him in power was neither impolitic nor surprising. Rabih by no means chose an outsider to be his representative, but rather he replaced one branch of the ruling line with another. Unlike the rise to power of many other slave-raiders and -traders in Ubangi-Shari and the southwestern Sudan, al-Sanusi's saga is not one of social mobility. Not only did he belong to the important Runga-Bagrim subgroup, but his father AbuBakr was Kobur's paternal brother, making the new sultan part of the religious lineage said to have founded the state. In fact, some sources suggest that al-Sanusi's father was also a faqih-trader, and that he named his son after the founder of the new Sanusiya brotherhood. As for the important women in al-Sanusi's life, his mother was the daughter of Salih, a sultan of Dar Runga (c. 1850–c. 1870), while his senior wife was ʿUmm Diwan, the daughter of Salih's son ʿAqid, who also ruled Dar Runga (c. 1870–73).[26]

If Rabih's choice did not represent a shift of power from one class to another, it probably did reflect the Sudanese kingmaker's personal prefer-ence for al-Sanusi. Oral traditions claim that Rabih first came to know al-Sanusi over a one- or two-year period when the invader lived in a camp near

Kali-Sha.[27] While Kobur chose to ignore Rabih as much as possible, al-Sanusi apparently showed every courtesy, sending him regular offerings of grain and other foodstuffs. Unlike his more religious relatives, the future sultan had a great propensity for commerce, ran a successful trading operation that included limited slave-raiding among the Banda, and was also able to provide Rabih with trade goods—including small quantities of gunpowder. After Rabih left for Sara country, al-Sanusi used his commercial connections to channel a trickle of munitions and other imports to his mentor. Apart from the deference and trade possibilities that al-Sanusi offered Rabih, he was a younger man with greater vigor and ambition than his uncle. He was an obvious candidate to rule Dar al-Kuti, and Kobur's continued dalliance with Wadai finally moved Rabih to action.[28]

Rabih's near-monopoly on military power in northern Ubangi-Shari made al-Sanusi sultan of Dar al-Kuti, and in this way the new ruler, like his benefactor, profited from the Egyptian secondary empire. But it was the transfer of military technology from another source that enabled him to end his reliance on Rabih and begin his independent rise to power. In April 1891, less than a month after the departure of the Sudanese war leader, the Crampel Mission arrived in the vicinity of Kali-Sha.[29]

The appearance of the French expedition led by Paul Crampel stands as a major event in the history of Dar al-Kuti for three reasons. First, it was a harbinger of later French interest and interference in the affairs of the sultanate, an involvement that progressed by fits and starts in the 1890s and was continuous only after 1901. Secondly, this encounter between al-Sanusi and the French ended in violence, thereby contributing to the climate of suspicion and hostility that characterized relations between the two parties for most of the remaining years of the sultan's life. The third reason was of the greatest immediate importance. Crampel arrived at al-Sanusi's camp with a stock of nearly 50 rapid-fire rifles of diverse brands (Kropatchek, Gras, Remington, Rubin), 175 flintlocks, 30,000 cartridges, at least 60,000 percussion caps, several hundred kilograms of powder, and a small cache of revolvers. At this time the sultan had only a few dozen weapons of all models.[30] He was looking for a means of asserting his independence, and Crampel unwittingly provided it.

Not only did the sheer size of the arsenal tempt the sultan, but Crampel's objectives as well as dissatisfaction among his Senegalese sharpshooters and other African porters also encouraged al-Sanusi to disrupt the mission. The Frenchman wanted to proceed northward to either Rabih's camp or Wadai. Neither destination pleased the sultan. If Crampel succeeded in reaching Rabih's camp, it was reasonable to think that the Sudanese commander would seize the arms, increasing both his own power and al-Sanusi's dependence on him. As for Wadai, al-Sanusi had taken power without Wadaian approval following the removal of a faithful Wadaian client. The Abeche sultan consequently regarded him as a rebel, and soon after his rise to power had instituted another blockade of Dar al-Kuti— shifting the flow of northern goods to routes that passed through Kresh lands to the east. Moreover, sickness, inadequate food supplies, and uncertainty plagued Crampel's expedition, created dissension, and made it unlikely that an attempt to interrupt its journey would encounter stiff resistance.

Al-Sanusi first tried unsuccessfully to talk Crampel out of continuing his voyage, but the Frenchman refused to alter his plans and left Kali-Sha. A few hours later, acting against the advice of Kobur and accepting the counsel of his more militant advisors, the sultan sent several detachments of soldiers to ambush the expedition. They killed Crampel along with most of his men, although at least one sharpshooter survived, joined the sultan's entourage, and trained his troops in the use of the newly acquired arms. Some days after the ambush, in May 1891, al-Sanusi ordered another force south to attack a second contingent of the mission commanded by Gabriel Biscarrat. The sultan's men seized more arms and supplies. By mid-1891, al-Sanusi was fully equipped with the means to independent power.[31]

Besides setting the stage for eventual hostility and conflict between the sultan and the French, the Crampel affair marked the apogee of the more militant faction among al-Sanusi's advisors. These men, along with their more cautious counterparts, greatly influenced al-Sanusi's attitudes to the French and Wadai, sources of his major "foreign policy" problems after Rabih's departure.

Muslim Political Advisors in Ndele

In his early years as ruler of Dar al-Kuti, the sultan tended to rely primarily on his Runga countrymen for advice, but as the scope of his raiding and trading increased, and as he came into closer contact with Muslim traders, pilgrims, and faqihs from other parts of Africa, he opened the inner circle to foreign Muslims. This strategy occasionally brought him into conflict with other factions within the Runga community, in particular the descendants of Kobur, who felt that Rabih had denied them their rightful inheritance by installing al-Sanusi.[32] By the time Julien arrived as the first French resident, and through the tenure of Modat, the last, the sultan's three closest counselors included a Fur, Hausa, and Fulani.

Faqih ⁽Issa, a Fur aged about forty in 1901, served as the sultan's personal *imam* or prayer leader. His house stood just outside the main gate to the palace, and each day he presented the Qur'an to al-Sanusi and led him in prayer. He also ran the Qur'anic school or *garai* in the royal compound, where he instructed adults as well as children. Conversant with the same magical practices as other faqihs, he often washed the writing boards of his students and offered the sacred water to the sultan, who drank it as a cure for all ills. Grech, French resident between 1902 and 1904, wrote, "Aissa [*sic*] is, in a manner of speaking, the archbishop of Ndele, and enjoys an excellent reputation."[33] But ⁣ᶜIssa's duties extended into other domains. Because he was an intimate of the ruler and because he was literate, the faqih took charge of the treasury. In addition, he oversaw the distribution of all weapons, enumerating guns and keeping records of those who had received arms and ammunition. As the imam and the *muezzin* or caller-to-prayer of the mosque, he had a large collection of books on religious subjects which he studied with al-Hajj Tukur and al-Hajj Abdo (Abdu), the sultan's other confidants.[34]

Al-Hajj Tukur, a Fulani, and al-Hajj Abdo, a Hausa, were learned men who also possessed a wide range of worldly experience acquired through commerce as well as the pilgrimage. Born in the 1850s, Tukur grew up in Sokoto, made his way to Mecca, and returned to the Nile region, where the Mahdists took him prisoner. He eventually escaped and made his way to Wadai, where he served sultan Yusuf between 1893 and 1895 as his commercial agent in Rafai, managing trade between this small Azande state on the Mbomu River and Abeche. But Tukur's activities failed to turn a profit, and out of carelessness or greed he dissipated the goods entrusted to him. Shortly thereafter he joined the ranks of al-Sanusi's counselors, becoming the architect of the policy of rapprochement with the French. He soon became the most important diplomat at the Ndele court, and along with al-Hajj Abdo coordinated communications between the palace and the French post. In 1897 and 1901 he led the sultan's delegation in talks with the Europeans and even went to Paris as al-Sanusi's personal representative in 1898. As the brushes with the Mahdists and Yusuf suggest, Tukur was adept at the art of self-preservation. Although neither Julien nor Grech liked him, he succeeded in becoming an interpreter for the colonial administration following the death of the sultan in 1911; he died in Ndele in 1929.[35]

Al-Hajj Ahmad Abdallahi, or Ajj-Abdo as he was called in Dar al-Kuti, was a Hausa born in Kano in about 1840. He, too, made the pilgrimage, traveling from Abeche to al-Fasher in Dar Fur with Nachtigal in 1873. Following his return from Arabia, he began trading in Dar Sila and then shifted his activities to Dar al-Kuti in 1885, where he met al-Sanusi. The sultan recruited him to be doctor, diplomatic advisor, and general aide. He was among the very few who had access to the harem, evidence of the trust placed in him; as noted, he also helped manage communications with the French.[36] Grech, who succeeded Julien in Ndele, held al-Hajj Abdo in high esteem:

Al-Hajj is the ambassador of al-Sanusi. Each evening he appears at the residence to transmit the communications of the sultan. He is charged with negotiations with the Resident; he deals with foreigners, the harvest, and the wives [of the sultan]; he is the chamberlain, trusted advisor, master of ceremonies, and intimate counselor. Al-Hajj Abdu has the sultan's ear and probably gives him good advice because he is a prudent and wise old man.[37]

Al-Sanusi took advantage of the expertise offered by foreign Muslims and felt he could trust them, undoubtedly in part because they had had greater experience in the larger Islamic world to the north. But these men, and others like them such as Cheggue Toum, a Bornoan married to the sister of Sultan Bakhit of Dar Sila who also sought the hand of Hadija, al-Sanusi's daughter and widow of Rabih's son, were not particularly pious. They reflected the more practical imperatives of the world in which they lived.[38] Learning was useful for business, and as a means of remaining in touch with the rest of the Islamic world. Yet it remained secondary, and the men in the sultan's service in no way constituted an *culama'*, a learned body conversant with the religious and philosophical literature of Islam. The scribes could write fairly well, a skill that promoted the management of everyday affairs. Al-Hajj Tukur and al-Hajj Abdo enjoyed fame and responsibility, not so much because they had acquired piety during their pilgrimages, but because they had learned a lot about the Middle East and other parts of Islamic Africa. They also knew about the French and the English; Tukur had witnessed the arrival of Belgian agents of the Congo Independent State in Rafai. Hence they could ably advise al-Sanusi, a man of limited travel, in dealing with European encroachment at the end of the century as well as relations with neighboring Muslim states such as Wadai.

Relations with Wadai and Regional Rivalries, 1890–1911

Over the twenty-year period that al-Sanusi ruled Dar al-Kuti, concern with Wadai, the French, and slave-raiding and slave-trading dominated the state's external relations. Throughout the 1890s Wadai loomed large, threatening the very existence of the sultanate; by the early 1900s, however, the armed presence of the French on the Gribingui River to the south and in the capital of the sultanate itself made them a more immediate source of aid and danger. During these two decades al-Sanusi not only managed to survive, but by playing Wadai and the French against one another, he even expanded his domains. He eliminated commercial rivals in northern Ubangi-Shari and raided for slaves among non-Muslims on an ever-expanding scale. But before al-Sanusi could maneuver freely between Wadai and the French, he had to loosen his ties with Rabih—a process that took several years.

In the early years of his rule, al-Sanusi, like his predecessor, was caught between Rabih and Sultan Yusuf of Wadai. Yusuf was anxious to invade Dar al-Kuti because the circumstances of al-Sanusi's rise to power made him a symbol of opposition to Wadaian hegemony in the south and encouraged revolt among other vassal states. As for Rabih, from 1891 to 1893 he camped in Bagirmi and Sara country, close enough to protect his client, but also near enough to punish him if he tried to make peace with Wadai. Such punitive action was a real possibility, particularly after the Crampel episode, which aroused Rabih's suspicions about his client's loyalty. The Sudanese commander heard of the massacre shortly after it happened and immediately sent messengers to Kali-Sha ordering that all captured arms be given to him. Al-Sanusi responded with a few weapons and a limited quantity of munitions, which angered Rabih. He sent a second delegation demanding more arms. The sultan is said to have reacted by sending additional rifles and ammunition, burying the rest, and swearing on a Qur'an that no other weapons were *on* the earth. Although Rabih chose not to attack, his suspicions were not allayed; al-Sanusi expected him at any time. Finally in 1893 Rabih turned west, vanquished Bagirmi, and headed for Borno. The two men remained in contact, and until Rabih's death in 1900 al-Sanusi feared his return, but the conflict never came. After 1893 the new ruler was thus free to cope with Wadai; he was also alone.[39]

Rabih's departure left large parts of Dar Runga depopulated, while his gift of the sultanate saddled al-Sanusi with a vast and vulnerable plains region that bordered directly on Wadai. The Wadaian ruler continued to claim both Dar Runga and Dar al-Kuti, raided north of the Aouk, and pressured al-Sanusi by recognizing a rival sultan in Runga. He also stirred up dissension among Kobur's sons in the south. Al-Sanusi's weakness was apparent, and his unprotected settlement on the Kuti flood plain at Kali-Sha invited attack.[40] The expected holocaust came with the dry season in late 1894 when Sharif al-Din, the Wadaian governor in the Salamat, attacked Kali-Sha with a force of over 1,000 horsemen and foot soldiers armed with firearms. Forewarned of the attack, al-Sanusi and many of his followers fled, leaving his battle commander, Allah Jabu, a Banda captive whom he had raised from childhood, to defend the settlements and delay Wadaian pursuit. The sultan meanwhile sought refuge in rock outcroppings at the edge of the Kuti plain, probably first at Kaga Gollo forty kilometers southeast of Kali-Sha near present-day Ndele, and then at Kaga Toulou fifty kilometers farther east. Soon after, Allah Jabu abandoned the plains and joined al-Sanusi in the highlands.

Sharif al-Din and his soldiers remained in Dar al-Kuti throughout the dry season of 1894–95, taking slaves among the Runga and Nduka, collecting ivory, and even pausing to harvest some of the millet that had ripened during the campaign. They also distributed Wadaian battle flags and pledged support to Banda and Kresh chiefs who opposed al-Sanusi. Finally, after unsuccessful attempts to locate and capture the sultan, the invaders withdrew to the north in early 1895 with a convoy of several thousand captives.[41]

In the wake of Sharif al-Din's rampage, al-Sanusi began to rebuild his state and put it on a more secure footing. During the next several years he achieved three important goals. He first sought an accord with Wadai recognizing the legitimacy of his succession. To this end he dispatched a Tunjur intermediary to the north in late 1895 who negotiated an agreement confirming him as sultan of Dar al-Kuti, but also requiring that he acknowledge the supremacy of Wadai with regular tribute. Al-Sanusi accepted the arrangement, Sharif al-Din sent a representative to reside in the sultan's camp, and Dar al-Kuti became a self-governing province of Wadai.[42] However, al-Sanusi's second project indicates that he still questioned Wadaian intentions. In 1896, after a long search, the sultan founded a new capital on the high, rocky Ndele plateau, a site secure from attack by Wadaian horsemen (for discussion of the name "Ndele," see appendix 3). The city grew very rapidly to become the largest settlement in Dar al-Kuti and the major trading center in northern Ubangi-Shari.[43]

Al-Sanusi's third achievement was the elimination of rival centers of power and trade in the region. There were two such settlements in the 1890s, Mbele and Jagara. Mbele was a major Kresh town located on the Gounda River eighty kilometers northeast of Ndele. Named for its founder and chief, a former associate of al-Zubayr, Mbele's inhabitants were mainly Kresh who had fled west to escape the Khartoumers in the 1870s, only to set up their own slave-raiding and -trading operation. Like Kali-Sha and Ndele, their city lay midway between the Wadaian capital and the Ubangi River sultanates, and was thus in a position to become a major collection and transit center for slaves and other exports and imports.

Mbele's day came in the 1880s when the sultan of Wadai shifted trade away from Dar al-Kuti during Rabih's occupation. Mbele became a Wadaian client, and an official Wadaian representative lived in the city. By the mid-1880s the population had grown to several thousand people including traders from both Wadai and the southern states of Rafai, Zemio, and Bangassou. Léon Hanolet, a Belgian who was the only European to visit the city, described it in 1894 as a thriving center, while in 1897 Victor Liotard, the chief French administrator on the upper Ubangi, labeled Mbele one of the three most important market centers in North Central Africa (after Shakka in southern Dar Fur and Dem al-Zubayr).[44]

Al-Sanusi's prosperity depended on removing this threat to Dar al-Kuti as well as attracting traders and long-distance commerce to his new capital. After making peace with Wadai, the sultan launched devastating attacks against Mbele in the late 1890s, prompting the Kresh chief to withdraw to the southeast. The Wadai sultan sent a few weapons and a small armed force to aid Mbele, but the detachment had not yet reached the city when it encountered a caravan of Dajo traders from Dar Sila returning home with Kresh captives purchased after al-Sanusi's latest attack. The force returned to Wadai since the aid it was to provide Mbele came too late. Wadai did not punish al-Sanusi for his actions, and sent little further help to Mbele. By 1902, when Chevalier visited the site, piles of rubble were all that remained of the once flourishing Kresh commercial center.[45]

The other rival center was the Banda Ngao capital of Jagara, located about seventy kilometers southeast of Ndele near the present village of Pata.[46] The Banda Ngao chiefs Ngono and Ara commanded Jagara and other nearby Ngao settlements. Ngono had attacked Kali-Sha in the 1870s. Both men reportedly had received military training in the forces of al-Zubayr or Rabih, and by the 1890s they were engaged in slave-raiding and long distance trade much in the manner of Mbele. Through the inter-mediary of the Nzakara sultan Bangassou in the south, they exchanged ivory for firearms from the Belgians; from the north they received trans-Saharan goods in return for slaves taken in ghazzias against other Banda peoples. Jagara, like Mbele, became an important meeting place for merchants, although few Muslims permanently resided there.

As in the Kresh case, al-Sanusi saw the Ngao center as a potential economic and military rival. To counter this menace he first tried to coax the Ngao and their leaders to move voluntarily to his capital, but his efforts failed, and in late 1897 he launched a three-month campaign against Jagara and nearby vil-lages. Ngono was killed in the fighting, and al-Sanusi's men removed most of the Ngao to Ndele. A blood covenant with Ara formally ended the hostili-ties and brought the integration of many Ngao into the sultan's forces.[47]

By the late 1890s, then, al-Sanusi had clearly established his hegemony over the Dar al-Kuti region. His achievements encouraged the migration of many northern Runga to Ndele, particularly since occasional Wadaian ghazzias continued to make life insecure in their homeland. The number of other Muslims in Dar al-Kuti also grew rapidly at this time. Most of them were traders, including Hausa, Bornoans, Jallaba, and even several Libyans.[48]

Later relations with Wadai were, with the exception of two notable crises, largely correct but cool. Up to his death, al-Sanusi paid tribute to Wadai fairly regularly, and for most of this period—even after he had signed treaties with the French disavowing links with the ruler in Abeche—a

Wadaian representative resided in his capital. But despite these ties, relations between Dar al-Kuti and Wadai never progressed beyond a frosty détente. Al-Sanusi did not encourage immigration from Wadai, and from time to time northern Wadaian marauders still attacked Runga and Nduka villages on the fringes of Dar al-Kuti. The sultan continued to fear Wadaian plots. This concern led al-Sanusi to seek countervailing support, which took the form of involvement with the French who had reappeared in the area in 1897. This move further strained relations with Wadai, especially after 1902 when anti-French adherents of the Sanusiya brotherhood became very influential in Abeche.[49]

Two periods of tension between al-Sanusi and Wadai underscore the fragility of their relationship between the late 1890s and 1911. The first began in 1899 with Rabih's defeat of the French in southeastern Chad. Al-Sanusi, fearing that either Rabih or Wadai would seize the occasion to punish him for his dealings with the Europeans, went so far as to partially evacuate Ndele. Rumors of a Wadaian conspiracy with the disgruntled sons of Kobur further heightened his concern.[50]

The second incident occurred in 1901 and 1902. By this time al-Sanusi's raiding and efforts to control long-distance trade had carried his forces far to the southeast, well beyond the old sites of Mbele and Jagara to the settlement of the Kresh chief Saᶜid Baldas near the Sudanese border.[51] Like Mbele and Jagara, this town was an important commercial center, mediating trade between three of the Azande states (Rafai, Zemio, Tambura) and Wadai and Dar Fur. Saᶜid Baldas had also signed a treaty with the French, and was a vassal of Wadai. Al-Sanusi wanted to rid himself of yet another rival, but Wadai had apparently decided that his sphere of influence should grow no further, and sent word for him not to oppose the Kresh leader. The ruler responded by refusing to pay tribute. He also sought aid from the French.

The conflict remained unresolved as Saᶜid Baldas went to Abeche to request assistance. But while he was there, al-Sanusi's detachments destroyed his settlement. At the same time a coup d'état in Abeche and widespread violence between opposing political factions prevented Wadai from punishing the dissident sultan. By the time order had returned to the capital, the sultan of Dar al-Kuti had presented his superiors with a *fait accompli*. Wadai accepted the situation, and eventually the period of confrontation passed, but an air of suspicion and hostility remained.[52] The Wadaian sultans could no longer control al-Sanusi, and he was beginning to challenge their historic dominion over the non-Muslim lands to the south. Ironically, the French aided him both directly and indirectly.

Al-Sanusi and the French,
1897–1911

Following the massacre of the Crampel Mission in 1891, there was a six-year hiatus in relations between al-Sanusi and the French. During this time, the sultan was very much aware of the expanding French presence along the Ubangi River south of the sultanate. Moreover, two expeditions—those of Jean Dybowski and Casimir Léon Maistre—entered border regions of Dar al-Kuti in late 1891 and 1892, but al-Sanusi apparently did not communicate with them.[53] In part, this situation was a result of the massacre. The sultan assumed that the French blamed him for Crampel's death, while the Europeans, not sure whether they should hold the sultan or Rabih responsible for the debacle, were hesitant to open direct relations with Dar al-Kuti.[54] But the break also stemmed from the fact that in the early and mid-1900s, al-Sanusi faced more immediate threats to his rule. Although he had learned from his foreign Muslim advisors that the French were a major power in spite of their weak presence in North Central Africa, he had to contend with Rabih and Wadai before turning to them.

The sultan maneuvered successfully between these Muslim powers in the early 1890s, survived devastating Wadaian attacks in the middle of the decade, and by 1896 had founded a more secure capital. The following year he raided the settlements of the Banda Ngao chiefs Ngono and Ara. It was in 1897 at Ara's village that he received Pierre Prins, a representative from the new French post on the Gribingui just beyond the southwestern limits of his domains. The Prins visit opened the era of direct European involvement in Dar al-Kuti. Within a year, a French commercial company established an outlet in Ndele, and in 1901, Julien arrived to serve as the first official French representative.[55]

The three treaties that al-Sanusi signed with the French in 1897, 1903, and 1908 reflect the overall direction of his relations with them in the last fourteen years of his rule. Their terms indicate the shifting balance of power in northern Ubangi-Shari from al-Sanusi to the French.[56] In 1897, the French position in North Central Africa was weak. Their stations in central and eastern Ubangi-Shari were largely confined to the riverbanks of the Ubangi-Mbomu and Gribingui rivers. To the north they confronted the Muslim powers of Wadai, Bagirmi, and Rabih's Borno, as well as Dar al-Kuti; to the east they were engaged in a fierce race with the British to establish claims on the Upper Nile. At this time the British posed a greater threat to ultimate French interests than the Muslims did, because British conquest of the Upper Nile would probably lead to international recognition of their occupation. And so, in 1897, the French directed their energies in Ubangi-Shari to pushing the Mission Marchand east to the Nile before the British arrived from the north.[57]

With French interest directed elsewhere, it is not surprising to see that the terms of the 1897 treaty with al-Sanusi greatly favored the sultan. In large measure, the Europeans simply wanted to make sure that the Dar al-Kuti ruler would not interfere with expeditions they hoped to send north to deal with Rabih; they signed a treaty with the sultan of Bagirmi at the same time for the same reason.[58] Negotiated by Emile Gentil and al-Sanusi's advisor, al-Hajj Tukur, at the sultan's camp on the Gribingui in December, the 1897 accord included no mention whatsoever of slave-raiding or slave-trading, thereby allowing the ruler of Dar al-Kuti to expand these activities without harassment.[59] In fact, the treaty actually supported increased marauding, for the French agreed to provide al-Sanusi with 200 Gras carbines and 2,000 percussion caps annually. The French also promised to station an official resident in Ndele to assist in troop training and other matters. And finally, they offered to protect the sultanate from invasion, a commitment that they were not really in a position to uphold in 1897, but one which provided some security against Wadai and Rabih.[60]

In return, al-Sanusi promised not to sign treaties with any other European powers, and gave the French a monopoly over European commerce in his lands. Muslim merchants were allowed to continue trading, but were to limit their European imports to French goods. Needless to say, the French had no means of enforcing this provision and al-Sanusi ignored it. As for the ban on treaties with other powers, this article helped to establish French territorial claims to northern Ubangi-Shari, and was hence a victory over the British in the colonial sweepstakes, but to al-Sanusi it meant little, since no other Europeans ever presented themselves. Thus the accord was perhaps a minor diplomatic coup for the French in the international arena, but from a local perspective, al-Sanusi had made the better deal.

By 1903, events in northern Ubangi-Shari had shifted the balance of power towards the French. Rabih no longer threatened their interests in the Chad basin, and Britain's assertion of control over the southern Sudan after a confrontation at Fashoda in 1898 led the French to redirect their attention northward to Ubangi-Shari and Chad.[61] But even at this time, they were still not in a position to dominate al-Sanusi completely. In part this was because the European presence remained limited and lines of administrative and military support were long—particularly to outposts as isolated as Ndele.

Moreover, the sultan also had at least two viable alternatives to submitting to the French. First, the continued independence of Wadai provided him room to maneuver, and the French did not wish to see a closer alignment of Dar al-Kuti with the larger state to the north. They also feared that if they tried to restrict his activities by making too many demands, he would simply abandon Ndele and shift his capital east to the still-uncharted no man's land between the French and British spheres of influence. After all, he had moved his center of operations from kaga to kaga in the mid-1890s before settling at Ndele in 1896, and on at least two later occasions— in 1899 when he felt boxed in by Rabih, Wadai, and the French, and in 1900 when the French and Wadai again pressured him—he had prepared to leave the new capital as well. Despite these threats, however, al-Sanusi still needed the French just as they needed him. The Europeans provided him with arms and munitions, and their presence gave him leverage in his dealings with Wadai.[62]

It was in this general context that the French in 1903 sought to renegotiate the treaty of 1897. In addition, two important specific aims motivated them: when the delegation arrived in Ndele early in the year, its members hoped to levy and fix the amount of a formal annual tribute payment from the sultan. They also wanted to limit his raiding, particularly in the zones far to the southeast, which French concessionary companies were beginning to exploit in their own nefarious ways. It is indicative of the more powerful and yet not all-powerful position of the French that while they attained the first goal, they fell far short of the second.[63]

Once again, the conditions of the accord serve to illustrate the situation. First, despite European intentions, mention of slave-raiding and slave-trading is again omitted from the text of the document, thus leaving untouched the economic underpinnings of the state. Second, however, the sultan assented to an annual tribute of 3 tons of rubber, along with 500 kilograms of ivory, 200 kilograms of coffee, 10 cattle, 20 sheep, 3 horses, and the grain needed by the post. He also agreed to supply porters and courier service. Third, al-Sanusi committed himself to sending one or more of his children to France or Algeria for advanced Muslim education under French supervision. He also said that he would support the French militarily, undoubtedly a reference to a possible conflict with Wadai. And fifth, he agreed to favor French commerce and African merchants from the French territories in North and West Africa. Other general terms of the accord repeated those of 1897.[64]

For their part, the French agreed to continue supplying arms, along with merchandise and cash in a yearly package of 5 Gras carbines, 30 1842 muskets, 3,000 cartridges, merchandise worth 3,000 francs, and 3,000 francs in specie (2,000 francs in Maria Theresa *thalers* and 1,000 francs in French currency). They also promised to increase the number of officers to instruct the soldiers of the sultan, and used this proviso as an excuse for agreeing further to station a permanent armed escort in Ndele. The French clearly struck a better bargain in this round of negotiations than they had in

1897 and increased their influence in Dar al-Kuti; but as before, the 1903 treaty not only did not limit the sultan's ghazzias, but abetted their spread.

Generally rising tensions punctuated by brief periods of détente characterized relations between Dar al-Kuti and the French between 1903 and 1908. For the most part, the sultan did not fulfill the substantive terms of the 1903 treaty, and his soldiers, frequently led by his son Adam, continually violated an informal later agreement to avoid raiding in the Kotto and Ouaka river regions where the commercial companies had by now set up a few trading posts. As a result of these infractions, the companies put pressure on the colonial administration to assert greater control over al-Sanusi. An armed contingent was sent to Ndele in 1905 to reinforce the resident's small detachment, but withdrew without bringing significant change. After 1906, the situation deteriorated further, and French administrators in Chad and Dar al-Kuti complained that the sultan would not keep the north-south routes open, delayed tribute payments, refused to deliver needed food supplies, and diverted the official French mail carried by his couriers.[65]

Finally, in early 1908, the French felt powerful enough to send a force of 150 men to Ndele to enforce the 1903 accord, negotiate an end to the raiding, and, if possible, take Adam prisoner so that he could be held hostage in Fort-Lamy or Bangui. Conditions in Wadai probably encouraged this decision; the French had not yet conquered the state, but they launched a series of attacks in 1907 that had undermined its strength, and it appeared that they might be able to set up a client in Abeche. In the end, this did not come to pass, and the French invaded the Wadaian capital the next year. By this time it was obvious that the northern state was in no position to aid al-Sanusi. The French, then, confidently dispatched a military detachment to Dar al-Kuti.[66] But when the unit arrived in Ndele, the Europeans found that al-Sanusi's men greatly outnumbered them. Most of the sultan's army of 3,500 men were in the capital, and he had mobilized them all. The French halted near the resident's quarters; neither they nor al-Sanusi attacked. After some hours, during which Adam pressed his father to massacre the contingent, the sultan broke the impasse by meeting the French officer in charge of the troops half-way between his palace and the European post. While the sultan knew he had the upper hand in the immediate situation, he also feared future reprisals, and offered to negotiate with the Europeans. The result was still another treaty.[67]

This round of talks produced an agreement that decidedly favored the French, but while it was indicative of the regional balance of power, it was not a measure of the relative strength of the two parties in Ndele. It is therefore difficult to determine why the sultan signed it. Either he felt compelled to acknowledge the overall superiority of the French in the

Ubangi-Shari and Chad areas, or he simply assented to the accord as the most expedient means of getting the French force to leave—figuring that he could simply ignore this treaty as he had earlier ones. In any case, he signed the document and the French force withdrew.[68]

Although al-Sanusi once more failed to conform to the demands of the treaty, its provisions were important. Not only did they provide the French with an excuse for further intervention in Dar al-Kuti, but they give an indication of how the colonial government reacted to the Congo Reform movement and its French counterpart—campaigns led by European journalists and socialist-leaning figures which, beginning in 1904, had revealed a widespread pattern of government-sanctioned atrocities and mismanagement in the French territories of North Central Africa as well as in the Congo Independent State. Debates on the matter had begun in the French parliament in early 1906, and among the many revelations was the fact that the French on the Gribingui had returned fugitive slaves to al-Sanusi in 1904.[69] Thus the 1908 treaty can be viewed in part as a French attempt to improve the image of the colonial administration.

Although the 1908 agreement repeated most of the articles of that signed five years before, the new text made major additions and omissions.[70] The most important items were clauses forbidding all trade in slaves, and making all raids and military expeditions subject to French approval. Second, the agreement insisted that the sultan impose a head tax, and further demanded that he pass on one-third of all levies and tribute to the French in currency or in kind, an effort designed to force rubber collection. Third, al-Sanusi agreed to adopt some French administrative procedures and take a census for tax purposes, and to furnish all the supplies for an expanded French garrison. Finally, the treaty required that he cut all commercial ties with the Muslim north.

In return, the French simply reiterated the general provisions of the earlier agreements. But the most important aspect of their position was not what they offered, but what they omitted. For the first time there was no promise to provide arms, munitions, instruction, or presents. At least on paper, the French came out ahead of al-Sanusi in this round. For the next three years, the Europeans pressured the sultan to turn his paper promises into reality. Continued raiding by the forces of Dar al-Kuti created much friction between the two parties, but given the economic bases of the state apparatus and al-Sanusi himself, he could not discontinue an activity so central to his wellbeing. The French suggested that he place greater emphasis on "legitimate" enterprise such as rubber collection, but despite European contentions, rubber was hardly as lucrative as the traffic in slaves. In addition, it would not have produced the quantities of imported goods that the sultan required for redistribution among his followers.

Hence in 1909 and 1910 slave-raiding went on as it had in previous years, but with one major exception. Following a major campaign against the Banda Linda on the Ouaka River in late 1909—during which the war leader Wald Banda marched his troops around and around the French post at Bria while the administrator looked on helplessly—the French resident at Ndele requested assistance from other posts, and pressured al-Sanusi to return the captives taken by the expedition. Al-Sanusi did so, and over the next year the French initiated a more aggressive policy characterized by the lieutenant governor of the colony as "peaceful hostility."[71]

The sultan responded to this increased European intervention by making plans to abandon Ndele. He sent Allah Jabu east to prepare the way for a move to the large rock outcropping at Ouanda-Djale not far from the Sudanese border. The major duty of the expedition was to defeat and remove the Yulu from the site. In years past, the Yulu had successfully resisted campaigns launched against them from Ndele, and they were not now ready to yield their kaga without a fight. Thus the expedition was away for a long time, and following an abortive assault on the Yulu settlement in 1910, al-Sanusi's forces settled in for a long siege.[72]

In early January 1911, faced with the Sultan's imminent departure, the French resident in Ndele decided to act. With Allah Jabu and his men out of the capital and not likely soon to return, it was an opportune time to try to take control of the city. But even with part of the army absent, al-Sanusi's men still outnumbered the Europeans, so the French devised a ruse. Advising the sultan that a large armed contingent would be passing in front of his compound on the way to the French post at Bria, the resident requested that he greet the commanding officer when the detachment passed by his palace on the way out of town. Al-Sanusi agreed, and at the appointed time came out of his compound with Adam. After talking briefly with the sultan, the French officer quickly drew a pistol and shot them both.[73]

In plotting their maneuver, the French had hoped that the removal of the sultan would create panic and provoke only minimal resistance.[74] In fact, some years earlier, fears of chaos had led them to reject a similar solution to their difficulties with al-Sanusi, since they did not have the personnel needed to rule the sultanate themselves. By 1911, however, the sultan had become recalcitrant enough to lead the French to change their minds. They had more or less subdued Wadai by this time, thus eliminating the final major obstacle in their drive to conquer the Ubangi-Shari and Chad regions. And so they risked chaos and assassinated al-Sanusi on 12 January 1911.

Indeed, European expectations proved to be accurate. With the eruption of violence many people fled into the bush. On the plateau at the heart of the city, a few hundred Muslim fighters resisted for a day, and then retreated to the east to join Allah Jabu at Ouanda-Djale. Within two days, Ndele was a ghost town, and only a third of the population ever returned.[75] Many people established new villages, but many more set out for their former homelands. Ndele's day was done.

Part 2
THE POLITICAL
ECONOMY OF A SLAVE-
RAIDING STATE

Chapter 4
Ndele: The Organization of a Slave-Raiding Capital on the Islamic Frontier

The founding in 1896 of a fortified capital nestled high on the side of a plateau at Ndele brought security to al-Sanusi and his followers. Located in the hilly region on the eastern limit of the Kuti floodplain, this new center was almost a prerequisite for the sultan's later activities as a slave-raider and slave-trader. The rapid development of the city during the next decade and a half is dramatic proof of his success in both endeavors. By the time of his assassination in 1911, the lands immediately around Ndele had become an ethnic mosaic with groups representing nearly all the peoples of central and eastern Ubangi-Shari.[1]

The city, and the state that grew up around it, were above all products of economic change occasioned by the integration of North Central Africa into the desert commercial system. As already detailed, the first tenuous links with lands north of the Islamic frontier were established when Muslim migrants from Dar Runga and Bagirmi settled in the region in the early nineteenth century. In the latter half of the century, more migrants and an influx of firearms strengthened these ties and tipped the balance of power in favor of the newcomers. These weapons permitted slave-raiding on a larger scale than ever before possible. Slave-raiding, in turn, allowed the mobilization of labor on a larger scale than previously possible, accompanied by appropriation of a greater part of its product. The small-scale household labor force characteristic of indigenous non-Muslim societies was not eliminated, but it became a component of a multifaceted system of forced labor that also included plantation production. The perpetuation of this system depended in part on continued access to firearms, powder, and other long-distance trade goods from the north which could be obtained only in exchange for slaves and ivory.

Islam provided the ideological underpinnings of the city and the state. It reinforced the common economic interests of the Muslim ruling class and proved attractive to non-Muslims, many of whom converted. And yet Islam in Ndele reflected the city's location on the fringes of the Muslim world. Muslims were indeed dominant, but their ability to impose their religious culture on all peoples in the capital was limited and their impact uneven.

Ndele is an exceptional subject for historical inquiry. The remains of the old fortified city, which was abandoned on French orders in the two days following al-Sanusi's assassination and never reoccupied, are largely intact on the plateau edge. A detailed survey that I made of these ruins serves as the basis for reconstruction. In addition, several dozen individuals alive in 1974—non-Muslims taken as captives, and Muslims whose parents were slave-raiders and -traders—lived in the city in their youth and clearly recall its history. Written records also exist. The first Frenchman visited the capital in 1898, and official French representatives lived there after 1901. Early French military and scientific missions sojourned in the region, and around 1900, when Ndele became a major entrepôt and center on the southern hajj route, a few European travelers passed through the city. Many of these visitors recorded their impressions of al-Sanusi's capital. Taken together, these sources constitute the most complete picture yet available of a major slave-raiding and slave-trading center in North Central Africa during the final, furious years of the commerce.

The Founding of the City

Following the Wadaian calvalry attack which devastated his settlement at Kali-Sha on the Kuti plain in 1894, al-Sanusi became an intinerant sultan, a ruler in search of a capital. Security was uppermost in his mind. For the next two years he moved from one place to another, setting up camp first at Kaga Banga, then at Kaga Yagoua, followed by sojourns at Ara and Kaga Toulou. Despite the peace with Wadai in 1895, he still feared Wadaian attacks from the north. He was also wary of assaults by the Banda Ngao from the south and uncertain about the strength and intentions of the French.[2]

Sometime during the next year, al-Sanusi settled at Ndele.[3] The major factor in the selection of Ndele was a concern for safety; the sultan chose the site primarily because it was very defensible. A high, well-watered plateau with rocky terrain to the east and north were its most prominent features. Low, fertile plains suitable for agriculture lay to the west and south.

Oral traditions dealing with the founding of the new capital conflict, and even though they can be partially reconciled, differences remain which make it impossible to know the precise sequence of events which led al-Sanusi to settle at Ndele. Several Banda and Nduka groups boast of a major role in the episode. The Banda Toulou of Kaga Toulou, a rock outcropping located about fifty kilometers east of the site, may have guided the sultan to the area; in any case, they soon joined him.[4] The Banda Ngonvo, a group closely related to the Toulou, were the original inhabitants of the Ndele plateau; their traditions insist that they invited al-Sanusi to join them.[5] The Banda Mbatta, whose villages lay in kagas southwest of Ndele, assert that they, too, were instrumental in the founding of the city.[6] To further complicate the picture, the Nduka Gollo, today found at Yangoundarsa five kilometers west of Ndele, also boast that they led al-Sanusi to the site.[7]

Interpreted very generally, these traditions are not mutually exclusive. The sultan had ties with all of these groups prior to settling among them. While still at Kali-Sha, he traded with both the Banda Toulou and the Banda Ngonvo. The Toulou version of the founding of the city is quite plausible for this reason, and also because al-Sanusi had sought refuge with them during his wanderings. The Ngonvo traditions do not dispute this claim. The Ngonvo and the Toulou claim a long history of intermarriage and alliance, so it is possible that the Ngonvo extended their invitation to the sultan with Toulou approval.[8] Banda Mbatta might well have joined al-Sanusi at the new capital, given their residence in the regions frequented by the sultan south of the Kuti plain. As for the Nduka Gollo, their claim is also believable. In the 1890s they lived just west of Ndele at the base of a large rock formation not far from their current village. They had close ties with Runga in the region, and with al-Sanusi in particular; he took several wives from among them.[9] The sultan made judicious alliances to establish working relationships with all of these local peoples. To be sure, he possessed greater firepower than all of them combined and clearly did not accept them as equals. They did not pose a threat, yet they were in a position to contribute to the stability of the new settlement, and provide security vital to the expansion of al-Sanusi's raiding operations.

These bonds had strategic value because the new capital lay on the Banda-Nduka frontier, a boundary that must have been known to a Muslim such as al-Sanusi who grew up in the region. The Nduka inhabit the lands to the northwest and west, while the Banda live south and southeast of the city. The names of the two major streams in the immediate vicinity of Ndele are the most apparent indications of this ethnic and linguistic border. A stream flowing west at the base of the plateau was (and is) called the "Ndele" by all peoples in the area; without exception they identify it as a Banda word. Banda, Nduka, and Runga wordlists suggest the same conclusion.[10] The name of the other stream, the "Miangoulou," is of Nduka origin.[11] "Mian" means stream, and "goulou" probably refers to the Nduka Gollo. "Miangoulou" thus translates as "stream of the Gollo." In fact it flows through the area inhabited by this subgroup. Thus the rocky plateau at Ndele was not only a critical site geographically; by locating the new capital there between the Banda and the Nduka, al-Sanusi acknowledged its political importance as well.

In cultivating ties with the indigenous peoples of the area, the sultan also reaped other worldly benefits. As possessors of the land in and around Ndele, the Banda Toulou, Banda Ngonvo, and the Nduka Gollo enjoyed a ritual preeminence that al-Sanusi accepted. Not only did he encourage them to continue traditional agricultural ceremonies to assure the fertility of the soil and the abundance of the harvest, but at times he even provided them with the necessary foodstuffs and sacrificial animals. Throughout his sojourn in Ndele, al-Sanusi exchanged offerings with local non-Muslim earth chiefs.[12]

The Setting and Growth of Ndele

Al-Sanusi built his new capital on a wide shelf on the flank of the high plateau. To the northeast and east, abrupt rock outcroppings and the summit of higher plateaux shelter the site. On the southwest and west the shelf drops off steeply to the plain thirty meters below. The steep and rocky approaches to the shelf sheltered it from mounted assault, while caves and passageways in the rocks afforded refuge.[13] Provided control of the higher plateau could be assured, the new city would be well-protected from all attacks.

The Ndele and the Miangoulou offered another natural advantage. Because the streams flowed throughout the year, Ndele seldom suffered the drought common to areas to the north and east in the October–March dry season. At the same time, the plateau and adjacent lowland are high enough to escape the inundation characteristic of the western Kuti plain during the rains. Situated between the extremes of drought and deluge, the site met the requirements for permanent settlement.

The level terrace on the plateau flank became the nucleus of the city. Al-Sanusi built his houses and compound there, and his sons and trusted *ajawwid* (advisors [Chadic Arabic]) settled near him. Initially some captives taken in raiding and incorporated into the sultan's fighting units built their villages on the terrace. Among the earliest of these were the Kresh of Mbele, the commercial center east of Ndele. After al-Sanusi's attacks destroyed their city, the sultan brought the survivors to the new capital where he settled them on the terrace, the higher plateau, and another kaga adjoining his own.[14]

The Kresh episode is but one illustration of the general settlement policy followed by the sultan throughout his years in Ndele. When his armed bands took captives, al-Sanusi sold some and settled others in the capital.

After raids in a particular area and the arrival of new war prisoners, al-Sanusi assigned each group its own parcel of land. In most instances he placed people of the same ethnic group together. Sometimes this practice led to the reconstitution of entire villages. In 1897, for example, when the sultan defeated his old Banda Ngao rival, Ngono, he resettled the leader's followers south of the plateau along the eastern reaches of the Miangoulou.[15] His bazingirs also enslaved a large group of Banda Marba around this time and relocated them on the Miangoulou as well, just west of the Ngao. The Banda Ngao, Banda Buru, and the Banda Ngaja soon joined these other groups.[16] Usually a surviving chief, chief's son, or some other influential individual became the leader of such settlements.

As time passed, houses spread from the plateau and terrace to nearby hills and the plain below. An overall settlement pattern consisting of four roughly concentric circles developed. The plateau was at the heart of the city. Immediately around it, spreading onto nearby hills and down to the streams, stood the houses of war captives newly incorporated into the sultan's following. Beyond these areas lay plantations and a close-settled zone dotted with permanent and seasonal agricultural villages.[17] The width of this band varied, extending through Runga lands in the north and northwest nearly to the Aouk River (one hundred kilometers distant), while in the west it merged with the Nduka homelands. To the south and southeast the belt contracted, reaching perhaps forty kilometers into Banda territory; in the east it barely penetrated the lands of the Kresh. The outermost circle formed an arc of deserted territory curving from the north-northeast to the southwest that separated the populated areas from the Kresh and Banda homelands. Dating at least from the years of Rabih's ghazzias in the Aouk region and perhaps from the earlier epoch of Wadaian raiding, this *cordon sanitaire* sheltered al-Sanusi's new capital. People feared to settle within it, in part because the sultan's raiders frequently crossed these lands on the way to more distant areas. He also maintained lookout posts within its confines.

The number of Muslim followers and incorporated captives who settled with al-Sanusi in Ndele in 1896 is unknown and difficult to estimate, but the population grew rapidly. Plots of land assigned to the Kresh and Banda settlers doubled the area of the city, and while the population increase may have been proportionally less than the increase in area during this time, the additions suggest substantial growth. For the remainder of the precolonial period, 1900–1910, population estimates are available, and with one exception display a marked uniformity (see figure 2). The figures suggest that Ndele and its immediate environs maintained a population of 25,000 during the decade preceding the French conquest. A careful reading of Kumm (e) indicates that his 8–10,000 figure—a substantially lower total

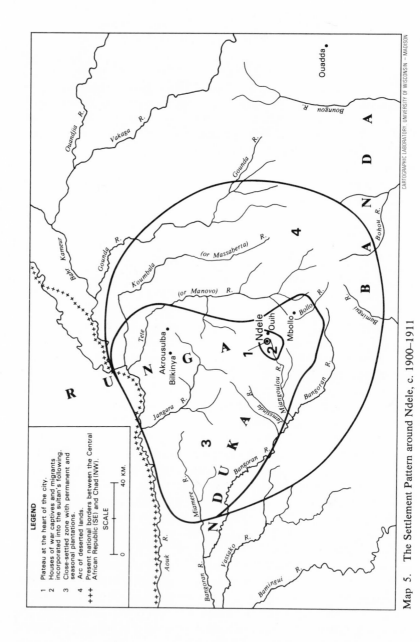

Map 5.   The Settlement Pattern around Ndele, c. 1900–1911

LEGEND

1   Plateau at the heart of the city.
2   Houses of war captives and migrants incorporated into the sultan's following.
3   Close-settled zone with permanent and seasonal plantations.
4   Arc of deserted lands.
+++   Present national borders between the Central African Republic (SE) and Chad (NW).

SCALE

0 ———————————— 40 KM.

84

CARTOGRAPHIC LABORATORY, UNIVERSITY OF WISCONSIN – MADISON

Figure 2

Population Estimates for Ndele, 1901–1910

Date	Estimate	Area
a) 1901	20–25,000	10 kilometer radius
b) 1902–3	25,000	20 kilometer radius
c) 1901–2	a) 15,000+	Ndele and agricultural villages
	b) 15,000	Kuti, Runga, Goula (that is, nearby)
d) 1905	30,000	in and around Ndele
e) 1909	8–10,000	in Ndele only
f) 1910	20,000	in and around Ndele

Sources:

a) Julien, "Mohamed-es-Senoussi" (1929), 49.
b) Chevalier, "Mission scientifique au Chari et au lac Tchad," 360.
c) H. Courtet, "Mission scientifique Chari–lac Tchad: Le pays Snoussi," *Revue des troupes coloniales* 3 (2nd semester, 1904), 485n1.
d) "Mohammed es-Senoussi," *AF* 21:3 (March 1911), 95.
e) Kumm, *From Hausaland to Egypt*, 170.
f) Modat, "Une tournée," 180.

than the others—refers to the core settlement of Ndele and not to the entire area of the capital. The French figures, however, are probably more accurate, since Julien, Chevalier, and Modat lived for extended periods in the city, while Kumm only passed through with a caravan of Hausa pilgrims. Courtet included "the Kuti"—that is, the Nduka peoples of the Kuti plain—in his 30,000 figure. His estimate consequently embraces the population of a larger area than the others. Ndele, then, sheltered about 25,000 people at the height of al-Sanusi's power. As such, its size rivaled that of Abeche to the north (28,000) and Bangassou to the south (31,000 inhabitants in the city and surrounding area), the termini of the major routes linking Ndele with the larger world.[18]

The limited fluctuation in population size suggests a conscious effort to control growth, since during this time the sultan's banners brought back a large number of captives each year. While some captives were settled in secondary centers away from the capital, others were purchased by foreign Muslim traders and exported.[19] Limited supplies of food and water do not appear to have been factors in containing the size of the city. Nor was space a problem, given the expanses of the Kuti plain to the west. Rather, al-Sanusi probably had to sell increasing numbers of prisoners in order to obtain weapons and munitions for his forces, whose ghazzias ranged farther and farther from the capital. He also had to sell more captives to acquire the long-distance trade goods needed to reward his subjects.

The Terrace

The basic plan of Ndele changed little between the founding of the city and the French conquest in 1911. Life revolved around the fortified terrace, which sheltered the government—the political and military nerve center of the capital. Major decisions emanated from the sultan's residence located there.

Measuring about 800 meters from east to west and 250 meters at its widest point, the terrace forms a natural shelf against a higher plateau which curves around and overlooks it from the northwest to the southeast. In the south and west, the area is delimited by steep drops to the lower plain and Ndele river stream-bed thirty meters below.[20] Space on the terrace is not completely open and unbroken, for numerous large boulders and occasional rock outcroppings limit visibility and movement; moreover, two small, spring-fed streams flowing south across the site to join the Ndele below have cut shallow ravines. Natural routes of access to the terrace are few and very narrow. On the northern side a few paths wind up through a broken façade to the summit of the higher plateau. To the south, the easiest descent lies through the rock-strewn beds of the small streams; in the west, the paths leading down to the plain are equally tortuous and narrow. Chevalier found the eastern approach to the site not much easier: "We returned to Ndele by way of the sources of the stream which gave its name to the city, passing through narrow corridors worn through blocks of sandstone to arrive within the hemicycle of rocks where Senoussi founded his capital."[21]

Al-Sanusi reinforced these natural characteristics to make the site even more secure. When he settled in Ndele, the memory of the Wadaian attack at Kali-Sha was undoubtedly still fresh. At Ndele this kind of attack could easily be repulsed. Only a very few paths were safe for horsemen, and even then they had to proceed slowly in single file. To protect the terrace further, the sultan built round guardhouses along its southern and western edges wherever there were breaks in the boulders. Guard posts at the eastern entrance to the site provided additional security. The streams assured a water supply adequate to withstand a long siege, while the caves and crevasses afforded cover.[22] The sultan had only to fear an attack reinforced by cannon. But this was not a real threat, since al-Sanusi possessed the only cannon in northern Ubangi-Shari.[23]

During his first several years in Ndele, the sultan had neither the time nor the resources to construct permanent buildings. After settling at the site in 1896, he lived for some years in a large house of straw surrounded by a woven straw fence similar to his earlier residence at Kali-Sha. Only with the accumulation of wealth and labor power through raiding in the last years of the century could he undertake more ambitious projects. Not until 1902, shortly before the arrival of Chevalier, did he complete construction of a new residence complex of rock-and-mud-walled houses surrounded by a high wall of the same materials.[24] Located on the western half of the site near one of the streams, this complex was the largest on the terrace. Pentagonal in shape, its longest sides measured roughly seventy meters in length. The walls were about four meters high and a meter thick at the base.

Within this compound, secondary walls—some of mud and rock, others of woven straw mats—divided the residence into several courtyards. Few trees were left in these areas, and straw shelters served as protection from the sun.[25] The first courtyard, reached through a large portal near the southeast corner of the compound, was an audience area. There the sultan greeted visitors, conducted business, and entertained his advisors. A number of small boys, generally non-Muslims taken in raids during infancy and raised as Muslims in the residence, acted as "court" messengers[26]

The harem enclosure, the only inner courtyard still visible today, lay in the southwest corner of the compound along with the personal quarters of al-Sanusi. The ruins of the home of the sultan's first wife, ᶜUmm Diwan, are found in this area. Access to these inner parts of the compound was limited to Faqih ᶜIssa, the sultan's Sudanese religious advisor who slaughtered cattle for the household and divided the meat among the women, and to al-Hajj Abdo, one of al-Sanusi's major counselors. Two servants, Faraj Allah (a Jallaba) and Ngusa Banda (a Banda), swept these inner courts. While the sultan's wives and concubines generally stayed within the compound, on festival occasions they sometimes danced just outside the entrance to the residence. And under a rudimentary straw shelter nearby, al-Sanusi frequently reviewed his troops and inspected recently arrived captives.[27] The remainder of the residence consisted of work space, granaries, storehouses, sleeping quarters perhaps reserved for guests or relatives, and open areas. Within the compound, too, small roundhouses of mud and stones served to store the millet needed to feed a household consisting of more than sixty women, their children, and the sultan's numerous clients and counselors.[28]

Other advisors, as well as major military leaders and al-Sanusi's sons, lived nearby. By 1911 at least, most had individual houses of the same mud-and-rock construction with courtyards enclosed by woven straw walls. Allah Jabu lived just to the west near the houses of Runga advisors Dabi and Muhammad Fufuni. In the same area, but farther north near the plateau face, stood the homes of Garaso, a Banda military leader, and Abi Sara, an Nduka banner commander. Momanguere, a Kresh chief who joined al-Sanusi after the destruction of Mbele, also had his compound there.[29]

Al-Sanusi's eldest son Adam and other followers lived south of the ruler's compound. Adam was the only other person who had a fortified compound. From a point just southwest of his father's residence, the walls

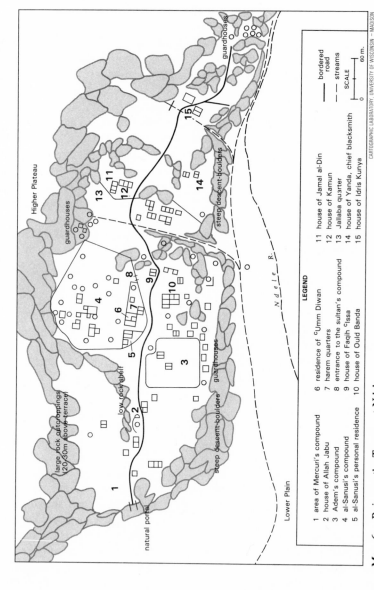

Map 6. Ruins on the Terrace at Ndele

LEGEND

1 area of Mercuri's compound
2 house of Allah Jabu
3 Adem's compound
4 al-Sanusi's compound
5 al-Sanusi's personal residence
6 residence of ʿUmm Diwan
7 harem quarters
8 entrance to the sultan's compound
9 house of Faqih ʿIssa
10 house of Ould Banda
11 house of Jamal al-Din
12 house of Kamun
13 Jallaba quarter
14 house of Yanda, chief blacksmith
15 house of Idris Kunya

CARTOGRAPHIC LABORATORY, UNIVERSITY OF WISCONSIN – MADISON

Higher Plateau

large rock outcroppings
(20-30m above terrace)

guardhouses

low rockshelf

natural portal

steep descent-boulders

guardhouses

guardhouses

steep descent-boulders

Lower Plain

N d e l e R.

bordered road
streams
SCALE
0   60 m.

88

of his enclosure extended to the line of guardhouses along the southern perimeter of the terrace. The compounds of father and son thus formed a secondary barrier nearly dividing the terrace from north to south.

West of these two residences stood the factory of the Société "La Kotto," the first French commercial company to station a permanent representative in Ndele. Mercuri, an Algerian who was the first agent in the city, supervised the building of the post along with storehouses for trade items such as beads, cloth, and manufactured goods.[30] The sultan apparently did not allow later French companies to construct depots on the terrace, and his display of hospitality towards Mercuri may have stemmed from the Algerian's knowledge of Arabic and his senior position as the earliest French agent; in any case, he and the sultan became good friends.[31]

East of Adam's compound lie the ruins of numerous other buildings. The largest of these, measuring nearly sixteen meters square, was the home of the important military leader Wald Banda. An adjacent house belonged to Mahammadi, a Sara from Chad who headed a war band and eventually became the governor of al-Sanusi's outpost at Ouadda.[32] Faqih ʿIssa also lived nearby, and the walls of his house are still visible today near the entrance to the sultan's residence. The ruins of small, single-room roundhouses and square dwellings are also found in this vicinity. Most sheltered lesser military figures. Oral traditions tell of a straw-walled mosque built here as well, but no traces of it are left.[33]

The mosque was not the only straw structure on this portion of the terrace. Although most of the enduring structures were of a military nature, not all military quarters were built to last. The map of the ruins suggests that large vacant areas separated the permanent buildings. In fact, clusters of straw houses inhabited by bazingirs and their families surrounded the compounds of the military leaders. Separated from each other only by narrow paths between compound walls of woven straw, these houses nearly filled the terrace west of the first stream. Potsherds blanket this entire area today, identifying it as a zone of dense population. Only a few open spaces remained, among them a small parade ground west of Adam's compound and the reviewing area near the palace entrance. Space was also left amid the houses for a road. Bordered by stones embedded in the ground, it ran west from the reviewing area to the terrace edge where it narrowed and passed under a high, overhanging rock—a natural portal—and continued down to the plain. From the sultan's residence an eastern extension of the route reached areas of the terrace beyond the streams, and passed through the eastern gateway to the site described above by Chevalier. A small path branched off to the south, led down to the Ndele stream-bed, and up to the Kresh quarter on the adjacent plateau.[34]

The east-central area of the terrace (between the two streams) was not as completely devoted to military activities. Guardhouses on the southern perimeter overlooked the Ndele, and ruins of a number of roundhouses show that, like the others, this part of the terrace was well watched. But most of the people who lived here were merchants, craftsmen, or relatives of the sultan with their followers. Judging from the ruins, fewer durable structures were built in this neighborhood.[35]

Immediately east of the first stream stand the remains of three large buildings. The most elaborate was the home of the sultan's son Jamal al-Din. Another was the residence of Kamun, a younger son who fled east after his father's death to Ouanda-Djale, where he resisted the French until 1912 when he sought refuge in the Sudan.[36] The third structure served as either a storehouse or a prison (the proximity of the merchant quarter suggests the former).[37] Along the stream north of these buildings stood the Jallaba settlement, although most traces of the houses that once crowded the site have disappeared. These traders were the only foreign merchant community to live on the terrace with the sultan, evidence of their special relationship to him. They traded foreign trade goods for ivory and slaves. As such, they were al-Sanusi's most important commercial partners, supplying the goods, arms, and munitions essential to the survival of Dar al-Kuti in exchange for the state's two major exports.[38]

The Jallaba probably also preferred to live on the terrace to avoid direct contact with the French. Official French residents in Ndele opposed the slave trade, and the treaty of 1908 specifically banned the traffic.[39] Given this political situation and al-Sanusi's dependence on the trade, it seems likely that he would have located the Jallaba and the French as far apart as possible. Since the resident lived on a high hill about a kilometer west of the plateau, across the valley and beyond the Ndele River, it made diplomatic sense to leave the Jallaba on the terrace near the palace where the French could not directly observe their activities. This arrangement also put the Jallaba near the eastern road out of the city, the route they took to return to the Sudan with their slaves. Although the French heard rumors concerning these caravans, they could not easily record their arrivals and departures. Many a group of recently captured slaves left Ndele under the cover of darkness.[40]

Craftsmen also lived between the two streams on this part of the terrace. Adjacent to the Jallaba were the houses of a small number of Hausa and Bornoan leatherworkers and shoemakers. Banda blacksmiths taken mainly from among the Ngao and Marba lived nearby. Jabda, the Ngao smith responsible for stenciling numbers on recently acquired rifles, had his house in this area.[41] Foremost among the ironworkers, however, was an Mbagga named Yanda, who as al-Sanusi's chief blacksmith possessed a large mud-and-rock residence. An enormous overhanging rock sheltered his workshop. The sultan and his lieutenants sent him rifles to be repaired along with requests for the fashioning of interchangeable parts. A prominent blacksmith who grew up on the plateau and lives in Ndele today acclaims Yanda's expertise: "There was nothing he did not know, . . . our fathers knew what they knew thanks to him."[42] In Ndele al-Sanusi relied on non-Muslim Banda smiths just as his forebears in Dar Runga had turned to their non-Muslim neighbors for ironworking.[43]

In addition to the Jallaba and the craftsmen, at least two military leaders and al-Sanusi's major counselor for foreign affairs had compounds in this vicinity. The Mbagga war leader Alwalla and Wamanguere, a Marba chief, lived near each other surrounded by bazingirs and members of their Banda groups. A large number of Banda Buru, a group closely related to the Ngao, settled with them.[44] But by far the most illustrious inhabitant of this part of the terrace was al-Hajj Ahmad Abdullahi (or al-Hajj Abdo, "Ajj Abdu" in Ndele parlance), the Hausa from Kano who arrived in Dar al-Kuti around 1885 and became a major counselor to the sultan a decade later. His house stood between the Jallaba quarter and the Hausa and Borno craftsmen. A small grove of banana trees belonging to the sultan also grew on this part of the terrace along the second stream and east of the settled areas described above.[45]

Beyond the second stream, the easternmost part of the terrace was smaller than the other two sectors. At this point the terrace shelf narrows considerably as the higher plateau face curves southward, eventually fusing with the rocks at the southern edge of the site. Roundhouses in a circle at the end of a narrow corridor of rocks guarded the eastern exit from the site. The ruins of the houses of Idris Kunya, another of al-Sanusi's sons, are the only traces of permanent structures in the area. As in the west, straw houses covered the other portions of the site. Once inhabited by a mixed population of Banda Marba, Kresh, and Runga, a blanket of broken pottery is all that remains.[46]

The terrace was thus the hub of al-Sanusi's new capital. The numerous military structures and their careful layout underscore the martial foundations of al-Sanusi's state. The mixed population of Runga, Kresh, and various Banda groups included the sultan's earliest supporters as well as the victims of his earliest raids, while the merchants residing on the terrace maintained the ties with the outer world that made everything else possible. In a sense, then, the terrace was a microcosm of the state, and like it, the core settlement fell to pieces after al-Sanusi's death. Today the site is abandoned and covered with dense undergrowth. In a famous epic poem of West Africa, the griot or court minstrel and historian of the medieval city of Niane recorded the destruction of Sosso, the stronghold of the sorcerer-king Soumaoro. He might well have described the fate of old Ndele:

All traces of the houses have vanished and of Soumaoro's seven
storey palace there remains nothing more. A field of desolation, Sosso
is now a spot where guinea fowl and young partridge come to take their
dust baths. . . . Many years have rolled by and many times the moon
has traversed the heaven since these places lost their inhabitants. The
bourein, the tree of desolation, spreads out its thorny undergrowth and
insolently grows in Soumaoro's capital. Sosso the Proud is nothing
but a memory in the mouths of the griots.[47]

The Higher Plateau

The sultan divided the space on the plateau above the terrace according to
the three functions it served. First, in a narrow band along the broken edge
of the plateau and atop the kagas overlooking the city core, he built yet
another line of guardhouses in order to survey activity below and to protect
the northern flank of the capital.[48] Second, some groups of people had their
homes on the plateau. Paramilitary villages of Kresh and Kara bazingirs,
their families, and common people lay directly north of the military
outposts. To the west, still on the plateau but overlooking the Kuti plain
beyond the western limit of the terrace, were other Kresh and Runga,
including several of Kobur's sons.[49] By settling his most loyal followers on
the higher plateau, al-Sanusi may have hoped to secure the most vulnerable
approach to the terrace. In any case, there was never an attack from this
direction. The Kresh, Kara, and Runga quarters resembled the terrace
settlements. Most houses were of straw and surrounded by walls of the same
material. The third function of the plateau was agricultural. Some of the
sultan's plantations lay to the northeast along with those of Adam.[50] Fields
of millet and other crops also grew among and north of the Kresh, Kara, and
Runga villages.[51]

The Lower Valley and the Plain

While the governmental and military center of al-Sanusi's capital lay on the
terrace and higher plateau, the bulk of the population lived in the lower part
of the city adjacent to the Miangoulou and Ndele. East of the Miangoulou
the sultan settled the vast majority of non-Muslim slaves not sold to slave-
traders. Between 1900 and 1910, this population included the groups listed
in figure 3.

Figure 3

Non-Muslim Captive Groups Settled at Ndele

Banda Marba	Banda Tombaggo	Kresh	Banda Toulou*
Banda Mbagga	Banda Linda	Sara Ngama	Banda Ngonvo*
Banda Ngao	Banda Ouassa	Sara Dinjo	Banda Mbatta*
Banda Buru	Banda Togbo	Sara Kaba	Nduka Gollo*
Banda Ngaja	Banda Ngapu	Goula	
Banda Dakpa	Banda Yakpa	Manza	

*As the earliest inhabitants of Ndele, these groups enjoyed a special relationship with al-Sanusi. They were not captives in the same sense as the other peoples listed above, but they were subject to the sultan's will.

Sources: OA4.1; OA9.1; OA9.2/10.1; OA15.2/16.1; Carbou, *La région*, 2:230.

Most Muslims living on the plain built their compounds west of the Miangoulou. A Runga community, including many migrants from Dar Runga attracted by al-Sanusi's prosperity, grew up at the base of the plateau in the first years of the century, and eventually spread west for several kilometers.[52] This part of Ndele remained a Runga domain throughout the colonial period, and it was here that al-Sanusi's two successors built their palaces under the watchful eyes of the French. Foreign Muslim merchants also resided in this area. Hausa and Bornoan traders had houses just east of the French post. And between them and the Runga lived a few Dajo from Dar Sila, Fezzanis and Tripolitanians from Libya, those Jallaba who did not live with countrymen on the terrace, and a small number of Bagirmi.[53] Muslim pilgrims on the way to Mecca also temporarily resided in this area.

Two other important areas below the terrace were the parade ground and the marketplace. Early maps locate these sites near each other, but no map includes both. Chevalier's map does not show a marketplace, but it does note the existence of a parade ground in the lower part of the city while Kumm's sketch omits any indication of a parade ground, but clearly identifies a market in approximately the same location.[54] As he went from the French post to al-Sanusi's palace, Kumm passed it, writing that there were "women of many nations, men with their rifles slung over their backs, sheep and goats, chickens and babies in artistic profusion."[55] Informants readily recall the market, describing it mainly as a place for the sale and purchase of foodstuffs; long-distance traders rarely appeared there with imported goods. The market's location at the foot of the plateau made it a meeting place for local people from the upper and lower parts of the city. Bazingirs and their families bought millet and other items from the peoples living on the plain.[56] All evidence considered, it thus seems likely that the sultan turned the review grounds into a marketplace sometime between the 1902–3 mission of Chevalier and Kumm's visit to Ndele in 1909.

This transformation of parade ground into marketplace may have been linked to increasing French interest in al-Sanusi's affairs, and his continued slave-raiding in particular. The sultan's actions perhaps reflected his own concern for privacy and security. While the review area on the plain offered much more space than the small site on the terrace west of Adam's compound, the French could easily have observed activity in this part of the city from their hilltop headquarters at the southwestern edge of the city. Consequently, even during Chevalier's visit, it was used primarily for ceremonial troop displays. Serious calls to arms for raiding expeditions went out from the terrace, and the bazingirs assembled there to avoid the French.[57] Eliminating the lower parade ground removed military activities to the terrace—completely out of the range of the French.

The founding of the market may also be taken as a sign of the penetration of the European market economy. By the middle of the first decade of the century, there were certainly present in Ndele a large number of people who were not part of the sultan's patron-client system. Significant quantities of European currency circulated as well. Moreover, the creation of a regular market for foodstuffs on the plain gave al-Sanusi greater freedom of action. Formerly the French went to his compound to obtain needed food supplies for themselves and their African troops. The marketplace discouraged these visits.

A description of the organization of Ndele in the first decade of the century would not be complete without further mention of the French post. Although the French did not assume direct control of the city until after al-Sanusi's death in 1911, the specter of European involvement was always present. From the time of Crampel's assassination in 1891 to the opening of the first French trading post in 1898, al-Sanusi was aware of the expanding French presence on the Ubangi. In this sense, the city of Ndele never had a precolonial history whose dynamics were totally independent of the French.

The potential for French interference in the affairs of Ndele and Dar al-Kuti increased greatly with Julien's arrival in June 1901. He first lived in a small house on the plain near the Miangoulou between the Muslim and non-Muslim parts of town. He described the site as "easily flooded and dominated [by higher land] on all sides."[58] By the time he left Ndele at the end of 1902, the Frenchman had directed the construction of the new post on a high, steep hill at the southwest limit of the populated part of the plain.[59]

High on their hill, the French were unaware of many events that took place on the terrace and higher plateau, and al-Sanusi did his best to see that

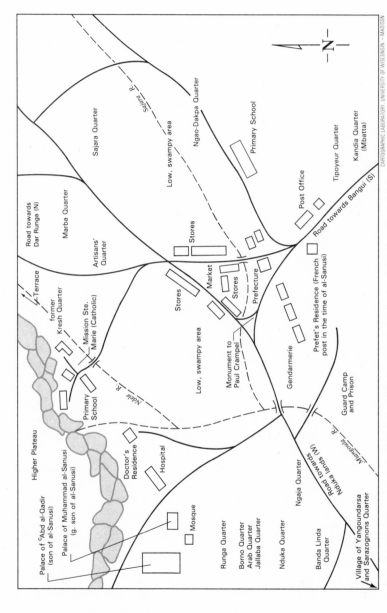

Map 7. The Organization of Ndele in 1974 (comprising only the lowland area of al-Sanusi's capital)

Palace of ʿAbd al-Qadir (son of al-Sanusi)

Palace of Muhammad al-Sanusi (g. son of al-Sanusi)

Higher Plateau

Mosque

Runga Quarter

Borno Quarter
Arab Quarter
Jaliaba Quarter

Nduka Quarter

Banda Linda Quarter

Village of Yangoundarsa and Sarazognons Quarter

Road towards Ndele (W)

Ngaja Quarter

Doctor's Residence

Hospital

Primary School

Ndele R.

Terrace

former Kresh Quarter

Mission Ste. Marie (Catholic)

Stores

Low, swampy area

Monument to Paul Crampel

Gendarmerie

Prefet's Residence (French post in the time of al-Sanusi)

Guard Camp and Prison

Mbaregoula R.

Prefecture

Stores

Market

Stores

Road towards Dar Runga (N)

Marba Quarter

Artisans' Quarter

Sajara Quarter

Sajara R.

Low, swampy area

Ngao-Dakpa Quarter

Primary School

Post Office

Road towards Bangui (S)

Tipoyeur Quarter

Kandia Quarter (Mbatta)

N

they remained in the dark. But the presence of the French post, which included a small armed detachment as well as the resident, impinged on the life of the city. Between 1908 and 1911, as relations between the French and the sultan deteriorated, the Europeans fostered client settlements of Hausa, Bornoans, and non-Muslims below the post. Africans who worked for them settled an area just southwest of the hill in a quarter that came to be called "Quartier Tipoyeur'" during the colonial period.[60]

As time passed, the post became a competing center of power. The French could never have defeated the forces of al-Sanusi in a pitched battle, but the post on the hill challenged his authority. After the assassinations of the sultan and his son in 1911, the center of power in Ndele shifted, dramatically and permanently, to the hilltop southwest of the city. Until 1911, however, the city's primary political, economic, and cultural ties bound it to the Muslim world north of the Islamic frontier. And Islam was the ideological cement which held the city together.

Islam in Ndele

Adherence to Islamic norms varied greatly in al-Sanusi's capital, and it was not always an indication of who was a Muslim and who was not. Many of the long-distance traders, pilgrims, and associates of the sultan were closely linked to more orthodox traditions; to a lesser extent this included the Runga, who lacked the worldly experience of these other Muslim groups, but whose long-term association with them produced similar effects. As for the Banda and Nduka, their exposure to Islam was less holistic and more recent. Muslim dress was prevalent among the more prominent non-Runga, but this reflected wealth and class as much as belief. The use of Arabic was not a reliable index of belief either, since it was the trade language for the entire region.

This discussion raises the broader question of conversion—how it can be authenticated, and the manner and degree in which it occurred.[61] Early studies of Islam in Africa devoted much effort to determining whether the faith was "pure" or "impure" when measured against practice in the Middle East or North Africa. In Ubangi-Shari, French travelers and administrators such as Julien, Modat, and Prins decried the degree to which local customs had, in their eyes, debased the pristine nature of Islam as they knew it from earlier experiences in North Africa.[62] Such prejudices divert attention from the deeper and far more interesting question of how peoples everywhere adapted Islam to their particular cultural contexts.[63] A Muslim in Africa, as anywhere, is best defined as one who identifies himself or herself as such regardless of the way he or she manifests the faith. This definition is not just an academic way of skirting an important issue; rather it mirrors the attitudes of Muslims themselves, most of whom believe that pronouncing the *shahada* (profession of faith) is sufficient to make one a Muslim:

> The Muslim coming from the heartlands of the faith may be amazed, shocked, or moved to contempt at what he sees in the outlying provinces, but he will not, in general, be inclined to contest the provincial claim to orthodoxy as long as he is satisfied of the community's determination to identify itself with the *ᶜumma Muhammadiyya* [community of Muhammad].[64]

It is in this light that Islam in Ndele at the turn of the century should be perceived. Most groups in the capital were touched by Islamic culture in one way or another, but important differences existed among them. Some, generally migrants from the Sahel where Islam arrived earlier, tried to protect and promote the more orthodox aspects of the faith, although their own understanding of it was not always accurate. Others, such as the Banda, and to a lesser degree the Nduka, adopted only those practices consistent with their own needs and beliefs.

In Ndele the terrace was the center of the more orthodox tradition. The forms and functions of the faith were more recognizable there because they more closely resembled standards of practice associated with Islam in other parts of Africa and the world. Hence it is a logical place to begin an examination of the role of Islam in al-Sanusi's capital. As noted, the only mosque in the city stood there. Its straw construction stands as a precarious testimony to the tenuous nature of the formal Islamic establishment in this frontier zone. The sultan and his close associates, both Runga and non-Runga Muslims, prayed in the building. The lack of mosques in other parts of town did not mean that no one else prayed; informants recall that the Jallaba, Bornoans, and Hausa gathered in their own quarters of the city and prayed outdoors just as elsewhere in Islamic Africa. Nonetheless, the major observance of the week, held at noon on Friday, took place on the terrace. And as might be expected in a martial settlement, a review of the troops accompanied it.[65]

Institutions and Agents of Islamization

Institutions of Islamization in al-Sanusi's capital, although rudimentary, also lay close to the seat of political power. Chief among these was the Qur'anic school, called the *garai* (from the Arabic *qara'a*, meaning "to

read"). Under the supervision of a faqih, usually Faqih ᶜIssa, students
gathered in the sultan's compound early in the morning and again late in the
evening to learn basic reading skills. Access to the school was limited to the
children of the sultan and a few important counselors, although non-Muslim
children taken in raiding and then attached to these households also
attended.

More advanced Islamic educational institutions did not exist in Ndele.
Those desiring further study had to go to Abeche, Dar Fur, or centers of
learning even farther away such as al-Azhar in Cairo or schools in the
Hijaz. These itinerant students were called *muhajirun*, or migrants,
presumably because they journeyed in search of knowledge. Julien
suggested that al-Sanusi had followed such a course of study, although informants in Ndele today deny it, maintaining that he was interested in
power (*mulk* [Arabic]) and not in learning, and that the two do not mix.[66] It
is generally acknowledged, however, that ᶜAbd al-Mintalib, the eldest son
of Kobur and a respected faqih in Ndele, had studied in Wadai.[67]

Dar al-Kuti also lacked the Islamic brotherhood or *tariqa*, an
institution common to Sahelian Africa, although a few northern Muslims
followed the Qadiriya and Sanusiya. Sidi al-Mahdi, leader of the latter,
wrote to the sultan in 1902, inviting him to join the brotherhood and offering
to send deputies, but partly out of fear of a hostile French reaction, al-
Sanusi refused his overtures. The Tijaniya, today the most popular tariqa,
arrived only late in the colonial era.[68]

Although Ndele's institutional links with the rest of the Islamic world
were tenuous, two groups of Muslims reduced the city's cultural isolation
and often served as agents of Islamization. Faqihs and pilgrims (*hujaj*
[Arabic]) visited the capital and settled there for a time. Their activities
varied, but many acted as mediators between Islam as it existed in North
Africa and the Middle East and the religious culture of Ndele. They stood
between the small Muslim religious and political class, which was aware of
the greater Islamic world, and the remainder of the population.

The term faqih in Dar al-Kuti was vague, referring generally to anyone
who could read the Qur'an or other religious literature.[69] Faqihs in Ndele
could read, although Grech reported that their unfamiliarity with elemen-
tary grammatical rules and orthography sometimes made it difficult to
decipher their writing.[70] Yet, because they possessed a modicum of
learning, al-Sanusi welcomed them and occasionally provided them with
women and slaves as was the custom elsewhere. Some served as educators
and religious counselors to the elite, but most catered to a larger clientele,
not as teachers but as suppliers of *hajab* or *warga*, Islamic charms for
protection and healing. Unlike Qur'anic instruction, which was confined to

the ruling circles and their dependents, these magical and medical services served a large part of Ndele's population. Most hajab were written charms; writing acquired a religious identity because its diffusion coincided with the spread of Islam. Some charms, generally consisting of an appropriate passage from the Qur'an transcribed on a slate, were used to treat sickness. Faqihs rinsed off the writing, collected the water and ink, and gave it to their clients to drink. The potion reputedly possessed the power of the words dissolved in it. They also produced amulets assuring long-term protection from ill-fortune, witchcraft, and violence. The written word was again the affective agent, appropriate verses being written on scraps of paper, sewn into leather pouches, and worn on the body.[71] Charms against iron fell into this category and were particularly popular. In a slave-raiding, slave-trading region such as Dar al-Kuti, such a shield from violence was very important. As one informant put it, "When a man goes to war, does he not take a stout stick?" Banda informants say that when worn in battle, Muslim amulets made the bearer a Muslim and the faith sheltered him.[72]

Although the historical evidence is too limited to classify faqihs in al-Sanusi's time, today in Ndele they definitely fall into two groups. Muslims go to one set, non-Muslims to another. Muslims of northern provenance such as the Runga expect a faqih to have studied *tafsir*, Qur'anic exegesis, and tend to avoid anyone claiming to be a faqih who has not followed this course of instruction. The Banda, on the other hand, are less acquainted with the conventions of Islamic learning, and their specifications are less stringent.[73] This does not mean that the non-Muslims did not respect and even revere Islam. Modat noted in 1911 that the Banda were famed for their loyalty to oaths sworn on the Qur'an.[74]

Pilgrims also fostered familiarity with Islam in al-Sanusi's capital. Most came from Hausaland or Borno, and they began arriving soon after Ndele was founded. Before this time most routes from West Africa to the holy cities passed well to the north, but as Dar al-Kuti became increasingly integrated into the Islamic world, travelers became more familiar with it. In addition, Rabih's conquests in Bagirmi and Borno, as well as French intervention in the Middle Shari valley and Wadai beginning in the 1890s, frightened Muslim travelers away from these northern routes.[75]

Although the Bornoans and Hausa appeared in Dar al-Kuti about the same time, they came for somewhat different reasons. Boukar Froumbala, a Bornoan who first spent a month in Ndele in 1910 and then returned in the 1930s to settle permanently, says that the Bornoans came to the city mainly to trade, although some eventually made the pilgrimage. The Hausa, on the other hand, viewed Ndele merely as a stopping point on the hajj. A survey of the prominent members of both communities confirms Boukar's judgment.

Of the four heads of the Bornoan settlement in Ndele between 1900 and 1974, only one made the pilgrimage. In contrast, the three most important Hausa in al-Sanusi's capital were all returned pilgrims.[76]

The volume of pilgrim traffic is difficult to estimate, although the numbers passing through the city certainly increased during the colonial era. Reports from Ndele for 1914 put their number at 480, and in November alone 551 passed through Gribingui, a post just to the southwest. By the 1930s, when Froumbala was chief of the Bornoan quarter in Ndele, several hundred Hausa and Bornoan pilgrims came through the city annually.[77] In al-Sanusi's time the numbers were fewer, but over a hundred pilgrims probably resided in the capital at any one time. Froumbala estimated that the Hausa numbered between 150 and 200 at the time of his sojourn in 1910, and the Bornoans between 50 and 60.[78] In any case, traffic was significant enough to merit the construction of rest camps capable of sheltering thirty pilgrims every twenty-five kilometers between Fort-Archambault, the major French post on the Upper Shari, and Ndele. Karl Kumm, a German who made his way from Hausaland to the Sudan in 1909, traveled with a party that included sixty Hausa heading for the Nile valley and Arabia. And Ndele was apparently known in the holy cities, for in 1907 the sultan received a holy flag from Mecca that he put on display in the mosque; when pilgrims went to worship, they often honored the memento with a kiss.[79]

Pilgrim activities in Ndele paralleled those elsewhere in the eastern Sudan in the late nineteenth and early twentieth centuries. Mobility gave birth to a common "hujaj culture" in the region, partly because of the length of the journey—which has been estimated at about seven years.[80] During the trek, many people settled temporarily, sowing and harvesting crops for a year or more in order to finance the next leg of the trip. This strategy sometimes brought important agricultural innovation. In Dar al-Kuti pilgrims are credited with the introduction of onions, and Hausa and Bornoans controlled the cultivation and marketing of the crop throughout the colonial era.[81]

Pilgrims also contributed to the permanent population of the city. Some eastbound Muslims abandoned their quest, settled, and married into local communities. Similarly, westbound travelers like al-Hajj Mouloukou often made the most of their achievement, finding fame and fortune along the way and never returning to their homelands. Fortune for many consisted of petty trade, and pilgrims frequently dealt in cowrie shells, natron, kola, beads, and other items purchased at one point on their itinerary and sold at another. In addition, most of the butchers in Ndele were Hausa or Bornoans, as in other urban centers of North Central and West Africa. Finally, like pilgrims throughout the Lake Chad–Nile region, some advertised themselves as faqihs, taught in local garai, and wrote charms.[82]

Al-Sanusi, himself a serious Muslim who never drank alcohol, encouraged these travelers. The rest camps along the route in western Dar al-Kuti were built at his behest. Moreover, he provided most newly arrived pilgrims with a meal or two before they settled or continued on their journey. Mindful of the prestige accorded those who had completed the hajj, he enticed many returning pilgrims to settle, offering them wives and wealth. Their knowledge of worldly affairs often surpassed his own, and pilgrims such as al-Hajj Abdo and al-Hajj Tukur were among his most trusted advisors.[83] This pattern also occurred elsewhere in the eastern Sudan, where political leaders frequently welcomed returned pilgrims as counselors, scribes, and people of experience. But the link was particularly important for a region so distant from Islamic centers as Dar al-Kuti. The pilgrims were a bridge to the heartlands of the Hijaz as well as to the more Islamized parts of the savanna and Sahel to the north and west. In 1900 Ndele's population included pilgrims, although most were on their way to somewhere else; faqihs offered their services, acting as mediators between Islam and African culture. But the city remained fundamentally a frontier community where day-to-day concerns militated against the growth of a truly learned community. The world of slave-raiding on the Islamic frontier was not the place to lead the reflective life.

Just as the schools, faqihs, and pilgrims communicated some aspects of Muslim culture to a broad part of Ndele's population, so did the observances of religious holidays. Major community observances marked the end of Ramadan, the month of fasting, and Karama, the anniversary of the birth of the prophet. Delegations came to the capital from outlying Banda and Nduka villages as well as the Muslim Runga settlements in northern Dar al-Kuti. People danced, and the sultan offered a feast for all assembled and gave gifts to important clients. Although these events embraced most groups in the city, the Muslim and non-Muslim communities understood them differently. The former tended to emphasize their religious nature, and on Karama faqihs read from the Qur'an and biographies of Muhammad; non-Muslims, however, saw them mainly as festive occasions, although today they recall them with awe, insisting that their own cultures had no comparable festivals.[84] In a larger sense, the celebrations also represented a redistribution of wealth from the sultan back to major groups within the community, as well as a way of reaffirming his authority; but because they occurred within an Islamic context, they also familiarized the city's population with the dominant culture.

While conclusions about psychological attitudes are extremely difficult to verify, it is apparent that the ascendancy of Islam in Ndele and Dar al-Kuti, and perhaps along much of the Islamic frontier, made local peoples aware of it as a pervasive world culture. In this sense the religion provided ideological support even among non-Muslims. This perception, the military prowess of the Muslims, and their monopoly over the prestigious goods of long-distance commerce, seem to have awed non-Muslims. Certainly, this was (and is) the case among the Banda of Ndele. Asked about traditional Banda ceremonial occasions, informants consistently replied that none compared to those of Islam.[85] A major non-Muslim informant responded to questions about these events by saying that "al-Sanusi made them [the Banda of that time] understand."[86] This sense of cultural inferiority extended into other spheres. People believed that Islamic magic was more powerful than their own, at least in certain circumstances. Not only did they purchase warga for protection against iron, but Muslim charms were also thought to provide protection from the nefarious actions of the *ngandro*, returned ancestors who disrupt Banda village life with witchcraft. Muslim military power and cultural domination on the frontier would probably have been perceived as divinely sanctioned in any event, since non-Muslims and Muslims alike associated worldly achievement with supernatural aid or acquiescence.[87] But the high regard of non-Muslims for Islam greatly "fortified" settlements such as that founded by al-Sanusi.

Chapter 5
Slave-Raiding, the Slave Trade, and Agricultural Production

The political economy of Dar al-Kuti rested on slavery and the raiding and trading in people that maintained it. This is to say, too, that it was founded on violence: the constant incorporation of captives furnished labor for intensive agricultural production around Ndele, along with additional manpower for the sultan's armed forces and raiding parties; and the continual export of other captives to Muslim zones north of the Islamic frontier brought the weapons and wealth necessary for further conquest and incorporation. Thus were articulated raiding, the production of foodstuffs for internal consumption, and long-distance exchange.

Early studies of precolonial Muslim states in Africa emphasized the vital role of long-distance trade in forming and maintaining political systems.[1] Later works dealt with internal agricultural production—for consumption as well as export—often within the context of indigenous slavery and the Muslim slave trade.[2] Still others, such as those of Lovejoy, Baier, Cooper, Terray, and Goody, scrutinized the links between these economic spheres.[3] This chapter and the next attempt to do the same, along with an analysis of how al-Sanusi manipulated both spheres to sustain and expand his power. The sultan's success stemmed in part from his ability to balance domestic needs for labor with the external demand for slaves that supplied needed items of long-distance commerce. Thus it seems appropriate to begin by considering the raiding that produced needed captives and the military apparatus which underlay al-Sanusi's state.

The Slave-Raiding of al-Sanusi, 1890–1911

Between the late 1880s when al-Sanusi became Rabih's client and his death in 1911, the sultan or his war leaders raided for slaves and ivory throughout northern and eastern Ubangi-Shari as well as the southeastern Chad basin. Initially the marauders attacked peoples in the lands adjacent to the Runga-

Nduka heartland of Dar al-Kuti, but each year they ventured farther afield. Their ghazzias eventually carried them as far as the southwestern Anglo-Egyptian Sudan. These raids affected virtually every major group of people living in this vast region (see figure 4).

Raiding campaigns generally occurred during the dry part of the year, after much of the agricultural work was done and when travel was easier. The dry season runs from October to April; hence the frequent two-year entries cited in figure 4.[4] The scale of these operations was in keeping with their long duration. They ranged in size from a hundred or two hundred to as many as a thousand or two thousand men, usually setting out within a couple of months after the end of the rains and moving slowly towards the target area. While the detachment remained within the immediate hinterland of Ndele, the sultan's agricultural villages provided grain; beyond this zone, numerous small hunting and foraging parties scoured the countryside for game, Shea butter nuts, and edible wild plants to supplement the food supplies carried by the expedition. In these outlying areas, minimally dependent on Ndele, the raiders plundered local farmers and their stores of grain.

Once they were in the region to be raided, the marauders constructed one or more zaribas that served as headquarters for the operation. From these bases lesser parties went out to raid the small and scattered non-Muslim settlements. Slaves taken in each encounter were then herded back to the zariba. After a sufficient number of captives had been acquired, they were tied together, and the expedition returned to Ndele. This procedure explains the large number of slaves taken in the few campaigns for which statistics are available (see figure 4, nn. i, r, u, w, gg). It also indicates the reason for the small known number of prisoners recorded for the Sara raids of 1902–3 (see figure 4, n. x); Chevalier accompanied al-Sanusi's men on this foray, and these figures refer to slaves taken in individual villages.[5]

Success depended on a combination of surprise, numbers, and the panic provoked by gunfire at close range. Unlike the raiding expeditions of Sahelian states such as Wadai, Bagirmi, and Dar Fur, al-Sanusi's forces included no cavalry detachments. In fact, there were only a few dozen horses in Ndele at any given time, and they belonged to the sultan and a few other influential officials. Generally these animals succumbed to sleeping sickness within a short time and fresh stock had to be brought in from the north.[6] Lacking horses, then, a large number of raiders usually made their way on foot to within striking distance of a village and set up camp for the night. The next morning they arose well before daybreak and set out after the dawn prayer. They attacked in the gray light of early morning with guns blazing. In most cases, villages were taken by surprise, and many people were killed or captured in the initial melee. Because others fled to hide in the

Figure 4

Peoples and Areas Raided by al-Sanusi or his Bands,
1890–1911

	Approximate Dates	Peoples	Homelands	Location Relative to Dar al-Kuti	No. Slaves Taken
a)	Early 1890s	B. Marba, B. Mbatta B. Mbagga, B. Mbi, B. Dakoa	Kaga Bongolo Bamingui- Bangoran and	S	Unknown
		B. Mbres	Koukourou R.		
b)	1892	Akouga (Nduka?)	Upper Gribingui R.	SW	Unknown
c)	1892 or 1893	Manza	Kaga Kazemba	SW	al-Sanusi defeated
d)	1892	W. B. Ngao	R. Ouham	SW	Unknown
e)	1894–1895	Kresh	Mbele on Gounda R.	E	Unknown
f)	1895	B. Mbi, B. Dakpa, Sabanga	Grimari region	S	Unknown
g)	1895–1896	Banda	Ouaka R. region	SE	Unknown
		Banda	Upper Kotto R.	SE	Unknown
h)	1895–1896	B. Mbra, B. Mbagga,	Kaga Mbra,	S	Unknown
		B. Marba	Kaga Ngouzera	S	Unknown
i)	1896	S. Ngama	Aouk-Bamingui confluence	W	2,000
		B. Bongo	Bongou R.	SE	Unknown
j)	1897	B. Tombaggo	Gribingui-Koddo confluence	SW	Unknown
		B. Ngao	NE of Bamingui R.	S	Unknown
		B. Banda	Kaga Bakongolo	S	Unknown
		B. Mbatta	Kaga Trogba	S	Unknown
k)	1897	Kresh	Mbele on Gounda R.	E	Unknown
l)	late 1890s	B. Toulou	Kaga Toulou	E	Unknown
m)	1898	B. Mbres, B. Mbra	Kaga Mbres, Kaga Mbra	S	Unknown
		Sabanga	N of Grimari	S	Unknown
n)	1899	Banda	Ouaka R. region	SE	Unknown
o)	1898–1900	Goula	Lake Mamoun	E	Unknown
		B. Ouadda,	Ouadda region	SE	Unknown
		B. Ngaja,	Ouadda region	SE	Unknown
		B. Tombaggo,	N of Grimari	S	Unknown
		B. Dakpa, B. Ngao	N of Grimari and	S	Unknown
		(also called Ngapu)	NE of Bamingui R.	S	Unknown

Figure 4 (Continued)

Peoples and Areas Raided by al-Sanusi or his Bands,
1890–1911

Approximate Dates	Peoples	Homelands	Location Relative to Dar al-Kuti	No. Slaves Taken
p) 1900–1902	Banda, Kresh, and Sabanga	Area N of Rafai, SE of Ouadda, to Sudanese border	Far E	Unknown
q) 1901	K., Sa꜀id Baldas	eastern Ubangi-Shari	Far E	Unknown
r) 1901	B. Linda, B. Yakpa,	Upper Kotto	SE	2,500
	Sabanga	N of Grimari	SE	Unknown
s) 1901	K. from Mbele	E of Gounda site	E	Unknown
t) 1901–1902	Hemat Arabs	N of Dar Runga	NE	Unknown
u) 1902	B. Linda,	Grimari	S	Unknown
	B. Tombaggo	Bambari	SE	Unknown
	B. Ouadda	Ouadda region	SE	Unknown
	K. Aja, K. Sauji	N of Rafai	Far SE	Unknown
	K., Sa꜀id Baldas	near Sudan border	Far SE	Unknown
	Vidri	Bria region	SE	Unknown
v) 1902–1903	B. Junguru	Upper Kotto	SE	Unknown
w) 1903	Goula	Aouk to Lake Iro	N	1,000
x) 1902–1903	S. of Mbanga	Village N of Aouk	N	40
	S. Ngaka, Sara (general)	SW of Lake Iro	W & NW	Unknown
	S. of Biro	Village SW of Iro	W & NW	100
	S. Dinjo, S. Kaba	W of Lake Iro		
y) 1903–1904 or 1905	B. Dukpu (Dakpa)	Chinko R. region	Far SE	Unknown
z) 1904	Kara	Birao region	NE	Unknown
aa) 1905	Hufrat al-Nuhas region	SW Sudan	Far SE	Unknown
bb) 1905	B. Ouassa	N of Rafai	Far SE	Unknown
cc) 1905–1906	B. Govvoro	W of Ouanda-Djale	E	Unknown
dd) 1906	B. Ouadda	Ouadda region	E	Unknown
ee) 1906	Goula	Lake Mamoun	E	Unknown
ff) 1907	Sabanga, Vidri	Grimari region	S	Unknown
	B. Ngaja	and east	SE	Unknown
gg) 1909	B. Linda	Upper Kotto and	SE	600 taken,
	B. of Bria region	Ouaka R. region	SE	200 arrive in Ndele
hh) 1910–1911	Banda and Kresh	Yalinga area	Far SE	Unknown
	Yulu	Ouanda-Djale	E	Unknown

B = Banda   K = Kresh   S = Sara

Figure 4 (Continued)

*Peoples and Areas Raided by al-Sanusi or his Bands,
1890–1911*

Sources:

a) OA3.2; OA15.2/16.1; OA17.2/18.1; OA19.1/20.1; Chevalier, *Mission*, 158; Julien, "Mohamed-es-Senoussi" (1929), 59; Grech, "Essai sur le Dar Kouti," 21.
b) Maistre, *A Travers L'Afrique centrale*, 129–31.
c) Vergiat, *Moeurs et coutumes des Mandja*, 28; Gaud, *Les Mandja*, 95–96; Kalck, "Histoire," 2:449–50.
d) Kalck, "Histoire," 2:449–50.
e) OA15.2/16.1; Grech, "Essai sur le Dar Kouti," 21–22; Julien, "Mohamed-es-Senoussi" (1929), 59; Santandrea, *A Tribal History*, 219–23.
f) Serre, "Histoire économique et sociale du district de Grimari," 22; Julien, "Mohamed-es-Senoussi" (1925), 142.
g) OA19.1/20.1; Julien, "Mohamed-es-Senoussi" (1925), 142.
h) OA3.2; OA17.2/18.1; OA19.1/20.1; ANF-SOM (Paris), Papiers Julien, 6P.A., "Rapport du Cap^{ne} Julien . . . du Ba-Mingui"; Julien, "Mohamed-es-Senoussi" (1925), 142.
i) OA22.1; OA23.1; Julien, "Mohamed-es-Senoussi" (1915), 142–43; (1929), 29.
j) OA9.1; OA9.2/10.1; OA19.1/20.1; ANF-SOM (Paris), Papiers Julien, 6P.A., "Rapport du Cap^{ne} Julien . . . du Ba-Mingui"; Prins, "Les Troglodytes du Dar Banda," 12–14, 22; Modat, "Une tournée," 232; Julien, "Mohamed-es-Senoussi" (1929), 59.
k) Modat, "Une tournée," 232.
l) OA17.2/18.1; Chevalier, *Mission*, 158.
m) Julien, "Mohamed-es-Senoussi" (1929), 59.
n) ANF-SOM (Paris), Papiers Julien, 6P.A., "Rapport du Cap^{ne} Julien . . . du Ba-Mingui"; Julien, "Mohamed-es-Senoussi" (1925), 167.
o) Julien, "Mohamed-es-Senoussi" (1927), 70–71, 100; (1929), 59; Modat, "Une tournée," 232.
p) ANF-SOM (Aix), 4(3)D11, "Rapport mensuel du mois d'Août," Bangui, 28 September 1904; Modat, "Une tournée," 232; Julien, "Mohamed-es-Senoussi" (1929), 59.
q) ANF-SOM (Paris), Tchad I, dossier 3, Prins, "Rapport d'un voyage de Raphai à Said Baldas."
r) Julien, "Mohamed-es-Senoussi" (1928), 65–66; (1929), 56, 80.
s) OA14.2; OA17.2/18.1; Julien, "Mohamed-es-Senoussi" (1928), 61.
t) ANT, W53.9, "Documents et études historiques sur le Salamat, réunis par Y. Merot: Rabah et Senoussi au Dar Rounga," 2.
u) ANF-SOM (Aix), 4(3)D9, Romiaux, "Rapport mensuel (septembre)," Rafai, 1 October 1902; ANF-SOM (Aix), 4(3)D9, Administrateur du Haut-Oubangui, "Rapport politique," Mobaye, 30 July 1902; Julien, "Mohamed-es-Senoussi" (1928), 76–77; (1929), 60; Kalck, "Histoire," 3:74–76; Kalck, *Réalités oubanguiennes*, 97–98.
v) Santandrea, *A Tribal History*, 250–51.
w) Chevalier, *Mission*, 304–6.

Figure 4 (Continued)

Peoples and Areas Raided by al-Sanusi or his Bands,
1890–1911

Sources:

x) OA4.1; OA22.1; OA23.1; Chevalier, *Mission*, 301–3; Julien, "Mohamed-es-Senoussi" (1929), 80; Modat, "Une tournée," 223, 274–75; Kalck, "Histoire," 3:77; Decorse, *Du Congo au lac Tchad*, 161, 172–73.

y) Santandrea, *A Tribal History*, 249, 259–61.

z) AMBB, No. 167 (Bangassou), Boucher, "Monographe sur le Dar Kouti oriental."

aa) Oppenheim, "Rapports sur le Ouadai, le Dar al-Kouti, et le Senoussia," *Etudes et documents tchadiens*, série B, No. 1 (1968), 135.

bb) Santandrea, *A Tribal History*, 254–55, 272.

cc) Ibid., 270.

dd) Ibid., 254–55. I dated this raid to 1906 because al-Sanusi founded his post at Ouadda at about this time, and it was commanded by the Sara lieutenant whom Santandrea mentions.

ee) OA21.4; CC, Cornet, "Au coeur de l'Afrique centrale," 69; Martine, "Essai sur l'histoire du pays Salamat," 22; Modat, "Une tournée," 277. The Dajo of Dar Sila raided the Goula of Mamoun at the same time. Since al-Sanusi and the Dajo sultan were allies, it is likely that these ghazzias were part of a joint campaign (see Martine, 25)

ff) Julien, "Mohamed-es-Senoussi" (1929), 81.

gg) OA17.2/18.1; AAV (Vincennes), A. E. F., Oubangui-Chari, série O^3, ctn. 1, dossier 3, Modat to Lt.-Gouverneur, Letter No. 43, Ndele, 6 October 1909; Modat to Lt.-Cmdt. le Cercle de Kouango, Letter No. 45, Ndele, 19 October 1909; ANF-SOM (Aix), 4(3)D17, "Razzias commises par les bandes de Senoussi de N'Délé," Brazzaville, 20 April 1910, 1–7; Tisserant, *Ce que j'ai connu de l'esclavage en Oubangui-Chari* (Paris, 1955), 17–18.

hh) OA5.1; OA11.1; AMBB, No. 108 (Bangassou), Langellier-Bellevue, Chef de la Circonscription de la Haute-Kotto, to M. le District Commissioner, Western Region, Anglo-Egypian Sudan, Letter, 24 May 1934; AAV (Vincennes), A. E. F., L'Oubangui-Chari, série O^3, ctn. 1, dossier 3, Modat to Gouverneur de L'Oubangui-Chari-Tchad, Letter No. 14, Ndele, 3 April 1910; Julien, "Mohamed-es-Senoussi" (1929), 83.

bush nearby, raiding parties frequently camped in the abandoned villages for several days to hunt for refugees. The marauders also took this opportunity to strip the settlement of stored food and items of value, such as ivory, that had been put aside for trading with itinerant peddlers. The raiding party then returned to the central zariba.[7]

Although al-Sanusi's forces triumphed in most encounters, they were not invincible, and they knew it. The use of surprise tactics suggests that the raiders feared defeat or unbearable casualties in a direct engagement. Another strategy also reflected concern over resistance. The sultan's men would sometimes approach a village slowly and quite openly, causing everyone to flee into the bush. They then withdrew. Thinking that the danger had passed, the villagers eventually returned. Shortly thereafter, however, the marauders abruptly reappeared, attacking and quickly subduing the village.[8]

It is difficult to gauge the effectiveness of these tactics. Certainly marauders on foot were more vulnerable than those on horseback. After the initial attack, their firearms were of little advantage, since most of them were not rapid-fire weapons. In this situation, one would expect that the marauders would sustain a fairly high number of casualties, occasionally even being routed, and indeed this was the case. The sultan's forces met defeat at the hands of the Manza in 1892 or 1893; his detachments suffered serious reversals in raids against the Sara Ngama in 1896 although they still managed to return with many prisoners; and in a campaign among the Banda Linda in 1901, the Linda attacked the central camp at night, forcing many of al-Sanusi's men to throw themselves into the nearby Ouaka River where they drowned (see figure 4, nn. c, i, r). In 1903, during his travels with the raiders in Sara country, Chevalier noted that the sultan's forces lost fifteen men in a single attack on a village of 120 people (see figure 4, n. x). In an assault on another settlement of similar size, two fighters were killed.[9]

The slave-raiders also employed terror to discourage opposition. It is impossible to tell how often or randomly such measures were used, but in several instances the entire male population of a village was bound and burned in piles of grass or severely mutilated and then slaughtered.[10] Used primarily against villages that chose to fight rather than to surrender, such methods probably had their desired effect. They also helped promote the belief that the sultan's forces could not be beaten—a myth that thrives in Ndele today.

As for the non-Muslims, they were most likely to be killed or injured at two times. The first was during the initial raid. As in the case of casualties among the raiders, there are little data on mortality rates among villagers in the fighting. But again, Chevalier offered a few statistics. In the Goula village of Tanako, al-Sanusi's men killed seventy men, while fifty men and women either disappeared or were taken prisoner; in an attack on another settlement, thirteen people died, eighty-four were enslaved, and fifty escaped. A third encounter resulted in the death of sixteen men, and captives numbered forty.[11] In these few cases, casualty rates ranged roughly from 10 to 60 percent. In addition to deaths in the fighting, particular groups of captives—mainly older adult men and elderly people of both sexes—were sometimes executed.[12]

The second time of danger came during the long return trip to Ndele. Fatigue, lack of sufficient food, injuries, and illness took their toll on the returning caravans. While heading back to Ndele in 1909 following a campaign among the Banda Linda, for example, a caravan lost 400 of 600 captives to these causes (see figure 4, n. gg). Outbreaks of smallpox sometimes afflicted returning expeditions. Of 2,500 slaves taken among the Banda Linda and Banda Yakpa in 1901, half reportedly died of the disease on the way to al-Sanusi's capital; and a year later between 600 and 1,000 of 2,000 Banda Linda and Banda Tombaggo slaves succumbed to the malady (see Figure 4, n. r).[13] There is no way of knowing whether these figures are representative for returning raiding expeditions as a whole, but the mortality rates range between 30 and 67 percent. Combining these figures with the mortality rates in the initial raiding yields an overall *approximate* death toll of between 37 and 87 percent for both phases of the operation.

A captive faced an additional major threat once in Ndele, for the sultan and his war leaders divided the new slaves into two groups, one destined for settlement and the other for sale to foreign Muslim slave-traders. A person sold to a merchant then faced the danger of another long trip—perhaps to Wadai or the Sudan, but maybe all the way across the Sahara.

The word *incorporation* best sums up al-Sanusi's disposition of the slaves in his capital. Much in the manner of al-Zubayr and Rabih, he encouraged boys and young men to adopt Islam and integrated them into his military forces. Most adopted Muslim dress and performed the most obvious duties of the religion; some became fervent followers of their captors' faith. Beginning as aides and gunbearers for seasoned fighters, they received military training and eventually became soldiers themselves. The girls and young women who remained usually became the wives or concubines of the sultan's soldiers.[14] Captives of both sexes also became part of the agricultural labor force in the capital. Older people who stayed in the city were either craftspersons whose skills the sultan needed, or beneficiaries of al-Sanusi's frequent practice of transplanting en masse the populations of entire villages to his capital (see chapter 4).

At this point it will be wondered how these policies worked, why large numbers of slaves never fled, and why there were apparently no known revolts among the populace. In response, it should be noted that some people did flee Ndele. Small scattered refugee communities appeared in the rock outcroppings southwest of Ndele along the Gribingui, particularly in the early 1900s when the proximity of the French discouraged raids in the area.[15] But these settlements never undermined the growth of the capital; the overwhelming impression that emerges from the entire range of data on Dar al-Kuti is that most people accepted their situation. That individuals would choose to remain with those who had destroyed their villages and killed their relatives is, at first view, surprising to say the least. And yet it was precisely because villages were destroyed and family members carried off that people stayed. There were no more homelands, and fellow villagers who had survived the violence either had been sold to northern traders or were themselves in Ndele. The experience of the guide who led Karl Kumm through the depopulated lands east of Dar al-Kuti clearly illustrates the situation faced by many of the inhabitants of al-Sanusi's capital: ". . . We came to the Mera rock at a place where there was formerly a large village. One of our guides, a slave of Sinussi, pointed out the place where his hut had stood, and the place where his father had lived who was killed in the slave raids."[16]

Proximity to the city also provided security, and security was rare in Ubangi-Shari in the time of al-Sanusi. The sultan was not the only slave-raider. Bands from Wadai, Dar Sila, the western Sudan, and the southern Azande and Nzakara states as well as the scattered Banda and Kresh enclaves, pillaged the region. Al-Sanusi's detachments devastated many settlements, but a person who survived the dangerous periods in the ordeal enjoyed safety in Ndele. Surveying the greatly reduced size of the city in 1937, over a quarter century after al-Sanusi's death, a French administrator in the former capital of Dar al-Kuti described the circumstances that had produced such a center:

This large agglomeration was composed mainly of fighters, captives, and other people of diverse origins who had fled before a stronger enemy and had come to a powerful and respected chief seeking refuge that they could not find elsewhere. Subsequently, after our presence reestablished peace, security, and tranquility, the larger part of the population rushed to return to the homelands which had been deserted earlier.[17]

Thus many people taken in the ghazzias were co-opted by events and came to benefit from, and hence have a stake in, al-Sanusi's slave-raiding and slave-trading enterprise. Among those who profited most were the Muslims and former captives who made up his military detachments.

Military Organization and Arms

The army of Dar al-Kuti was the source and the guarantor of al-Sanusi's wealth and power. Like the forces of Rabih in the 1880s, the sultan's detachments engaged primarily in raiding for slaves and ivory, providing the ruler with people to settle as well as people and products to exchange for arms, munitions, and long-distance trade goods—imports necessary for further expansion. In addition, the army guaranteed the security of the state by discouraging other powers, notably Wadai and the French, from intervening in its affairs.

The army consisted of individual detachments, each called a *birek*, a Turkish word meaning "banner" whose usage derives from the Muslim military custom of providing each unit with a battle flag bearing Qur'anic inscriptions.[18] Each banner included between 100 and 200 men under the command of a war leader and a lieutenant (*wakil* [Arabic]). Between campaigns or in minor raids, the commander directed the activities of his men, while for larger expeditions the units joined together in varying combinations under a single leader. On a few occasions early in his reign, the sultan led these combined forces, but most of the time he delegated this responsibility to his eldest son Adam or Allah Jabu, the Banda who was his chief military officer. When they were not marauding, most detachments remained in Ndele, although al-Sanusi sometimes established temporary posts in the countryside, and after 1906 he set up permanent secondary settlements with their own garrisons at Ouadda and Mouka southeast of the capital.[19]

It is impossible to chronicle the expansion of the sultan's forces in great detail, but the scattered estimates of the size of his army that date from 1899 do confirm that the number of soldiers increased—from 900 in 1899 to 2,000 in 1901, 2,500 in 1902, and 3,000 or 3,500 between 1908 and 1910.[20] The recruitment of fighters brought the creation of new banners. In mid-1901, for example, al-Sanusi added four detachments to the army, bringing the total number of units to seventeen. This expansion might well have been related to Rabih's defeat and death the previous year in an encounter with the French at Kusseri in the Lake Chad region, since many Muslim survivors of the battle sought refuge in Ndele.[21]

As a result of al-Sanusi's policies of training young captives and incorporating them into his banners, membership in the army as a whole was very cosmopolitan. Internally, however, it was segregated, each detachment having its own ethnic identity. In most cases fighters from ethnic groups long associated with Islam such as the Runga served in banners apart from recently converted recruits taken from traditionally non-

Muslim peoples. Among the latter, large groups such as the Kresh and the Banda had their own units.

The ethnic mix of the armed forces thus reflected the state at large. There is only one contemporary listing of this force by population group, so it is not possible to see how it changed over time. But this set of observations indicates how the army was organized in 1901–2. It also shows the degree to which al-Sanusi relied on battle leaders who had received military training in the Sudan and then peddled their know-how beyond the Sudanese frontier. The first two banners included Runga, foreign Muslims, and the most loyal Sara, Banda, and Kresh; they had excellent arms. Abbo Izzo, the commander of the first unit, was related to the royal family of Dar Runga, while his wife was al-Sanusi's sister, and his daughter was married to one of the sultan's sons. The leader of the second detachment, ᶜAbd al-Rahim, was a Sudanese who had served with al-Zubayr and Rabih before joining al-Sanusi in the mid-1890s.

The third banner belonged to Adam. Composed of his brothers, other individuals of Bagirmi ancestry, and young Nduka, Banda, Kresh, and Sara converts raised with him, it was the youngest, best-equipped, and best-trained unit. Adam's lieutenant was Wald Banda, described as the most courageous of al-Sanusi's soldiers. The fourth detachment was led by Allah Jabu, and his troops belonged to a variety of Banda groups; his assisting officer came from Dar Fur and had served for three years with the Anglo-Egyptian army in Egypt.

Kresh made up the fifth and sixth banners. The fifth was led by Soumit, an influential leader from Mbele who had thrown in his lot with al-Sanusi. Soldiers from a variety of Banda groups (Marba, Bru or Toulou, Mbres, Ngao, and Ngaja) composed the seventh through twelfth, as well as the sixteenth and seventeenth units; their commanders also came from these groups. The thirteenth detachment included Tunjur (Muslims) and Runga led by Tum, a childhood companion of the sultan, and the fourteenth was predominantly composed of Bornoans and Runga.[22]

Apart from these detachments, al-Sanusi also had a personal guard called the Ghafar Mbang. Its members came primarily from the first two banners, and accompanied the sultan whenever he traveled. Although there were a few Runga in this contingent, most of the guards were Banda converts raised, trained, and armed by the ruler. Its banner was made of green silk bordered with white and inscribed with verses from the Qur'an.[23]

In order to control the armed forces, al-Sanusi attempted to maintain a monopoly on all trade in munitions and firearms. He authorized permanent possession of rapid-fire weapons only for family members and a few trusted leaders, and kept track of the distribution of arms by having a Banda blacksmith, Jabda, stamp numbers on new guns arriving in the city. The arms were then carefully checked in and out of the arsenal located in the sultan's compound. As a further control, the ruler tightly regulated the supply of munitions—to the point of having Faqih ᶜIssa record all assignments. Julien reported that while family members and some foreign counselors had the right to an ammunition belt of between 100 and 200 cartridges, fighters in the ranks were allowed a few rounds at most. The powder supply was also watched carefully.[24]

Contemporary estimates provide a general picture of the sultan's accumulation of arms between 1891 and 1911. On the basis of inquiries in Ndele shortly after 1900, Julien guessed that al-Sanusi had 100 guns when he took control of Dar al-Kuti in 1890. This number roughly doubled following Crampel's assassination in 1891, and then increased steadily by about 100 firearms each year until 1899 and 1900, when, according to the terms of a treaty signed in 1897, the French gave the sultan 335 weapons. This put his arsenal at 1,200.[25] After this time the rate of arms acquisition increased, and Frenchmen in Ndele in 1902–3 estimated that al-Sanusi then had between 2,000 and 2,500 firearms, including more than 500 rapid-fire weapons.[26] Modat placed the total number of arms at 3,000 in 1908 and 6,000 two years later, just before the sultan's death.[27]

Munitions estimates are even more vague. Julien wrote that al-Sanusi had between 15,000 and 20,000 cartridges along with a ton of powder in 1901, whereas in 1902 Grech cited figures of 10,000 cartridges, 20,000 firing caps, and only 200 kilograms of powder. Much later in 1910, Modat estimated the number of cartridges (Modèle Gras) at 20,000, and reported stores of powder and firing caps "in quantity."[28]

Al-Sanusi's arsenal was diverse.[29] Among the rapid-fire rifles, Kropatcheks predominated, but the arms also included Remingtons, Albinis, and Winchesters. In addition, the sultan had numerous Gras carbines and a few revolvers. But the vast majority of weapons were double-barreled muskets (Abu-Ruhain [Chadic Arabic]) and single-shot flintlocks (Abu-Lufta [Chadic Arabic]), both muzzle-loading guns. In 1901 Julien estimated that al-Sanusi had 1,700 firearms, and that among these weapons there were 900 flintlocks and 400 double-shot muskets. Only 400 guns, less than one-fourth, were rapid-fire arms. Later sources confirm this distribution pattern, suggesting that while the overall numbers of weapons increased after 1901, rapid-fire rifles remained relatively rare.[30]

Julien calculated in 1901 that in the case of the rapid-fire weapons, one-fourth were acquired after the Crampel and Biscarrat massacres and Rabih's defeat; another quarter resulted from purchases from Belgian interests in the Congo Independent State and the southern states of Bangassou, Rafai, and Zemio; one-fourth came from the Sudan after the fall of the Mahdiya in 1898; and the remainder were bought from Libyan and Jallaba traders. As for the double-barreled muskets, a quarter were taken in raiding while three-fourths came from the Libyans and the Jallaba.

But it is the provenance of the flintlocks in Ndele that is perhaps most surprising, and even ironic in the light of later events: one-third came from the French post at Fort Crampel on the Gribingui—in the form of gifts following the signing of the treaty between the French and al-Sanusi.[31] Indeed, looking at the entire roster of weapons, it is clear that in one way or another the French provided al-Sanusi with a large part of his arsenal in the first decade of his rule, the years when he was building the power base that would eventually enable him to raid throughout eastern Ubangi-Shari.[32] The Europeans then spent the last half of the sultan's reign trying to contain the power that they had helped unleash.

The Sale and Settlement of Slaves in Ndele

Slave-raiding gave way to slave-trading when the sultan's banners arrived in the capital with their captives. Many of these were already owed to the Jallaba, whose provisioning of al-Sanusi was frequently on credit. But before the Muslim merchants could claim the slaves due them, two selections occurred: prisoners were first divided between al-Sanusi and his bazingirs; the owners then decided which captives to sell and separated them from those destined for settlement in and around Ndele.

One-third to one-half of the prisoners went to the sultan, while between one-half and two-thirds remained the property of their captors.[33] This division was common practice in the outlying parts of al-Sanusi's domains as well. Kalck records the testimony of a hundred-year-old man in Ouadda, in eastern Dar al-Kuti, who said that half of the captives belonged to al-Sanusi and half to his raiders.[34] Ndele informants said that when a party of raiders returned to the city, they presented their prisoners to the sultan in the small clearing just outside the portal to his compound.[35] The ruler usually had first choice. In part he claimed this privilege as the sovereign of the land, but informants insist that this right also grew out of al-Sanusi's ownership of the firearms used by his fighters: "Because you had suffered, you took four [of six slaves] and he took two—because he had power and the guns, the guns were all his."[36] The right to first choice meant that al-Sanusi acquired the best of the prisoners. And even if he did not exercise his privilege to take the most desirable of the captives, he often ended up with them anyway, since it was common practice to curry favor by giving him the most able-bodied young men and the most attractive young women. This custom was common throughout northern Ubangi-Shari, where quality firearms were seldom found in large quantities, and ownership of a stock of such weapons brought privileges. Ngono, the Banda Ngao chief and al-Sanusi's long-time adversary, also had first claim to the captives taken by his followers because they had employed his firearms in their raids.[37]

Once the sultan and his men had divided the captives, they gave some to slave traders as payment for imports, and settled others, incorporating them into the permanent population of the capital. Estimates of the proportion of prisoners sold and prisoners settled vary widely. Julien wrote that up to 1901–2 al-Sanusi sold two-thirds of his captives to foreign merchants; shortly thereafter Grech estimated that the ruler exchanged about half of the prisoners for long-distance goods and livestock.[38] Oral sources, Muslim and non-Muslim, present a different picture, claiming that the sultan's primary interest was to increase the size of his following, and that to this end he kept most of the captives in Ndele.[39] The most obvious explanation for this discrepancy is that the proportion of prisoners sold varied according to time and circumstances. If a large number of Jallaba were awaiting payment for goods extended on credit, the sultan might well have given them a large part of the next contingent of captives. Wadaian demands for tribute had the same effect. On the other hand, al-Sanusi was likely to keep most prisoners who reached the city at times of planting or harvesting.

Some individuals and groups were more likely prospects for sale than others. Al-Sanusi preferred to give the traders the least desirable of the prisoners—the old, infirm, and deformed. He retained as many of the young men and women as possible, even though he could not keep all of them since they were in greatest demand.[40] Because the traders had already extended goods on credit, they had no choice but to accept captives offered them. It might be argued that al-Sanusi risked alienating the merchants by this behavior, driving them to other regions, but he actually ran little risk since neighboring slave-exporting states followed a similar policy whenever possible. In Kuka, the capital of Borno, Nachtigal observed some years earlier that "old slaves who had outlived their usefulness" were frequently offered to pay debts.[41] And in Bagirmi he noted that the sultan sent his "oldest, ugliest, and most useless slaves" to Wadai as tribute.[42] But there were limits beyond which this practice would not be tolerated, for Nachtigal reported, too, that the deplorable condition of the captives included in tribute from Bagirmi helped provoke a Wadaian attack in 1870.[43]

Other factors influenced the selection of prisoners for sale in Ndele. Resistance was important. If a village opposed the sultan's raiders, its people were often exported. If a settlement surrendered and peacefully agreed to migrate to Ndele, al-Sanusi usually made blood covenants with its leaders and settled the people around the capital. Sometimes the sultan's fighters raided a village to even an old score, in which case the inhabitants were sold as punishment. The ruler also rid himself of individuals deemed to be troublesome and lazy by turning them over to foreign slave buyers.[44] This practice, too, was common in other parts of North Central and West Africa.[45]

In addition to taking whatever captives they could get from al-Sanusi, slave traders in Ndele sometimes resorted to kidnapping. The victims were usually children unfortunate enough to be in the fields or on the outskirts of town after nightfall whom the kidnappers spirited away inside large woven sacks. Yadjouma Pascal, a Banda informant who lived in the sultan's compound as a boy, recalls that when he and his companions went out in the evening to collect firewood for the nightly Qur'anic school they were always cautioned to be on the lookout for Jallaba kidnappers.[46] They particularly avoided the nearby Jallaba quarter. To be sure, the sultan opposed kidnapping and severely punished any trader caught taking children. He did not want Muslim children taken into slavery, and obviously preferred to sell his own captives to the merchants.[47]

Categories and Prices of Trade Slaves

Captives sold in Ndele fell into several categories distinguished by sex and age. Young men were categorized by height (expressed in spans), which was taken as an indicator of age. For women, adult males, and eunuchs, height did not necessarily reflect either age or desirability, and descriptive terms were used for these groups. Young prisoners brought better prices than older ones. Perhaps because they could bear children, but more likely because the sexual division of labor in Africa made them more suitable for labor-intensive tasks, young women were worth more than young men.[48] If they were pretty and virginal they brought an even better price. Boy eunuchs commanded the best prices of all, but they were rare, at least during al-Sanusi's first few years in Ndele. Julien and Chevalier recorded a fairly complete listing of slave categories and current prices when they were in the city (figures 5–6).

These categories and prices served only as the basic guidelines for the sale of prisoners. Individual sales were still subject to bargaining. A particularly beautiful young woman usually brought an above-average price for her category. Similarly, an adult slave skilled in a craft such as ironworking, weaving, or leatherworking was worth more than his unskilled counterpart. Al-Sanusi retained as many of these exceptional prisoners as he could, but sound business practice dictated that he not keep them all.

Julien and Chevalier failed to include adult captives and eunuchs in their lists. They may have omitted these groups simply because they lacked information about them, but there are other possible explanations. From the viewpoint of the buyers, older slaves were the least desirable captives. They did not easily withstand the rigors of the long trip to North Africa or the Middle East, and were not as malleable as young girls and boys, who could be readily converted to Islam and incorporated into harems, households, and military forces. Because adults were not in great demand, then, more price negotiations may have accompanied their sale.

Figure 5

Slave Categories and Prices in Ndele, 1901–1902

Type (males)	Price (thalers)	Price (magta^c)
a) *rebai*, 4 spans (Arabic *ruba^c i*, fourfold)	Not Given	
b) *khemassi*, 5 spans (Arabic *khumasi*, fivefold)	10	5
c) *sedassi*, 6 spans (Arabic *sudasi*, sixfold)	20	10
d) *sebai*, 7 spans (Arabic *suba^c i*, sevenfold)	30	15

Type (females)	Price (thalers)	Price (magta^c)
a) ordinary young girl	20–40	10–20
b) pretty and pure young girl	40–100	20–50
c) young woman	20–50	10–25

Source: Julien, "La situation économique du Dar-el-Kouti," 39.

Figure 6

Slave Categories and Prices in Ndele, 1902–1903

Type	Price (thalers)	Price (magta^c)
a) small girl (6–8 yrs.)	16–20	8–10
b) young woman (15 yrs.)	30–36	15–18
c) adults	6–8*	3–4*

*Chevalier noted that two adult slaves equaled the value of one horse, but did not record the price of a horse. These price calculations are thus based on Julien's 1901–2 price list which places the value of a horse at 30–40 *magta^c* (see Julien, "La situation économique du Dar-el-Kouti," 39).

Source: Chevalier, *Mission*, 157–58.

As for eunuchs, they were perhaps not available in Ndele in 1901–2. Informants recall that castration was mainly a form of punishment for adultery with the sultan's wives or concubines. Because mature men rarely survived the operation, an economic motive did not lie behind this form of punishment. One source claims that al-Sanusi had formerly put adulterers to death, but substituted the practice of emasculation at the behest of Faqih ᶜIssa and other Jallaba.[49] A few years later, however, the sultan did begin to produce eunuchs for sale, again with Jallaba encouragement, and the trade was quite lucrative despite the high mortality rate. Survivors fetched two-and-a-half or even three times the price of a young *sudasi* (six-span) male captive.[50] For surgical expertise, al-Sanusi drew on neighboring regions, importing practitioners of the art from Bagirmi and the Sara lands to the west; by the sultan's time, Bagirmi had long been famous as an exporter of eunuchs. Experts in the operation also migrated to Dar al-Kuti from Dar Runga, an area noted for the production of eunuchs a century earlier when al-Tunisi visited Dar Fur.[51] The most notorious of all the specialists was Mahammadi, the Sara who eventually became the sultan's governor at Ouadda. He continued to make eunuchs after he moved to this eastern post, sending some to Ndele and exporting others directly.[52]

It is not possible to see in any detail how or whether slave categories and prices changed during the years al-Sanusi ruled Dar al-Kuti. Chevalier recorded only a few facts about the actual sale of captives in Ndele in 1902–3. Overall, the outlines of the commerce as presented by these observers suggest that the trade remained much the same during the first decade of the century.

The data presented in figures 5–6 do not correspond on an item-by-item basis. They might be expected to be mutually reinforcing, since they both deal with the slave trade in Ndele and overlap chronologically. But they instead complement each other because, with one exception, they refer to different groups of captives. The first and third categories of Figure 6 do not appear in figure 5; conversely, Julien's four male categories and second female group are missing from Figure 6. The two Frenchmen whose sojourns in al-Sanusi's capital partially coincided thus collected different data, with the exception of information about young women; in this instance the two charts support each other. Julien's first and third female categories correspond with Chevalier's second division, and the prices quoted for all three groups are about the same. To get a more complete picture of all categories and prices in Ndele for the period 1901–3, then, these two tables should be considered together.

Modat's data on Ouadda—which he visited on the way to Kafiakingi—in 1910 suggest that slave categories and prices in Dar al-Kuti did not undergo any great change during the first decade of the century. Figure 7 (1910) does not list the first, second, or fourth male divisions found in figure 5 (1901–2), but Modat's use of the term *sedasi* [*sic*] suggests that the classification scheme had not altered. The prices of a sudasi captive in 1901–2 and 1910 were the same—barring a major shift in the purchasing power of the *thaler* or *magta^c*. Captives described as young girls also appear in both lists; in this case, too, prices were comparable. But there are some discrepancies between figures 5–6 and figure 7. For example, the latter lists a separate adult male category not specifically mentioned in the other tables. Adult male captives fall into only one adult grouping in figure 6. In addition, figure 7 includes a boy eunuch category missing from the other tables. As mentioned above, the production of eunuchs probably began in earnest only in the later years of al-Sanusi's reign. This addition of a significant trade in eunuchs was one of the more notable changes in the price structure and categories of captives in the Dar al-Kuti slave trade between 1901–3 (figures 5 and 6) and 1910 (figure 7). The decline in the demand for adult prisoners may also be significant, although the low price quoted for them in figure 6 shows that they were the least desirable captives in 1901–3 as well. In fact, overall preferences for the various categories of slaves in Ndele changed very little in the final decade of al-Sanusi's rule.

Figure 7

Slave Categories and Prices in Ouadda, 1910

Type	Price (thalers)	Price (magta^c)
a) *sedasi*, 6 span male (12–15 yrs)	20–25	10–13
b) *sourrija* (pl., *serrari*), or *nadifa* (concubine or "unclean," "soiled" girl)*	50–100	25–50
c) *adim* or *taouachy* (boy eunuchs)	50–80	25–40
d) *gourzem* (adult males)	No demand	

*The terms *surriya* and *nadifa* are problematic ones. Nachtigal never defines their usage in Central Africa; in Arabic they simply mean "concubine" and "unclean, soiled"; see Maan Z. Madina, comp., *Arabic-English Dictionary of the Modern Literary Language* (New York, 1973), 310, 672; Hans Wehr, *A Dictionary of Modern Written Arabic* (Ithaca, 1966), 405, 972. Humphrey J. Fisher offers the following comment on this category (personal communication, 20 February 1978): "The use of the term *surriya* here is interesting; does it mean simply any 'virginal girl at puberty,' or does it imply one who is somehow specially suited to become a concubine? My hunch is that something special was involved, particularly since the prices run above those for eunuchs, who were themselves very expensive."

Source: Modat, "Une tournée," 182n2.

The categories and relative values of captives in Dar al-Kuti at the end of al-Sanusi's reign were common to a large part of the eastern and central Sudan throughout the nineteenth century. Al-Tunisi wrote that he had two sudasi slaves during his sojourn in Wadai shortly after 1800.[53] During the course of a visit to Shendi on the Upper Nile in 1814, Burckhardt reported that slaves sold there came primarily from the west, and were divided into three categories: "*khomasy*, ... *sedasy*, ... and *balegh*, or grown-up."[54] When European travelers finally reached the western lands a half-century later, they found similar systems of classification still in use. Nachtigal noted the use of the term *sedasi* to refer to six-span young male captives when he visited Wadai in 1873–74.[55] Schweinfurth included the same grouping—" *'sittahsi'* (literally, six spans high)"—in his description of the slave trade among the Khartoumers and Jallaba of the southwestern Sudan in 1871.[56] Farther west at Kuka, the capital of Borno, Nachtigal recorded a lengthy list of slave categories closely resembling that of Julien.[57] Earlier, the English traveler James Richardson had described a very similar system of slave classification used at Kano in the 1850s. His list featured female categories corresponding to the sudasi and khumasi male groupings of Burckhardt, Nachtigal, and Julien. These divisions were denoted by the Arabic feminine equivalents *sudasia* and *khumasia*.[58] Buyer preferences also remained quite consistent over this entire zone, generally favoring youths over adults and young women over young men.

The Volume of the Slave Trade in Dar al-Kuti

It is impossible to determine the number of captives exported from Ndele between 1896 and 1911 with much precision. The estimates scattered through the documents are apparently all based on one source: Julien in 1901 wrote that the sultan had taken by raids, and then kept or sold, 40,000 captives between 1891 and 1901.[59] The French resident believed that an equal number of people had been killed, injured, or uprooted by the ruler's bazingirs during the same period. In 1901, the population of Ndele was 20–25,000 people, suggesting that al-Sanusi had exported about 15–20,000 captives up to this time—or an average of 1,500 to 2,000 individuals each year ($40,000 - 20-25,000 = 15-20,000 \div 10$ years $= 1,500-2,000$). This average is a very rough calculation that fails to take into account such obvious factors as birth and death rates among the settled population, the effects of the several smallpox epidemics that hit the city, and the number of voluntary Muslim migrants from Dar Runga and elsewhere who were attracted to Ndele.[60]

For the final decade of al-Sanusi's rule, there are no slave export totals whatsoever. Modat—the European observer in the best position to make such a calculation—contented himself with repeating Julien's earlier total.[61] Ndele remained the same size, and the foreign merchant communities remained intact. Given Modat's own descriptions of the vast tracts of deserted territory and devastated villages he encountered while traveling to Kafiakingi in 1910, it seems unlikely that the number of captives taken decreased between 1901 and 1911. If anything, al-Sanusi's men—supplied with more firearms of greater sophistication—took a larger number of prisoners.[62]

The history of the sultan's raiding activities supports this conclusion. Following a single expedition against the Banda Tombaggo in 1902, for example, bazingirs rounded up nearly 2,000 captives (one-half of whom died of smallpox on the way to Ndele).[63] For this decade, then, 40,000 can be taken as a minimum estimate. But because the population of Ndele did not grow appreciably during this time, a greater proportion of these prisoners may have been exported. The average annual sale of slaves to foreign traders was probably higher than that for the earlier decade, but somewhat less than 4,000. Again, this calculation ignores birth and death rates and outbreaks of disease, as well as voluntary Muslim immigration.

If 1,500 to 2,000 captives were exported each year between 1891 and 1901, and less than 4,000 prisoners annually in the ten years after 1901, then the total for the twenty-year period ranged from 30,000 (minimum estimate of 15,000 for each decade) to 50,000 (maximum estimate of 20,000 plus 30,000). Perhaps future work in the North African, Turkish, and Sudanese archives, research in the old fortified lodges (*zawiyas*) of the Sanusiya along the Wadai-Benghazi caravan route, and further exploration of the voluminous French and British consular reports concerning these regions will permit a more accurate calculation of slave exports from Dar al-Kuti.[64] (Kalck writes that Banda captives were known in the slave markets of Tunis in 1900, raising the possibility of finding further data in Tunisia.)[65]

Labor and Agricultural Production

Apart from supplying slaves for sale, raiding also produced slaves for settlement. The migrants' main contribution to the Ndele economy was their labor power, mainly in agriculture. In his broad survey of slavery in Africa, and in his research on the Muslim plantation system on the East African coast, Frederick Cooper observed that enslavement was one of the only ways to mobilize a large permanent labor force in a region of abundant land, limited population, and subsistence agriculture.[66] With most of the labor force tied to kin-based units of production, and without the mobility of a wage economy, labor was mobilized through violence. And the threat of further violence kept the work force intact.

In northern Ubangi-Shari all of the above conditions prevailed. Before the arrival of Rabih and the rise of al-Sanusi, most peoples in the region—the Muslim Runga as well as the non-Muslim Nduka, Banda, and Kresh—lived in dispersed villages. The labor force was based on the domestic group. Occasional warfare between groups produced war prisoners, but they were either ransomed by their kinsmen or integrated into the domestic labor force of their captors.[67] They were never numerous enough to constitute a separate servile class. And in any case, recipient societies had neither the monopoly of violence nor the human power to control a subordinate class; eventual social incorporation offered the only means of profiting from captured labor. The coming of Rabih and al-Sanusi brought significant changes. Military superiority and access to goods unavailable or available only in limited quantities to local leaders enabled them to begin recruiting a subordinate work force.

Slave-holders in Dar al-Kuti failed to implant a plantation system as monolithic as those in the Americas or even East Africa—if indeed that was their aim. Only al-Sanusi deployed part of his captives in this manner, and even he lacked the means to transform the entire work force and maintain a closed slave class. In Dar al-Kuti, as along other stretches of the Islamic frontier south of the Sahara and in East Africa, conversion to Islam and incorporation into the military (in the case of men) or marriage to a Muslim (in the case of women) offered escape from slave status. The constant resettlement of new captives, changes in status within the settled community, and mixed kinds of work forces make it impossible to classify the population into neat categories. Moreover, the fall of al-Sanusi in 1911 brought a return to earlier patterns of work which the colonial presence began to alter only in the 1920s. Informants had only vague recollections of how the sultan deployed his captives. A general picture of agricultural production in Dar al-Kuti can be reconstructed, however, by coupling their accounts with written evidence.

The fields of Ndele lay all around the city (map 5). In the north and west, they extended far into Runga and Nduka lands, while in the east and south they formed a discrete band bordered by the "no man's land" separating Ndele from the Banda homelands. Fields covered the land for ten kilometers in every direction when Chevalier visited the region in 1901–2, and isolated agricultural settlements lay as far away as twenty-five kilometers in the east and south. Other tribute-paying villages were even more distant. All of these settlements were linked to the city by a maze of paths. A decade later Modat confirmed Chevalier's observations, reporting plantations scattered for thirty kilometers around the Ndele plateau. The similarity of the Frenchmen's descriptions lends credence to what the population figures in chapter 4 suggest—the number of people in Ndele did not increase appreciably between 1900 and 1910 despite intensified raiding.[68]

Five general types of agricultural land supplied the foodstuffs—particularly the grain—consumed in al-Sanusi's capital. Each was clearly distinguished by the area(s) it occupied and by the combination of laborers who worked it. Two generalizations can be made, however, about all agricultural labor in Ndele: it was both individual and communal; and it included personal slaves, incorporated captives (resettled prisoners of war), and free people (mainly Muslims, but also privileged non-Muslims such as the Nduka).

The first category of fields, consisting mainly of individually held plantations in the immediate vicinity of the city, formed the continuous band of cultivated land described by Chevalier. The different ethnic communities in Ndele—the Banda, Kresh, Nduka, and Runga—each cultivated a separate part of this zone. Al-Sanusi assigned fields to each new group of residents after its resettlement in Ndele, and as a rule these plots were located as close as possible to the newcomers' residential quarters.[69] For example, the Banda Ngao and Banda Dakpa who lived on the plain in the southeastern part of the capital along the stream today called the Sajara worked land just beyond the hills near their homes.[70] The Runga who resided on the plain west of the Miangoulou on the other side of town had their fields farther west, whereas their countrymen on the upper plateau cultivated plantations farther north in the highlands. On the northeastern edge of the city beyond al-Sanusi's fortified terrace, the Banda Toulou raised crops near their settlement at Ouih. To be sure, Ndele was so large that some groups, such as the Kresh and Banda living in the central areas of the city, had to work fields some distance from their homes. But by and large, their fields, too, were within walking distance of the capital.[71]

Local residents and/or their personal slaves usually worked these fields.[72] Among the Banda, these landholders included settled captives who had escaped sale to foreign slave-traders, formerly independent village heads who had become clients of the sultan, and other Banda incorporated into the military forces of al-Sanusi. Among the Muslim Runga, landholders consisted of the large number of common people from Dar Runga attracted to Ndele by the success of al-Sanusi.[73] They joined long-time Runga residents of Dar al-Kuti who had left villages such as Kali, Sha, and Kolanjanga to resettle in the city. Among the foreign Muslims, only the Hausa and Bornoans had their own fields.[74]

The second category of fields lay farther away towards the Banda lands east and south of Ndele. Although within twenty-five kilometers of the city, these plantations were beyond easy walking distance. They required a resident work force during the growing season, labor which al-Sanusi provided by establishing seasonal agricultural villages. At the beginning of the rainy season (April), settled captives went out to live in these hamlets near the fields; during the dry season after the harvest (September–October) they returned to Ndele.[75]

The number of these villages in al-Sanusi's time remains unknown. In 1901–2 H. Courtet estimated their total population to be about 3,000, but he visited only two settlements besides Ndele.[76] Many were abandoned after the sultan's assassination. Such was the case with Torogo, a Banda village twenty-five kilometers from Ndele built on stilts for protection from wild animals, which Chevalier visited in 1901. Ndofouti, an agricultural village on the Tete River about twenty-five kilometers southeast of Ndele, also visited by the Frenchman, suffered the same fate.[77] But some of the seasonal settlements became permanent villages during the colonial period. Mbollo, the administrative center of one of the two *cantons* (now called *communes*) in the Ndele subprefecture twenty-three kilometers southeast of the city, began as a seasonal settlement inhabited by Banda Ngao captives in the time of al-Sanusi. The Banda villages of Kilibiti (Banda Ngao–Ouadda), Sokoumba (Banda Mbagga–Marba), Koutchikako (Banda Linda), and Bavongo (Banda Ngao–Marba), all south of Ndele, were founded in the same way.[78]

In al-Sanusi's time the work force of these settlements consisted mainly of settled Banda slaves who labored under the watchful eyes of armed Muslim agents of the sultan as well as their own leaders. Although theoretically al-Sanusi had absolute power over these prisoners of war, they were not held by force. Seldom were they locked up or kept in irons. Occasionally, fieldworkers escaped—such as those who lived in the resistance communities along the Gribingui southwest of Ndele—but most elected to accept resettlement peacefully.[79] It brought security and the possibility of material advancement, sometimes following years of hiding and flight.

The villages of the Banda Mbatta, the Banda Toulou, and the Banda Mbagga were a third source of food for the capital. Like the settlements described above, they lay outside the main population center at Ndele. But these hamlets were inhabited throughout the year. While subject to al-Sanusi, they enjoyed a status different from the seasonal agricultural hamlets where the resettled captives resided. Like the Runga and Nduka settlements (discussed below), the Mbatta, Toulou, and Mbagga villages sent tribute to the sultan, but retained some freedom of action. This status, unusual for Banda villages, probably stemmed from the fact that these peoples were the original inhabitants of the immediate area. They were in their homelands, the Mbatta fifteen kilometers southwest of the city; the

Mbagga farther southwest near the Bangoran and Bamingui rivers; and the Toulou to the east. (The Banda Ngonvo and the Nduka Gollo were from within the limits of Ndele proper and remained there.) Originally these peoples had lived in or near kagas in the bush for protection against raiding by the Runga, the Wadaians, and Rabih. Al-Sanusi forced them to resettle on lower land, but allowed them to live outside the capital.[80]

From their rural locations all of these peoples sent food to Ndele. The Toulou periodically sent offerings of forty or fifty baskets of grain from Ouih just northeast of Ndele; the Mbatta sent parties of youths to the capital bearing baskets of millet from their villages at Bissingou. The Mbagga made similar tribute payments, and also housed and fed bazingir patrols in the region. Such patrols were frequent because the route from Ndele to the French post at Gribingui (Fort-Crampel) passed through the area, and the sultan watched it carefully.[81]

Plantations belonging to Runga villages north of Ndele, and Nduka fields to the west, constituted a fourth source of foodstuffs for the capital. When al-Sanusi founded his city, he insisted that Runga from most villages leave their homes and join him. But he allowed Runga from Akrousoulba, Bilkinya, and several other hamlets in the north towards the frontier with Dar Runga to remain there. Similarly, he permitted Nduka subgroups such as the Doggo and Kutikovo to stay in their traditional homelands on the Kuti plain west of Ndele.[82]

Political and economic considerations led the sultan to treat the Nduka as he did. The Nduka had long been associated with the Runga migrants in Kuti, many of whom had married Nduka women.[83] They did not have a history of raiding and were militarily weak. Informants suggest that Wuda, the earth chief of the Nduka Kutikovo, and his counterpart among the Nduka Doggo preferred to remain in their own villages;[84] as ritual chiefs of the land, their power depended on remaining in their traditional territories. Leaving them in the bush did not pose a threat to al-Sanusi. In fact he profited from it in several ways. Their rural setting enabled them to hunt ivory and gather bush products more readily. They also provided shelter for raiding parties of the sultan heading west to attack the Sara Dinjo or the Sara Ngama. Moreover, this location allowed the Nduka to plant large fields of grain. They regularly sent gathered products and grain to Ndele as tribute.[85]

The Runga case was more complex, but once again the important factors were political and economic. Because the sultan's succession created discontent among the Runga-Bagrim of Kali who were directly related to Kobur, al-Sanusi probably relocated them in Ndele so that he could watch them. And he wanted his associates from Sha with him. There is no obvious reason why he resettled the Runga of Kolanjanga in the city. As for the Runga of Akrousoulba and Bilkinya and neighboring villages, they were not

Runga-Bagrim; they were less likely to oppose al-Sanusi's rule.[86] Politically it was safe to leave them outside Ndele.

This decision was also economically sound. Because these Runga settlements lay astride a route north towards Dar Runga, Dar Sila, Wadai, and Dar Fur, they provided food and shelter for some of the merchants that linked Ndele to the trans-Saharan and Sudanese trading networks.[87] Then as now, Akrousoulba and Bilkinya also served the needs of regional commerce by welcoming the itinerant livestock traders who brought cattle to Ndele and Kuti from Dar Sila.[88] Finally, these villages, along with Doum and Akrousoulba Dil nearby, were important agricultural and fishing centers. Moving their inhabitants to Ndele would have deprived the city of a main source of food.

Thus al-Sanusi left these particular Runga in their villages to cultivate extensive plantations and send regular offerings of foodstuffs to Ndele. Today informants identify these payments to al-Sanusi as *zakat* or a tax, and equate them with levies imposed by the national government (*impôt*). The Runga of Bilkinya and Akrousoulba also provided the sultan with wild game and smoked and dried fish from the nearby Aouk River, for which they received gifts of imported trade goods and slaves. These captives—only a few in number and attached to Runga households—joined the free Runga in the fields, increasing agricultural production and tribute. But the link with Ndele was closer than a tribute relationship. The leaders of Akrousoulba and Bilkinya became close associates of the sultan. Chiefs such as Jar Barit (Akrousoulba), Garoua (Akrousoulba), Bilyan (Bilkinya), and Sudur (Akrousoulba Dil) periodically visited al-Sanusi in Ndele. When he announced a campaign, they sent him fighting men. In return, military service often brought additional slaves, since a bazingir could keep a portion of all prisoners seized in raiding or warfare.[89] Despite military assistance, however, the real support offered by these villages was not the men they sent to Ndele, but the baskets of grain they supplied.

The labor force in the village fields, as well as that in the Nduka plantations, consisted of free persons and slaves. But slave laborers were more numerous among the Runga than among the Nduka, a difference which probably stemmed from the fact that the Nduka seldom raided for slaves themselves.[90] Nor did the Nduka serve in al-Sanusi's forces in large numbers, depending rather on the sultan to provide them with slaves as gifts in recognition of their status as autochthonous peoples. As a result, slaveholding was not extensive. Nduka ritual leaders such as Wuda (Nduka Kutikovo and Abnarbe (Nduka Gollo) received captives who worked the fields, but many Nduka did not have this assistance.[91]

The extensive plantations of al-Sanusi and his eldest son Adam constituted a fifth source of grain. Sorghum was the main crop, although it is unlikely that the entire area was planted with a single item. Banda peoples in the central Ubangi-Shari traditionally grew several crops in association with each other; they also rotated planting regularly.[92] Data on Ndele provide little detailed information regarding these practices in the fields of the sultan and his son, but those fields were also probably planted with crops other than sorghum. Stretching for six kilometers east of the city, the plantations lay along both sides of a road between the Banda Toulou village of Ouih and the Gime (Nduka) settlement at Aliou. Even today people speak in awe of the enormous size of these fields—no agricultural scheme in the region has equaled them since the days of al-Sanusi.[93]

Two different groups of laborers worked these fields. The sultan's and Adam's personal slaves comprised one group. They lived in temporary shelters around the edges of the plantations and did routine tasks. At other times, particularly during clearing, planting, and harvesting, the slaves were aided by contingents from throughout the capital which came together to work in the fields. Large parties of Runga, Nduka, and incorporated Banda, sometimes accompanied by their own slaves, came to work for short periods on a rotating basis from each quarter of the capital.[94]

Even though their presence in the sultan's fields was a form of forced labor, people of all ethnic groups in Ndele today recall these periods of group work as great festive occasions over which the sultan personally presided. Chevalier described one such occasion in 1902 when the rains came in late March. Deliberately set bush fires had already cleared the land for planting. One morning al-Sanusi left his compound with great pomp and circumstance surrounded by his advisors and faqihs, and proceeded to the center of his fields where a great tent had been set up. There, under his supervision, a work party of 500 men and women began planting.[95] In the days that followed people came from each part of town led by their local leaders. The military detachments also came, and all parties worked a day or two before returning to plant their own plantations.[96]

At the end of a day of group labor in his fields, the sultan offered food to everyone. He even had cattle slaughtered and roasted; beef was a rare treat for most residents of the city.[97] He passed out large quantities of trade goods such as cloth, sugar, and tea to leaders of the working parties, who in turn redistributed part of their reward among their following. After the meal, people drank millet beer and *douma*, a Banda mead, and danced into the night. Yadjouma Pascal, the Banda raised in the compound of al-Sanusi, recalls these celebrations with pleasure: "They cultivated like that until he gave the command. Then they knew that he would give out food in grand fashion. He fed the people. . . . They ate until they could not eat anymore, until they were tired of eating. Then came the sound of drums, and people danced."[98]

While the economic value of group labor in al-Sanusi's fields must not be underestimated, these occasions may also be viewed as periodic reaffirmations of the sultan's power and the unity of his diverse following. In the most obvious sense, al-Sanusi offered food and goods as symbolic compensation to his people for services rendered. But these occasions also provided an opportunity for the constituent groups of Ndele to display their loyalty to the ruler; by using these times as occasions for the distribution of long-distance trade goods among the people in a great show of generosity, the sultan proved himself worthy of this loyalty and trust. The festivities also brought together the Muslims and non-Muslims. Al-Sanusi brought religious advisors such as Faqih ^cIssa to the fields with him; at the same time he provided ritual leaders of the indigenous Banda Ngonvo with the animals and millet necessary to make the sacrifices and offerings to nature spirits which formed part of their traditional agricultural ceremonies.[99]

Agricultural Production in Secondary Centers

Between 1903 and 1908, when he was at the height of his power, the sultan founded satellite centers at Ouadda on the Pipi (or Ippy) River and at Mouka on the Zamza (or Boungoul). Both probably furnished food to Ndele; in any case, they supplied raiding parties from the capital. Ouadda lay 225 kilometers from Ndele, Mouka was about 160 kilometers away. At the time these ancillary centers were established, al-Sanusi's continuing and expanding need for captives carried his banners farther away, well beyond the deserted zone surrounding Ndele. These new outposts offered security and shelter for forces raiding in the region.[100]

At Ouadda al-Sanusi built a residence surrounded by a palisade and appointed Mahammadi, a former Sara slave, to serve as his agent or ^caqid. Mahammadi used a force of fifty men armed with rifles to subdue the Banda Tombaggo peoples living in the area. When Kumm passed through Ouadda in 1909, he estimated that 1,000 people lived at the post. Nearby stood a captive Banda village whose inhabitants raised a variety of foodstuffs including guinea corn, maize, manioc, and sweet potatoes. They also offered tribute in ivory and rubber to al-Sanusi in Ndele.[101]

The Mouka post was smaller but served essentially the same function. As early as 1901 most of the ivory from the area went north to Ndele; by 1903 the sultan had set up an armed camp and appointed an ^caqid who collected ivory and raided among the Banda Tombaggo, Banda Linda, and Sabanga.[102] In 1905, Peron, director of the Société "La Kotto" in the region, described al-Sanusi as the sovereign over the Tombaggo. He explained the situation to French colonial officials in Bangui: "You should know that apart from [dealing] through al-Sanusi, the Tombaggo haven't the right to buy a spool of thread directly from the factory, much less a rifle."[103] Food from Mouka probably made its way to the capital with other tribute, and the post indirectly supplied the city by feeding al-Sanusi's bazingirs.

Food arrived in Ndele from adjacent fields and from plantations far from the city. Some harvests, such as those from the captive villages and al-Sanusi's personal fields, were entirely the property of the ruler, but only portions of the yields of other settlements belonged to him. Writing in 1934, long after the elaborate system of agricultural production in the Ndele region had fallen apart, French administrator Rogué noted that the land surrounding the Miangoulou flowing through Ndele was rich in fluvial deposits from the era when it was a large stream. He suggested that this fertile valley was the sole source of foodstuffs for the city.[104] From the above picture—put together entirely through reference to oral data—it is clear that the Ndele agricultural supply system was much more complex and highly organized, and it has not been duplicated since the sultan's death.

Food Crops

Sorghums (or millets) dominated the crop complex cultivated around Ndele during the time of al-Sanusi. Eleusine, maize, and sesame were also common grain crops. Other foodstuffs included beans, sweet potatoes, and groundpeas. People extracted oils and made sauces from Shea butter nut (*Butyrospermum*), castor beans, palms, peanuts, and okra (*Hibiscus esculentus*) which they seasoned with dried red pepper (*Capsicum annum* or *Capsicum frutesceus*) and a large variety of gathered plants.[105] At the behest of the French representatives, and Julien in particular, the sultan planted small fields of rice and wheat after 1901.[106] As noted, onion cultivation was introduced to the region by Hausa and Bornoan traders and pilgrims; shallot and garlic bulbs imported from Wadai also thrived.[107] Manioc, or cassava, a staple in the Ubangi River region to the south, was not raised in the rural regions of Dar al-Kuti at this time, but small scattered patches of the crop grew in stream beds near Ndele.

Numerous varieties of sorghum were found in the region. Chevalier, a noted botanist, identified at least ten types on plantations in the agricultural belt around al-Sanusi's capital.[108] The many sorghum strains cultivated around Ndele and throughout the northern Central African Republic and southern Chad suggest a long history of domestication.[109] Rituals surrounding the planting and harvest of sorghum are an integral part of life among the Sara peoples (including the Nduka and Goula of Dar al-Kuti) as well as the Runga and the Banda.[110] Among the Banda, the traditional calendar and agricultural rituals all center around the sorghum-growing season.[111] The millet harvest is usually celebrated on a day in January designated by the chief. The night before, men and women sleep apart. In the morning a young male relative of the chief goes to the field to cut several "heads" of millet. He brings them back to the chief for ritual inspection. Following this ceremony each man examines the sample grain before setting out to harvest his own fields.[112]

People in Dar al-Kuti separate the sorghums into two major groups distinguished by color. Plants bearing white grains are called *ghalla* (Chadic Arabic). Large white grain is produced by *Paniciuum sorgho*, and smaller white grain (*ghalla dukhun*) comes from a related plant (*Penicillaria spicata*).[113] Red millet grain (probably *Sorghum bicolor*), referred to as *nyemdi* by both Runga and Banda informants, is used to make beer (*marisa* in Chadic Arabic). Boiling and fermentation produce a filling drink commonly known in the Ndele region as the "to-drink-is-to-eat" ("boire-à-manger") beverage; the beer also has ritual functions.[114]

Dar al-Kuti was self-sufficient in staple food production in 1900. Informants suggest that the elaborate system of fields produced enough sorghum for the population of the sultanate. Referring to the era of al-Sanusi, one man exclaimed, "The fields went on and on; there was no hunger."[115] Another was even more emphatic: "Fields!? They were everywhere! The place was f-u-l-l!"[116] Reinforcing this assessment is the impression that the fifteen years of al-Sanusi's reign in Ndele were spared from drought and other natural disasters.

Chevalier offered the only contemporary estimate of sorghum production. Estimating a consumption of one kilogram per person each day, he multiplied this figure by the population of the city, which he put at 15,000 people (at another place in his travel account, he suggested a population of 25,000). He concluded that Ndele's inhabitants required 5,475 metric tons of sorghum each year. Figuring the net yield of a hectare of sorghum at 1,200 kilograms, he determined that fields with a total area of 4,562 hectares (or about 45 square kilometers) were necessary to supply the city's population.[117] The fields of the capital and hinterland almost certainly amounted to an area considerably in excess of this. At any rate, Chevalier's rough estimate confirms the generally positive picture of agricultural production in the Ndele region presented by informants.

Fortune has not been so kind to the area since al-Sanusi's assassination in 1911. After his death many people fled, and the French resettled others in rural locations. The population of the city dropped to between 7,000 and 8,000 where it has remained ever since. Ndele frequently had difficulties feeding itself during the colonial period, and this problem continues today.[118]

The Diffusion of Manioc or Cassava

While the growth of Ndele under al-Sanusi greatly expanded the production of long-established food crops in the Dar al-Kuti region, the resettlement policies of the sultan also introduced manioc, an important new staple, in the vicinity of the capital. In addition, slave-raiding by the ruler's military units encouraged the spread of the plant throughout eastern Ubangi-Shari. In 1891, when Dybowski traveled in Dar al-Kuti, manioc was not cultivated, but by 1901, when Chevalier visited the area, it had gained a foothold around Ndele. Promoted by the French during the colonial period, manioc cultivation spread to southern Chad and all parts of Ubangi-Shari. Today it would not be inaccurate to call it, as indeed one writer does, the "national dish" of the Central African Republic.[119]

Manioc is not an indigenous African crop. The Portuguese first learned of it during their American explorations, and introduced the plant to the Kingdom of Kongo on the western African coast at the beginning of the seventeenth century.[120] From there it diffused steadily up the river valleys and trade routes used to export slaves and ivory from the interior.[121] The plant probably reached the lower Ubangi basin sometime in the eighteenth century, and in the late 1880s and 1890s it attracted the attention of the first French expeditions to reach the area. But it was not yet a major crop. Along the river, bananas and plantains remained the staple food items. While manioc assumed greater importance in the savanna immediately north of the river valley, even there it was usually raised in association with the sorghums, which continued to be the major staple.[122] In the 1890s peoples such as the Ouadda who lived along the "route du Tchad" grew manioc to sell to the European expeditions.[123] Because the crop grows best in a humid, sunny environment, it did not displace plantains in the forest along the river; nor did it spread readily to the drier northern savanna. It had reached the limits of its most favorable zone of cultivation.

But other factors encouraged its further diffusion northward. In the latter nineteenth century in the Ubangi region, manioc became a reserve food crop. Prioul associates this development with the expansion of slave-raiding after 1870 by al-Zubayr, Rabih, the sultans of the Mbomu River zone (Bangassou, Rafai, and Zemio), al-Sanusi, and the many lesser raider-traders who obtained a small stock of arms and ammunition which they used to take captives.[124] Charles Tisserant estimated that cultivation of the plant began in the Ouaka River region (Bambari) around 1880, roughly the time that slave-raiding became a major problem.[125] As violence became a regular feature of life in central and eastern Ubangi area, so did manioc.

Manioc cultivation spread in part because it was well adapted to the precarious conditions of life in time of war. The plant's ability to grow in the poorest of soils made it attractive to the refugee populations in the rocky kagas of the northern savanna of Ubangi-Shari, while its great yield made possible the cultivation of scattered, small plots which could be concealed more easily than extensive sorghum plantations. Moreover, unlike sorghum, manioc does not have to be harvested during a short period at the end of its growth cycle. The roots are generally ready to be eaten after 18–24 months, but can be left in the ground for a longer time. In fact, it is not uncommon in some areas to exploit a field up to three years after planting.[126] Thus people could safely abandon their fields during a period of raids and return later to harvest the roots.

In addition, manioc was less vulnerable to attack than sorghum. If stripping ripened sorghum plants of the "heads" of grain took little time, emptying a full granary was even easier. In the case of manioc, though, people did not gather the roots until they needed them. The roots then had to be soaked, dried, and pounded into a meal. The work was difficult and very time-consuming. Depending on the type of manioc and the method of preparation, the task frequently yielded a final product that spoiled within a short time. Raiding parties, usually composed of Muslim peoples who did not particularly enjoy the plant's bitter taste anyway, were not likely to pillage the manioc patches.[127] Thus the plant was insurance against famine.

Other characteristics of the plant made it attractive. First, growing manioc did not require the rejection of sorghum. Indeed, the two plants complemented one another. Manioc thrives in the moist soils and high humidity of lowlands and river valleys, while sorghum grows best in higher and drier areas. The work cycles of the two crops are also easily integrated. Manioc cuttings are planted at the beginning of the rainy season in April–May, whereas sorghum is sown in June–July. The sorghum harvest occurs in January about halfway through the dry season, while manioc is dug up at the grower's convenience. Today in Dar al-Kuti and elsewhere, people frequently plant the two crops in the same field in the rainy season, sometimes adding other foodstuffs such as cucumbers.[128] Second, manioc is desirable because most of the plant can be eaten. The roots may be roasted, or meal can be boiled to produce a paste served with a sauce. The leaves are crushed and boiled to make a dish resembling spinach (*gabo* or *kangali* [Banda]).

Finally, manioc was somewhat more resistant than sorghum to plagues of locusts, grasshoppers, and crickets.[129] When the Belgian explorer Hanolet visited the lands of the Kresh east of Ndele in the early 1890s, he noted that swarms of caterpillars and grasshoppers invaded the region at the end of the rainy season. They devastated the sorghum plantations.[130] These pests also frequently devastated sorghum fields during the colonial period in districts stretching from Kouga and Mangueigne in Dar Runga (Chad) to

Bangassou. Manioc plants usually fared better than sorghum under the onslaught, possibly because their foliage replenished itself more rapidly. In the 1930s the situation was critical enough to warrant a joint Anglo-French project for the exchange of information about the insect invasions.[131] In Dar al-Kuti the problem promoted the cultivation of manioc:

> . . . unfortunately clouds of grasshoppers moving from south to north still pass through the region and cause substantial damage. The local people manage to save their small plots of maize planted on the edges of the villages, but they cannot do anything about the millet plantations which are larger and farther away. In some fields, the young stalks have been completely ravaged by the grasshoppers. . . . Instructions have been given to plant major fields of sweet potatoes [*patates*] and manioc in each village.[132]

Although this report dates from the colonial era, plagues of insects almost certainly afflicted the Ubangi-Shari region in the precolonial period as well, and encouraged people to turn to manioc.

From the Ubangi River area manioc diffused north to the southern Shari basin—to the territories drained by the Gribingui, Koukourou, Bamingui, and Bangoran rivers. Early French explorers reported the presence of the plant. Gaston Jules Decorse mentioned that manioc was an important part of the diet of the Banda Ndri of Krebedje (today's Sibut) south of the Gribingui; Pierre Prins noted the abundance of the plant in the Gribingui valley south of Kaga Balidjia; Paul Brunache and Jean Dybowski both wrote that farther north the Banda Ngapu raised it in the early 1890s; Félix Chapiseau found manioc farther west among the Manza as well.[133] It should be emphasized once again that except among the Banda Ndri, manioc by no means supplanted sorghum. But it is important to note that these were the areas of al-Sanusi's earliest raids. Many peoples had fled for protection to the kagas where conditions favored manioc cultivation. Dybowski described the situation succinctly:

> . . . security does not reign here. All work on the land is done in haste, in any fashion. One senses that those who do it are constantly on the lookout for an enemy. Quickly they scratch at the soil, throw a few seeds into it that they have saved from the meager sustenance of each day, and then seek refuge to avoid being seized. Little ragged fields are scattered everywhere to assure that something can be salvaged in flight—in any direction.[134]

In the vicinity of Ndele, a region secure from raiding, manioc never became a major crop. In 1901–2 Chevalier saw only a few patches of the plant around the city, and neither Julien nor Grech, early French representatives at al-Sanusi's capital, even mentions it.[135] Rather, all three were impressed by the extensive fields of sorghum. Oral testimonies agree that manioc was rare in Dar al-Kuti during the era of al-Sanusi. And accounts collected from the Banda Toulou, the Banda Mbatta, the Banda Ngonvo, and the Nduka indicate that sorghum was the traditional staple before the coming of the sultan.[136] In fact, the few plots of manioc that did grow around Ndele in al-Sanusi's time owed their existence to raiding in a most direct way: they belonged mainly to southern Banda peoples settled in the city following their capture.[137]

By the first decade of the century, then, manioc had reached the domains of al-Sanusi but was not the dominant crop. In the course of the colonial period, however, cultivation spread greatly, both around Ndele and throughout Ubangi-Shari. The French fostered its diffusion both directly and indirectly. In administrative centers like Fort Crampel (today's Kaga Bandero), Ndele, and Yalinga, they took official action, planting demonstration fields and distributing manioc plants. In addition, colonial policies of forced rubber collection, forced labor, and the impressing of workers for the Congo-Océan railroad indirectly encouraged the spread of manioc cultivation. Africans saw these policies as enslavement and responded as they had to the Muslim slave raiders the previous century—by fleeing to the bush—to kagas and caves. Once again people had to hide, planting and harvesting their fields in haste. And this time manioc did replace sorghum as the major food crop in large parts of the colony.[138]

Chapter 6
Long-Distance Commerce in Ndele

Long-distance commerce was the lifeblood of Ndele. With it the city grew and prospered. Trade attracted foreign merchants who provided unprecedented quantities of North African, Middle Eastern, and European goods. During the course of the nineteenth century these items had come to signify wealth, prestige, and patronage in Dar al-Kuti, much as they had in other parts of Sahelian Africa. The internal exchange of these goods—by sale, exchange, or gift—played a vital role in knitting together the elaborate network of economic, political, military, social, and ritual relationships that underlay the state. As Ndele became an important commercial center, it drew Muslim migrants from Dar Runga and elsewhere. And as the sultan's slave-raiders and slave-traders expanded the scope of their operations, more captives became available for sale or settlement. In the words of one informant, whose opinion was shared by many: *Dar bigi hilwa, nas katir beju godu* ("the land was magnificent, and many people came to settle").[1]

For al-Sanusi, control over this expanding commerce translated into power. He maintained as strict a monopoly as possible over imports and exports. Imports included the usual items of the desert trade—cloth, tea, sugar, and assorted European manufactured goods. Ivory and odoriferous plants such as *jamsinda* and *kombo* also figured among the exports, although the economy of Dar al-Kuti rested primarily on the slave trade. The sultan's power and monopoly trading position depended on his continued ability to deliver enough prisoners to satisfy the demands of the foreign Muslim merchants. Without captives there would have been no imports—neither firearms nor other goods. Without large quantities of such weapons and luxury items, al-Sanusi would have been simply one more Muslim *farrashi* (peddler [Arabic]) among the many who made their way from village to village in the Islamic borderlands of Dar Runga and Dar al-Kuti.

That considerations of foreign trade influenced the layout of the city is clear. The proximity of the Jallaba quarter to the sultan's compound on the terrace dramatized the importance of these merchants. The guardhouses along the edges of the terrace and higher plateau also reflected the prominent role of the army in Dar al-Kuti, a force that depended upon long-distance commerce for arms and ammunition. In addition, foreign trade was articulated with agricultural production. The cloth, tea, sugar, and other goods distributed by the sultan during group labor activities arrived in the capital by way of the commercial networks. The rare and costly nature of these goods also made them appropriate gifts for the ritual leaders of the indigenous Banda and Nduka peoples. Sometimes al-Sanusi offered such products as direct compensation for foodstuffs, other goods, or services— such as the performance of local planting and harvest rituals. On other occasions he gave them as gifts or rewards in exchanges that carried social, political, and/or ritual connotations as well as economic value; the payment of bridewealth and gifts to blood partners fell into this category. This trade indirectly created bonds of community solidarity.

Al-Sanusi's Conduct of Trade

Al-Sanusi did his best to control all foreign trade in Ndele. To this end he dealt directly with most foreign merchants. These negotiations followed a prescribed pattern which demonstrates the sultan's authority. When a trader arrived in the city, he first sought shelter with his countrymen residing there. Shortly thereafter, refreshed and presumably acquainted with recent news about local commerce, he presented himself to al-Sanusi in one of the outer courts of the ruler's compound. Following tea and sometimes a meal, he presented letters of introduction to the sultan. Generally written by prominent officials in neighboring Muslim domains, such documents described the business of the bearer and probably attested to his character. These letters were important for the peaceful conduct of commerce in the region. They also served the commercial interests of the rulers of nearby states such as Dar Runga, Dar Sila, Wadai, Bagirmi, Dar Fur, and the Mbomu territories, most of whom also tried to maintain a monopoly over long-distance trade.[2] The trader then brought out samples of his wares. These goods were at the same time gifts preliminary to serious bargaining and the beginning of actual exchange. Since the merchant was familiar with the bargaining procedure, he undoubtedly included the value of these goods in the financial calculations for his entire lot of merchandise, while at the same time the custom of giving gifts at the outset of talks implied recognition of al-Sanusi's authority.[3]

Actual negotiations were not lengthy, since in most cases both parties knew the approximate value of the imported goods, and the merchant had little immediate choice but to accept the sultan's offer.[4] Ultimately, of course, he could decide not to return, but once in the city with his goods, he was not likely to leave without striking a deal. In Ndele the trader could not easily turn to another buyer in a ploy to maximize his profits, since the sultan was the only officially sanctioned purchaser in the capital, as well as the most reliable source of desired exports.[5] Hence al-Sanusi wielded considerable economic clout. But as a shrewd ruler and trader himself, he also knew that a bad reputation among the northern merchants could discourage commerce, ultimately diverting it to other areas.

Al-Sanusi's efforts to monopolize long-distance trade in Ndele were largely successful. When asked about local traders in the precolonial period, many informants replied emphatically that there were none apart from the sultan. French visitors such as Chevalier and Auguste Terrier agreed.[6] As he was the sole commercial agent in the capital, a high proportion of long-distance trade passed through his hands. When the local Banda Ngonvo followers of the sultan took captives, for example, they gave him his share plus those prisoners they wished to sell. He sold them to foreign Muslim traders in exchange for cloth, which he then distributed among Ngonvo leaders. They in turn redistributed some of the goods to their subordinates. Among local Muslims, the procedure was much the same: "... everything, everything, everything, to his soldiers, to his dependents, to whomever ... everything—he alone gave it, he alone gave it, he alone gave it!"[7] This system brought wealth and patronage power to the sultan, and the patterns of distribution and redistribution linked all classes of Ndele society.

The sultan also made most payments to foreign merchants. Most transactions were done on a credit basis. After negotiations, al-Sanusi usually took the imported goods, storing some in his compound and distributing the remainder; long-distance commodities rarely appeared in the Ndele market.[8] Merchants then had to wait for their exports. Often they waited several months, since the sultan usually sent his banners out to collect ivory, captives, and other items only after the dry season began in October. During this hiatus, the merchants lived with their resident countrymen. This long delay in payment did not discourage long-distance trade in the city; al-Tunisi noted that it was a long-established procedure in the raiding and trading zones on the southern frontiers of the trans-Saharan network.[9]

Despite close surveillance in Ndele, al-Sanusi's monopoly was not totally effective. In outlying parts of Dar al-Kuti, particularly in the east near the Sudan, he exercised only sporadic control. Peoples such as the Yulu of Ouanda-Djale dealt directly with traders from the Sudan, even though they acknowledged al-Sanusi as their superior and paid tribute for a few years before 1910.[10] At posts such as Ouadda and Mouka, the local representatives of the sultan traded surreptitiously on their own, although most ivory and slaves from the region still tended to go to Ndele.[11] Even in the capital, other leaders probably engaged in limited trade with foreign merchants. Such clandestine commerce was also common elsewhere. In the Wadaian capital of Abeche, for example, the ruler also enjoyed a royal monopoly over certain goods, but the first Hausa settler there traded ivory and slaves without the sultan's approval; a Mejabra caravaneer dealt regularly in contraband gunpowder in Abeche in the 1890s.[12] Because Ndele was a smaller city, the sultan may have exercised control more successfully than the Wadaian ruler, yet some transactions probably still passed him by.

Today most people perceive al-Sanusi's time as a commercial era completely different from any other.[13] The effectiveness of the sultan's monopoly can be judged by the fact that informants today characterize him as the great provider. All major goods theoretically belonged to him, and these items came mainly from him. In return, his advisors, military leaders, and the common people provided labor, exports, and foodstuffs. Chevalier viewed these exchanges as one-dimensional economic transactions.[14] In fact, by funneling most long-distance trade into his compound and then redistributing varying portions of its rewards among the diverse elements of his following, the sultan effectively employed commerce to build community solidarity.

The peoples of Ndele certainly saw the distribution of goods as something more than a mere commercial transaction. Muslims and non-Muslims alike called al-Sanusi *abuna* ("our father" [Arabic]), or *miri* (local parlance for *amir*, "the commander" [Arabic]). People continue to use these deferential terms today when talking about the sultan.[15] When Santandrea collected oral testimonies from Banda in the Sudan who had sought refuge there following al-Sanusi's death, he was surprised to find that they revered the sultan and considered him a great man. In the 1950s among the Banda in the Sudan, Santandrea reached a conclusion consistent with findings in Ndele in 1974: "It is evident from their common confession that—if it were possible—they would willingly change their present condition with the old one."[16]

Merchant Communities

To use long-distance trade as he did, al-Sanusi had to attract merchants to Ndele. His success as a slave-raider and slave-trader aided him in this endeavor, and by the turn of the century several groups of foreign traders had settled in the city. Although each ethnic group had its own identity and interests, all shared the features of diaspora trading communities found in other parts of Africa and the world. Each group was divided into two parties: permanent residents and visiting merchants who came to trade for a limited time and then returned to their homelands. The former acted as hosts and agents or landlord-brokers for the latter, who ceded them part of their profits as payment for their assistance.[17] The creation of a series of landlord-broker communities spread along a trade route helped solve many of the problems inherent in the conduct of long-distance commerce in the premodern era. A landlord provided shelter and information about commercial conditions. He usually had personal contacts with local authorities that aided the visiting merchant. In addition, he could vouch for the honesty of his countryman. The continuous presence of the landlord-broker also was a guarantee that commercial agreements would be honored, since his business fortunes depended in large measure on the reliability of his recommendations.[18]

In Ndele the Jallaba were the most important foreign merchants. As earlier chapters indicate, they were by no means newcomers to long-distance commerce. Browne (1792–98), al-Tunisi (1803–15), Barth (1849–55), and Nachtigal (1869–71) all noted their presence in Muslim areas to the north; Schweinfurth (1868–71) encountered them in his travels in the southern Sudan.[19] In Dar al-Kuti, a few Jallaba lived at the Runga villages of Sha, Kali, and Bringel, centers of small-scale commerce before the founding of Ndele. They also frequented Jagara, the capital of the Banda Ngao leader Ngono. But the largest permanent Jallaba settlement in Dar al-Kuti developed at Ndele.

Prominent among the traders were ʿAbd al-Rassul, Rashid, al-Nagar, Zaruk, ʿAbd al-Kerar, and ʿIssa Wald al-Ribb.[20] These resident Jallaba merchants, and the first four in particular, were the major landlord-brokers in the city. They housed itinerant Jallaba traders and stored their goods. They seldom traveled to the Sudan themselves, but some of their countrymen returned each dry season, thereby maintaining regular communication between the Jallaba enclave in Ndele and the homeland.[21]

The Ndele Jallaba were in an excellent position to introduce visiting countrymen; kinship ties linked the most prominent among them to the sultan. ʿAbd al-Rassul, Rashid, al-Nagar, and Zaruk all married daughters of al-Sanusi. These bonds were even more significant than might initially be supposed, because the women were the offspring of legitimate Runga wives and not the children of concubines.[22] These strategic marriages, probably along with others that are not remembered, brought advantages both to the Jallaba and to al-Sanusi. To the former they brought security, prestige, and access to the ruler. To the sultan they brought bridewealth in the form of long-distance trade goods;[23] but more important, the marriage ties gave him added influence over the Jallaba, who played the most independent role in the economic system supporting his hegemony. After all, he could not incorporate them into his following by promises of long-distance imports; they already had access to them. And there were other sources for the slaves, ivory, and additional exports that they sought. Marriage bonds afforded al-Sanusi an easy way of expanding his base of power and wealth to embrace the foreign merchants so essential to his good fortune.

Other Jallaba became agents of the sultan engaged in noncommercial activities, although it is likely that they traded on the side. Most notable in this group were Faqih ^cIssa, al-Sanusi's major religious advisor; Faqih ^cAli, another religious figure; and Adam Fartak, a former trader in Banda country captured by a raiding party in about 1895. Taken to Ndele, Fartak became an aide to the sultan, and today he is remembered as the tailor of the sultan's battle flags. Still others served as scribes, penning the letters al-Sanusi sent to neighboring Muslim rulers and the French.[24] A few Jallaba also served as military leaders and advisors. Faraj, a former houseboy to General Gordon in Khartoum, led al-Sanusi's personal guard (the Ghafar Mbang), while Dahiye, a deserter from the Egyptian army, was second in command to Allah Jabu. ^cAbd al-Karim, formerly in the service of al-Zubayr, joined the sultan in 1895; Shaikhu was a former soldier in Rabih's legions. These men played a crucial role in the military successes of al-Sanusi, who had no fighting experience himself. They acquainted the sultan and his forces with the more advanced firearms and military techniques of the Nile region.[25] Jallaba participation in the armed forces was in keeping with their traditional identity as traders. Speaking of the era of al-Sanusi, informants refer to war and commerce in the same breath. Assakin Muhammad, a Runga-Jallaba (Sharia), says that the Jallaba trader Rashid was interested in war as well as commerce in slaves and ivory: "Everything was commerce to him"; that is, war and violence brought the slaves and tusks which were the major trade items.[26]

Although they shared the religion of the Jallaba, the Hausa and Bornoans occupied a different commercial niche. While small trading parties had circulated in Dar al-Kuti in the late nineteenth century, larger numbers of Hausa and Bornoans came to Ndele only following Rabih's conquest of Borno in 1894 and the French campaigns against Bagirmi after 1900. As in the case of the Jallaba, settled traders acted as landlord-brokers for their fellows. Although they occasionally trafficked in slaves, the Hausa and Bornoans were more involved in petty commerce and the *hajj*—as hostelers or as pilgrims themselves. As traders, they dealt mainly in ivory, livestock, skins, finished leather goods, beads, salt, natron, kola nuts, and cowries. Their ranks also included craftsmen and butchers.[27]

Hausa and Bornoans also raised condiment and legume crops in the lowlands along the Miangoulou. Maiduku, the title and possibly the name of the head of the Bornoan community in the first decade of the century, is said to have inaugurated onion cultivation in the region, which made him a wealthy man. In fact, it appears that the migrants introduced the crop as only one facet of the marshland cultivation technique common to Borno and Hausaland known as *fadama* agriculture.[28]

Other settled Hausa and Bornoans figured prominently in the life of the capital: Al-Hajj Abdo and al-Hajj Tukur were his two major political advisors. Other successful Hausa and Bornoans in Ndele included ᶜAli Bimini, a Bornoan merchant who on at least one occasion gave several horses to the sultan. (For his trouble, al-Sanusi presented him with a house on the terrace.)[29] Cheggue Toum also exercised considerable influence during Julien's soujourn. He was described as "polite, well-informed, distinguished, and an artful conversationalist." Little else is known about him except that his prominent position, like that of the major Jallaba merchants, was associated with strategic marriage; he was married to the sister of the sultan of Dar Sila and aspired to the hand of al-Sanusi's daughter Hadija, the widow of Rabih's son Fadlallah.[30]

Important members of the Hausa settlement in about 1900 included Abdu, a Hausa client and a jack-of-all-trades whose occupations read like the employment section of a newspaper: mason, blacksmith, carpenter, cobbler, tailor, cannoneer, and gardener. During a stint as a trader, he went to Dar al-Kuti to peddle goods entrusted to him by a Fezzani merchant in the north; after frittering away the merchandise of his patron, he entered the service of al-Sanusi. Another Hausa, Muhammad, arrived in Ndele in 1901 fresh from the pilgrimage. In Mecca, he was among a large group of black pilgrims whom the Ottoman sultan invited to Istanbul for a six-month stay. Showered with gifts on their departure, the African Muslims voyaged by sea to Suez and dispersed for the overland trip home. In Ndele, where Muhammad eventually made his way, his travels brought him much prestige.[31]

Other groups were neither as large nor as influential as the Jallaba or Hausa and Bornoans. A Tripolitanian named Salih acted as an emissary between al-Sanusi and the French mission of Gentil in 1897.[32] A few Fezzanis trafficked in slaves and ivory, but the community possessed no real economic power. Julien included only two Fezzanis in his listing of influential personalities in Dar al-Kuti, a trader named Hamonde from the oasis of Qatrun and another peddler called Jamaᶜ from Murzuk; his description of their activities makes them sound more like Islamic propagandists or Sanusiya missionaries than genuine merchants.[33] That there were few North African merchants in Ndele is not surprising. In most cases these traders limited themselves to the trans-Saharan routes and the lands immediately adjacent to their southern termini. Imports destined for points farther south were usually put in the hands of black African merchants, like the Hausa trader Abdu, who were familiar with these regions. Towns in the northern states of Borno, Wadai, and Dar Fur thus functioned as the transfer points joining the desert and Sahel-savanna trading networks.[34]

Informants likewise recall only a few Wadaians in Ndele during the time of al-Sanusi. The absence of a large number of settled Wadaians probably grew out of the long history of hostility between al-Sanusi and the sultans in Abeche. In 1895, the year following the devastating Wadaian attack against al-Sanusi at Sha, the sultan offered his submission to Abeche, but relations between the two powers remained troubled throughout al-Sanusi's years in Ndele.[35] Even today Runga accounts of the history of the period emphasize the unscrupulous character of the Wadaians. This ill-feeling discouraged the formation of a large Wadaian community. Moreover, such a group would have aroused the ire of the French in Ndele, who counted Wadaians among their major adversaries in the Chad basin.

Several other small parties of foreign merchants visited or lived in Ndele during this period. Chief among them were Bagirmi, Runga refugees from the north, and Dajo from Dar Sila. Given the close ties between Bagirmi and Dar al-Kuti, and the continuing links between the Runga of Dar Runga and their southern counterparts, these two groups did not have the distinct identity of the Jallaba or Hausa-Bornoan communities.

The Dajo brought cattle, horses, and other livestock to exchange for slaves, ivory, and other exports. The sultan usually sent his followers to Goz Beida, the capital of Dar Sila, with letters requesting livestock, and the Dajo sultan responded either by giving the animals to people from Ndele or by sending Dajo subjects to Dar al-Kuti with the herds.[36] Most of these imported animals went to al-Sanusi, who owned the only herds in the city. Although he occasionally allowed meat to be sold in the market, he tried to maintain a monopoly over these imports just as he did over cloth and trans-Saharan goods.

The Currencies of Dar al-Kuti

The growth of foreign Muslim settlements in Ndele is a tangible indication of the progressive integration of Dar al-Kuti into the economy of the Sahara and Mediterranean basin. Certainly the demand for slaves and, to a lesser extent, ivory in the north, and the need for weapons, powder, and luxury items in the south, were the determining economic factors in this process. As elsewhere along the Islamic frontier in North Central and West Africa, this exchange was reckoned in, and carried on with the aid of, a variety of currencies which circulated together. Woven cloth strips, beads, and several varieties of coins figured most prominently in Ndele, although some descendants of Muslim traders today include slaves as currency, snidely saying that "the Banda were our money in the time of al-Sanusi."[37] There was no highly formalized system of separate spheres of exchange, although in practice more highly valued currencies tended to be used in transactions involving more highly valued items. Slaves apart, these currencies fit Hopkins' criteria for general purpose currencies; that is, they acted as media of exchange, common measures of value, means of storing wealth, and, albeit less regularly, standards for deferred payment.[38]

Long strips of cotton woven in Dar al-Kuti, Dar Runga, and adjacent Muslim zones in the north were the most common currency and measures of value employed in precolonial Ndele.[39] Both Julien and Grech noted that al-Sanusi kept his financial records in cloth units.[40] Slaves and all costly import items were calculated in terms of rolls of cloth strips measured in *durah* (forearm lengths [Arabic]).[41] Middle-valued imports such as sugar, tea, salt, and soap were also frequently reckoned in terms of cloth. But the strips were rarely used in market commerce in foodstuffs, mainly because they could not be subdivided into units small enough for easy exchange. Theoretically the cloth could have been reduced to single threads, but this means of making "small change" was not customary in Dar al-Kuti. In fact, a survey of the travel literature for the entire region suggests that threads were used as currency only in one part of Dar Fur, where *rubat* (bundles [Arabic]) of twenty cotton fibers were needed to purchase some goods.[42]

Discussion of the specific types of cloth currencies found in precolonial Dar al-Kuti must be prefaced by several comments on terminology (also see appendix 4). First, most colonial documents on Dar al-Kuti refer to the cloth currency of the capital as *megta* (variously *mekta, magta^c*, or *makta*) and indicate that it was a specific variety of cotton strip. Yet these European sources do not describe the currency in the same way. Taken alone, they suggest great fluctuations in the size of the *megta* without pattern or reason. The oral sources clear up the problem quite readily. From them it is clear that the term is a very general one, meaning simply "piece of cloth." This definition is entirely consistent with Arabic usage, since the word derives from the classical Arabic *qata^c a* (*gata^c a*, [Chadic Arabic]), meaning "to cut."[43]

A second semantic problem issues from frequent European use of the term *gabak*. In most cases, the written sources give it specific but also inconsistent definitions (see appendix 4). The term is not found in most oral testimony from Dar al-Kuti, but does turn up in an interview with a Bornoan. It is also found in Barth's writings on Borno, suggesting that French military officers and their interpreters picked up the word during their expeditions around Lake Chad in the 1890s and carried it with them to northern and eastern Ubangi-Shari a few years later. The cloth woven in Dar al-Kuti and neighboring regions resembled the Bornoan *gabak* described by Barth, but it was not the same.

Finally, the words *gumash*, *farda*, *khaleg* (pl. *khulugan*), and *tob* (or *taub*), all of which derive from the names of specific articles of clothing somewhere in the Arabic-speaking world, meant (and mean) cloth and clothing in general in Dar al-Kuti. Complete reliance on the written sources confuses the meanings of these terms as well.

Of the many types of cloth found in Ndele when al-Sanusi was sultan, four varieties—*tukia* (pl., *tekaki*, *attagia*), *tombassia*, *tarrak*, and *shakka*—served as the principal currencies. As with the terms discussed above, disparate data on these cloth types create problems of definition. It is nonetheless clear that both oral and written sources are describing specific kinds of cloth. The currencies shared a few characteristics: all were long cotton strips stored in large rolls and all were woven in Dar al-Kuti or nearby sub-Saharan regions from locally produced fiber. None arrived in Ndele from north of the desert, although North African and Sudanese traders frequently bought and sold them within the region. Finally, most sources divide the types into narrow and wide varieties.

Tukia was the most widely used cloth currency in Dar al-Kuti. Usually described as the narrowest of these currencies, it was woven on a loom consisting of two sticks implanted in the ground about fifteen centimeters apart with a warp strung between them. The Runga were the principal weavers of the cloth in Ndele, but in time the Banda also began to make it. It was also produced in Wadai and elsewhere in the north. Tukia strips were woven of coarse cotton and usually retained the natural color of the fiber, although occasionally the cloth was dyed with indigo.

Tukia had many uses in Ndele. Producers could give it to al-Sanusi in payment of *zakat* (tax [Arabic]) or in exchange for long-distance trade goods.[44] It also was a major item in bridewealth payments among the Runga and other Muslims. Banda and Nduka welcomed the inclusion of tukia as part of marriage exchanges, too, but it was not compulsory. Ivory, slaves, and domestic animals could be bought with the currency, although the large amounts of cloth involved may have discouraged such transactions. (Chevalier reported that one eight-year-old slave cost between eight and ten tukia strips, each fifteen meters long.[45] It is unlikely that individuals not already possessing slaves could produce sufficient quantities of cloth to buy a following. Tukia manufacture was not the easiest way to social advancement in Dar al-Kuti; joining the ranks of the raiders brought greater reward.) Tukia could also be exchanged for other cloth; only very rarely was it used to buy foodstuffs. In addition, people frequently sewed strips together to make clothing. Such dress marked a Muslim as a common person, whereas among the Banda it indicated a modicum of wealth and brought prestige. Tukia was also a sign of the sultan's favor, since he sometimes rewarded followers with it.

Little is known about the organization of tukia production in Ndele. It seems unlikely that the sultan grouped large numbers of weavers together, for evidence of such a large-scale project would have turned up in the oral or written sources. Rather, al-Sanusi probably accepted whatever tukia his personal slaves and subjects made as taxes or in exchange for goods. The cloth was also imported from northern areas in exchange for the aromatic plants of Dar al-Kuti, ivory, and slaves.

It does not appear that the sultan controlled production or imports in order to maintain a fixed value for the cloth currencies, and yet during al-Sanusi's years in Ndele inflation does not seem to have been a problem. This stability may have stemmed in part from the simple fact that the sultan did not rule very long in Dar al-Kuti. But the fact that the various cloth types were commodity currencies—that is, currencies whose value was largely determined by an investment of labor—was the most important factor in preventing inflation. This conclusion is consistent with Marion Johnson's analysis of cloth currencies in areas farther west:

> The state normally played no part in controlling the issue of cloth money, though it often accepted taxes in cloth; cost of production and demand between them controlled the quantity of cloth entering the system. Cloth currency was thus admirably suited to operate across state frontiers and in stateless or near-stateless societies. Where more than one type of cloth currency was found in the same market, there appear to have been standard rates of exchange between them, based on the area of cloth rather than on its quality.[46]

Tombassia, tarrak, and *shakka* may be grouped together, not because they are identical but because the sources do not make clear distinctions among them. The term *tombassia,* for example, is found only in the oral sources, and its descriptions resemble those recorded for tarrak and shakka, suggesting that it may simply be another name for one of these cloth types. In any case, all of these currencies were much wider than tukia, obviously indicating the use of wider looms. Unlike tukia, the bulk of this cloth came to Ndele from Dar Runga, Dar Sila, Wadai, and Dar Fur. Shakka may well have come from the area just south of Dar Fur bearing the same name. One informant even identifies it with *sabah* (east [Chadic Arabic]), the name given to another kind of cloth imported into Dar al-Kuti from the Sudan, but sabah was not usually used as a medium of exchange.[47] The uses and distribution of tombassia, tarrak, and shakka in Ndele followed the same lines as those described for tukia, although since these three kinds of cloth were imported goods, they were somewhat rarer and more expensive.

Beads were another form of currency common in Dar al-Kuti and indeed in the entire Ubangi-Shari and eastern Sudanic region at the end of the nineteenth century. Generally referred to as *suk-suk*, *kharaz*, or *khaddur* (Chadic Arabic), and *krizi* or *kidji* (Banda), they were desirable as jewelry and media of exchange.[48] There were many different types of beads, and not only did each type have its own value, but bead preferences shifted from people to people and region to region. Written materials provide little detailed information concerning bead types, and the oral sources are also vague, perhaps because coins supplanted beads as currency early in the colonial period.

In Dar al-Kuti and the Banda homelands the Banda had a much higher regard for beads than did the Muslims. Both in Ndele and in the Banda's own lands, beads comprised a major portion of bridewealth payments; they also were accepted in exchange for captives and ivory.[49] The Muslims of Dar al-Kuti, on the other hand, insisted that marriage payments be made in cloth and the highly valued items of long-distance trade. Beads were "too light" (*khafīf* [Arabic]) to be counted as bridewealth; rare and valuable beads such as the *soumit*, one of which was worth two slaves in Wadai in the time of al-Tunisi, apparently did not circulate as far south as Dar al-Kuti.[50] In Ndele, some types of beads were also exchanged for foodstuffs and other low-value items in the marketplace below the terrace.[51]

Although cloth and beads moved together in a single exchange system, the more highly valued cloth currencies circulated more commonly among the Muslims, while most non-Muslims dealt primarily in low-value currencies such as certain types of beads. The reason for this division is quite simple. Because the Muslims comprised the wealthier segment of the population, they possessed greater quantities of highly valued exchange items than did the poorer non-Muslims. In addition, the highly valued currencies were generally exchanged for other highly valued media of exchange, slaves, and expensive goods, or were used as bridewealth. While conversion from low-value currencies to highly valued media was possible, it was not easy. As noted, this difficulty stemmed in part from the great difference in value between the exchange items. Cloth currencies were not divisible into units small enough to be exchanged for foodstuffs and the inexpensive goods of daily consumption. Moreover, the bulk of these commodities was produced by household units for internal consumption, and thus lay outside the monetized sector of the economy.

The different uses of beads among the non-Muslim Banda and the Muslims, both in Ndele and the Banda homelands, created a basis for trade between these two groups. Because the Muslims had access to the world market, they could supply beads to the Banda peoples of Dar al-Kuti and other areas beyond the Islamic frontier. They were willing to do so because by furnishing varieties of beads that had low utility in the Sahel, they could acquire slaves and ivory, items that had a very high utility in the Muslim zones. As for the Banda, in the short term they were satisfied with this arrangement because beads had a high utility among them. It may well be argued that in terms of prestige exchange, at least, the currency system of Ndele was inherently unstable, and that the Banda would soon have ceased to regard beads as a high utility commodity for which they would exchange ivory and slaves.[52] However, this shift did not happen during al-Sanusi's brief tenure in Ndele, and colonial conquest soon undermined the entire system. But along with this functionalist explanation, it must be remembered, too, that superior Muslim power reinforced this system of unequal exchange.

Coins of various provenance also made their way to Ndele from Muslim lands to the north and French-controlled districts to the south. European coins such as the Spanish, Russian, and Maria Theresa thalers occasionally appeared in the city, but never in sufficient quantities to become a major medium of exchange.[53] But the sultan did accept these coins from northern merchants, using them to pay other traders when he was short of slaves or ivory, or to acquire goods from the French commercial agent in Ndele.[54] French currency was not at all common as a medium of exchange in Ndele during the sultan's lifetime, although a five-franc coin—called *chinko* in Dar al-Kuti—was sometimes seen in the city.[55]

The Ivory Trade in Ndele

Ivory ranked after slaves in importance among the exports of Dar al-Kuti in al-Sanusi's time. But while yearly slave exports probably increased during the sultan's years in Ndele, ivory exports fell markedly. Julien estimated that up to 1900 al-Sanusi received between twelve and sixteen tons of ivory each year from diverse sources (see figure 8). By 1902 the volume of ivory receipts had dropped over 50 percent to between five and six tons each year. Shortly thereafter, Grech echoed this figure, reporting that the sultan could amass only five to eight tons of ivory annually.[56]

In explaining the decrease in ivory exports, Julien stressed the role of the French, theorizing that the ivory trade to Ndele was interrupted by the French occupation of the Upper Shari and the delegation of extensive lands in central and eastern Ubangi-Shari to concessionary companies. To substantiate his explanation, the Frenchman noted that by late 1902, al-

Figure 8

Quantities and Sources of Ivory Exported
Annually through Ndele before 1900

Quantity	Source(s)
2–3 tons	elephant hunts and ivory gathered within the sultan's domains
2–3 tons	raids
3–4 tons	Ubangi sultanates and slave traders
5–6 tons	purchases from Dar Sila, Dar Salamat, and from non-Muslims outside Dar al-Kuti
12–16 tons	total

Source: Julien, "La situation économique du Dar-el-Kouti," 39.

Sanusi no longer received ivory from the Ubangi states which had fallen under the jurisdiction of the Compagnie des Sultanats du Haut-Oubangui in 1899.[57]

These French actions may have discouraged the flow of ivory to Ndele, but they were probably not the determining factors. By 1902, the Compagnie des Sultanats had barely begun to occupy its lands; it never succeeded in controlling all commerce within its vast concession. And the French presence on the Upper Shari did not significantly modify indigenous commercial patterns in the Dar al-Kuti region until well into the colonial era.[58] Julien made the mistake of overemphasizing the impact of his countrymen on the Africans around them, a common miscalculation according to Prins: "The error common to all Europeans who cross . . . Africa is to believe that the echo of their feats and movements carries far beyond them and impresses itself profoundly on the memory of the local peoples."[59]

Other explanations for the drop in ivory exports seem more likely. First, the Europeans may well have simply overestimated the volume of the earlier trade. The French made this error in their calculations of ivory "production" throughout Ubangi-Shari in the early years of the colonial period. Before their arrival, chiefs, clan heads, and other important individuals or groups frequently amassed a store of ivory. It was saved for passing caravans. With the increase in violence in the late nineteenth century, many owners sold all their ivory to European buyers in exchange for guns, munitions, and alcohol. These agents concluded that their purchases approximated the annual volume of ivory exports, when in reality they represented the liquidation of a fixed stock. Such miscalculation led to exaggerated estimates.[60] In Dar al-Kuti, the sultan's Muslim trading partners preferred slaves over ivory, and al-Sanusi paid his debts in ivory only when enough slaves were not available.[61] So before the establishment of the French post it is possible that he received more ivory than he disbursed. He then may have drawn heavily upon the accumulated store of ivory in trade with the Europeans, since they refused to deal in slaves.

Secondly, a breakdown in al-Sanusi's relations with Hetman of Rafai and Bangassou in 1901–2 contributed to the interruption of ivory supplies from the Ubangi states. Al-Sanusi charged that Hetman had mistreated traders from Dar al-Kuti in Rafai; he retaliated by detaining two bazingirs his neighbor had sent to Ndele to buy cattle. The sultan also took 100 thalers from them as compensation for injuries suffered by his own agents in the south.[62] At about the same time, relations with Bangassou deteriorated following an attack on the northern Muslim quarter in the Nzakara capital. Some of al-Sanusi's followers died in the melee, including ᶜAbd al-Samat, who was a son of a former sultan of Dar Runga, al-Sanusi's first cousin and a brother-in-law of the sultan of Dar Sila.[63] The sultan wrote to Bangassou protesting the violence. He also blamed Bangassou for later attacks on trading parties traveling from Ndele to the Ubangi, charging that the Nzakara attacks had encouraged local peoples all along the routes to pillage northern caravans. These disruptions caused al-Sanusi to block all dealings with the southern regions for a time.[64]

A third factor behind the fall in exports may well have been a decision by al-Sanusi to place less emphasis on ivory collection than in earlier years. At the time of the troubles with Hetman and Bangassou, the sultan also cut ivory purchases from other sources by half; the amount of ivory acquired in raiding also dropped. Because his bazingirs had to travel farther in search of captives than ever before, al-Sanusi probably found it necessary to devote a correspondingly larger share of his forces to slave-raiding. And ivory brought only one franc per kilogram (one magtaᶜ per 2½ kilos) in Ndele at this time, a decline related to the 1902 drop in the world price of ivory.[65]

While foreign purchases and raiding provided al-Sanusi with the largest part of his ivory, the importance of ivory hunted and gathered within Dar al-Kuti itself should not be underestimated. The quantity may have been small, only two to three tons annually, but ivory acquired in this manner had political and social significance as well as economic value. Among both the Nduka and the Banda, a portion of ivory taken from elephants killed or found dead on the land traditionally had belonged to the earth priest of the region. In some cases, the tusk which first touched the ground went to him; at other times he simply claimed a portion of all tusks taken.[66] Early in al-Sanusi's career Nduka and Banda groups in the Dar al-Kuti region began presenting him with tusks. At first, local earth priests brought offerings.

Banda Toulou and Ngonvo leaders took him ivory even before he moved to Ndele; in the new capital, resettled slaves also presented tusks directly to him.[67] Far from their homelands and recently arrived in a land completely dominated by al-Sanusi, they perhaps ascribed to him some of the characteristics associated with traditional ritual leaders in their homelands. Voluntary migrants may have regarded him similarly, for this practice also coincided with the traditional Banda custom of giving a portion of the rewards in any hunting or gathering expedition to all who had participated in it either directly or indirectly by providing arms.[68]

These non-Muslim customs fit well with al-Sanusi's own notion of his prerogatives as sultan. Rulers of nearby and older Muslim states such as Wadai, Dar Fur, and Dar Runga had long claimed a monopoly over ivory trade. Al-Sanusi did the same in Dar al-Kuti. In the eyes of the sultan, his followers owed him ivory because they were his subjects. To the Banda and Nduka, his position was analogous to those of their customary ritual and war leaders. By offering ivory, they acknowledged al-Sanusi's authority. Such recognition also brought economic rewards, since the sultan usually responded by presenting gifts of cloth and imported goods.[69] These exchanges, like those associated with agriculture and the slave trade, helped hold together a diverse following.

Exports of Aromatic Plants and Coffee

Aromatic plants—principally *jamsinda* (*Ischaemum brochyatherum*), *fil-fil* (*Capsicum* family), *kombo* (*Xylopia oethiopica*), *dorot* (*Entada sudanica*), and coffee (*Coffea excelsa*) were also among the important exports from Dar al-Kuti.[70] The plants went mainly to Wadai, the Sudan, and other Muslim lands north of Ubangi-Shari where they served as major ingredients in incenses and perfumes. Coffee was consumed as a beverage. Judging from the frequent mention in the travel literature of the importation of sandalwood, perfumes, and other scented items from Europe and the Middle East into the Muslim lands of the Sahel, such products must have enjoyed considerable popularity. These items were attractive to traders because they were easy to transport; to consumers they were attractive in part because of their association with Islam. Some were also thought to be powerful healing agents or aphrodisiacs.[71] In the case of Dar al-Kuti these exports are seldom mentioned in the written sources. Unlike ivory, they were not in demand in Europe, and unlike slaves, they did not attract European attention. Data come largely from oral testimony, which adequately describes the collection and preparation of the products for export but gives little precise indication of prices or trade volume.

Jamsinda or *su^cda* (Classical Arabic) was and is the major aromatic plant exported from northern Ubangi-Shari. It is a green aquatic grass which grows in the sandy, swampy lowlands adjacent to many streams in the region.[72] Yusuf Dingis, the major jamsinda merchant in Ndele in 1975, said that the plant was found all around the city at the turn of the century. It also thrived in a marshy area about twenty kilometers west of al-Sanusi's capital; additional quantities came from the swamps of the Bahr Aouk River separating Dar al-Kuti and Dar Runga, and from Lake Mamoun and the lowlands around Mangueigne in Dar Runga itself. Sudanese and Wadaian merchants referred to this entire region as the "land of jamsinda."[73]

The valuable part of the jamsinda plant is not the grass but the root. The entire plant must be pulled up or dug out of the ground. This operation takes place in the dry months, when the plants can be most easily extracted from the sandy soil, and continues until the rains begin in April. At that time, the increased moisture causes the soil to stick together; the grass also grows very rapidly to a height that hinders its collection. This optimal period coincides with the least busy months of the agricultural year in Dar al-Kuti. After gathering, the plants are burned, leaving only the roots, which are placed in the sun, dried until brittle, and then stored in large sacks pending the arrival of Sudanese and Wadaian buyers.[74]

Jamsinda commerce probably began as a regional trade based on ecological differences: southern Dar Runga and Dar al-Kuti possessed an environment favorable to the plant, while areas farther north did not. Informants generally agree that the trade expanded following al-Sanusi's arrival in Ndele. It was only then that large numbers of Jallaba merchants came to Dar al-Kuti, and they were the principal buyers of jamsinda. In addition, the sultan's presence brought security to the areas near his capital, thereby encouraging people to collect the plant. Because he could sell it quite readily, al-Sanusi accepted jamsinda as tribute. Common people also gathered the plant and exchanged it for imported cloth and beads, items necessary for bridewealth.[75]

Fil-fil, kombo, and dorot from Dar al-Kuti also found a market in the north.[76] They were perhaps as important as jamsinda, but much less is known about their collection and sale. Fil-fil is a pepper seed found in pods on a small shrub. It is roasted, ground, and used in tea, coffee, and sauces. Boiled in water and gargled, it is useful as a gastric stimulant. Dorot refers to the aromatic sap from a tree (*Entada sudanica*). In Dar al-Kuti it is gathered principally from trees infested with termites. The sawdust that the insects bring out of the tree is scented with the sap, and people collect it for sale in the marketplace. When burned, the powder gives off a very sweet smell. As for kombo, sometimes called Ethiopian pepper, it is a seed that grows in black pods on a slender tree. Pulverized and mixed with other ingredients, it adds scent to oils used to anoint the body. In rural areas where the supply of soap and water is limited, people wash themselves with kombo oil and perfume their clothes with it. In the early colonial period in Chad, a French administrator noted that kombo was more expensive than jamsinda: "Kombo, bought mainly . . . at Ouadda, Ouanda-Djale, and Ndele, has become as costly as ivory in Wadai, Sila, and Batha. Even in El-Obeid it is fifty francs per kilo" (jamsinda sold for one franc per kilogram at the time).[77]

All of these plants were widely purchased in the Sudan and Wadai. Their uses were many and various: They were thought to foster good health. Women perfumed their bedclothes with jamsinda, dorot, and kombo before and after childbirth. With the exception of dorot, these plants were mixed into sauces and gruels. Herdsmen in districts infested with tse-tse flies burned jamsinda at night to scent the air and keep the insects away from their animals; other people burned it beneath their beds during the rains to repel mosquitos. Clothes were scented with the smoke as well. In Dar al-Kuti today, the Runga warm and perfume themselves by sitting over scented fires during the cool evenings of the rainy season. Pallme observed a similar practice in Kordofan in the 1840s:

> In the houses of the married, there is a small elevation of about one foot and a half in height, in which an earthen pot is immured up to its embouchure. This is . . . for the purpose of fumigating the person. Wood cut into thin shavings . . . is placed in the pot, and ignited, whereupon the person performs the fumigation. This smoke is very tonic in its operation, and so astringent that it corrugates the skin. The shirts are also fumigated with sandalwood over this pot.[78]

Coffee also grew in Dar al-Kuti, and al-Sanusi exported it northward. Although Julien wrote that coffee was unknown before his arrival, and boasted of introducing its collection and sale, oral tradition and Chevalier dispute this claim, suggesting that Muslim traders bought coffee along with ivory, slaves, and aromatic plants in the late nineteenth century. Some of this coffee may have ended up in the markets of Tripoli, where the French consul Rivière noticed it in the 1880s.[79] Chevalier estimated that al-Sanusi could harvest a ton of coffee beans annually, enough to satisfy two-thirds of French needs in the whole Shari valley. Indeed, in a single month in 1902, the sultan's followers collected 200 kilograms of coffee and dispatched it to the French post at Fort-Crampel.[80]

The coffee of Dar al-Kuti was of a variety unknown to Europeans before the arrival of the botanist Chevalier. He called it *excelsa*, probably in reference to the great height of the tree, which frequently attained fifteen or twenty meters. The roasted and ground beans had an exquisite aroma, much superior to the smaller *Coffea congensis* variety the French found in the river valleys of southern Ubangi-Shari. But despite the better quality of excelsa coffee, it was not exploited to its fullest potential; the sultan harvested the beans by cutting down the trees.[81]

The Imports of Long-Distance Trade

The major products imported into Ndele at the turn of the century were the familiar goods of desert commerce, and ranked in importance as follows: cloth of all kinds, glassware (including beads), rifles, powder, firing caps, salt, natron, sugar, tea, candles, sabers, domestic animals, tin and copper jewelry, perfumes, soaps, a few thalers, and northern foodstuffs such as dates.[82] The volume of trade in each item remains unknown, but cloth, salt, beads, and firearms probably made up the bulk of it. Julien recorded the prices of several of these imports along with an estimate of the sultan's yearly needs (see figures 9–10).

Julien did not indicate how he arrived at these figures, and they cannot be easily verified, but Chevalier made a passing reference to al-Sanusi's import needs which permits comparison (figure 11). There are important differences between the two estimates. The sets of figures given for cloth are much closer than those listed for salt and beads. But Julien's lower estimate is still 20 percent higher than Chevalier's figure (15,000 m versus 18,000 m), whereas his upper amount is almost double (15,000 m versus 27,000 m). Julien's salt figure is smaller than that of Chevalier, 1,000 kilograms compared to 12,000 kilograms; his bead total amounts to only 40 or 60 percent of the other quantity (600–900 kg versus 1,500 kg).

The estimates thus yield little conclusive evidence. The cloth estimates are close and can probably be accepted as a minimum figure. It may well be that more salt arrived in Ndele from Chad than Julien suspected— Chevalier traveled extensively in this northern area and was in a better position to observe this traffic. From this disparate information it is apparent that the French possessed little hard data concerning the flow of imports to Dar al-Kuti from the Muslim zones outside their control. Given the isolated location of the French post in Ndele and the clandestine nature of the slave trade, this is not surprising.

Neither Chevalier nor Julien say much about the origin of imports. In general, Dar al-Kuti was not totally dependent on trans-Saharan trade. Much of the merchandise arriving in al-Sanusi's capital did come from across the desert or from the Nile region, but many items were the products of regional trade with immediately adjacent Muslim lands. Cloth currencies

Figure 9

Prices of some Imported Goods in Ndele, 1901–1902*

Item	Price (magta^c)
1 horse	30–40
1 mule	40–60
1 cow	4–5
1 pregnant cow	8–10
1 calf	2–3
1 sheep	2
1 donkey	5
1 kg powder, according to fineness	2–4
1 box of 100 firing caps	2
1 barrel-loading rifle, according to model	15–20
1 rapid-fire weapon, according to model	40–100
1 kg loaf sugar	1 (or 1 kg ivory)
1 kg black tea	4 (or 4 kg ivory)
1 kg salt	1 (or 1 kg ivory)

*Other products, such as perfumes, luxury soap, cloth for turbans, shoes, stockings, etc., were bargained for item by item.

Source: Julien, "La situation économique du Dar-el-Kouti," 39.

were largely of regional or local origin, while other hand-woven material came from sub-Saharan areas as far away as Kano.[83] Salt came from Chad in *dirdimi* (cones [Chadic Arabic]), along with natron.[84] The horses and cattle sold in Ndele also came from the Sahel. At the turn of the century, most other goods came from across the desert, but by 1912, a year after the sultan's assassination, Hausa and Bornoan peddlers brought significant quantities of cloth, salt, and sugar to Ndele from French settlements such as Bangui and Fort-Sibut in the south and Fort-Archambault in the west.[85]

This chapter and chapter 5 present a detailed examination of economic life in al-Sanusi's Ndele. Of the many themes treated here, perhaps two emerge as the most central for understanding the social, political, and economic dynamics of Dar al-Kuti's history. First, the sultan maintained control of his domains by carefully directing the flow of prestige goods. Near-monopoly of the export and import trade brought economic and military power. Through commerce he acquired the products necessary to satisfy and support his following; he also obtained the firearms and munitions needed to continue slave-raiding. Power brought prestige and the popular belief that he was attuned to the spiritual forces that were believed

Figure 10

Julien's Estimate of al-Sanusi's Annual Import Requirements

Item	Amount
Guinea-blue cloth, light and wide	20–30 *ballots*[a] (bundles, French), totaling 6–9,000 m
Guinea-blue cloth, heavy	20–30 *ballots*, totaling 6–9,000 m
Heavy white cloth	20–30 *ballots*, totaling 6–9,000 m
Salt	1,000 kg
Tea	300 kg
Sugar	600 kg
Soap	300 kg
Blue *bapterose* beads[b]	20–30 cases, totaling 600–900 kg
Chechias (fezes)	200–300
Firearms	Unknown

a) DeMezières gave the length of a *ballot* as 300 meters. See ANF-SOM (Aix), 2(D)21, "Rapport de M. A. Bonnel deMezières, chargé de Mission sur le Haut-Oubangui, le M'Bomou et le Bahr-el-Ghazal," Paris, 31 December 1900.

b) DeMezières suggested that 30 kilograms of beads were usually packed in one case, which would give a total of 600–900 kilograms. See deMezières reference above.

Source: Julien, "Mohamed-es-Senoussi" (1929), 74.

Figure 11

Chevalier's Estimate of al-Sanusi's Annual Import Requirements

Item	Amount	Price (magta[c])	(francs)
Cotton cloth	15,000 m	8,000	20,000
Salt	12,000 kg	10,000	25,000
Beads	1,500 kg or 50 cases	2,000	5,000

Source: Chevalier, *Mission*, 153–54.

to decide human fate. Among the Banda, death in battle was an indication that the *lingu* (protector spirit) of the victim was weak and out of harmony with the supernatural forces abroad in the world. People who fell into slavery were thought to suffer the same deficiency.[86] To his followers, al-Sanusi's success must have been proof that he was in accord with these forces.

Secondly, the economic system of which al-Sanusi was a part did not allow any choice concerning slave-raiding and slave-trading. The northern merchants and markets sought slaves and ivory, and to get what he needed, the sultan had to supply these exports. There was no alternative. French claims to the contrary, rubber was not a viable "legitimate" trade good. It required too much labor, brought too low a price, and was not plentiful enough.[87] Within Dar al-Kuti, the story was the same. Agricultural production depended upon slave labor and the sultan's fighting forces were replenished by raiding. The French belief that al-Sanusi could rapidly and without upheaval beat his swords into ploughshares simply shows how little they knew about the internal dynamics that held the sultanate together. Al-Hajj Tukur clearly understood the situation, and responded to Chevalier's inquiries about ending the slave trade with the following assessment:

What would you have us do without slaves? . . . Where would you want the sultan to obtain the porters necessary for your travels? Who would cultivate the fields? Look at our arms (and he showed me the thin arms of a Fulbe), do you think that they are strong enough to turn over the soil? Where would you have us find the cattle that your government requests if we had no slaves to give to the northern Arabs in exchange for their herds?[88]

Conclusion

The history of Dar al-Kuti and eastern Ubangi-Shari shows how regions peripheral to the European core of the expanding international economy came to be indirectly but increasingly linked to it in the nineteenth century. In North Central Africa, as in East Africa, Muslims forged and maintained the crucial links articulating the local and international spheres—funneling items of European manufacture into the area along with goods from the Islamic world. The exports provided in exchange were not of direct importance to European economies. Certainly ivory was in great demand in late nineteenth century Europe, but it was not an essential import—such as were, for example, the vegetable oils of West Africa. And as for slaves, the other major export, they were either employed in Central Africa itself or in adjacent Muslim lands. There was no market for them in Europe, and no links with the Caribbean and South America, where countries such as Cuba and Brazil continued to import captives after 1850. Thus North Central Africa lay, like West Africa in the era of the Atlantic slave trade, on the periphery of a periphery of the international economy.[1] It was peripheral to the Muslim economies of the Sahara and the Nile, themselves peripheral to Europe.

Despite its indirect nature, this integration brought enormous change to North Central Africa during the century. Beginning in the 1820s, Muhammad ᶜAli, the ruler of Egypt, and his successors used European weapons and links with the international economy to stake out an empire in the Upper Nile basin; by the 1860s, and particularly after the rise of the Mahdist state in the 1880s, numerous individuals associated with Egyptian conquest carried weapons and other imports westward, where they also had great effect. Some tried to maintain ties with the Nile region, but most established new connections with the international economy, northward through Muslim states of the desert edge such as Dar Fur and Wadai. By this time these states had also carved out their own spheres of influence in North Central Africa.

This general theme has, of course, been identified elsewhere. For example, articles on Rabih document the connections between Egyptian military modernization and conquest and the Sudanese leader's campaigns in the Lake Chad region. But the career of al-Sanusi in particular, as well as the activities of Ngono, Mbele, Sa^cid Baldas, Rafai, Zemio, Tambura, Bangassou, and other local warlords in northern and eastern Ubangi-Shari, show how ripples from the Egyptian conquests washed over regions and peoples directly incorporated neither into Egyptian domains nor the territories of al-Zubayr and Rabih. These individuals took advantage of European military technology and Muslim commercial networks to establish raiding and trading centers well beyond the Islamic frontier. Although few of these operations outlived the men who began them, they shed light on the impact of the international economy on this part of Africa.

The analysis of the rise of Dar al-Kuti shows *how* integration into the international economy, albeit indirect, affected the societies of North Central Africa. Changes were many and major. As far as is now known, prior to Muslim penetration the predominant mode of production among the non-Muslim societies of the region was domestic, each unit producing largely for itself with surpluses accruing to the group. With the slow infiltration of Muslim traders in the early nineteenth century, the arrival of marauders from the Nile basin, the conquests of Rabih, and the rise of al-Sanusi as sultan of Dar al-Kuti, the large-scale use of slave labor became common in northern and eastern Ubangi-Shari. Yet, as the agricultural history of Ndele suggests, great plantations such as those of al-Sanusi and his son Adam were not the rule; most slaves worked in smaller groups and probably on smaller plots. In the case of villages transplanted whole to Ndele, the organization and composition of the work force probably remained much as before; kin units were also the units of agricultural production. But despite continuity, there were important changes. Mixed relations of production now existed, and the product of labor was divided differently, much of it accruing to slave owners, to overseers who often held military positions, and to the sultan himself. This pattern was replicated elsewhere[2]—in the regions around Mouka and Ouadda; in the settlements of other Muslim marauders; and even in the centers of non-Muslim raiders, places like Jagara (founded by the Ngao leader Ngono). Agricultural production on a larger scale became possible, as did the appropriation of a larger surplus which could be used to support a slave-owning ruling class and a military force.

A second theme concerns the interrelationships of domestic production, long-distance exchange, and the redistribution of wealth in Dar al-Kuti.[3] The first two kinds of economic activity were interdependent; neither can be understood without the other. Farmers were taken from their villages and either put to work in Dar al-Kuti or exported northward; ivory was either reinvested in the domestic economy or given to foreign merchants in exchange for luxury goods. In most cases, the relationships between slaves as producers and slaves as commodities, between slavery as an economic system and slavery as a system of political clientage and assimilation, were worked out within the context of state power. The sultan decided whether to export slaves or to resettle them in new villages dependent on his military units for security. The same kinds of decisions were also made by other members of the Dar al-Kuti ruling class. For example, military leaders— either Runga or more recently Islamized Banda—decided whether to pay bridewealth in the form of slaves or ivory for free wives, or to take slave wives who required no bridewealth instead and put their wealth to other uses.

In addition, valid analysis of the political economy of the sultanate requires study of the redistribution of wealth. Within Dar al-Kuti economic activity included both market transactions and non-market exchange. The latter, consisting of the redistribution of goods among constituent groups, brought such intangible rewards as loyalty and prestige; yet this exchange very obviously functioned with reference to market transactions.[4] Al-Sanusi enjoyed a near-monopoly in the trade and distribution of long-distance goods, and was aware of the price they would bring if released into the market sector of the economy. This knowledge obviously influenced his decisions regarding the redistribution of wealth among his followers.

Thus market and non-market exchange both occurred.[5] Moreover, the percentage of goods circulating in the latter sector must have been great enough to influence prices. At the same time, the Ndele economy was an appendage of the greater trans-Saharan trading system; as such, prevailing prices in this network—for ivory, slaves, and long-distance imports—must have affected the quantity and value of similar commodities changing hands in Dar al-Kuti.

Thirdly, the historical experience of Dar al-Kuti illuminates a theme that preoccupies historians of other parts of the continent: the effects of the slave trade on individual African societies and specific regions.[6] This study has explored three facets of this question in some detail—slave-raiding, slave-trading, and demographic change. In North Central Africa, or at least in Dar al-Kuti, the human costs of the trade were frightfully high for non-Muslim societies. These costs included the depopulation of entire districts, the disruption of agriculture, and severe social dislocation as people fled from one place to another.

The demographic implications of these upheavals are of particular importance. Although in-depth local studies will perhaps one day provide more precise indications of how raiding and trading affected specific groups of people in Ubangi-Shari, it is already apparent that migration occurred on a large scale. Some of this movement was voluntary. For example, Muslim Runga moved south from Dar Runga to join countrymen and countrywomen in Dar al-Kuti, while commercial opportunities drew Hausa, Bornoans, and

Jallaba to the region. But most migration was forced. Some non-Muslims ended up in Ndele because the sultan's raiding parties captured them and took them there. Others moved apparently of their own volition, although in reality they had little choice; confronted with an ultimatum from a raiding party to migrate or be annihilated, many Banda, Kresh, and Goula chose the former. Still other groups moved to the vicinity of the capital because it offered security in an era of increasing and more widespread violence. The period thus brought greater concentrations of population; and, as noted, this permitted changes in the relations of production, producing the surpluses necessary for the reproduction and extension of the system itself.

It is also apparent that the greatest impact of the slave trade in North Central Africa came in the late nineteenth century, an era identified with abolition and the rise of "legitimate commerce" in many earlier standard histories. This characterization was probably a result of the historiography of the slave trade itself. Research began with the Atlantic slave trade to the near exclusion of the Muslim commerce or the expanding use of slaves within Africa—undoubtedly because the evidence was more plentiful, as well as because this aspect of the trade most directly affected the New World, which was of major concern to American scholars. Furthermore, study of the Atlantic trade tended to concentrate on its external features— how Europeans acquired captives, how many captives there were, and how well they survived the crossing. It is true that the Atlantic trade had more or less ended by the 1860s, but the Muslim trade to the Middle East and North Africa, and within Africa itself, actually intensified in the later years of the century. Certainly this was the case in North Central Africa after 1890.[7]

Fourthly, the history of Dar al-Kuti challenges the prevailing image of the spread of Islam in North Central Africa. General histories of the early Muslim conquests of North Africa, as well as European accounts of the expansion of Muslim influence in sub-Saharan Africa, frequently create the impression that followers of Muhammad conquered everyone in their way, arrogantly obliterating preexisting religions and social institutions.[8] Recent studies, however, reject such simplistic analyses. Nehemia Levtzion, for example, suggests that "although it is difficult to assess the relative importance of forced conversions in the general process of Islamization, they seem to have weighed less than is implied in non-Muslim sources and more than is admitted by Muslims."[9] The Islamization of Dar al-Kuti obviously supports Levtzion's observation. Moreover, it conforms to a pattern visible along most of the Islamic frontier in North Central and West Africa, where traders and men of religion created a climate conducive to nonviolent initial conversion. Beginning with the earliest immigrants in the sultanate, and continuing into the era of al-Sanusi, Muslims accommodated themselves to non-Muslim peoples and cultures, because the demands of daily existence made such peaceful coexistence necessary. Local peoples also took on some customs and beliefs associated with Islam. Thus began, in the words of Levtzion, "a long process toward greater conformity and orthodoxy."[10] Elsewhere along the Islamic frontier in Africa, this brought "the growth of Islamic learning, communications with the central lands of the Muslim world through the pilgrimage to Mecca, socioeconomic changes, all [of which] led to improved observance of the precepts of Islamic worship and law."[11] In Dar al-Kuti this transformation was interrupted by the French conquest. And while Islam continued to spread during the colonial era, the absence of an Islamic institutional framework slowed it down.

The history of the sultanate also offers evidence with which to assess the impact of slave-raiding on the spread of the faith. Writers on other regions have argued that such violence retarded Islamization.[12] While this may have been the case in regions such as the southern Sudan, it was not so in Dar al-Kuti proper and northern Ubangi-Shari. Even at the height of al-Sanusi's raiding, Islam gained adherents; among peoples such as the Goula—one of the most heavily raided groups in the area—nearly everyone became a Muslim. Today, long after the disappearance of the Muslim threat, most of these people have Arabic names and profess Islam. The same is true of other peoples in northern Ubangi-Shari, such as the Nduka, Kara, Yulu, and some Sara and northern Banda groups. Part of the reason why these people accepted and retained the faith may be that Islam already enjoyed prestige and respect in the area before the great expansion in slave-raiding and slave-trading under Rabih and al-Sanusi. Indeed, the generation of these positive attitudes may well be the most lasting contribution of al-Sanusi's predecessors, such as Kobur. In addition, and probably as important, was the fact that the disruption of territorially rooted classical African religions caused by the slave trade made the non-Muslim populations of northern Ubangi-Shari more susceptible to Islam.

These are some of the major conclusions to be drawn from the history of Dar al-Kuti. Voluminous as that history may be, it is only a beginning in reconstructing the history of the Lake Chad-Nile region; even for northern Ubangi-Shari and Dar al-Kuti much remains to be done. It is hoped that this book will encourage others to do research in North Central Africa—to help fill this great gap in African history before oral traditions like those that have contributed so much to understanding other parts of the continent are lost forever.

REFERENCE MATERIAL

Appendix 1
The Fulani and the
Islamization of Bagirmi

The early history of Islam in Bagirmi is associated with a Fulani cleric or clerics named Ould Dede, Waldede, or Waldid. In the *Infaq al-Maysur*, written from the geographical and religious perspective of post-jihad Hausaland, Muhammad Bello links Ould Dede with the founding of Bidri. He is said to have arrived in Bagirmi in about 1500 in search of his father, who had left Borno on the pilgrimage some years earlier. Upon learning that his father had died in Bagirmi on the way home and was buried there, Ould Dede abandoned his quest and founded Bidri.[1]

Adding traditions from the Fulani of Kalfu, southwest of Bagirmi, Mohammadou Eldridge confirms this version of Ould Dede's arrival. Following Gustav Nachtigal, Henri Gaden, and Viviana Pâques, he suggests that a Fulani *modibbe* (the Fulani equivalent of the Hausa *mallam* or Islamic teacher) named Dede participated in the founding of Massenya. The Kalfu traditions go on to emphasize the role that Dede and his village of teachers played in the Islamization of the area. Mohammadou's interpretation likewise links Ould Dede directly with Bidri.[2]

The *Infaq* includes another tradition regarding a Fulani cleric named Waldede who is also linked with the pilgrimage. This account suggests that Waldede was born while his mother was on the hajj. She became separated from her traveling companions, was nearly overcome with thirst, and then gave birth to the future teacher. After three days, traders found her and took her to their land. There Waldede learned to read the Qur'an and traveled widely in search of knowledge. He reportedly died in 999 a.h., shortly after 1590.[3]

The third figure, Waldid, also appears in the *Infaq*. Bello reported that he was a Fulani mallam whose preaching attracted a large following in Borno at the end of the sixteenth century. Mai ᶜUmar Idrisu, said to be the ruler at the time, felt threatened by the mallam's exhortations to purify the faith and retaliated by killing al-Jarmiyu, a cleric associated with Waldid. The mallam then fled to Bagirmi.[4]

Needless to say, the traditions concerning these figures are both incomplete and contradictory. They may all refer to one individual, or there may have indeed been two or three Fulani Muslim leaders with similar names. For purposes of this study it is not necessary to sort out the traditions; citing the various accounts is sufficient to demonstrate the importance of links between Bagirmi and Fulani teachers from Muslim lands farther west. These migrants settled at Bidri and elsewhere in Bagirmi.

Appendix 2
Genealogies of the
Rulers of Precolonial
Dar al-Kuti

In keeping with the short history of formal Muslim rule in the area south of the Aouk, Julien's genealogy is brief, consisting of only three rulers. This is the genealogy almost always found in the French sources as well as in French and English secondary works, where it is presented as the absolute truth. It is therefore apt to be duplicated without qualification in future histories of the Central African Republic unless a few words of caution are injected.

Multiple sources confirm the existence of Kobur and Muhammad al-Sanusi, and indicate that they ruled during approximately the periods calculated by Julien. There is serious doubt, however, about the historical character of the supposed first ruler, ^cUmar Jugultum al-Bagirmai. Although two of the other lists mention him, neither of them suggests that he was the father of Kobur; rather, they relegate him to the more distant past, and treat him as an almost mythic figure. Perhaps he was just that, for Chevalier's information on the rulers of Dar al-Kuti, collected about the same time as Julien's data, makes no mention of him whatsoever.[1] (For further comment, see chapter 2.)

Chevalier collected his version of the genealogy of the rulers of Dar al-Kuti during his sojourn in 1902. As such, it is as old as Julien's list but much less accessible, since it is buried in the 800-page report of the mission. Chevalier acquired his data from the son of ^cAbd al-Mintalib (Kobur's son). The inclusion of Guni as Kobur's father on this list accords with all other versions of the list except that of Julien. But it is perhaps important to note that Barth, Martine, and Santerre suggest that the term *Goni* may simply be another term for *faqih* or *marabout*,[2] in which case Guni, like *al-hajj al-kabir*, may not be a proper name at all. It is apparent from the list that the number of generations is erroneous, because Sultan ^cAbd al-Qadir ruled Bagirmi in 1846–58 according to Nachtigal, and al-Sanusi was born in the 1850s.[3]

The Yacoub and Khrouma versions are similar and can be considered together. The use of the name Jugultum in the Khrouma version is the only important distinction between them, although the Yacoub version also differs in its inclusion of the name of the earlier sultan of Dar Runga (Bokur) and that of Sultan ^cAqid's daughter (Amin), who married Guni. In both versions, Guni was reportedly born in Bagirmi and arrived in Dar al-Kuti by way of Dar Runga. His father was left in

Figure 12   *Julien Version*

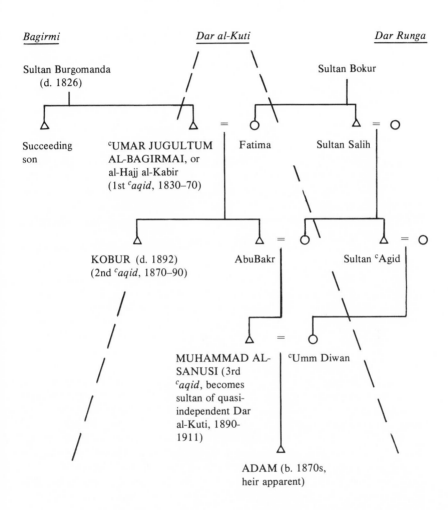

Source: ANF-SOM (Paris), Papiers Julien, 6P.A. (Papiers d'Agent), ctn. 1, pièce N° 1,
"Historique des Etats Senoussiens (Dar-el-Kouti), Annexe N° 1: Généalogie
des Sultans Baghirmiens et Senoussiens," 104–5, 152–53. This information was
later published: see Julien, "Mohamed-es-Senoussi" (1925), 125–27.

Figure 13 *Chevalier Version*

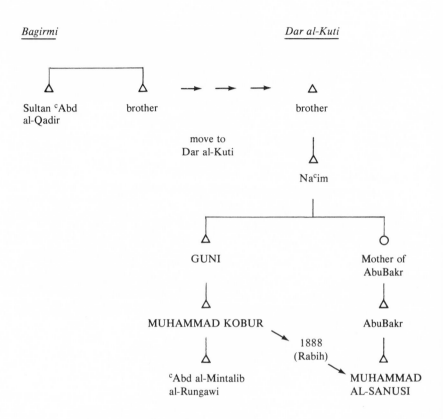

Bagirmi   *Dar al-Kuti*

Sultan ᶜAbd   brother   brother
al-Qadir

                        move to
                        Dar al-Kuti   Naᶜim

                              GUNI   Mother of
                                                     AbuBakr

                    MUHAMMAD KOBUR   AbuBakr
                                          1888
                                         (Rabih)
                    ᶜAbd al-Mintalib   MUHAMMAD
                    al-Rungawi   AL-SANUSI

Source: Chevalier, *Mission*, 130–32.

Figure 14 *Yacoub Version*

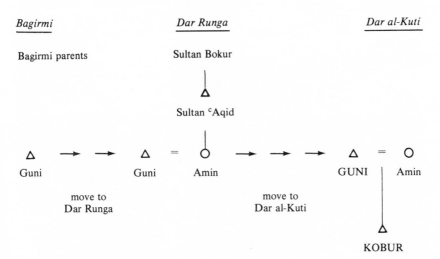

Bagirmi   *Dar Runga*   *Dar al-Kuti*

Bagirmi parents   Sultan Bokur

Sultan ᶜAqid

Guni   Guni   Amin   GUNI   Amin

move to   move to
Dar Runga   Dar al-Kuti

KOBUR

Source: OA5.1; OA5.2/6.1

Bagirmi. In the Yacoub version the data on the Runga rulers are probably not accurate since another sultan, Salih (son of Bokur and father of ꜤAqid), should be included.[4]

A final version of the genealogy serves as the frontispiece to this volume (see illustration opposite title page). This list or *nasaliya* was not meant to be a list of the rulers of Dar al-Kuti. It traces instead the ancestry of SumaꜤin, a faqih in Kali early in the colonial period. But because the religious families in Kali (who live today in Koundi) all claim descent from Guni or Guni and Kobur, the early parts of the nasaliya can be viewed as a "kinglist." The immediately obvious problem with the list is the great number of generations it includes. Jugultum and Guni are separated by two generations that do not appear in any other versions. As for the list of the Bagirmi sultans, it does not agree with Nachtigal in names, generations, or order. The Abbasid connection only reflects the desire for a respectable Islamic background. The nasaliya is valuable mainly because it shows how the faqihs of Koundi (Kali) view their past. It undoubtedly contains seeds of truth, but they are not readily apparent.

Figure 15 *Khrouma Version*

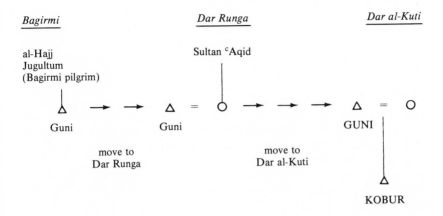

Bagirmi

al-Hajj
Jugultum
(Bagirmi pilgrim)

Guni

move to
Dar Runga

Dar Runga

Sultan ᶜAqid

Guni

move to
Dar al-Kuti

Dar al-Kuti

GUNI

KOBUR

Source: OA13.1; OA14.2; OA23.2.

Figure 16   *Koundi Nasaliya*

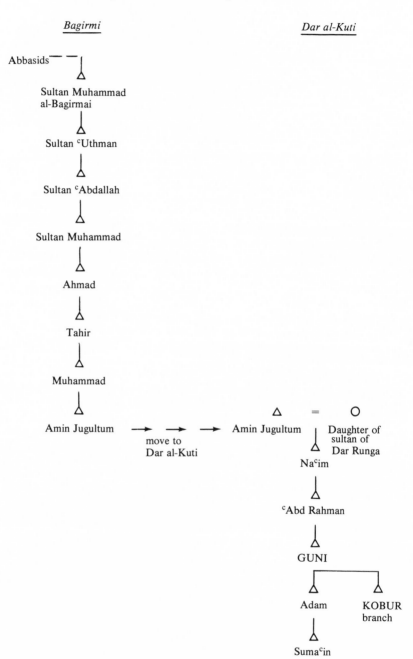

Bagirmi   *Dar al-Kuti*

Abbasids

Sultan Muhammad
al-Bagirmai

Sultan ᶜUthman

Sultan ᶜAbdallah

Sultan Muhammad

Ahmad

Tahir

Muhammad

Amin Jugultum → → → Amin Jugultum = ◯
                  move to   Daughter of
                  Dar al-Kuti   sultan of
                                   Naᶜim   Dar Runga

                                   ᶜAbd Rahman

                                   GUNI

                              Adam   KOBUR
                                        branch

                              Sumaᶜin

Source: Koundi *Nasaliya* manuscript (see frontispiece).

Appendix 3
The Name of the
New Capital

Explanations of the word *ndele* are as various as accounts of the city's founding. Three of the most common etiological traditions are presented here, together with commentary.

The first etymology is the most inventive and the least likely. As the story goes, when al-Sanusi was choosing building sites on the plateau, he noticed bats flying about the mouths of caves in the rocks. Summoning a Banda follower to his side, he asked what bats were called in Banda. The man replied, *nde*. Hence the name. Although two informants tell this story, and another confirms that a particular species of bat is called *nde* in Banda, this explanation of the name of the city is not common in Ndele today.[1] And since al-Sanusi grew up in the area and apparently spoke local Banda dialects fluently, he probably would not have needed to inquire about the word in any case.[2]

According to the second derivation, *ndele* is a combination of two Sango words: *ndo*, meaning "high" or "on top of," and *lé*, meaning "face." *Ndo lé* refers to the forehead. Thus *ndele* could be a Sango reference to the high, mushroom-shaped rock outcroppings north of the core of the old city on the terrace.[3] The explanation rings true and the Sango items are correct,[4] but Sango has been commonly spoken in the Ndele area only since the beginning of colonial administration. In al-Sanusi's time Banda and Chadic Arabic were the major languages, and even today it is not uncommon to find old Runga (Muslims) and Banda who do not speak Sango. That this interpretation enjoys any currency at all in Ndele today is perhaps its most salient characteristic, because it illustrates the breadth and speed of the diffusion of Sango in the last half-century.

Of all the explanations, the most probable is that the sultan named his capital for a large boulder balanced on a tower of rocks just south of the major plateau.[5] Identified as *ndele* by most peoples currently living in the city, the formation is located just above the stream of the same name. It was a sacred site where the Banda Ngonvo made libations of Shea butter nut (*karité*) oil both before and during al-Sanusi's sojourn in the area.[6] This practice was not unique to the Ngonvo. Banda groups throughout Ubangi-Shari traditionally ascribed ritual importance to particular rocks, trees, and other natural features of their environment.[7] Al-Sanusi's choice of a Banda name for his new capital is further evidence of his desire to seek accommodation with the indigenous peoples of the region.

Appendix 4
Cloth in Dar al-Kuti in the Time of al-Sanusi (descriptions and sources)

A. Cotton Cloth used as Currency and for Consumption

magta^c (megta, magta, makta, magta)

cotton currency in Dar al-Kuti	Kalck, 1970, 2:529–31.
mention, no description	Kalck, 1970, 3:63–64.
4 m–long, locally produced cloth	Kalck, 1959, 90.
tukia, 20 cm × 30 *durah* (elbow-lengths)	Grech, 1924, 41.
light cloth 12 *durah* in length	Chevalier, 1907, 154.
cloth, 10 *durah*, from Dar al-Kuti, Dar Runga, Wadai, Bagirmi; also *tob*	Rouget, 1906, 826–27.
local cloth, 15 cm × 15 m	Julien, "La situation," 39.
cloth 15 cm × 15 m, also called *chakka*	Julien, 1929, 71–73.
narrow band of cotton serving as currency in Wadai, equal to a certain number of *tukia*	Carbou, 1913, 197.
maqta tromba or *maqta kham*, customary currency in Wadai, consisting of pieces of European cotton cloth 65 cm × 17 m which came from Egypt via the Nile; also found in Kobe in western Dar Fur	Nachtigal, 1971, 55, 253–54.
general term, cottons	Derendinger, 1923, 48.
locally produced cloth, including *tukia* *shakka, tombassia* (narrow *magta^c* called *tukia*, wide *maqta^c* called *tombassia*), term also used for *shakka* cloth	OA17.1.
"piece" of cloth	All informants.

matta (may be same as magta^c)

matta, cloth currency woven and used in southern Wadai (Oum-Hadjer), 1 *durah* × 12 *durah*;	Burthe d'Annelet, 1939, 2:1038.

Exchange rates were as follows:

200 *matta*	slave 10 years old
20–150	adult slave (according to age)
20–400	female slave 10 years old (adult females found no buyers)
10–40	bull or cow
300–500	horse
100–200	camel
1	one sheep
1	one bullock load of millet at highest price of year

gumash

general term for cloth	Lethem, 1920, 283.
cloth, sometimes vest	Derendinger, 1923, 57, 135.
gumadji, a type of short shirt; *gumach*, cloth, "toile de coton"	Carbou, 1913, 198 and n1.
general term for cloth in Egypt	ANF-SOM (Paris), Gabon-Congo III, dossier 13b.
general term for cloth	All informants, Dar al-Kuti, 1974.

gabad, gabak, gabag, gabaga

gabak, narrow cloth	Muraz, 1926, 29.
gabak, cloth currency used in Bagirmi, 10–12 cm wide	Burthe d'Annelet, 1939, 2:1282.
gabag, also called *tokiye*, locally woven cloth in narrow strips	Lethem, 1920, 283.
gabaga, narrow bands of cotton cloth from Chad, sometimes exported to Nigeria	Bruel, 1930
gabaga, cotton strips used as currency	Barth, 1851, 2:55.
indigo-colored bands, 5 cm wide, popular in Bagirmi and Borno	Decorse, *AF-RC*, May 1905.
gabaga, locally woven bands of cloth, used as currency in Bagirmi	Gaden, 1909, 81.
gabaga kilso, gabaga 4 *durah* long which served as currency in Bagirmi as well	Gaden, 1909, 81.
gabag, 6 cm wide cotton band, sometimes used as currency	Derendinger, 1923, 39, 133.
gabagae, gabagaya (pl., *gabag*), narrow band of indigenous cotton cloth, smaller than *shakka* and used as money	Carbou, 1913, 197.

gabad, gabak, gabag, gabaga (Cont'd.)

> *gabag*, cloth currency in western   Kalck, 1970, 2:529–31.
> Central African Republic,
> 44 cm × 42–44 m
> *gabak*, bands of cotton   AMBB, No. 95 (Bangassou),
>   Barthélémew, "Rapport
>   général," December 1920.
> *gabak*, strips of woven cloth whose   AMBB, No. 95 (Bangassou),
> production the colonial govern-   "Tissage du Gabak," 26
> ment wished to encourage in 1938   November 1938.
> *gabad*, long rolls of locally   OA1.1; OA13.1.
> produced cloth from Chad

farda, ferda, parda, ferdah

> *farda*, cloth or *pagne*   Derendinger, 1923, 57.
> *ferda*, subdivision of the *maqta*   Nachtigal, 1971, 203–4.
> *tromba* equaling 1/2 *tukia*
> *farda*, strips of cotton cloth   Barth, 1851, 2:511.
> about two *durah* in length and a hand-
> span wide, currency in Bagirmi
> *farda*, collective noun for clothing,   Carbou, 1913, 197–98.
> 2-piece woman's outfit (1 for chest and
> shoulders, 1 for rest of body)
> *ferdah*, sash worn by Runga women   Modat, *AF-RC*, July, 1912,
>   272.
> *parda*, coarsely woven band of canvas   Chevalier, 1907, 362.
> *farde zarak*, cloth, no detailed description OA7.2/8.1 (no other
>   informants mentioned it)

khaleg (pl. *khulugan*)

> *khalak*, general term for cloth,   Lethem, 1920, 284.
> but properly refers to coat, gown
> *khalag*, shirts used to purchase   Barth, 1851, 2:511.
> larger items in Bagirmi (equaled 70–150
> *farda* depending on quality)
> *khaleg*, a *boubou* or flowing robe   Muraz, 1926, 34.
> *khaleg*, piece of men's clothing,   Carbou, 1913, 198.
> used interchangeably with *tob* (pl. *tiban*)
> *khallaq* (pl., *rhulgan*), *boubou*   Derendinger, 1923, 41, 149.
> cotton currency bands sewn   Kalck, 1970, 2:529–31.
> together to serve as clothing (pants and
> shirts)

khaleg (pl. *khulugan*) (Cont'd.)

    classic men's garment in Chad
      made of cotton bands resembling
      a priest's vestment
    general term for cloth

Jean Ferrandi, "Abéché,
    capitale du Ouadai,"
    362, n1.
OA5.1; OA9.1; OA9.2/10.1;
    Ndele market, 1974.

tob, taub, toub, tobes, tobe, tsaub

    tob, large garment worn by the Muslims
    tob, general term, also used for gown
    toub, light, imported cloth
    toub, light cloth pieces equaling
      2 *magta^c*
    tobes, robes of Manchester cotton
      cloth of the poorest quality,
      used as "money standard"

    taub, simple black shirt valued
      at about 20 piasters (5F20 in 1850s)
    taub, large expansive garment that
      covers a woman head to foot, can be
      made of various types of cloth
    tobe, standard men's garment in Borno,
      finest quality *tobe* came from Nife on
      the Niger; derived from Arabic *thawb*,
      a large robe in Egypt worn by women
      and men
    tob, piece of men's clothing,same as *khaleg*
    taub, piece of cloth draped over body

    tsaub, tob, clothing
    tobes, and half-*tobes*, single strips of
      cotton cloth 7 cm × 3–4 *durah*, used as
      currency in Bagirmi

Rouget, 1906, 827–28.
Lethem, 1920, 282.
Kalck, 1970, 3:63–64.
Chevalier, 1907, 154.

F. Sidney Ensor, *Incidents on
    a Journey through Nubia to
    Darfoor* (London, 1881),
    112.
Al-Tunisi, 1845, 492.

Al-Tunisi, 1845, 205–7.

Fisher and Fisher, "Glossary,"
    in Nachtigal, 1971, 416–17.

Carbou, 1913, 198.
Modat, *AF-RC*, July 1912,
    272.
Derendinger, 1923, 171.
Barth, 1851, 2:479.

tombassia, tombassi

    cloth about 25 cm wide, locally made in Dar
    al-Kuti, Dar Runga, and by the Dajo,
    Fongoro, Wadaians, and Kibet; wider
    than the *tukia*, which is about 8 cm in
    width

OA8.2.

tombassia, tombassi (Cont'd.)

same as above (same informant), with these added details: not frequently made by Runga, but usually made in northern areas and imported; wide and white	OA17.1.
locally made wide cloth, 30–40 cm in width	OA6.2.
cloth that generally came from Chad, but which was sometimes made in Dar al-Kuti	OA11.1.
cloth made by the Runga and brought to Ndele from Dar Runga, common in Ndele in 1911; locally (or regionally) produced cloth 20–25 cm wide, came in great rolls	OA1.1 and OA2.1 (same informant)
cloth woven by the Runga, who also taught the Banda to make it; made of cotton and came in large rolls	OA4.1 and OA15.2/16.1 (same informant)

Note: *Tombassia* is not mentioned in any written source examined in the course of compiling this appendix.

targa, taraga, tarak, terek, tirke

tarak, pieces of wide cloth	Muraz, 1926, 29.
tirke, pieces of ordinary grey shirting, cut into lengths of 3 m, one dark blue, the other light blue (see *jawaz khadar* entry)	John Petherick, *Egypt, the Soudan, and Central Africa* (London, 1861), 305–6.
terek, small dark or light blue pieces of dyed cloth, 1 m × 1.5 m, woven very loosely, useless for clothing and used only for currency in large market centers and nearby villages; used as small change for *maqta tromba* and *thalers*; dark blue pieces are more valuable	Nachtigal, 1971, 253–54.
tarak, sturdy cloth similar to khaki, produced in Dar al-Kuti, Dar Sila, Fongoro, Kibet areas in north; about 1 m in width, similar to *tombassia*	OA8.2 and OA17.1 (same informant)
taraga, locally produced cloth from Chad and Dar al-Kuti	OA11.1.
tarak, locally produced wide cloth	OA13.1.
tarak, wide cloth (about 25 cm) made by the Banda of Ouadda	OA22.3.
tarak, cloth made in Chad by the Dagur near Am Timan and used for pants; made	OA23.2.

targa, taraga, tarak, terek, tirke (Cont'd.)

    also by a people called the Nuba (not
    Sudanese Nuba)

tarak, cloth woven in the Salamat   Martine, 1924, 80, 82–83.
    (Chad), 30 cm × 2 *durah*

tarak, cloth currency in Bagirmi;   Burthe d'Annelet, 1939,
    two types, one 30 cm wide and the other   2:1282.
    50 cm wide

targa, long strips of cloth, wide   OA3.2 and OA15.2/16.1
    but not the widest woven, sewn together   (same informant)
    for clothing and exchanged for slaves in
    al-Sanusi's time; wider than *shakka*

shakka, tchaka, chykeh

    narrow (12 cm) bands of locally woven   Chevalier, 1907, 154.
      cotton cloth, 32 *durah* in length

    narrow band of cotton cloth woven in   Rouget, 1906, 827–28.
      southern Chad, Dar al-Kuti, Dar Runga,
      about 12 cm × 32 *durah*, 6 rolls equaled
      the price of one 6–7-year-old female slave

    wide cotton cloth also called *tarak*   Muraz, 1926, 29.

    indigenous cotton cloth 15 cm × 15 m,   Julien, 1929, 71–73.
      also called *megta*; used as currency for all
      transactions in the area

    loosely woven cloth strips about 40–50 cm   Nachtigal, 1971, 234.
      wide

    shaka, chaka, bands of cotton wider   Carbou, 1913, 197.
      than the *gabag*

    band of cotton cloth 20 cm wide,   Derendinger, 1923, 39, 79.
      also means "to weave"

    tchaka, "to weave"   Assemblées Chrétiennes du
                               Tchad, *Dictionnaire
                               Français-Arabe* (Doba,
                               Tchad, n.d.), 123.

    woven cloth   OA5.2/6.1.

    cloth made by the Runga, Wadaians,   OA8.2.
      Dajo, Kibet, Fongoro

    locally made white cloth   OA17.1.

    locally made wide, white cloth   OA4.1 and OA15.2/16.1
      that came in rolls   (same informant)

    locally made narrow cloth   OA6.2.
      (20 cm wide)

    cloth from the east, also called *sabah*   OA9.1.

shakka, tchaka, chykeh (Cont'd.)

cloth like *sabah*, worn by local leaders in al-Sanusi's time	OA15.1.
cloth from Chad, regions near Mongo, Aboudeia, Am Timan; also called *tukia shakka*	OA13.1.
white cloth, made and commonly worn in Dar Sila	OA14.1.
cloth made by the Runga of Dar Runga, not commonly made in the south	OA22.3.
cloth of local manufacture used as currency	OA5.1.
cloth from Chad, although it was also made in Dar al-Kuti by the Runga and a few Banda; wide like *blingetti* (blankets [Banda])	OA11.1 and OA11.2/12.1 (same informant)
chykeh, one of two types of *tukia*, made of a light material; 4 *chykeh* equaled 1 Spanish *thaler;* other type is called *katkat* (see *tukia* entry)	Al-Tunisi, 1845, 314–15.

tukia, toukia, toqqiya, tokiye (others below)

tekaky, teikau, godany, strips of narrow, black cloth sewn together by Wadaians to make a large, billowy garment; sometimes used as money; sometimes refers to bundles of cotton fibers	Al-Tunisi, 1851, 394–492.
toukkiyeh (pl., *tekaki*), cotton strip of two types: 1) *chykeh*, light and slack material; 2) *katkat*, sturdy and tightly woven material; both are used as currency (4 *chykeh* equaled 1 Spanish *thaler;* 4-1/2 *katkat* equaled the same); used at Ran el-Fyl as "higher" currency, for expensive items	Al-Tunisi, 1845, 314–15, 318–21.
tekaki, cloth tax collected by sultan ᶜAli Dinar of Dar Fur	Theobald, 1965, 215–16.
toqqiya, teqaqi, cotton strips worth 4–5 *terek* in Wadai; 12 *teqaqi* equaled 1 *maqta tromba*, another cloth currency used only for prestige items; "strips of coarse cloth sewn together"	Nachtigal, 1971, 46, 203–4, 253–54.
toqqiya dibdoba, a durable type of *toqqiya*	Nachtigal, 1971, 234.

tukia, toukia, toqqiya, tokiye (others below) (Cont'd.)

toqqiya, strips of cotton cloth;
the *melik al-teqaqi* cared for
the royal stores of *teqaqi* in Wadai,
amassed frequently as tax payments
(*teqaqi* is the plural form of *toqqiya*)

Fisher and Fisher, "Glossary,"
in Nachtigal, 1971, 417.

toukia, a cloth analogous to
shakka and about 24 cm × 16–17
durah; of local manufacture

Chevalier, 1907, 154.

toukia, cloth woven in the Salamat
(Chad), 10 cm × 33 *durah*

Martine, 1924, 80, 82–83.

toukia, locally woven cotton cloth
pieces 24 cm wide and 30 *durah* long

Rouget, 1906, 827–28.

toukia, locally produced cotton
cloth bands 24 cm × 16–17 *durah* and
used as currency in eastern Ubangi-Shari

Kalck, 2:529–31; 3:63–64.

toukia, locally produced bands of cotton
cloth of varied widths and lengths; very
popular and worn as clothing by both men
and women; coarse but solid, a *toukia*
20 cm × 30 *durah* was called a *toukia*
megta; 7–8 *toukia megta* equaled the
price of a 7–8-year-old slave; also used as
currency to purchase items such as foodstuffs, honey, millet beer

Grech, 1924, 41.

toqqiye, indigenous cloth

Derendinger, 1923, 48, 171.

toqqiye, tokkiye, bands of indigenous
cotton cloth used as currency in Wadai

Carbou, 1913, 197.

takyeh, cloth produced by the Runga

Modat, 1912, 272.

tokiye, also called *gabag*, locally woven
cotton cloth in narrow strips

Lethem, 1920, 283.

tokiya, units of cloth currency in Wadai
consisting of 2 long strips of cotton cloth
(3 *durah* × 18 *durah*) made up of smaller
pieces; 1 *tokiya* was valued at 3–4 sheep
among the Mahamid Arabs or 4–5 bul-
lock-loads of millet at high prices

Barth, 1852, 2:660–61.

takiya, bands of homespun cotton
cloth used to pay taxes in the Hausa
quarter in Abeche early in the century

Works, 1976, 70.

tukia, a type of cloth brought from areas
just to the east of Dar al-Kuti; came with a
black cloth called *sabah*

OA1.1.

tukia, toukia, toqqiya, tokiye (others below) (Cont'd.)

narrow and locally made cloth, produced and used apart from the cloth imported by the Jallaba in Dar al-Kuti	OA15.1.
tukia, cloth from Chad, not from across the desert	OA7.2/8.1.
tukia, narrow and fairly light cloth, black in color; two pieces sewn together would be sufficient to make a robe; used as currency among the Runga and some Banda	OA8.2.
tukia, locally produced black cloth, 7 cm to 14 cm in width and produced on looms consisting of a warp strung between two sticks planted in the ground; made in Dar al-Kuti, but imported from Dar Runga, Dar Sila, Wadai, Kibet territory, and Fongoro lands; grouped with *tombassia* and *shakka* as locally produced cloth as opposed to imported cloth; narrower than *tombassia*	OA17.1 (same informant as OA8.2)
tukia, a black, locally produced cloth	OA14.1.
tukia, cloth made in Chad at Aboudeia, Mongo, Am Timan, which cost 2F50 per piece in the early colonial period; available in Chad at that time in exchange for *kombo, jamsinda*, or *dorot*; a roll of this cloth was called a *gabad*	OA13.1.

B.   Cloth imported into Dar al-Kuti and not usually used as currency

chah

chah, muslin or chiffon for turbans	Chevalier, 1907, 154.
chah, muslin or chiffon for turbans	Rouget, 1906, 827–28.
chah, muslin or chiffon for turbans	Kalck, 1970, 3:63–64.

harir

harir, silk	Carbou, 1913, 200.
harir, light silk-like cloth brought to Dar al-Kuti by Jallaba and Fezzanis (same as *tralala* or *hammam tar*)	OA15.2/16.1.
haril, term for silk used in Bagirmi	Gaden, 1909, 85.

masriye, masria bleu, mekiyya

masriye, properly used to refer to cloth in general	Lethem, 1920, 283.
masria bleu, cloth from Cairo (hence the name "Egyptian blue")	Chevalier, 1907, 154.
mekiyya, loosely woven, dark blue rectangular cotton cloths from Egypt	Nachtigal, 1971, 84.
masriye, mekkiye, blue cottons from Egypt	Carbou, 1913, 199.
cotton cloth from Cairo	Rouget, 1906, 827–28.
masria bleu, cloth from Cairo	Kalck, 1970, 3:63–64.

Note: This cloth may be the same as *targa* and/or *jawaz khadar;* see these entries.

jawaz khadar

sets of two pieces of cloth, one blue and the other dark blue or black; translates as "married blues"	OA, notes on a conversation with Abakar Tidjani, Ndele, 8 July 1974.
jawaz khadar, two pieces of black and blue cloth, sold by Jallaba and Fezzanis	OA17.1.

Note: This cloth may be the same as *targa* and/or *masriye*; see these entries.

abu dagig

abu dagig, a kind of white cloth	Lethem, 1920, in Roth-Laly, 1969, 1:17.
abu dagig, a white cloth which when unrolled has a light covering of white powder, hence the name "possessor of flour"	OA, notes on a conversation with Muhammad Abakar, Ndele, July, 1974.

askandriyya, skandriyya

a type of cloth from Egypt, no further description	OA6.2.

langelterra

cloth of English manufacture sold by Fezzanis (perhaps calico)	OA6.2.
black cloth sold by Sudanese traders and worn by women	OA17.1.

kalafarous, calafarous, lafalarous

light yellow trade cloth	Chevalier, 1907, 154.
light yellow trade cloth	Rouget, 1906, 827–28.
light yellow trade cloth	Kalck, 1970, 3:63–64.

sabah, zarak, azrak

sabah, same type of cloth as *zarak*, from east, black in color, called *zarak*	OA11.1.
sabah, black cloth from the east, similar to *bablin*, but wider than cloth sold in Ndele today; same as *shakka*, worn by important people in al-Sanusi's time	OA15.1.
khaleg azraq hafif, light-weight, dark-colored cloth from the Sudan and other northern areas; term is interchangeable with *gabak*; used for bridewealth	OA1.1.
farde zarak, mentioned, no description	OA7.2/8.1.
zarak or *azrak*, black cloth, and the black cloth that went with *jawaz khadar*	OA6.2; OA, notes on a conversation with Abakar Tidjani, Ndele, 8 July 1974.
zarag, blue cotton cloth	S. Hillelson, *Sudan Arabic Texts with Translations and Glossary* (Cambridge, 1935), in Roth-Laly, 1969, 2:204.

sotar

sotar, calico in Bagirmi	Gaden, 1909, 115.

firke, baizun

mentioned, no description,	OA8.2.
multicolored cloth	OA4.1.
silk-like light cloth, sold by Jallaba and Fezzanis	OA6.2.
multicolored cloth, called by both names	OA17.1.
large, colored *pagne*	Kalck, 1970, 3:63–64.
large, colored *pagne*	Chevalier, 1907, 154.
large, colored *pagne*	Rouget, 1906, 827–28.

americani, mericaniyya

mentioned, no description,	OA6.2.
wide and white cloth	OA11.2/12.1.
wide, white manufactured cotton cloth	OA17.1.

dablan, daplan, dabalan, dabelan

white cloth sold by the Jallaba	OA6.2.
white, sturdy cloth	OA17.1.
blue, imported cloth	OA11.2/12.1.

dablan daplan, dabalan, dabelan (Cont'd.)

good, white cotton cloth, superior to *mahmudi*	Fisher and Fisher, "Glossary," in Nachtigal, 1971, 406.
white, cotton cloth; one 30 m piece cost 12 Maria Theresa *thalers*	Nachtigal, 1971, 373–74.
daplan, white calico	Grech, 1924, 39.
dabalan, calico	Lethem, 1920, in Roth-Laly, 2:155.
dabelan, calico	Hillelson, 1935, in Roth-Laly, 2:155.

demour, dammur, bacha-koua

dammur, locally produced cotton cloth	Hillelson, 1935, in Roth-Laly, 2:169.
demmour, shiny lustrous cloth, also called *bacha-koua*	Chevalier, 1907, 154.
demmour, shiny lustrous cloth, also called *bacha-koua*	Rouget, 1906, 826–27.
demmour, shiny lustrous cloth, also called *bacha-koua*	Kalck, 1970, 3:63–64.
dammour, coarse cotton cloth made near Sennar in the Nile region	Burckhardt, 1822, 216.
damour, cotton cloth found in Kordofan, usually woven in Dongolah	Escayrac de Lauture, 1851, 361.
damoor, durable home-woven cloth found in Dem Sulayman (formerly Dem al-Zubayr); said to be as good as cloth from Sennar	Wilson, 1882, 2:216, 274.
dammur, strips of blue and white home-woven cloth used to pay taxes in Dar Fur; white cloths were called *tob*, and blue ones were called *faradieh*; exchange rates were as follows:	Wilson, 1882, 2:276.
40 small *damur* cloths (10 cm x 25 cm) sewn together	1 white *tob*
2 white cloths	1 thaler (= 4s2d–9s9d, English currency)
1 *thaler*	1/2 thaler
1 small blue cloth	Gessi, 1892 translation, 376.
damur, gray cloth woven by the Mandala of southern Dar Fur; the Mandala were said to be the products of intermarriage between non-Muslim slaves and Bagirmi immigrants	

demour, dammur, bacha-koua (Cont'd.)

> *damur*, strips of coarse cotton cloth   Comyn, 1911, 55.
> woven on hand looms in El-Obeid in the
> Sudan; was worn as clothing and also
> served as currency; one strip was valued at
> one shilling in 1911

white, red, and black cloth from Dar al-Kuti

> no further description, but Crampel's   ANF-SOM (Paris), Gabon-
> communications suggested that these   Congo III, dossier 13b,
> types of colored cloth arrived in Dar   Dolisie, notes from the
> al-Kuti from English lands (Nigeria   Paul Crampel expedition
> or the Sudan), and were brought by   (1891).
> Bornoans, Hausa, and Jallaba traders

Note: These types of cloth probably fall into several of the other categories listed in this appendix. Crampel did not give local names for the cloth, so identification is impossible.

toile de treillis

> name given in Crampel's notes for a sturdy,   ANF-SOM (Paris), Gabon-
> white cloth used to make trousers in   Congo III, dossier 13b,
> Dar al-Kuti in 1891; a type of heavy linen   Dolisie, notes from the Paul
> or canvas   Crampel expedition (1891).

Note: This type of cloth probably falls into the categories of locally produced cloth of the same description found elsewhere in this appendix.

Notes

Introduction

1. Studies of the emerging international economy, or the "world system," are numerous. For a broad introduction to the topic and its all-embracing mode of analysis, see Immanuel Wallerstein, *The Modern World-System I: Capitalist Agriculture and the Origins of the European World-Economy in the Sixteenth Century* (New York, 1974), 7–11 and throughout. For a discussion of the links between Africa and the "intercommunicating zone," see Curtin's chapter, "Africa and World History," in *Africa and Africans*, Paul Bohannan and Philip Curtin, eds. (rev. ed.: Garden City, 1971), 223–41.

2. There is as yet no general history at all of Libya or Chad, and only one historical survey of the Central African Republic. While histories of the Sudan are more numerous, none make the effort to relate the Sudanese past to this large area. For the Central African Republic, see Pierre Kalck, "Histoire de la République Centrafricaine des origines à nos jours" (doctorat d'état, Université de Paris, Sorbonne, 1970). Kalck has published three shorter overviews of the history of the Central African Republic with varying emphases (see bibliography). For the Sudan, see P. M. Holt, *A Modern History of the Sudan* (New York, 1961); A. J. Arkell, *A History of the Sudan: From the Earliest Times to 1821*, 2nd ed. (London, 1961); Naᶜum Shuqayr, *Tarikh al-Sudan wa Jughrafiya* (Beirut, 1967).

3. Eric de Dampierre, *Un ancien royaume Bandia du Haut-Oubangui* (Paris, 1967).

4. Neither colonial nor post-independence sources report the extensive ruins at Ndele. When I arrived in Ndele early in 1974, I was surprised to find the remains of numerous buildings and walls strewn over a plateau site roughly 800 meters long and 250 meters wide. In the limited time available before the onset of the rainy season, I located, measured, and photographed many of the buildings on the site. In addition, a cursory survey of pottery remains over various parts of the site served to give an indication of population density. Eventually, however, the rains and rapidly growing vegetation prevented further work that year.

Chapter 1

An Overview: The Lake Chad–Nile Region
and Ubangi-Shari, 1750–1900

1. For a very detailed, although dry, survey of the physical milieu of the Central
    African Republic, see Gérard Grellet, Monique Mainguet, and Pierre
    Soumille, *La République centrafricaine* (Paris, 1982), 5–49.
2. Georges Bruel, *L'Afrique équatoriale française* (Paris, 1930), 80, 84–85;
    Bruel, *La France équatoriale africaine: le pays, les habitants, la colonisa-
    tion, les pouvoirs publics* (Paris, 1935), 38, 54–55. For a very detailed
    description of the *kagas* of the Bamingui River area southwest of Ndele, see
    Pierre Prins, "Les troglodytes du Dar Banda et du Djebel Méla," *Bulletin de
    géographie historique et déscriptive* (1909), 12–26.
3. For a broader consideration of these issues, see Dennis D. Cordell, "The
    Savanna Belt of North Central Africa," in *History of Central Africa*, David
    Birmingham and Phyllis Martin, eds. (London, 1983), 1:30–74.
4. Christian Prioul, *Entre Oubangui et Chari vers 1890* (Paris, 1981), 101–18.
5. On the Kotoko, see Annie M. D. Lebeuf, *Les principautés Kotoko* (Paris,
    1969).
6. The limited linguistic and anthropological research done in this region suggests
    that the peoples living in the sultanates are closely related to each other. See
    A. N. Tucker, *The Eastern Sudanic Languages* (London, 1940), vii–xv,
    1–21; Marie-José Tubiana, *Survivances préislamiques en pays Zaghawa*
    (Paris, 1964). The history of these small states is only now being written,
    thanks in large measure to the work of Ludwien Kapteijns. See her "Mahdist
    Faith and Sudanic Tradition: History of Dar Masalit, 1870–1930" (Doctoral
    dissertation, Universiteit van Amsterdam, 1982); "Dar Sila: The Sultanate
    in Precolonial Times, 1870–1916," *Cahiers d'études africaines* (in press).
    Carbou includes a few paragraphs or pages on each area dealing mainly with
    the history of relations among local peoples, Wadai, and the French; see
    Henri Carbou, *La région du Tchad et du Ouadai* (Paris, 1912), vol. 2. More
    detailed sources include, for Dar Runga: ANT, W53.4, Lt. Fouchet,
    "Généalogie des sultans du Rounga, et historique de la pénétration française
    dans ce pays," Am Timan, 5 August 1911; ANT, W60.1Aa, "Rapport sur
    l'unification des tribus du Dar Rounga," Am Timan, 8 August 1934; for Dar
    Masalit: R. Davies, "The Massalit Sultanate," *Sudan Notes and Records*
    7:2 (1924), 49–62; for Dar Sila: ANT, W52, Capitaine X, "La subdivision
    de Goz-Beida," 1922; ANT, W52.29, Lt. Chambon, "Renseignements sur
    le Sila," Am Dam, 11 July 1911; ANT, W52.34, Chef de la subdivision de
    Goz-Beida, "Renseignements monographiques sur le Sila," Goz-Beida, after
    1926; Lt.-Col. de Burthe d'Annelet, *A travers l'Afrique française du Sénégal
    au Cameroun par les confins libyens*, 2 vols. (Paris, 1939), ch. 3 ("D'Adré
    à Goz Beida"), 1164–1206; Hilaire, "L'Occupation du Dar-Sila: rapport du
    Colonel Hilaire sur les opérations du 13 au 17 mai 1916 et la ré-occupation

de Goz-Beida," *AF-RC* 27:5–6 (1917), 105–18; for the Salamat: F. Martine, "Essai sur l'histoire du pays Salamat et les moeurs et coutumes de ses habitants," *BSRC* 5 (1924), 19–88; ANT, W45, W46, W49, W53, W60, series of colonial reports on the area.

7. OA7.2/8.1; OA12.2; OA20.2; OA20.3; Paul Brunache, *Le centre de l'Afrique—autour du Tchad* (Paris, 1894), 218; Joseph Fortier, ed., *Le mythe et les contes de Sou en pays Mbai-Moissala* (Paris, 1967), 11–16, 21–22. On the precolonial history of the Sara, see in general, Gaya J. Kogongar, "Introduction à la vie et à l'histoire pré-coloniale des populations Sara du Tchad" (doctoral thesis [3e cycle], Université de Paris, Sorbonne, 1971).

8. In the literature, these units would be classified as "stateless societies" in great distinction to state organizations like Dar Fur. In fact, they were probably quite similar to the core Fur society. See the meticulous survey by Stefano Santandrea, *Ethno-Geography of the Bahr el Ghazal (Sudan): An Attempt at Historical Reconstruction* (Bologna, 1981), 57–124.

9. George Murdock, *Africa: Its Peoples and Their Culture History* (New York, 1959), map in pocket at end; Joseph H. Greenberg, *The Languages of Africa* (Bloomington, 1966), 172, 174, 176.

10. Prioul, *Entre Oubangui et Chari*, 31–48.

11. Frederick Jackson Turner, *The Frontier in American History* (New York, 1920); Leonard Thompson and Howard Lamar, "Comparative Frontier History," in *The Frontier in History: North America and Southern Africa Compared*, Lamar and Thompson, eds. (New Haven, 1981), 3–13.

12. Thompson and Lamar, "Comparative Frontier History," 7.

13. Ibid., 9.

14. Ibid.

15. OA7.2/8.1; OA9.2/10.1; OA11.1; OA11.2/12.1; OA19.1/20.1; OA22.1.

16. Grech, "Essai sur le Dar Kouti au temps de Snoussi," *BSRC* 4 (1924), 51.

17. For surveys of Arabic sources relating to Africa, see Joseph M. Cuoq, ed. and trans., *Recueil des sources arabes concernant l'Afrique occidentale du VIIIᵉ au XVIᵉ siècle (Bilad al-Sudan)* (Paris, 1975); Tadeusz Lewicki, *Arabic External Sources for the History of Africa to the South of Sahara* (London, 1974); Nehemia Levtzion and J. F. P. Hopkins, eds., *Corpus of Arabic Sources for West African History* (Cambridge, 1980).

18. Mohammed ibn-Omar El-Tounsy (Muhammad ibn ᶜUmar al-Tunisi), *Voyage au Ouaday*, trans. S. Perron (Paris, 1851), 276–81 and maps; M. Jomard, "Préface," El-Tounsy (al-Tunisi), *Voyage au Darfour*, trans. S. Perron (Paris, 1845), xxvii–xxviii; M. U. J. Seetzen, "Nouveaux renseignements sur l'intérieur de l'Afrique," *Annales des voyages, de la géographie, et de l'histoire* 21 (1813), 179. By the late nineteenth century, the ethnic significance of the term Fertit was completely lost. Describing the peoples south of Dar Fur, Nachtigal wrote that "all these Pagan tribes are comprised under the name of the Fertit, and we cannot at present distinguish them from each other, either physically or ethnographically." See Gustav Nachtigal, *Sahara and Sudan IV: Wadai and Darfur*, trans. Humphrey J. Fisher and Allan G. B.

Fisher (Berkeley, 1971), 357.

19.   Al-Tunisi listed the following peoples south of Wadai and Dar Fur: Chala, Raunga, Sila, Binga, Routou, Kara, Goula, Faraougueh, Fangorah (or Fongoroh), Bendallah, Baya (divided into Baya-Fara and Baya-Kereitcheh), Bendah (divided into Bendah-Djoukou and Bendah-Yamyam), Djenakherah, Kirdy, Dengo, and Kouka (all *sic*). See al-Tunisi, *Voyage au Ouaday*, 280–81.

20.   Al-Tunisi, *Voyage au Ouaday*, 271–72; Kalck, "Histoire," 1:150; Félix Chapiseau, *Au pays de l'esclavage: moeurs et coutumes de l'Afrique centrale, d'après les notes recueillies par Béhagle* (Paris,1900), 159.

21.   Al-Tunisi, *Voyage au Ouaday*, 275. In an effort to determine the limits of the non-Muslim lands, the Furians headed south until they came to a body of water so wide that it was impossible to discern individuals on the opposite shore. Because they had no boats, the northerners turned back. Al-Tunisi wrote that this mission took place during the reign of Sultan ᶜUmar of Dar Fur, a brother of Sultan Tyrab, but the only Sultan ᶜUmar related to Tyrab was a cousin named ᶜUmar Lel who ruled from 1730 to 1752/53. Al-Tunisi claimed to have talked with an old man who accompanied the expedition, which suggests that the mission occurred late in ᶜUmar's reign. See Rex S. O'Fahey and J. L. Spaulding, *Kingdoms of the Sudan* (London, 1974), 129–33.

22.   On the infiltration of the Jallaba into the southwestern Sudan, see Robert O. Collins, "Sudanese Factors in the History of the Congo and Central West Africa in the Nineteenth Century," in *Sudan in Africa*, Yusuf Fadl Hasan, ed. (Khartoum, 1971), 160; Richard Gray, *History of the Southern Sudan, 1839–1889* (Oxford, 1961), 65–66. For a succinct history of the Islamic frontier south of Dar Fur, see R. S. O'Fahey, "Fur and Fartit: The History of a Frontier," in *Culture History in the Southern Sudan: Archaeology, Linguistics and Ethnohistory*, John Mack and Peter Robertshaw, eds. (Nairobi, 1982), 75–87.

23.   Edmond de Cadalvene and J. de Breuvery, "Observations sur quelques points géographiques de la carte du Dar-Four, par le Sultan Teima, d'après les renseignements fournis par les Djellabs," in their *L'Egypte et la Turquie de 1829 à 1836*, 2 vols. (Paris, 1836), 2:522.

24.   William George B. Browne, *Travels in Africa, Egypt, and Syria from the Year 1792 to 1798* (London, 1806), 325, 354–57, 570, map.

25.   Al-Tunisi, *Voyage au Ouaday*, 280–81, 485; Seetzen, "Nouvelles recherches sur l'intérieur de l'Afrique," *Annales des voyages, de la géographie, et de l'histoire* 19 (1812), 180; John Lewis Burckhardt, *Travels in Nubia* (London, 1822), 290.

26.   Heinrich Barth, "Account of Two Expeditions in Central Africa by the Furanys," *Journal of the Royal Geographical Society of London* 23 (1853), 120–22. These expeditions are not mentioned in Barth's monumental *Travels and Discoveries in North and Central, Africa*, 3 vols. (London, 1857–59). This edition was reprinted in 1965 (London: Frank Cass). Barth's Muslim colleague, like those of al-Tunisi, said that the river in the far south was so wide that it was impossible to distinguish people on the opposite bank. More-

over, the expeditions also turned back because they could not cross to the other shore.

27. Fulgence Fresnel, "Mémoire sur le Waday: notice historique et géographique sur le Waday et les relations de cet empire avec la côte septentrionale de l'Afrique," *Bulletin de la société de géographie de Paris*, 3ᵉ serie, N° 11 (1849), 16, 25; N° 13 (1850), 97.

28. Ignatius Pallme, *Travels in Kordofan* (London, 1844), 293, 346–47.

29. O'Fahey and Spaulding, *Kingdoms of the Sudan*, 173, 176–79; R. S. O'Fahey, "Slavery and the Slave Trade in Dar Fur," *JAH* 14:1 (1973), 37, 39–42. Some Fur clearly saw Egyptian military and administrative innovations as sources of Egypt's power. A claimant to the Fur throne who arrived in Cairo in hopes of convincing Muhammad ᶜAli to make him sultan met S. Perron in the Egyptian capital and invited him to visit the sultanate following his installation. He promised great changes: "When I return to Dar Fur, you must come visit the land. I will inaugurate there the modes of warfare that I have seen here; I will introduce another method of administration. I have seen Egypt and Muhammad ᶜAli." See Perron's note in al-Tunisi, *Voyage au Darfour*, 156n1.

30. Nachtigal, *Sahara and Sudan IV*, 308–13; O'Fahey and Spaulding, *Kingdoms of the Sudan*, 176–79.

31. El-Zubeir Pasha, *Black Ivory, or the Story of El-Zubeir Pasha, Slaver and Sultan, as Told by Himself*, trans. H. C. Jackson (New York, 1970), 32; O'Fahey and Spaulding, *Kingdoms of the Sudan*, 179.

32. Nachtigal, *Sahara and Sudan IV*, 365. For a discussion of the "Forty-Day Road," one of the major trans-Saharan routes that connected Dar Fur with Egypt, see W. B. K. Shaw, "Darb al-Arbaᶜ in," *Sudan Notes and Records* 12: 1 (1929), 63–71; Terence Walz, *Trade between Egypt and Bilad as-Sudan, 1700–1820* (Paris and Cairo, 1978), 3–9.

33. El-Zubeir, *Black Ivory*, 68; O'Fahey and Spaulding, *Kingdoms of the Sudan*, 179–83, 186.

34. For a history of Dar Fur during the Mahdiya, see Musa al-Mubarak al-Hasan, *Tarikh Darfur al-siyasi, 1882–1898* (Khartoum, c. 1970). The largely unsuccessful efforts of the Mahdists to conquer the non-Muslim Bahr al-Ghazal region are chronicled in Robert O. Collins, *The Southern Sudan, 1883–1898: A Struggle for Control* (New Haven, 1962), 22–42, 51–54, 172–81.

35. There are at least six divergent kinglists for Wadai, and to date few efforts have been made to reconcile them. Further efforts to reconcile these varying chronologies will probably have to await further fieldwork and research. For the kinglists, see Marie-José Tubiana, "Un document inédit sur les sultans de Wadday," *Cahiers d'études africaines* 2 (1960), 96–109.

36. See Dennis D. Cordell, "Eastern Libya, Wadai, and the Sanusiya: A Tariqa and a Trade Route," *JAH* 18:1 (1977), 21–36, for a detailed study of Wadaian trade with North Africa along this route in the nineteenth century.

37. Al-Tunisi, *Voyage au Ouaday*, 165–67, 171, 193–95, 205–6; Burckhardt, *Travels*, 435, 440; Barth, *Travels*, 2:551–53, 644–45; Nachtigal, *Sahara and Sudan IV*, 214–15; Henri Gaden, "Les états musulmans de l'Afrique

centrale et leurs rapports avec La Mecque et Constantinople," *Questions diplomatiques et coloniales*, t. 24 (1907), 439. It should be strongly emphasized here that this narrative is based on information collected by the authors in Wadai or from Wadaians resident in other Muslim states of the desert fringe. Data from Dar Sila, Dar Tama, and Dar Runga may well challenge the Wadaian point of view. My work in the southern sultanate of Dar al-Kuti highlights some discrepancies. To cite but a minor example dealing with the areas invaded by Sabun, sources in Dar Sila recall a clash with the sultan, but maintain that the Wadaians were defeated. See ANT, W.52, Capitaine X, "La Subdivision de Goz-Beida," 1922, a history of Dar Sila partially based on oral traditions collected locally.

38. Burckhardt, *Travels*, 440.
39. Modat, "Une tournée en pays Fertyt," *AF-RC* 22:7 (July 1912), 271.
40. Nachtigal, *Sahara and Sudan IV*, 215–21; Fresnel, "Mémoire sur le Waday," (1849), 64–65.
41. Emile Julien, "Le Dar-Ouadai," *AF-RC* 14:2 (February 1904), 52–53; P. H. S. d'Escayrac de Lauture, *Mémoire sur le Soudan* (Paris, 1855–56), 1:78 (reprinted from the *Bulletin de la société de géographie de Paris*, 4ᵉ série, N° 10 [1855–56]); Nachtigal, *Sahara and Sudan IV*, 221–24.
42. Fresnel, "Mémoire sur le Waday" (1850), 84–86.
43. For a survey of these problems, see Jeffrey E. Hayer, "A Political History of the Maba Sultanate of Wadai: 1635–1912" (M.A. thesis, University of Wisconsin, Madison, 1975), 29–32.
44. For details, see Nachtigal, *Sahara and Sudan IV*, 56–57, 68–69, 128–30; Carbou, *La région*, 2:122–24; Julien, "Le Dar Ouadai," 56–57.
45. Nachtigal, *Sahara and Sudan IV*, 225–26.
46. ANF-SOM (Paris), Papiers Julien, 6P.A. (Papiers d'Agents), ctn. 1, pièce 1, "Annexe No. 2: Généalogie des Sultans Roungas et Senoussiens," 153; Julien, "Le Ouadai," 56; Carbou, *La région*, 2:124, 126; Gustav Nachtigal, *Sahara und Sudan: Ergebnisse Sechsjähriger Reisen in Afrika*, 3 vols. (1879–89; Graz, 1967), 2:723. Estimates of the number of captives vary. The twenty to thirty thousand figure comes from Carbou. Nachtigal put the total between twelve and fifteen thousand, but admitted that his figures were perhaps too low (Nachtigal, *Sahara and Sudan IV*, 67).
47. The French archives and colonial publications are filled with accounts of these campaigns after 1900. For a review of early French military efforts in Chad, see Pierre Gentil, *La conquête du Tchad (1894–1916)*, 2 vols. (Château de Vincennes, 1971).
48. Nachtigal, *Sahara and Sudan IV*, 98, 177, 182; Hayer, "A Political History of the Maba Sultanate of Wadai," 60, 62.
49. For details, see Cordell, "Eastern Libya, Wadai, and the Sanusiya," 31–32.
50. Julien, "Le Dar Ouadai," 57; John A. Works, Jr., *Pilgrims in a Strange Land: Hausa Communities in Chad* (New York, 1976), 65.
51. Georg Schweinfurth, *The Heart of Africa: Three Years' Travels and Adventures in the Unexplored Regions of Central Africa, 1868–1871*, trans. Ellen Frewer (New York, 1874), 2:410–11; ANF-SOM (Aix), 2D58, M.

Defrance (Ministre plenipotentiare de la République Française au Caire) to M. Poincaré (Président du Conseil, Ministre des Affaires Etrangères), "Entretien avec Abdallah Kahhal, arrivé au Caire avec des caravaniers senoussis chargés d'acheter des armes pour Ali Dinar," Cairo, 25 March 1912. Defrance's informant reported that North African and Cairene merchants carried on a rich trade with North Central Africa in the 1880s. But as European pressure mounted—in Egypt in the 1880s and in the Sudan in the following decade—the trade routes shifted westward to Wadai, Benghazi, and Tripoli. According to the informant, some routes also went through Dar Fur at this time.

52. Works, *Pilgrims in a Strange Land*, 59.
53. Julien, "Le Dar Ouadai," 61. Kalck writes that the Wadai sultan had a minister for "pagan affairs in the south" who was responsible for commercial relations between Abeche and the Ubangi area. I suspect that he is referring to the *caqid al-Salamat* or one of his *kursis* (representatives [Arabic]) and not to an official responsible for commercial affairs only. See Pierre Kalck, *Réalités oubanguiennes* (Paris, 1959), 70.
54. ANF-SOM (Aix), 4(3)D55, nine Arabic letters between Wadaian merchants and Sultan Rafai, Rafai, April–May, 1896. The letters do not indicate what Rafai was to send north in exchange for the animals, but given the prevailing pattern of trade in the region, slaves, ivory, and firearms acquired from Belgian traders in the Congo Independent State probably comprised an important portion of the exports.
55. Stefano Santandrea, *A Tribal History of the Western Bahr el-Ghazal* (Bologna, 1964), 229–30; Modat, "Une tournée en pays Fertyt," *AF-RC* 22:5 (May 1912), 193; Maurice Delafosse, *Enquête coloniale dans l'Afrique française* (Paris, 1930), 109.
56. AMBB, no. 167 (Bangassou), Boucher, Chef de la Circonscription du Dar Kouti oriental, "Monographe sur Dar Kouti oriental," Birao, 31 December 1934; Modat, "*Une tournée*," 277.
57. Browne, *Travels*, 356; Modat, "Une tournée," 275–76.
58. Barth, *Travels*, 2:657; Fresnel, "Mémoire sur le Waday" (1849), 19.
59. Delafosse, *Enquête coloniale*, 119.
60. The Kresh are also sometimes called the Kpala or Gbaya, names of important subgroups. These Gbaya are distinct from the western Gbaya who live in the Cameroon and western Central African Republic.
61. Santandrea, *A Tribal History*, 191, 207; Adolphe de Calonne-Beaufaict, *Azande: Introduction à une ethnographie générale des bassins de l'Ubangi-Uélé et de l'Aruwimi* (Brussels, 1921), 132.
62. D. C. E. Comyn, *Service and Sport in the Sudan* (London, 1911), 258; Carbou, *La région*, 2:232; Modat, "Une tournée," 285; Tucker, *The Eastern Sudanic Languages*, 51. With the exception of Goula, Greenberg puts these languages and their various dialects together as a northwestern cluster of the Central Sudanic languages (II.E.2), themselves a subgroup of the Shari-Nile family. Greenberg's lexical data were probably not extensive, yet he apparently discerned sufficient similarity to classify them together. See Greenberg,

The Languages of Africa, 85–129, 162–71, 177.

63. The assassination of al-Sanusi in 1911 led many of the Kresh in Ndele to re-
     turn to their homelands in the east. By 1915, most of the remaining Kresh
     lived once again in the watershed region, which by then roughly delimited the
     border between the French Congo and the Anglo-Egyptian Sudan. But the
     raids and forced migrations had taken their toll on the Kresh population, and
     in the 1950s, the tax-rolls of the Sudan included only 1,769 Kresh taxpayers
     (heads of households) for this entire area. In the Central African Republic
     today the Kresh are of historical importance only; no more than a few Kresh
     villages remain in the entire country. Santandrea, *A Tribal History*, 193,
     197, 199, 204, 206; Pierre Kalck, *Central African Republic: A Failure in
     de-Colonisation*, trans. Barbara Thomson (London, 1971), 18.
64. Al-Tunisi, *Voyage au Ouaday*, 275; Jomard, "Préface," xxvii–xxviii.
65. Kalck, "Histoire," 1:171–72, 212–13, 244. In 1958 the population of the
     Mobaye district, which encompasses most of this region, was 12.1 individ-
     uals per square kilometer, and the population density of the Ubangi-Shari
     colony as a whole was 1.86 persons per square kilometer.
66. Casimir Léon Maistre, *A travers l'Afrique centrale du Congo au Niger,
     1892–1893* (Paris, 1895), 35; Kalck, "Histoire," 1:213; 2:403. A lengthy
     list of the migrations of many of the Banda subgroups is included in Modat,
     "Une tournée," 277–80. Delafosse quoted Modat and condensed his list in
     1930, and Tucker in turn quoted Delafosse quoting Modat; Bruel published a
     list partially based on Modat as well. See Delafosse, *Enquête coloniale*, 99;
     Tucker, *The Eastern Sudanic Languages*, 52–53; Bruel, *La France
     équatoriale africaine*, 285–87. For a discussion of the early history of the
     Banda and related Ubangian peoples, see Douglas E. Saxon, "Linguistic
     Evidence for the Eastward Spread of Ubangian Peoples," in *The Archaeo-
     logical and Linguistic Reconstruction of African History*, Christopher Ehret
     and Merrick Posnansky, eds. (Berkeley and Los Angeles, 1982), 66–77.
67. Nachtigal, *Sahara and Sudan IV*, 318–19; ANF-SOM (Paris), Gabon-
     Congo II, dossier 5; Grech, "Travail d'inspection: Soudan central, sultans
     zandés, et l'occupation française," Dem Ziber, 25 June 1897; Richard Hill,
     A Biographical Dictionary of the Anglo-Egyptian Sudan (London, 1951),
     390–91; Kalck, "Histoire," 1:213. For al-Zubayr's own version of events
     during these years, see El-Zubeir, *Black Ivory*, 9–73.
68. Collins, *The Southern Sudan*, 14–16; Santandrea, *A Tribal History*, 30; El-
     Zubeir, *Black Ivory*, 32; Modat, "Une tournée en pays Fertyt" *AF* 22:6
     (June 1912), 224–25; Gray, *History of the Southern Sudan*, 68; Kalck,
     "Histoire," 1:252.
69. Emile Julien, "Mohamed-es-Senoussi et ses états," *BSRC* 7 (1925), 106;
     El-Zubeir, *Black Ivory*, 73; Kalck, *Central African Republic*, 35; Modat,
     "Une tournée," 225, 227–28; R. A. Adeleye, "Rabih b. Fadlallah, 1879–
     1893: Exploits and Impact on Political Relations in Central Sudan," *Journal
     of the Historical Society of Nigeria* 5:2 (June 1970), 225–26; Hill, *A Bio-
     graphical Dictionary*, 390–91.
70. For other traditions, see Fernand Gaud, *Les Mandja (Congo-Français)*

(Brussels, 1911), 97, 107.

71.   Later the group split and some Ngura went back to the Ouaka River where they accepted Linda domination. See BENA (Bangui), Circonscription du Kémo-Gribingui, folder entitled "Les Ungourras: correspondance départ (19-4-1906 au 21-2-1908)," Le chef de poste, "Ngouras 1906—correspondance départ" (livre de poste, district des Mbrès). (The archival documents at ENA are not classified or numbered, necessitating this lengthy form of citation.) For a survey of these documents as well as those in the national archives in Chad, see Dennis D. Cordell, "Archival Report: Research Resources in Chad and the Central African Republic," *History in Africa* 2 (1975), 217–20.

72.   Modat, "Une tournée," 221, 279. The raiders in this case may have been from Dar Fur and not the Khartoumer settlements. Modat, who collected oral traditions among these Banda, claimed that the movement took place ten generations earlier, in which case the marauders obviously would not have been Khartoumers. But given the shallow depth of most Banda traditions, it seems very unlikely that the migrations occurred this long ago. Until further evidence turns up, a more cautious dating to the era of al-Zubayr seems in order. Marba in Ndele today make little distinction between the Fur and the Khartoumers, and this may have been the case in Modat's time as well.

73.   OA9.1; OA9.2/10.1.

74.   OA3.2; OA4.1; OA9.1; OA11.1; OA11.2/12.1; OA15.2/16.1.

Chapter 2

Dar al-Kuti: Early Muslim Settlement, Commerce, and Islam

1.   The dates used to delimit the periods should be thought of as times of transition, and not as exact indicators of beginnings and ends. This approach recommends itself for three reasons. First, it accurately reflects the nature of the written sources, which seldom give precise dates for events in the nineteenth century. Second, this periodization coincides well with the interpretation offered by Muslim and non-Muslim informants concerning the history of Dar al-Kuti. Finally and most important, the major political and economic shifts affecting the area rarely occurred abruptly.

2.   Barth, *Travels*, 2:652; Nachtigal, *Sahara and Sudan IV*, map at end.

3.   All informants, but see OA3.2 in particular.

4.   Grech, "Essai sur le Dar Kouti," 30–31; Auguste Chevalier, *Mission Chari–lac Tchad, 1902–1904: L'Afrique Centrale Française, récit du voyage de la mission* (Paris, 1907), 209–11; Auguste Chevalier, "Exploration scientifique dans les états de Snoussi, sultan du Dar-el-Kouti," *La Géographie* 8 (1903), 89–90.

5.   This misunderstanding was reflected in the administrative schema in the early colonial period. The plan included a "Dar-Kouti" district stretching eastward

to the Sudanese border. The French later redrew the administrative boundaries, and provided for a Dar al-Kuti subdivision whose area was restricted to the lands adjacent to the Aouk. Since independence, the Central African Republic government has administered the region as the "Commune de Moyen Exercice du Dar-el-Kouti." ANF-SOM (Aix), 4(3)D21, Schmoll, "Rapport de tournée, nord-est du Dar-Kouti," Affaires politiques N° 78, Ndele, 26 March 1914; ANF-SOM (Aix), 4(3)D27, Diette, "Rapport du 1er trimestre 1920," Bangui, 1 December 1920, 1–9; Bruel, *L'Afrique équatoriale française* (Paris, 1930), 233; APBB, Préfecture du Bamingui-Bangoran, "Rapport sur la Préfecture pour la conférence des Préfets, 1970," Ndele, 1970.

6. OA3.2; OA5.1; OA5.2/6.1; OA11.2/12.1; OA13.1; OA14.2; OA17.2/18.1; OA21.1; OA22.1; Emile Julien, "Mohamed-es-Senoussi," *BSRC* 10 (1929), 60; Auguste Chevalier, "De l'Oubangui au lac Tchad à travers le bassin du Chari," *La Géographie*, 9 (1904), 353; Modat, "Une tournée," 230.

7. Most of this information comes from personal observation. Chevalier included similar descriptions in his writings on the area. For a summary, see Chevalier, "Exploration scientifique dans les états de Snoussi," 89–90. Detailed information on the region may be found in Chevalier, *Mission*, 165–224; and a general discussion of gallery forests is appended to the same volume (747–53). Also see Roger Sillans, *Les savanes de l'Afrique centrale* (Paris, 1958).

8. OA5.2/6.1; OA6.2; OA7.2/8.1; OA8.2; OA21.1.

9. OA8.2; OA14.2; OA20.2; OA20.3; OA21.1; OA21.4; OA22.1. Also personal observation; and ANF-SOM (Aix), 4(3)D21, Schmoll, "Rapport de tournée," 11; Chevalier, *Mission*, 224; H. Courtet, "La mouche tsétsé," appended to Chevalier, *Mission*, 730–31.

10. Among them, OA3.2; OA5.1; OA8.2; OA20.3; OA21.1; OA21.4; Modat, "Une tournée," 275–76; Bruel, *La France équatoriale africaine*, 281–82.

11. The Lutos are probably the Routou mentioned in al-Tunisi, *Voyage au Ouaday*, 280–81; Modat, "Une tournée," 275–76; and Gaston Jules Decorse, *Du Congo au lac Tchad: la brousse telle qu'elle est, et les gens tels qu'ils sont (Mission Chari-lac Tchad, 1902–1904)* (Paris, 1906), 77–78. Since no single transcriptions for these names predominate in the written sources on Dar al-Kuti, I have generally relied on my informants' pronunciations as guides in spelling.

12. Prioul, *Entre Oubangui et Chari*, 47.

13. Maurice Gaudefroy-Demombynes, *Documents sur les langues de l'Oubangui-Chari* (Paris, 1906), 24–63 (extract from the *Actes du XIVᵉ Congrès International des Orientalistes*, vol. 2); Henri Gaden, *Essai de grammaire de la langue baguirmienne, suivi de textes et de vocabulaires baguirmien-français et français-baguirmien* (Paris, 1909), 1–2, 35–38; OA7.2/8.1; OA12.2; OA, notes on a conversation with R. P. DeMoustier, priest at Miamane (118 kilometers west of Ndele), Ndele, 26 August 1974. Comparing what I know of Sara Majingay (learned as a Peace Corps volunteer in southeastern Chad) with Nduka spoken in Dar al-Kuti, I come to the

same conclusion. Greenberg also classifies these languages together. See Greenberg, *The Languages of Africa*, 162–77.

14. For a sampling, see Fernand Rouget, *L'expansion coloniale au Congo-français* (Paris, 1906), 391–94; AAV (Vincennes), A.E.F., L'Oubangui-Chari, serie O³, ctn. 1, "Lettre N° 19 du 18 Avril 1910 du Capitaine Modat, Commandant la Circonscription de N'Dele à Monsieur le Lieutenant-Gouverneur de l'Oubangui-Chari à Bangui, Notice ethnographique sur les populations du Dar-Kouti," Ndele, 18 April 1910 (copy made 10 October 1955 by J. Carré in Ndele); Modat, "Une tournée," 275–76; Decorse, *Du Congo au Lac Tchad*, 77–78; Bruel, *La France équatoriale africaine*, 281–82; Tucker, *The Eastern Sudanic Languages*, ii–iii, 11–12; J. P. Caprile and J. Fédry, *Le Groupe des langues "sara" (République du Tchad)* (Lyon, 1969), throughout.

15. It is highly unlikely that the Nduka peoples are a mixed Banda-Kresh group as Kalck suggests. Only Modat posited close ties between the Nduka and Banda, and then changed his mind, grouping the Nduka with the Sara and the Barma (Bagirmi). See Kalck, "Histoire," 1:98; Modat references are included in the preceding note.

16. The names of six of these groups appear in the oral testimonies: Gollo, Vanga or Baie, Kutikola, Kutikof(v)o, Doggo, and Mavline. See OA6.2; OA7.2/8.1; OA8.2; OA20.2; OA20.3; OA22.1; OA22.2; OA, notes on a conversation with Abakar Tidjani, Runga-Nduka, Ndele, 1 June 1974; OA, notes on a conversation with Souia, Nduka Doggo, Village of Manga, 1 October 1974 (collected by Moussa Josef-Puskas Riky). In light of the earlier discussion of the word *kuti*, it is interesting to note that Souia claimed that the name Kutikola referred to the woods where this Nduka group resided.

17. OA6.2; OA8.2; OA22.1. The names of many of these groups corresponded with names of prominent topographical features in the neighborhood. For example, the Gollo lived near the Miangoulou ("stream of the Gollo"), while the Kutikola were located in or near the woods (kuti) of the same name (OA9.1; OA, notes on a conversation with Souia).

18. OA7.2/8.1; OA13.1; OA14.1; OA20.2; OA20.3; OA21.4; OA22.1; OA22.3; OA23.1; OA, notes on a conversation with Zacharia Kouzoubali, Nduka Doggo, Village of Manga, 30 September 1974 (collected by Moussa Josef-Puskas Riky); OA, notes on a conversation with Souia. Gaudefroy-Demombynes recorded a very similar Nduka word for chief (*garije*) in his Barma language group vocabulary. See Gaudefroy-Demombynes, *Documents*, 28.

19. Robert Jaulin, *La mort Sara* (Paris, 1967), throughout, but see particularly 16–35, 45, 58–119, 121–23, 141–57, 194–210. For a broader survey, see Cordell, "The Savanna Belt of North Central Africa." During the colonial era, political power among the Sara became more centralized with the appointment of local chiefs by the French and the delegation of wide-ranging powers to them. Among the Nduka, this change also occurred, but not to so great a degree.

20. Gabriel Gosselin, *Travail et changement social en pays Gbeya (R.C.A.)*

(Paris, 1972), 82–87; William Samarin, personal communication, 15 June 1983.

21. Pierre Kalck, "Les savanes centrafricaines," in *Histoire générale de l'Afrique noire*, Hubert Deschamps, ed. (Paris, 1971), 2:197. François Ramm, "Le peuplement des savanes de l'Afrique centrale: essai historique," transcription of a lecture delivered 13 December 1972 and printed in *Cahiers du Centre Protestant de la Jeunesse* (Bangui, n.d. but probably early 1973), unpaginated (p. 18 of transcription). The continued existence of a parent Runga group in Dar Runga, and the existence of basic linguistic differences among the Runga, Sara, and Banda languages, show that the Runga were originally a distinct population. Recognizing these differences, Modat, Gaudefroy-Demombynes, and Carbou all placed the Runga in a category apart from the Sara and Banda, while at the same time noting a high degree of intermarriage among them in Dar al-Kuti. See OA5.2/6.1; OA13.1; OA21.4; OA22.1; Gaudefroy-Demombynes, *Documents*, 1–70, 144–52; Modat, "Une tournée," 271; Carbou, *La région*, 2:222–23, 227–29.

22. Greenberg, *The Languages of Africa*, 163–64, 170, 178; Browne, *Travels in Africa*, 357–59; Jomard, "Préface," lii–liii; Gaudefroy-Demombynes, *Documents*, 1–70, 144–52. Bruel also opted for classing Sara, Banda, and Runga in separate families. See Bruel, *La France équatoriale africaine*, 159–60.

23. OA5.1; OA7.1; OA, notes on a conversation with Sultan-Maire Muhammad al-Sanusi, Ndele, 3 May 1974.

24. For the Runga *kunus*, see OA5.2/6.1; OA7.2/8.1; OA14.2. On the Zaghawa, see Tubiana, *Survivances préislamiques*, 198. The earliest description of Runga religion, by Pallme, may be in large measure fanciful, but is a clear indication of Runga religion's non-Islamic character: "The religion of the natives is exceedingly simple; they believe in the existence of an invisible deity who produces water, namely rain, and makes their fruit to grow. They pay, further, great respect to persons afflicted with fatuity, and believe them to be prophets of the invisible God. They build peculiar huts for these beings, more like birdcages than houses, where they are confined, and provided with food. Before sunset, the populace visits them to consult them for advice, and every answer, be it ever so nonsensical, is regarded as an oracle, and firmly believed" (*Travels in Kordofan*, 350–51, notes).

25. As with the Nduka, the list of Runga subgroups is not entirely consistent from informant to informant, but there is a high degree of agreement among them. The Runga of Dar al-Kuti are divided into the Bagrim (also called Bagari), Issa-Tinia, Mangele, and Adimi; Dewau, Bua, and Tunjur populations live in both Dar al-Kuti and Dar Runga; and the northern Runga include the ᶜAgid and the Assamoya (OA6.2; OA8.2; OA13.1; OA21.1; OA22.1; OA, notes on a conversation with Abakar Tidjani, 1 June 1974). Information collected in Dar Runga itself would undoubtedly yield the names of other subgroups in the north.

26. OA13.1; OA14.1. Again, research in Dar Runga might reveal that the northern Runga view their southern counterparts very differently, given the

high degree of intermarriage between the Runga and non-Muslims in Dar al-Kuti.

27. Personal observation; OA11.1; OA13.1; OA14.2; OA15.2/16.1; OA19.1/20.1; OA23.2; OA24.1; Harold D. Nelson et al., *Area Handbook for Chad* (Washington, 1972), 62; ANT, W45.11A, "Rapport trimestriel du Salamat," 2ᵉ trimestre, Am Timan, 1928; ANT, W45.32B, "Rapport de la tournée effectuée du 10 février au 2 mars 1933 inclus par M. le Chef de la Circonscription du Salamat," Am Timan, 1933; ANT, W46.8, Chef de Subdivision de Mangueigne, "Rapport de tournée N° 1, 11 mai–22 mai 1941," Mangueigne, 1941; ANF-SOM (Aix), 4(3)D21, Ripault, "Rapport sur la reconnaissance executée dans la région Aouk-Kameur du 4 au 21 février 1914," Ouanda-Djale, 24 February 1914, in file "Dar-Kouti 1914"; Carbou, *La région*, 2:224–25; Modat, "Une tournée," 271–73; Chevalier, *Mission*, 229–30; Nachtigal, *Sahara and Sudan IV*, 141–42.

28. The references are admittedly vague for this early period. Al-Tunisi, for example, mentioned the "Routou," the "Banda Djoukou," and the "Dengo," locating them all in the approximate area of Dar al-Kuti. As suggested earlier (note 11), "Routou" is probably a reference to the Lutos, an Nduka subgroup. "Djoukou" may well refer to the Nduka, since it is clear that al-Tunisi thought them to be different from other Banda. "Dengo" has a more obvious referent: the large Sara subgroup called the Dinjo who live in western Dar al-Kuti. See al-Tunisi, *Voyage au Ouaday*, 280–1.

29. OA5.1; OA7.2/8.1; OA8.2; OA13.1; OA17.2/18.1; OA21.4; OA, notes on a conversation with Moustapha Seleman, Nduka Doggo, Village of Manga, 3 October 1974 (collected by Moussa Josef-Puskas Riky); Chapiseau, *Au pays de l'esclavage*, 124–25; Carbou, *La région*, 2:223. During his stay in Wadai in the early nineteenth century, al-Tunisi noted that the sultan sent out raiding parties each year to take captives among the non-Muslim peoples in the south. He did not indicate where these ghazzias took place, but the limited nature of his information on the region beyond Dar al-Kuti suggests that raids there were intermittent at best. For al-Tunisi's description of Wadaian raiding procedures in the early 1800s, see *Voyage au Ouaday*, 467, 488.

30. OA7.2/8.1; OA14.2; OA15.2/16.1; OA17.2/18.1; Bruel, *La France équatoriale africaine*, 239. On ironworking among the Banda, see OA3.2; OA4.1; OA14.2; OA15.2/16.1; Prioul, *Entre Oubangui et Chari*, 58–60; Prioul, "Le Velad el-Kouti et le seuil Oubangui-Chari, 1830–1892," paper prepared for the Ecole Nationale d'Administration (Bangui, n.d., c. 1972), mimeographed, 14; P. Daigre, "Les Bandas de l'Oubangui-Chari," *Anthropos* 26 (1931), 655; Jean Dybowski, *La Route du Tchad du Loango au Chari* (Paris, 1893), 304–5; Dampierre, *Un ancien royaume Bandia*, 338; Kalck, "Histoire," 2:529.

31. OA24.1; ANF-SOM (Aix), 4(3)D21, Ripault, "Rapport sur la reconnaissance executée dans la région Aouk-Kameur du 4 au 21 février 1914," Ouanda-Djale, 24 February 1914, in file "Dar Kouti 1914." The Runga in Dar Runga were famed fishermen as well, and carried on a considerable commerce in dried fish during the colonial period. See ANT, W45.11A,

"Rapport trimestriel du Salamat," 2ᵉ trimestre, Am Timan, 1928; ANT, W45.32B, "Rapport de la tournée effectuée du 10 février au 2 mars 1933 inclus par M. le Chef de la Circonscription du Salamat," Am Timan, 1933; ANT, W46.8, Chef de Subdivision de Mangueigne, "Rapport de tournée N° 1, 11 mai–22 mai 1941," Mangueigne, 1941; Burthe d'Annelet, *A travers l'Afrique française*, 2:1193.

32. OA11.1; OA15.2/16.1; OA19.1/20.1; Browne, *Travels in Africa*, 304–49; Burckhardt, *Travels*, 442; Pallme, *Travels in Kordofan*, 351n; Barth, *Travels*, 1:521; 2:488; Schweinfurth, *The Heart of Africa*, 2:372; Nachtigal, *Sahara and Sudan IV*, 81, 83, 139, 140, 354, 414; Kalck, "Histoire," 1:262–63, 272 and note.

33. R. Ciocardel, Birlea, and Gbakpoma, *Eléments pour la géologie de l'Afrique*, 3 vols. (Bangui, 1974), 3:345–47; Grellet, Mainguet and Soumille, *La République centrafricaine*, 16.

34. OA5.2; OA5.2/6.1; OA6.2; OA7.2/8.1; OA8.2; OA14.2; OA21.1; OA21.4; OA22.1; OA, notes on a conversation with Moustapha Seleman; Carbou, *La région*, 2:223.

35. Julien, "Mohamed-es-Senoussi" (1925), 105. The rulers of Bagirmi assigned great importance to the Shari; so much so, that a major official at the Bagirmi court, the Alifa Ba, was made responsible for overseeing activities along it. (In the Sara, Nduka, and Bagirmi or Barma languages, *ba* means "river.") See Barth, *Travels*, 2:499; Devallée, "Le Baghirmi," *BSRC* 7:2, 3, 4 (1925), 26. The people of Bagirmi should technically be called the Barma, but in this study they are referred to as Bagirmi, both for the sake of clarity and because the inhabitants of Dar al-Kuti use this term.

36. Barth, *Travels*, 2:486, 521, 543, 557–62, 623, 652, 677. A complete translation from the Nduka would yield "forest (or thicket) chiefs."

37. OA1.1; OA2.1; OA5.1; OA6.2; OA8.2; OA14.1; OA21.1; OA21.4; OA22.1; Modat, "Une tournée," 273; Carbou, *La région*, 2:225–26; Chevalier, "Exploration scientifique dans les états de Snoussi," 95. The practice of Muslim migrants and traders taking wives from non-Muslim peoples was common in the Sahel and farther south along the Islamic frontier.

38. OA13.1; OA23.2.

39. Major sources of information on Bagirmi history are limited to the Devallée article cited in note 35; H. Lanier, "L'ancien royaume du Baguirmi," *AF-RC* 35:10 (October 1925), 457–74; Nachtigal, *Sahara und Sudan*, 2:691–728; Gustav Nachtigal, *Sahara and Sudan II: Kawar, Bornu, Kanem, Borku, Ennedi*, trans. Allan G. B. and Humphrey J. Fisher (London, 1980), throughout, but particularly 290–91, 296, 298–99, 302–3, 311–12; Barth, *Travels*, 2:543–57.

40. OA4.1; OA5.1; OA5.2/6.1; OA6.2; OA7.2/8.1; OA8.2; OA13.1; OA14.1; OA14.2; OA21.1; OA21.4; OA22.1; OA22.2; OA22.3; OA23.3. Julien and Grech both say that there were a few Bagirmi in Ndele shortly after 1900; Modat and Carbou, however, report that the Bagirmi had a long history of intermarriage with the Runga and Nduka, and had lost their distinct identity. See Julien, "Mohamed-es-Senoussi" (1929), 49; Grech, "Essai sur le Dar

Kouti," 45; Carbou, *La région*, 2:225–35; Modat, "Une tournée," 273. Additional Bagirmi migrants made their way to Ndele following the campaigns pitting Rabih against the French and Bagirmi in their homeland in the late 1890s (OA15.2/16.1). This later migration stream makes it difficult to identify the residue of earlier Bagirmi migration to Dar al-Kuti, but it also confirms a history of ties between the two areas.

41.   For a study of this demographic problem in recent years, see Steven Perry Reyna, "The Costs of Marriage: A Study of Some Factors Affecting Northwest Barma Fertility" (doctoral dissertation, Columbia University, 1972).

42.   Burckhardt, *Travels*, 440; Carbou, *La région*, 2:126; Barth, *Travels*, 2:547–58; Nachtigal, *Sahara and Sudan II*, 296, 298–99, 501; Nachtigal, *Sahara and Sudan IV*, 67–68, 171, 231, 355.

43.   OA12.1; Burckhardt, *Travels*, 435; Barth, *Travels*, 2:513–14, 559; Chapiseau, *Au pays de l'esclavage*, 119–20, 159–61; Brunache, *Le centre de l'Afrique*, 230–1, 244–45; Annie M. D. Lebeuf, *Les populations du Tchad au nord du dixième parallèle* (Paris, 1959), 70; Jacques LeCornec, *Histoire politique du Tchad de 1900 à 1962* (Paris, 1963), 18–19.

44.   Mohammadou Eldridge, "Kalfu ou l'Emirat Peul de Baguirmi et les toorobbe Sokkoto," *Afrika Zamani: revue d'histoire africaine/Review of African History*, N° 4 (July 1975), 49, 103-4; Barth, *Travels*, 2:539, 549. Barth called Bidri the "first seat" of Islam in Bagirmi.

45.   Nachtigal, *Sahara und Sudan*, 2:693, 696–99; Barth, *Travels*, 2:643, 3:432–433, 505, 528, 592; Henri Gaden, *Manuel de la langue baguirmienne* (Paris, 1908), 56–57; Mohammadou, "Kalfu," 73–75, 101, 104, 109. Other studies support these conclusions. See Annie M. D. Lebeuf, "Boum Massenia: capitale de l'ancien royaume de Baguirmi," *Journal de la société des africanistes* 37:2 (1967), 219, 232–36; Viviana Pâques, "Origine et caractères du pouvoir royale au Baguirmi," *Journal de la société des africanistes* 37:2 (1967), 183–214.

46.   Mohammadou, "Kalfu," 103n66; OA, notes on a session with Khrouma Sale, Village of Koundi, 21 June 1974; OA5.1; OA6.2; OA8.2; OA14.1; OA14.2; OA21.1; OA21.4; OA22.1; OA22.3; OA, notes on a session with Père DeMoustier, Ndele, 26 August 1974; Carbou, *La région*, 2:129, 130n.

47.   Works, *Pilgrims in a Strange Land*, 9–11; J. S. Birks, *Across the Savannas to Mecca: The Overland Pilgrimage from West Africa* (London, 1978), 8–16, ᶜUmar al-Naqar, *The Pilgrimage Tradition in West Africa* (Khartoum, 1972), 92–94, 99, 104, 109–13.

48.   Nachtigal, *Sahara und Sudan*, 2:720–23. For a chronology of the al-Kanemi dynasty in Borno, see Louis Brenner, *The Shehus of Kukawa: A History of the Al-Kanemi Dynasty of Bornu* (London, 1973), 63, 78.

49.   Martin Z. Njeuma, "Adamawa and Mahdism: The career of Hayatu ibn Saᶜid in Adamawa, 1878–1898," *JAH* 12:1 (1971), 63-64. Njeuma suggests that an effort to extend the jihad to Bagirmi failed. He does not provide an exact date for this endeavor, but in the following paragraph he begins with jihad leader Modibbo Adama's receipt of a flag from dan Fodio in 1809,

which makes it likely that the Bagirmi jihad occurred before this time. Mohammadou definitely identifies 1815–20 as the dates of Lamiinu's assault on Bagirmi. It would therefore appear that there were two efforts to conquer Bagirmi for Sokoto. Mohammadou, "Kalfu," 69–71, 109–11.

50. Mohammadou, "Kalfu," 109–11.

51. Ibid., 108–11; Nachtigal, *Sahara und Sudan*, 2:713.

52. OA7.2/8.1; OA13.1; OA14.2; OA21.1; OA21.4.

53. Al-Tunisi, *Voyage au Ouaday*, 149: "toutes les fois qu'il approachait d'un village, d'un bourg, il envoyait dire aux ulémas et aux principaux de l'endroit, de venir le trouver; puis, il leur parlait avec bienveillance, et leur donnait quelques présents. Lorsque Saboun arrivait à un lieu sacré, révéré par la piété publique, au santon d'un saint, il y faisait des aûmones, et laissait quelques dons pieux à ceux qui étaient chargés des soins des lieux saints."

54. Personal observation; OA5.1; OA5.2/6.1; OA7.1; OA14.1; OA14.2; OA24.1; OA, notes on a conversation with Khrouma Sale, Runga-Bagrim, Village of Koundi, 21 June 1974; ANF-SOM (Aix), 4(3)D45, Rogué, "Rapport trimestriel, 3ᵉ trimestre, année 1934," Subdivision autonome de Ndele, Ndele, 1934.

55. OA5.1; OA22.1; OA22.3; OA24.1; Carbou, *La région*, 2:223; Prioul, "Le Velad el-Kouti," 1–3. Prioul suggests that 3,000 Muslims inhabited Dar al-Kuti at this time, although it is not clear how he arrived at this figure. As for possible reasons behind accelerated migration into Dar al-Kuti, a period of drought and famine between 1830 and 1835 in Wadai reportedly led many people to emigrate (see Barth, *Travels*, 2:646; Nachtigal, *Sahara and Sudan IV*, 218–19). But the Wadaian heartlands lay 700 kilometers north of Dar al-Kuti, and there are no indications that these movements affected the area south of the Aouk. By way of comparison, the prolonged drought in the Sahel in the 1970s affected Wadai severely, but had little impact on the northern Central African Republic.

56. OA5.1; OA5.2/6.1; OA6.2; OA8.2; OA13.1; OA14.1; OA14.2; OA21.4; OA22.1; OA24.1; Pierre Prins, "Voyage au Dar Rounga: résultats scientifiques," *La Géographie* 1:3 (1900), 196; Julien, "Mohamed-es-Senoussi" (1925), 104–5, 125–27; Grech, "Essai sur le Dar Kouti," 19; Chevalier, *Mission*, 130–32; Modat, "Une tournée," 221–24; Santandrea, "Sanusi, Ruler of Dar Banda and Dar Kuti in the History of the Bahr el-Ghazal," *Sudan Notes and Records* 28 (1957), 151.

57. Kalck, *Central African Republic*, 34; Kalck, "Histoire," 1:208–10; Pierre Kalck, *Histoire de la République centrafricaine des origines préhistorique à nos jours* (Paris, 1974), 95; Prioul, *Entre Oubangui et Chari*, 121; Jacques Serre, "Histoire économique et sociale du district de Grimari (1907–1958)," Salle de documentation, document N° 82, Ecole Nationale d'Administration, Bangui, 1960, 1:12 (written as a *doctorat du 3ᵉ cycle* for a French university); Adeleye, "Rabih b. Fadlallah, 1879–1893: Exploits and Impact on Political Relations in Central Sudan," 227; also see citations in note 56 above.

58. For discussion and further examples of this phenomenon, see P. H. S.

d'Escayrac de Lauture, *Le Désert et le Soudan* (Paris, 1853), 448–49; Nachtigal, *Sahara and Sudan IV*, 206–7; Prins, "Voyage au Dar Rounga," 196; Santandrea, "Sanusi, Ruler of Dar Banda and Dar Kuti," 151; Tubiana, "Un document inédit sur les sultans du Wadday," 62–65; R. J. Elles, "The Kingdom of Tegali," *Sudan Notes and Records* 18:1 (1935), 2, 7–9; R. C. Stevenson, "Some Aspects of the Spread of Islam in the Nuba Mountains (Kordofan Province, Republic of the Sudan)," in *Islam in Tropical Africa*, I. M. Lewis, ed. (London, 1966), 209, 214; Yusuf Fadl Hasan, "The Penetration of Islam in the Eastern Sudan," in *Islam in Tropical Africa*, 150; I. M. Lewis, "Introduction," in *Islam in Tropical Africa*, 36.

59. Nachtigal, *Sahara und Sudan*, 2:693; Barth, *Travels*, 2:551–55.

60. This view is supported by Henige's broader comparative study of chronologies and oral tradition, which suggests that assigning longer reigns to early, probably nonhistorical, figures is a common form of distortion in both oral traditions and written kinglists. See David P. Henige, *The Chronology of Oral Tradition: Quest for a Chimera* (Oxford, 1974), 49–51. The thirty-nine-year reign of Bagirmi sultan Bourgomanda (1807–46) is an exception to this general pattern, and may itself be problematic. See Nachtigal, *Sahara und Sudan*, 2:693.

61. This judgment is based mainly on personal observation. For a sampling of names from southern Chad, see Nelson, *Area Handbook for Chad*, throughout; Chad, Direction générale de l'information, *Annuaire officiel du Tchad* (Paris, 1972), 63, 80, 83, 94–95, 103.

62. Devallée, "Le Baghirmi," *BSRC* 7 (1925), 31.

63. Henige, *The Chronology of Oral Tradition*, 51–55.

64. OA5.1; OA5.2/6.1; OA9.1; OA9.2/10.1; OA13.1; OA14.2; OA15.2/16.1; OA17.2/18.1; OA21.1; OA21.4; OA, notes on a conversation with Mahamat Ngouvela Dodo, Banda Ngao, Village of Mbollo, 5 June 1974; Charles Tisserant, *Essai sur la grammaire Banda* (Paris, 1930), 10; Martine, "Essai sur l'histoire du pays Salamat," 23–24; Julien, "Mohamed-es-Senoussi" (1925), 106–7, 113, 124–25; Georges Toque, *Essai sur le peuple et la langue Banda* (Paris, 1904), 14–15; Chevalier, *Mission*, 131–32; Modat, "Une tournée," 180, 272; Carbou, *La région*, 2:129–30; Kalck, "Histoire," 1:250; 2:305, 451.

65. OA5.1.

66. OA5.1; OA5.2/6.1; OA7.1; OA11.2/12.1; OA13.1; OA14.2; OA15.2/16.1; OA21.1; OA21.4; OA22.3; Julien, "Mohamed-es-Senoussi" (1929), 47. Today at least eight great-grandsons live in the village of Koundi where they all are religious leaders. Some have studied outside the area, mainly in Abeche and al-Geneina (Sudan). Faqih Muhammad Na^{c}im, however, studied for eight years in Cairo at al-Azhar.

67. The post–1890 political situation has encouraged emphasis on the differences between the two figures, since that allows the descendants of Kobur to explain satisfactorily their loss of power. During al-Sanusi's reign, Kobur's sons were a focal point for dissension, yet they never regained control. Later,

the French appointed several of al-Sanusi's sons and grandsons to politically influential positions, and the independent Central African Republic government has continued this practice. Because the two lines are closely related—al-Sanusi's father and Kobur were brothers—pointing out the differing areas of strength of their forebears has perhaps served to minimize disagreement. OA3.2; OA5.1, OA5.2/6.1, OA11.2/12.1; OA13.1; OA14.2; OA21.1; OA21.4; OA22.3; ANF-SOM (Paris), Papiers Julien, 6P.A., "Historique des états Senoussiens (Dar-el-Kouti), Annexe N° 3; Renseignements sur la famille Mohamed-es-Senoussi," 155; Julien, "Mohamed-es-Senoussi" (1925), 124–25; Carbou, *La région*, 2:224–25; Modat, "Une tournée," 272; Kalck, "Histoire," 3:55–56. Asked if Kobur's family was bitter following al-Sanusi's rise to power, one informant (related to both lines by marriage) replied: "Ah, they were of the same family, they had the same grandfather. When someone takes [power], his force surpasses your own, what are you going to do? If he has many guns? And so, they [Kobur's people] all left, and settled down, ate millet. . . . They [al-Sanusi's descendants] came, and government there, it was in the same family. What was to be done? They were agreeable" (OA5.1). Or, from another informant: "Kobur was more interested in his religious activities than in becoming sultan; power and faqihs do not go together" (OA21.4).

68.   OA5.1; OA5.2/6.1; OA7.2/8.1; OA14.2; OA17.2/18.1; OA21.1; OA21.4.
69.   ANF-SOM (Paris), Papiers Julien, 6.P.A., "Historique des états Senoussiens (Dar el-Kouti)," 3; Julien, "Mohamed-es-Senoussi" (1925), 105–7; Prioul, "Le Velad el-Kouti," 4. In a contemporary reference to Dar Runga and Dar al-Kuti, Nachtigal noted that the Wadaian ᶜaqid in the Salamat, the official responsible for the southern part of the empire, made an extended tour of the south each year, taking slaves and collecting ivory to be sent to Abeche (see Nachtigal, *Sahara and Sudan IV*, 140–41).
70.   OA5.1; OA7.2/8.1; OA21.1; Julien, "Mohamed-es-Senoussi" (1925), 105–7.
71.   Nachtigal, *Sahara and Sudan IV*, 139–41, and map at end.
72.   ANF-SOM (Paris), Gabon-Congo III, dossier 13b, Dolisie to M. le Commissaire-Générale, "Mission Crampel," Brazzaville, 20 July 1891. Information for the earlier decades is based entirely on informants' testimonies. It is impossible to assign an exact date to the situation they describe, but they all make a clear distinction between the period of Kobur's rule and the years when Dar al-Kuti was under the sway of Rabih and al-Sanusi. See OA1.1; OA1.2; OA3.2; OA5.1; OA5.2/6.1; OA6.2; OA7.2/8.1; OA8.2; OA9.2/10.1; A13.1; OA14.1; OA14.2; OA17.1; OA17.2/18.1; OA20.2; OA20.3; OA21.1; OA21.4; OA22.1; OA23.2; OA, notes on a conversation with Khrouma Sale, 21 June 1974.
73.   Although Kali was the major Muslim center in Dar al-Kuti before the founding of Ndele, its existence in the precolonial period is noted in only two published sources, both of which appeared after al-Sanusi's rise to power. Neither work describes the settlement, and hence the sketch presented here is

based on oral data collected in 1974. For the published sources, see Romolo Gessi Pasha, *Seven Years in the Sudan, being a Record of Exploration, Adventures, and Campaigns against the Arab Slave Hunters* (London, 1892), map at end; Chevalier, *Mission*, 131. For the oral traditions, see OA5.1; OA5.2/6.1; OA7.2/8.1; OA8.2; OA13.1.

74. Unlike his uncle Kobur, al-Sanusi had no special reputation for piety.

75. OA1.1; OA1.2; OA3.2; OA5.1; OA5.2/6.1; OA6.2; OA7.2/8.1; OA8.2; OA9.2/10.1; OA13.1; OA14.1; OA21.1; OA22.1; ANF-SOM (Aix), 4(3)D45, Rogué, "Rapport trimestriel, 4ᵉ trimestre, et rapport annuel, année 1934," Ndele, 30 November 1934; Julien, "Mohamed-es-Senoussi" (1925), 105–6, 108–23.

76. OA6.2; OA7.2/8.1; OA21.1 "Karnak" is a loan word into Chadic Arabic of unknown origin. The term is commonly used in Chad to describe a capital or major settlement. In the mid-nineteenth century, Perron noted that the people of Bagirmi sometimes referred to their capital at Massenya as Karnak. See M. Perron's "Introduction" to al-Tunisi, *Voyage au Ouaday*, 24; Arlette Roth-Laly, comp., *Lexique des parlers arabes tchado-soudanais/An Arabic-English-French Lexicon of Dialects Spoken in the Chad-Sudan Area*, 4 vols. (Paris, 1972), 4:416.

77. The name Kuti appears in many documents and travel accounts from the early colonial period, although it is not usually clear whether the term refers to the Kuti-Kali-Sha complex or to a single settlement. See, for example, Dybowski, *La Route du Tchad*, 70–71; Harry Alis, "L'Expédition Crampel," *AF* 1:9 (September 1891), 4–5. Mungo (*sic*) appears only in one source, and it may not refer to the same village. See Karl Kumm, *From Hausaland to Egypt, through the Sudan* (London, 1910), 165–67. Oral sources on Mongo-Kuti are: OA3.2; OA5.1; OA5.2/6.1; OA6.2; OA7.2/8.1; OA8.2; OA13.1; OA14.1; OA14.2; OA17.1; OA20.2; OA20.3; OA21.1; OA21.4; OA22.1; OA22.2; OA22.3; OA23.1; OA23.2; OA, notes on a conversation with Moustapha Seleman, 3 October 1974.

78. OA1.2; OA5.2/6.1; OA13.1; OA14.2; OA17.1; OA18.2; OA21.1; OA21.2; OA21.4; OA22.1; OA23.2; ANF-SOM (Aix), 4(3)D45, Rogué, "Rapport trimestriel, 4ᵉ trimestre, et rapport annuel, année 1934," Ndele, 30 November 1934.

79. OA6.2; OA13.1; OA14.2; OA21.1; OA22.1; OA, notes on a conversation with Abakar Tidjani, 23 June 1974; OA, notes on a conversation with Zacharia Kouzoubali, 30 September 1974; ANF-SOM (Aix), 4(3)D23, Leprince, Lt.-Gouv. p. i., Colonie de l'Oubangui-Chari-Tchad, "Rapport politique, ler trimestre, 1916," 8–9. Despite these upheavals and others provoked by forced labor recruitment during the colonial period, the descendants of the earlier inhabitants of Kali, Sha, and Mongo-Kuti have reconstituted their communities along the road to Haraze (Chad) north of Ndele. The Runga groups who lived in Kali now inhabit Koundi; those originally from Sha are now found at Sokoumba; and the Nduka from Mongo-Kuti reside at Djobossinda. Although these settlements are now located

between forty and fifty kilometers from their original sites, the three villages have recreated their original configuration. Koundi (Kali), Sokoumba (Sha), and Djobossinda (Mongo-Kuti) are located near one another along a nine-kilometer stretch of the road (personal observation; OA6.2; OA14.2; OA, notes on a conversation with Khrouma Sale, 21 June 1974).

Chapter 3

Dar al-Kuti: The Formation of the Sultanate

1. Julien, "Mohamed-es-Senoussi" (1929), 60.
2. *Plaque tournante*: Eric de Dampierre, personal communication, 10 February 1977.
3. Romolo Gessi, *Seven Years in the Sudan* (London, 1892), 322. I added the word "probably" in dating Rabih's arrival because there are at least seven published itineraries detailing his migration from the Sudan (1878) to Borno (1894). The itineraries fall into two sets separated by chronological differences. For example, one set (Modat-Oppenheim-Decorse and Gaudefroy-Demombynes-Julien) suggests that Rabih first appeared in Dar al-Kuti in 1879, while the other (Babikir-Hallam-Adeleye) dates his arrival to 1882. A recent book by Dampierre has shed new light on this chronological problem, leading to my choice of 1878. See Dampierre, *Des ennemis, des Arabes, des histoires* (Paris, 1983). For the various itineraries, and sources of other information included in this paragraph, see Modat, "Une tournée," 226–30; Max Adrian Simon freiherr von Oppenheim, *Rabeh und das Tschadseegebiet* (Berlin, 1902), 14–33; Gaston Jules Decorse and Maurice Gaudefroy-Demombynes, *Rabah et les arabes du Chari: documents arabes et vocabulaire* (Paris, 1906), 5–13; Julien, "Mohamed-es-Senoussi" (1925), 108–14; Arbab Djama Babikir, *L'empire de Rabeh* (Paris, 1950), 30–32; W. K. R. Hallam, *Life and Times of Rabih Fadl Allah* (Devon, 1977), 54–56, 69–72, 83, 86–91; Hallam, "The Itinerary of Rabih Fadl Allah, 1879–1893," *Bulletin de l'Institut Fondamental de l'Afrique noire*, série B, t. 30, N° 1 (1968), 170–78; Adeleye, "Rabih b. Fadlallah, 1879–1893," 223–42.
4. OA3.2; OA5.1; OA5.2/6.1; OA7.1; OA8.2; OA13.1; OA14.2; OA15.2/16.1; A17.1; OA21.1; OA21.4; OA22.3; Chevalier, *Mission*, 117; Carbou, *La région*, 2:223. Later in Borno, Rabih's raiders continued to take slaves from Muslim as well as non-Muslim villages. See Hallam, *Rabih Fadl Allah*, 160, 173n12.
5. Chevalier, *Mission*, 226; Modat, "Une tournée," 226.
6. OA15.2/16.1; OA22.3.
7. OA22.3.
8. OA21.4.
9. ANF-SOM (Paris), Gabon-Congo II, dossier 5, Grech, "Travail d'inspec-

tion: Soudan central, sultans zandés, et l'occupation française," Dem Ziber, 25 July 1897; ANF-SOM (Paris), Tchad I, dossier 3, Prins, "Rapport d'un voyage de Raphai à Said Baldas, aux Djebels Mélla et Guyamba du 3 février au 15 mai 1901; Julien, "Mohamed-es-Senoussi et ses états," *BSRC* 9 (1928), 92–93; Modat, "Une tournée," 229; Hill, *A Biographical Dictionary*, 389; Santandrea, *A Tribal History*, 36; Hallam, "The Itinerary," 168.

10. Bohannan and Curtin, *Africa and Africans*, 279, 288.

11. Ibid., 278–81, 293–94; Joseph Smaldone, "The Firearms Trade in the Central Sudan in the Nineteenth Century," in *Aspects of West African Islam*, Daniel F. McCall and Norman R. Bennett, eds. (Boston, 1971), 170. For a general discussion of the impact of firearms in the nineteenth century in Africa, see Daniel R. Headrick, *The Tools of Empire: Technology and European Imperialism in the Nineteenth Century* (New York, 1981), 83–114.

12. P. M. Holt, "Egypt and the Nile Valley," in *The Cambridge History of Africa, Volume 5, c. 1790-c. 1870*, John E. Flint, ed. (Cambridge, 1976), 13–50.

13. ANF-SOM (Paris), Gabon-Congo II, dossier 5, Grech, "Travail d'inspection"; ANF-SOM (Paris), Tchad I, dossier 3, Prins, "Rapport d'un voyage de Raphai à Said Baldas"; Chevalier, *Mission*, 226; Santandrea, *A Tribal History*, 267; Hallam, *Rabih Fadl Allah*, 160; Bohannan and Curtin, *Africa and Africans*, 287–89. For mentions of slave recruitment in West Africa, see Robert S. Smith, *Warfare and Diplomacy in Pre-Colonial West Africa* (London, 1976), 56, 82.

14. Hill, *A Biographical Dictionary*, 312–13; PRO (London), FO2/118, XJ6230, Wingate, "Memo on the Western Sudan." An informant in Dar al-Kuti provided a very similar account of Rabih's career (OA21.1).

15. Emile Gentil, *La chute de l'empire de Rabah* (Paris, 1902), 258; Babikir, L'empire de Rabeh, 7–9, 28–29; Adeleye, "Rabih b. Fadlallah, 1879–1893," 225, 227; Julien, "Mohamed-es-Senoussi," 1925, 107–8.

16. OA3.2; OA4.1; OA15.2/16.1; ANF-SOM (Paris), Papiers Julien, 6P.A., "Rapport du Cap^ne Julien . . . du Ba-Mingui"; Chevalier, *Mission*, 226; Toque, *Essai sur le peuple et la langue Banda*, 47; Bruel, *La France équatoriale africaine*, 283–84; Babikir, *L'empire de Rabeh*, 28–29, 62; Hallam, "The Itinerary," 172; Kalck, "Histoire," 2:307–8.

17. OA18.2; Julien, "Mohamed-es-Senoussi" (1925), 114–15; Modat, "Une tournée," 230. The census is included in Jean Ferrandi and Capitaine Lame, "Fort-Lamy, chef-lieu du territoire du Tchad," *AF-RC* 22:3 (March 1912), 105, and reproduced in Works, *Pilgrims in a Strange Land*, 105.

18. ASPN, District de Ndele, "Journal des tournées du 20–3–1948 au 31–12–1953," Ndele, 1948–1953, not paginated, entry for 29 September 1951; Casimir Léon Maistre, "Rapport de la Mission Maistre," *AF* 3:6 (June 1893), 6; Chevalier, *Mission*, 120; Modat, "Une tournée," 230; Gaud, *Les Mandja*, 97; Toque, *Essai sur le peuple et la langue Banda*, 16–21; Charles Tisserant, "L'Agriculture dans les savanes de l'Oubangui," *Bulletin de l'institut des études centrafricaines (Brazzaville)*, nouvelle série, N° 6 (1953), 214; Kalck, "Histoire," 2:398.

19. Chevalier, *Mission*, 356–66, 371.
20. ANT, W53.9, "Documents et études historiques sur le Salamat, réunis par Y. Merot: Rabah et Senoussi au Dar Rounga"; Carbou, *La région*, 2:223; Modat, "Une tournée," 196, 228, 271; Martine, "Essai sur l'histoire du pays Salamat," 23–24; Bruel, *La France équatoriale africaine*, 281; Dampierre, *Un ancien royaume Bandia*, 430n1.
21. ANT, W53.9, "Documents et études historiques sur le Salamat, réunis par Y. Merot: Note au sujet du Rabah au Salamat," 3; PRO (London), FO2/118, XJ6230, Wingate, "Memo on the Western Sudan"; Chevalier, *Mission*, 365–66; Modat, "Une tournée," 228–30; Martine, "Essai sur l'histoire du pays Salamat," 23–24; Hallam, *Rabih Fadl Allah*, 99–100; Adeleye, "Rabih b. Fadlallah, 1879–1893," 227–32; Joseph Smaldone, *Warfare in the Sokoto Caliphate: Historical and Sociological Perspectives* (Cambridge, 1977), 101.
22. OA5.1; OA13.1; OA14.2; OA21.1; Julien, "Mohamed-es-Senoussi" (1925), 113; Carbou, *La région*, 2:129–30; Kalck, "Histoire," 2:296, 305–6, 357–58; Hallam, "The Itinerary," 175–76.
23. Julien, "Mohamed-es-Senoussi" (1925), 113; Modat, "Une tournée," 230; Carbou, *La région*, 2:130; Kalck, "Les savanes centrafricaines," 202.
24. Julien, "Mohamed-es-Senoussi" (1925), 111–13, 115, 125–27, 141; Prioul, "Le Velad-el-Kouti," 7; Hallam, "The Itinerary," 177, 180; Hallam, *Rabih Fadl Allah*, 99; Adeleye, "Rabih b. Fadlallah, 1879–1893," 231–32, 234–36.
25. OA5.1; OA13.1; OA14.1; OA17.2/18.1; OA18.2; OA19.1/20.1; OA21.1; AMBB, No. 167 (Bangassou), Boucher, Chef de la Circonscription du Dar Kouti oriental, "Monographe sur Dar Kouti oriental," Birao, 31 December 1934, unpaginated (section on Goula); Julien "Mohamed-es-Senoussi" (1925), 113, 115, 125–27, 134–35; Chevalier, *Mission*, 132, 365–66, 371; Carbou, *La région*, 2:130; Modat, "Une tournée," 195, 230–31; Santandrea, "Sanusi, Ruler of Dar Banda and Dar Kuti," 152; Prioul, "Le Velad-el-Kouti," 7; Kalck, "Histoire," 2:305–7.
26. OA1.1; OA3.2; OA5.1; OA11.2/12.1; OA13.1; OA19.1/20.1; OA21.1; OA21.4; ANF-SOM (Paris), Papiers Julien, 6P.A., "Annexe N°1: Généalogie des Sultans Baghirmiens et Senoussiens," 152; "Annexe N°2: Généalogie des Sultans Roungas et Senoussiens," 153; "Annexe N°3: Renseignements sur la famille Mohamed-es-Senoussi," 154; Julien, "Mohamed-es-Senoussi" (1925), 106; Prins, "Voyage au Dar Rounga," 196; Santandrea, "Sanusi, Ruler of Dar Banda and Dar Kuti," 151; Serre, "Histoire économique et sociale du district de Grimari (1907–1958)," 12.
27. OA5.1; OA11.1; OA13.1; OA14.2; OA21.1; OA21.4. The conflicting itineraries make it impossible to date Rabih's stay in the Kali-Sha area with confidence. Hallam suggests that Rabih was there in the dry season of 1882–83, but he then locates the camp on a stream that is not in Dar al-Kuti (see Hallam, "The Itinerary," 172). The other itineraries display similar inconsistencies.
28. OA5.1; OA11.1; OA14.2; OA17.2/18.1; OA21.1; OA21.4; Toque, *Essai*

sur le peuple et la langue Banda, 8; Chevalier, *Mission*, 131–32; Santandrea, "Sanusi, Ruler of Dar Banda and Dar Kuti," 152.

29. There are numerous published and unpublished accounts of the Crampel Mission. The best of these are: Anonymous, "L'Expédition Crampel," *AF* 1:1 (January 1891), 2–5; Harry Alis, "La Mission Paul Crampel," *AF* 1:3 (March 1891), 3–6; Harry Alis, "L'Expédition Crampel," *AF* 1:9 (September 1891), 2–5; ANF-SOM (Paris), Gabon-Congo III, dossier 13b, Dolisie, "Mission Crampel," Brazzaville, 20 July 1891; Albert Nebout, "La Mission Crampel," *Bulletin de la société normande de géographie*, N° 14 (1892), 217–47; Nebout, "La Mission Crampel," *Tour du Monde* 64 (1892), 1–65; Louis Jules Fredéric Kieffer, "Le Kouti: le massacre de la mission Crampel," *Bulletin de la société de géographie d'Alger et d'Afrique du Nord* (1905), 290–303; Kalck, "Paul Crampel, le centrafricain," *L'Afrique littéraire et artistique* 2 (1968), 60–63. The articles and books by Chevalier, Julien, and Modat also include scattered references to the Crampel Mission, and Kalck has written a lengthy, but as yet unpublished, biography of the explorer.

30. These approximate figures are included in the following sources: ANF-SOM (Paris), Gabon-Congo III, dossier 13b, Dolisie, "Mission Crampel"; Dybowski, *La Route du Tchad*, 76; Chapiseau, *Au pays de l'esclavage*, 184; Julien, "Mohamed-es-Senoussi" (1925), 118.

31. OA1.1; OA5.1; OA11.1; OA15.2/16.1; ANF-AE, *Correspondance politique des consuls (Turquie: Tripoli de Barbarie 1895, et Benghazi, 1891–1895)*, vol. 31, Vice-Consul Ricard to Ribot, Benghazi, 8 December 1891; ANF-SOM (Paris), Gabon-Congo III, 13b, Dolisie, "Mission Crampel"; PRO (London), FO2/118, XJ6230, Wingate, "Memo on the Western Sudan"; Kieffer, "Le Kouti," 294–95; Brunache, *Le centre de l'Afrique*, 39–40, 104; Dybowski, *La route du Tchad*, 68–74; Nebout, "La Mission Crampel," 240–47; Chevalier, *Mission*, 131–37, 272; Julien, "Mohamed-es-Senoussi" (1925), 116–20.

32. Julien, "Mohamed-es-Senoussi" (1925), 145; Modat, "Une tournée," 272; Carbou, *La région*, 2:224–25.

33. OA3.1; OA3.2; OA7.1; OA14.2; OA21.4; ANF-SOM (Paris), Julien, Papiers Julien, 6 P.A., "Annexe N° 4"; Grech, "Essai sur le Dar Kouti," 45.

34. OA3.2; ANF-SOM (Paris), Julien, Papiers Julien, 6 P.A., "Annexe N° 4"; Grech, "Essai sur le Dar Kouti," 52.

35. OA, notes on a conversation with Ahmadu Tukur (al-Hajj Tukur's youngest son), Ndele, 31 May 1974; OA2.1; OA8.2; APBB, A. Perrière, "Notes et Errata," 28 October 1971, appended to "Les rapports du Capitaine Julien," copy of Julien's reports made in Bangui, 20 March 1923; AAV (Vincennes), Modat, "Notice ethnographique sur les populations du Dar-Kouti"; ANF-SOM (Paris), Papiers Julien, 6P.A., "Annexe N° 4"; Georges Bruel, "Mohamed-es-Senoussi et ses états (Lettre de rectification)," *BSRC* 11 (1930), 99–100; Grech, "Essai sur le Dar Kouti," 47.

36. OA2.1; OA8.2; ANF-SOM (Paris), Julien, Papiers Julien, 6 P.A., "Annexe N° 4"; Julien, "Le Dar Ouadai," 58; Grech, "Essai sur le Dar Kouti," 26.

37. Grech, "Essai sur le Dar Kouti," 46.
38. ANF-SOM (Paris), Julien, Papiers Julien, 6 P.A., "Annexe N° 4."
39. OA5.1; OA13.1; OA21.4; PRO (London), FO2/118, XJ6230, Wingate, "Memo on the Western Sudan"; Chevalier, *Mission*, 134–37, 372; Julien, "Mohamed-es-Senoussi" (1925), 120; Modat, "Une tournée," 231 and n. 2; Adeleye, "Rabih b. Fadlallah, 1879–1893," 228–39; Jean Malval, *Essai de chronologie tchadienne (1707–1940)* (Paris, 1974), 30.
40. Modat, "Une tournée," 230–32; Julien, "Mohamed-es-Senoussi" (1925), 134–35; Carbou, *La région*, 2:224–25; Kalck, "Histoire," 2:306, 357–58, 448–51. Al-Sanusi obviously ruled Dar Runga in name only. Runga informants in Ndele denied that he ever controlled the area, although one said that on at least one occasion, the sultan sent his forces to Dar Runga. See OA7.1; OA13.1; OA21.4; OA, notes on a conversation with Abakar Tidjani, 26 June 1974.
41. OA1.2; OA8.2; OA14.2; OA17.1; OA17.2/18.1; OA19.1/20.1; OA20.2; OA20.3; OA23.2; OA, notes on a conversation with M. Thomassey, Ndele, 30 August 1974; CC, Cornet, "Au coeur de l'Afrique centrale," (n.p., n.d.), 12 August 1916 (printed report without publishing data); Anonymous, "Es-Senoussi," *AF* 21:3 (March 1911), 94; Grech, "Essai sur le Dar Kouti," 21, 23; Chevalier, *Mission*, 137–38; Julien, "Mohamed-es-Senoussi" (1925), 136–37, 142; Carbou, *La région*, 2:132; Modat, "Une tournée," 196; Martine, "Essai sur l'histoire du pays Salamat," 21–22, 24.
42. ANF-SOM (Paris), Papiers Julien, 6P.A., "Annexe N°4," 157; Julien, "Le Dar Ouadai," 139; Julien, "Mohamed-es-Senoussi" (1925), 142; Carbou, *La région*, 2:132; Modat, "Une tournée," 231.
43. Auguste Terrier, "Snoussi d'El-Kouti," *AF* 13:12 (December 1903), 394; Modat, "Une tournée," 231; Grech, "Essai sur le Dar Kouti," 23; Julien, "Mohamed-es-Senoussi" (1925), 142–43.
44. Léon Hanolet, "L'Exploration du commandant Hanolet vers les sources du Chari," *La Belgique coloniale* 2:23 (7 June 1896), 272; ANF-SOM (Paris), Gabon-Congo IV, dossier 14c, Liotard, Letter N°117, "Resumé de la situation politique du cercle de Dem Ziber (Août, 1897)," Dem Ziber, 10 August 1897; ANF-SOM (Paris), Gabon-Congo I, dossier 61c, Letter from Liotard to Dolisie, Djéma, 6 May 1897; ANF-SOM (Paris), Gabon-Congo I, dossier 63a, Letter from Liotard to the Minister of Colonies, Paris, 2 November 1898; ANF-SOM (Paris), Gabon-Congo II, dossier 5, Grech, "Travail d'inspection"; Julien, "Mohamed-es-Senoussi" (1925), 138–40, 152–53; Grech, "Essai sur le Dar Kouti," 21–23; Santandrea, *A Tribal History*, 201, 221–23.
45. OA3.2; OA15.2/16.1; ANF-SOM (Paris), Gabon-Congo I, dossier 61a, Liotard, Letter N° 37, "Envoi de quatre copies de pièces relatives à la Mission Marchand et renseignements divers," Rafai, 11 January 1898; Chevalier, *Mission*, 174–78; Auguste Chevalier, "Mission scientifique au Chari et au lac Tchad," *La Géographie* 7 (1903), 358; Grech, "Essai sur le Dar Kouti," 22–23; Santandrea, *A Tribal History*, 219–23; Julien,

"Mohamed-es-Senoussi" (1925), 153. On the basis of the ruins he saw in 1902, Chevalier estimated that the population of Mbele had been 10,000 people, whereas Hanolet suggested a figure of only two thousand in 1894 (see preceding note for Hanolet citation); Dampierre has recently suggested that they did not visit the same settlement (see Dampierre, *Des ennemis*, 57n6). Thomassey says that ruins of the city are still visible on the Gounda River today; the entire region is uninhabited (OA, notes on a conversation with M. Thomassey, Ndele, 30 August 1974).

46. The settlement is variously referred to as Jagara, Ngirke, or Durnata after small streams in the area.

47. OA1.2; OA3.2; OA5.2/61; OA9.1; OA9.2/10.1; OA11.1; OA11.2/12.1; OA14.2; OA15.1; OA15.2/16.1; OA17.2/18.1; OA19.1/20.1; OA21.4. Almost all the data on Jagara are taken from oral sources, but sparse written evidence corroborates a number of crucial details concerning Ngono and Ara, the date of al-Sanusi's attacks, and the location of the Ngao settlements. See Prins, "Voyage au Dar Rounga," 194, map between pp. 196 and 197; Prins, "Les troglodytes du Dar Banda," 12–14; Julien, "Mohamed-es-Senoussi" (1925), 154; Chevalier, *Mission*, 173–74, 176 and n. 1, 226–27; Modat, "Une tournée," 180; Santandrea, *A Tribal History*, 253–54.

48. The families of several Runga informants migrated to Ndele in the late 1890s, and almost all informants agree that the Muslim population of Dar al-Kuti mushroomed during these years. See OA3.2; OA7.2/8.1; OA13.1; OA17.1; OA19.1/20.1; OA21.1; OA22.1; OA22.3.

49. OA7.1; OA21.4; OA22.1; OA23.2; Modat, "Une tournée," 234n2; Carbou, *La région*, 2:178. For an account of Wadaian political history in the years between 1898 and 1911, see Carbou, *La région*, 2:133–98; Hayer, "A Political History of the Maba Sultanate of Wadai," 39–47. Chevalier described a visit in 1903 to an Nduka village (Ngara) surrounded by elaborate palisades for protection against "Jallaba" raiders. I suspect that the marauders were Wadaians, and not Jallaba, since the latter traded in slaves, but rarely raided for captives themselves. See Chevalier, *Mission*, 202–6.

50. ANF-SOM (Paris), Gabon-Congo IV, dossier 18, H. Bobichon (Délégué du Commissaire-Général) à M. E. Gentil (Commissaire du Gouvernement au Chari), Bangassou, 5 February 1900; Julien, "Le Dar Ouadai," 89; Julien, "Mohamed-es-Senoussi et ses états" *BSRC* 8 (1927), 70–71; (1929), 79–80; P. Gentil, *La conquête du Tchad*, 1:113; Kalck, "Histoire," 3:52–56.

51. See Cordell, "Secondary Empire and Slave Raiding beyond the Islamic Frontier in Northern Equatorial Africa: The Case of Sa^{c}id Baldas and Bandas Hakim," paper presented at the annual meeting of the American Historical Association (Dallas, December 1977).

52. Like Rabih, Zemio, Mbele, and perhaps Ngono, Sa^{c}id Baldas and Tambura were former soldiers in the legions of al-Zubayr. Their careers are further examples of the wide-ranging effects of secondary empire in North Central Africa in the late nineteenth and early twentieth centuries. ANF-SOM (Paris), Tchad I, dossier 3, "Rapport d'un voyage de Raphai à Said Baldas";

ANF-SOM (Paris), Gabon-Congo II, dossier 9, Letter from Secretaire-Général de la Société antiesclavagiste de France to the Ministre des colonies, Paris, 20 June 1908; ANF-SOM (Paris), Gabon-Congo II, dossier 5, Grech, "Travail d'inspection"; ANF-SOM (Aix), Liotard to the Ministre des colonies, "Renseignements sur les derviches, occupation de Tamboura," Zemio, 10 December 1895; ANF-SOM (Aix), 4(3)D8, Prins, "Resumé du rapport sur l'inspection du Cercle de Rafai, Sultanat de Said Baldas," Said Baldas, 12 March 1901; ANF-SOM (Aix), 4(3)D15, Lt.-Gouverneur de L'Oubangui-Chari-Tchad, "Ancien groupement de Said Baldas," 25 June 1909; Pierre Prins, "L'Islam et les musulmans dans les sultanats du Haut-Oubangui," *AF* 17:6 (June 1907), 163–68; Julien, "Mohamed-es-Senoussi" (1928), 56–57, 62, 82, 92–93; Julien, "Le Dar Ouadai," 91; P. Gentil, *La conquête du Tchad*, 1:142; Modat, "Une tournée," 286 and n. 1; Hill, *A Biographical Dictionary*, 355.

53. Prioul based much of his description of Ubangi-Shari in the 1890s on Dybowski's travel account. See Prioul, *Entre Oubangui et Chari*, throughout.

54. Julien, "Mohamed-es-Senoussi" (1925), 145; Modat, "Une tournée," 232.

55. Prins, "Voyage au Dar Rounga," 193–96. The almost daily fluctuations in relations between the sultan and the French are chronicled in the following sources: Julien, "Mohamed-es-Senoussi" (1925), 104–77; (1927), 55–122; (1928), 49–96; (1929), 45–88; P. Gentil, *La conquête du Tchad*, vols. 1–2, throughout; Modat, "Une tournée," 177–98, 218–37, 270–89; Bruel, "Mohamed-es-Senoussi et ses états (Lettre de rectification)," 93–101; Bruel, *L'Afrique équatorial française* (Paris, 1930), 56–59.

56. AAV (Vincennes), A.E.F., L'Oubangui-Chari, série O³, ctn. 1, dossier 1, "Copie du Traité de Commerce et d'Alliance entre chiek Mohamed-es-Senoussi et la France (représentée par l'administrateur Gentil)," 24 August 1897; "Copie du Traité en date du 18 Février 1903 entre le sultan Senoussi et la France completant le traité signé le 24 Août 1897"; "Copie du Traité en date du 26 Janvier 1908 revisant le traité passé le 18 Février 1903 (traité signé par le Capitaine Mangin, représentant le Lt.-Colonel Largeau, et Mohamed-es-Senoussi)."

57. On the Marchand Mission and Franco-British rivalry on the upper Nile, see the following: Marc Michel, *La Mission Marchand, 1895–1899* (Paris, 1972); Roger Glenn Brown, *Fashoda Reconsidered* (Baltimore, 1969); Robert O. Collins, *King Leopold, England, and the Upper Nile, 1899–1909* (New Haven, 1968), 1–7, 47–56, 69; Ronald Robinson and John Gallagher with Alice Denny, *Africa and the Victorians* (New York, 1961), 339–78.

58. Carbou, *La région*, 2:132; Chevalier, *Mission*, 138–39; Kalck, "Histoire," 2:455–56.

59. See note 56 above.

60. Julien, "Mohamed-es-Senoussi" (1925), 116–17, 149; Modat, "Une tournée," 232.

61. On Rabih's defeat, see E. Gentil, *La chute de l'empire de Rabah*; Oppenheim, *Rabeh und das Tshadseegebiet* (Berlin, 1902), 99–117.

62. Julien, "Mohamed-es-Senoussi" (1927), 110–12, 114–17; (1928), 61–63;

(1929), 45–46; Chevalier, *Mission*, 139–41; Modat, "Une tournée," 233.

63. Julien, "Mohamed-es-Senoussi" (1928), 73, 83; Kalck, "Histoire," 3:76–77. As early as January 1902, the sultan had agreed in principle to pay tribute to the French, but thought the assessment too high. See Grech, "Essai sur le Dar Kouti," 25–29; and Julien, "Mohamed-es-Senoussi" (1928), 73, 83.

64. See note 57 above. There is no evidence that any of al-Sanusi's children actually made their way to Europe or North Africa.

65. ANF-SOM (Paris), Tchad I, dossier 4, Largeau, "Rapport général au début de 1908"; Bruel, *L'Afrique équatoriale française*, 57–58.

66. ANF-SOM (Aix), 4(3)D13, Largeau, "A/s du rattachement de N'Délé au territoire militaire du Tchad," Fort-Lamy, 30 May 1907; Modat, "Une tournée," 234; Kalck, "Histoire," 3:189; Hayer, "A Political History of the Maba Sultanate of Wadai," 43–45.

67. Modat, "Une tournée," 234; Carbou, *La région*, 2:158; Charles Tisserant, *Ce que j'ai connu de l'esclavage en Oubangui-Chari* (Paris, 1955), 16–17.

68. Modat, "Une tournée," 234.

69. Kalck, "Histoire," 3:189.

70. See note 57 above.

71. ANF-S0M (Aix), 4(3)D17, "Razzias commises par des bandes de Senoussi de N'Délé"; ANF-SOM (Aix), 4(3)D17, Lt.-Gouv. à M. le Gouv.-Général, "Resumé des rapports mensuels arrivés à Bangui depuis novembre 1910," Bangui, 6 December 1910.

72. Modat, "Une tournée," 234–37. The Yulu were defeated in this campaign, but after Allah Jabu's departure the survivors reoccupied the kaga.

73. There are several sources on the assassination and the immediate events leading up to it. See OA3.1; OA4.1, for eyewitness African accounts. See also OA17.2/18.1; ANF-SOM (Aix), 4(3)D49, Département du Dar-el-Kouti, "Rapport semestriel, 2ᵉ semestre 1937," Ndele, 10 February 1938; "Une nouvelle version du combat de N'Délé," *Revue indigène* 6:65 (September 1911), 521–23; Carbou, *La région*, 2:176–85; Anonymous, "Les derniers événements des territoires du Tchad," *AF* 21:2 (February 1911), 53–56; Kalck, "Histoire," 3:222–24.

74. ANF-SOM (Aix), 4(3)D13, Largeau, "A/s du Rattachement de N'Délé au territoire militaire du Tchad."

75. OA2.1; OA3.1; OA4.1; OA5.1; OA7.1; OA15.2/16.1; OA21.1; OA22.1; OA24.1; also see citations in note 73.

Chapter 4

Ndele: A Slave-Raiding Capital on the Islamic Frontier

1. AAV (Vincennes), A.E.F., L'Oubangui-Chari, "Lettre N° 19 du 18 Avril 1910 du Capitaine Modat, Commandant la circonscription de N'Délé, à Monsieur le Lieutenant-Gouverneur de l'Oubangui-Chari à Bangui, "Notice

ethnographique sur les populations du Dar-Kouti."

2. OA17.1; Chevalier, *Mission*, 137–38. For a photo of Kaga Toulou, see Bayle des Hermens, *Recherches préhistoriques en République Centrafricaine* (Paris, 1975), plate 28, between 96–97. Grech gives a slightly different itinerary: see "Essai sur le Dar Kouti," 23.

3. Terrier, "Snoussi d'El-Kouti," 394.

4. OA15.2/16.1; OA17.2/18.1; OA19.1/20.1.

5. OA9.1; OA9.2/10.1; OA11.1; OA17.2/18.1; OA19.1/20.1; OA20.2; OA20.3; ANF-SOM (Aix), 4(3)D51, "Rapport politique, 2ᵉ semestre, année 1939," Ndele, 25 January 1940. All sources with the exception of Julien agree that the Ngonvo were the indigenous inhabitants of the Ndele plateau. But there are some differences. For a more lengthy discussion, see Dennis D. Cordell, "Dar al-Kuti: A History of the Slave Trade and State Formation on the Islamic Frontier in Northern Equatorial Africa (Central African Republic and Chad) in the Nineteenth and Early Twentieth Centuries" (Ph.D. dissertation, University of Wisconsin, Madison, 1977), 228n5.

6. OA15.1.

7. OA20.2; OA20.3; OA, notes on a conversation with Abakar Tidjani, Runga-Nduka, Ndele, 23 June 1974.

8. OA17.2/18.1; OA19.1/20.1. Both Toulou and Ngonvo informants say that they are "one race." The Ngonvo were an exogamous group and frequently went to the Toulou for their marriage partners.

9. OA6.2; OA20.2; OA20.3; OA21.1; OA22.1.

10. OA9.2/10.1; OA13.1; OA17.2/18.1; OA19.1/20.1. See Gaudefroy-Demombynes, *Documents*, for Banda, Runga, Nduka, and Kresh wordlists.

11. OA6.2; OA7.2/8.1; OA9.1

12. OA7.2/8.1; OA15.1; OA19.1/20.1; OA20.3; OA, notes on a conversation with Zakharia Kouzoubali, Nduka Doggo, Village of Manga, 30 September 1974.

13. OA, notes on a tour of the Ndele ruins with Abudullu, Banda Ngao–Banda Marba, Ndele, 17 June 1974.

14. OA3.1; OA, notes on a tour of the Ndele ruins with Abudullu, Banda Ngao–Banda Marba, Ndele, 17 June 1974; Chevalier, *Mission*, 177–78; OA, notes on a conversation with M. Thomassey, Ndele, 30 August 1974.

15. ANF-SOM (Aix), 4(3)D51, "Rapport politique, 2ᵉ semestre, année 1938," Ndele, 25 January 1940; OA3.1; OA9.1; OA9.2/10.1; Julien, "Mohamed-es-Senoussi" (1925), 153.

16. OA3.1; Julien, "Mohamed-es-Senoussi" (1927), 100; AAV (Vincennes), A.E.F., L'Oubangui-Chari, Modat, "Notice ethnographique."

17. The phrase "close-settled zone" recalls the area of dense yet dispersed settlement around Kano in today's northern Nigeria. There are some similarities between this area and the Ndele region in al-Sanusi's time; both, for example, were populated by migrants many of whom were of non-Muslim slave ancestry. However, the Kano close-settled zone is of much earlier origin. In addition, activities within the region ranged from local, regional, and long-

distance commerce to manufacturing and agricultural production. The Ndele area was much less diversified. It is, however, intriguing to speculate about the proliferation of economic activity that might have occurred in the Ndele zone had the city continued to be a major center in the savanna of North Central Africa. On the Kano close-settled zone, see M. J. Mortimore and J. Wilson, *Land and People in the Kano Close-Settled Zone* (Zaria, 1965), throughout; Polly Hill, *Rural Hausa: A Village and a Setting* (Cambridge, 1972), 303, 333; Polly Hill, *Population, Prosperity and Poverty: Rural Kano, 1900 and 1970* (Cambridge, 1977), 4, 7, 44, 55–57, 59, 60, 65–69.

18. Bruel, *L'Afrique équatoriale française, 157–59*; Jean Ferrandi, "Abéché, capitale du Ouadai," *AF-RC* 22:10 (October 1912), 349; AMBB, N° 101 (Bangassou), Lucien Fourneau, "Au sujet du recensement de la population de la circonscription du M'Bomu," Bangui, 20 April 1910.

19. In Dar al-Kuti and other areas of Muslim Africa, a prisoner was in greatest danger of being sold into the trans-Saharan trade immediately after his or her capture. Once settled, a person was secure unless he or she incurred the wrath of a superior, in which case he or she might be sold as punishment. OA3.2, OA4.1, and OA15.2/16.1. See also Allan G. B. Fisher and Humphrey J. Fisher, *Slavery and Muslim Society in Africa* (New York, 1971).

20. For the elevations of various parts of the city, see Chevalier, *Mission*, map between 140–41.

21. Chevalier, *Mission*, 170.

22. OA, notes on a tour of the Ndele ruins with Abudullu, Banda Ngao–Banda Marba, Ndele, 17 June 1974; OA6.2; OA7.2/8.1.

23. Grech, "Essai sur le Dar Kouti," 52; Julien, "Mohamed-es-Senoussi" (1925), 161. Bangassou acquired a cannon in 1892; it can still be seen in his former capital (Eric de Dampierre, personal communication, 4 February 1983).

24. Kumm, *From Hausaland to Egypt*, 174; Chevalier, *Mission*, 142.

25. OA3.1; OA5.1; OA5.2/6.1; OA7.1.

26. Grech, "Essai sur le Dar Kouti," 50–51. Among the messengers was Yadjouma Pascal, who was about eighty years old in 1974. A retired Chef de Canton, he was one of my most important informants.

27. OA3.1; OA4.1; OA, notes on a tour of the Ndele ruins with Abudullu, Banda Ngao–Banda Marba, Ndele, 17 June 1974; Grech, "Essai sur le Dar Kouti," 50–51. Chevalier suggests that the sultan's wives were not sequestered, but rode about the city on donkeys, even traveling out to inspect agricultural villages. During these outings they wore long veils of blue cloth that covered their heads and most of their bodies. The Frenchman did observe, however, that young wives remained in the residence (see Chevalier, *Mission*, 145). Yadjouma, who grew up in the sultan's palace, insists that only servant women left the compound regularly.

28. OA3.1; Chevalier, *Mission*, 144–45.

29. OA3.1; OA6.2; OA7.2/8.1; OA11.1 and 11.2/12.1; OA, notes on a tour of the Ndele ruins with Abudullu, Banda Ngao–Banda Marba, Ndele, 17 June 1974.

30.   OA3.1; OA15.2/16.1; OA, notes on a tour of the Ndele ruins with Abudullu,
       Banda Ngao–Banda Marba, Ndele, 17 June 1974; Grech, "Essai sur le Dar
       Kouti," 36–37; Chevalier, *Mission*, 156–57 and map between 140–41.
31.   Kieffer, "Le Kouti," 292–93. During a second tour in Ndele, this friendship
       led to conflict between Mercuri and Julien, the first official French resident in
       the city. According to Julien, the Algerian wanted a free hand to deal with the
       sultan as he had during his first stay in Ndele when he often acted as the in-
       formal representative of the French government. See Julien, "Mohamed es-
       Senoussi" (1928), 67–68.
32.   OA3.1; ANF-SOM (Aix), 4(3)D13, Fourneau, "Rapport mensuel du mois
       de décembre 1906, Congo-Français: L'Oubangui-Chari-Tchad," Bangui, 12
       February 1907; Kumm, *From Hausaland to Egypt*, 184–85.
33.   OA1.1; OA3.1; OA, notes on a tour of the Ndele ruins with Abudullu, Banda
       Ngao–Banda Marba, Ndele, 17 June 1974.
34.   OA3.1; OA3.2.
35.   It is possible that these remains have been more disturbed in the years since
       the site was abandoned, although the evidence does not support this conclu-
       sion. Because this area is farther from inhabited portions of colonial and con-
       temporary Ndele than the western part of the terrace, there is less chance that
       people carried rocks away for later construction. While people have raised
       millet near the ruins of the sultan's compound, close examination of the ter-
       rain suggests that no crops were planted east of the first stream.
36.   OA3.1; ANF-SOM (Aix), 4(3)D19, "Résumé des rapports mensuels de
       l'Oubangui-Chari pour le mois de décembre 1911," Bangui, 19 February
       1911; Santandrea, "Sanusi, Ruler of Dar Banda and Dar Kuti," 153. In
       August 1974, Kamun's son Ibrahim returned to Ndele after the death of his
       cousin, the reigning sultan-mayor (named Muhammad al-Sanusi after his
       illustrious grandfather). Ibrahim assumed the traditional office of sultan.
       However, the government chose the occasion to reassert its direct authority in
       the Ndele subprefecture by redesignating the office of mayor a civil post as it
       had been during the colonial period. Despite discontent, the government
       appointed a functionary to the position. In this manner the sultan was stripped
       of most legal and administrative powers.
37.   OA3.1.
38.   Ibid. As is the case for western parts of the terrace, numerous potsherds sub-
       stantiate traditions reporting a dense population in the past.
39.   AAV (Vincennes), A.E.F., L'Oubangui-Chari, "Copie du traité en date du
       26 janvier 1908 revisant le traité passé le 18 février 1903." Modat and
       Tisserant claim that the 1903 treaty also outlawed the trade, but such a ban is
       not included in copies of the treaty that I have read. See Modat, "Une
       Tournée," 233; Tisserant, *Ce que j'ai connu de l'esclavage en Oubangui-
       Chari*, 16–17; AAV (Vincennes), A.E.F., L'Oubangui-Chari, "Copie du
       traité en date du 18 février 1903 entre le Sultan Senoussi et la France com-
       pletant le traité signé le 24 août 1897."
40.   OA3.1; OA3.2; OA4.1; OA8.2; OA15.2/16.1; OA17.1.

41. OA1.1; OA3.1. Not all Muslim craftsmen lived on the terrace. My eldest in-
    formant, ninety-five-year-old Boukar Froumbala, was a Bornoan who first
    came to Ndele in 1910 where he sold shoes (*markub* [Arabic]). He lived in
    the Bornoan quarter on the plain below the French post.
42. OA15.2/16.1. Yadjouma's ironworking abilities led the French administra-
    tor in Ndele in the early 1930s to send him to France to display smithing tech-
    niques at one of the colonial expositions. Yadjouma likes to tell the story of his
    trip, always ending with "my forge took me to France."
43. OA3.1.; OA11.1; OA14.2; OA15.1; OA15.2/16.1; OA17.2/18.1; OA19.1/
    20.1; Daigre, "Les Bandas de l'Oubangui-Chari," 655; Grech, "Essai sur le
    Dar Kouti," 41.
44. OA3.1; OA, notes on a conversation with Mahamat Ngouvela Dodo, Banda
    Ngao, Village of Mbollo, 5 June 1974.
45. OA3.1; ANF-SOM (Paris), 6P.A., Papiers Julien, "Annexe N° 4: Renseigne-
    ments sur les personnages du Dar-El-Kouti."
46. OA3.1.
47. D. T. Niane, *Sundiata: An Epic of Old Mali*, trans. G. D. Pickett (London,
    1965), 69–70.
48. OA3.1; OA, notes on a tour of the Ndele ruins with Abudullu, Banda Ngao–
    Banda Marba, Ndele, 17 June 1974. The testimonies of these two informants
    are in dispute over whether guardhouses bordered the plateau edge directly
    above al-Sanusi's compound. If they did, the guards could easily have observed
    the harem quarters below. How much protection the guardposts afforded is
    uncertain in any case.Mordrelle thought the sultan's residence could be
    captured from the bluffs above despite the sentry posts. See ANF-SOM
    (Aix), 4(3)D19, "Rapport du Colonel Mordrelle," 27 October 1910.
49. Kumm, *From Hausaland to Egypt*, 171. Kumm labels these areas
    "Manguele" and "Ernago." They can be classed more generally as Runga
    and Kresh; the Manguele were a Runga subgroup, and Ernago was a Kresh
    war leader. OA3.2; OA5.1; OA5.2/6.1; OA6.2; OA7.1; OA8.2; OA13.1;
    OA17.1; OA21.3; OA22.1; OA23.2. OA, notes on a conversation with
    Abakar Tidjani, Runga-Nduka, Ndele, 1 June 1974.
50. OA, notes on a conversation with Abakar Tidjani, Runga-Nduka, Ndele, 1
    June 1974; OA6.2; OA7.2/8.1.
51. Grech, "Essai sur le Dar Kouti" 31; Kumm, *From Hausaland to Egypt*, 171.
52. OA5.1; OA8.2; OA17.1; Kobur's sons, descendants of the earliest Runga in
    Dar al-Kuti, lived on the higher plateau just above this quarter.
53. OA1.2; OA2.1; OA5.1; OA8.2; OA14.1; OA17.1; ANF-SOM (Paris),
    6P.A., Papiers Julien, "Annexe N° 4: Renseignments sur les personnages du
    Dar-El-Kouti."
54. Chevalier, *Mission*, map between 140–41; Kumm, *From Hausaland to
    Egypt*, 171.
55. Kumm, *From Hausaland to Egypt*, 173.
56. OA1.2; OA3.1; OA4.1; OA5.2/6.1; OAl3.1; OA15.1; Rouget, *L'expansion
    coloniale au Congo-Français*, 826; Chevalier, *Mission*, 153.

57. OA3.1.
58. Ibid.; Julien, "Mohamed-es-Senoussi" (1928), 55.
59. Julien, "Mohamed-es-Senoussi" (1928), 95–96.
60. *Tipoyeur* refers to Africans who carried the Europeans' sedan chairs. By extension, the quarter also housed other Africans who worked for or were associated with the French.
61. A fruitful discussion on Christianity and Islam in Africa is that between Humphrey J. Fisher and Robin Horton. The series of their articles is as follows: Horton, "African Conversion," *Africa* 41:2 (1971), 85–108; Fisher, "Conversion Reconsidered: Some Historical Aspects of Religious Conversion in Black Africa," *Africa* 43:1 (1973), 27–40; Horton, "On the Rationality of Conversion, Part I," *Africa* 45:3 (1975), 219–35; Horton, "On the Rationality of Conversion, Part II," *Africa*, 45:4 (1975), 373–99. See also Nehemia Levtzion, ed., *Conversion to Islam* (New York, 1979); Dennis D. Cordell, "Review of Nehemia Levtzion, ed., *Conversion to Islam*," *Canadian Journal of African Studies* 16:2 (1982), 419–22.
62. Julien, "Mohamed-es-Senoussi" (1929), 46–47, 64–65; Modat, "Une tournée," 273; Prins, "L'Islam et les musulmans," 137.
63. Studies of Christianity, Islam, and other world religions show that to be viable they must accommodate themselves to local cultures. On Christian conversion, see Arthur Darby Nock, *Conversion* (London, 1933), 4–5, 8. Wolfhart Pannenberg goes even further in citing the ability of world religions to incorporate local traditions as the source of their strength. See *Basic Questions in Theology* (London, 1971), 2:86, 93–94. Fisher cites both authors in "Conversion Reconsidered," 26nn3,4; 33nn31, 33; 38n51.
64. Gustav von Grunebaum, "The Problem: Unity in Diversity," in *Unity and Variety in Muslim Civilization*, von Grunebaum ed., (Chicago, 1955), 20–21, 28.
65. OA7.2/8.1; Julien, "Mohamed-es-Senoussi" (1929), 55; John Spencer Trimingham, *Islam in West Africa* (London, 1959), 70.
66. OA5.1; OA13.1; OA14.2; OA22.3; Julien, "Mohamed-es-Senoussi" (1929), 63; A. G. B. Fisher and H. J. Fisher, "Glossary," in Nachtigal, *Sahara and Sudan IV*, 413, *muhajirun* entry.
67. OA5.2/6.1; OA7.1; OA11.2/12.1; OA21.4; ANF-SOM (Paris), Julien, "Annexe N° 3: Renseignements sur la famille Mohammed-es-Senoussi," 6P.A., ctn. 1, pièce 1, 155. The limitations of Islamic learning in Ndele were illustrated in 1902 when the sultan sent a delegation of religious leaders to Grech, then the French resident. He had studied Arabic and Islamic sciences in Algeria, and the party invited him to offer courses in Arabic poetry, literature, and philosophy at the Ndele mosque. Grech declined, saying that he would only give French language instruction. The delegation rejected his offer, firmly stating that they wished the city's children to be taught Arabic and Muslim beliefs. Advanced learning was not available in Ndele, but a definite desire existed to perpetuate and extend the great tradition of Islam. See Grech, "Essai sur le Dar-Kouti," 25. Learning remains limited. Several faqihs in Koundi, Kobur's natal village, studied in Wadai and the Sudan,

while the most learned among the younger teachers, Faqih Moukhtar, spent eight years at al-Azhar, returning to Dar al-Kuti in 1973. OA, notes on a session with Faqih Moukhtar, Village of Koundi, 21 June 1974; also see OA13.1; OA14.2.

68. OA6.2; OA13.1; OA, notes on a session with Issa Boukar, Ndele, 7 May 1974; Julien, "Mohamed-es-Senoussi" (1929), 63–64; Djian, "Notes sur les populations musulmanes," 12. The Tijaniya arrived in the Sudan around 1850, and the last sultan of Dar Fur, ^cAli Dinar, joined the order near the end of the century. See Jamil M. Abun-Nasr, *The Tijaniyya: A Sufi Order in the Modern World* (London, 1965), 158–59; Works, *Pilgrims in a Strange Land*, 54, 137, 159–60.

69. Counterparts in other parts of Africa include the terms *cerno* and *karamoko* in the Futa Jaalo, *serigne* among the Lebu and Wolof of Senegal, and *moodibbo* in northern Cameroon. For these terms and others, see Renaud Santerre, *Pédagogie musulmane d'Afrique noire* (Montréal, 1973), 45, 63, 171.

70. Grech, "Essai sur le Dar-Kouti," 45–46.

71. None of these conventions were unique to Dar al-Kuti. Al-Tunisi reported analogous practices in both Wadai and Dar Fur in the early nineteenth century; Burckhardt described similar amulets made by the faqihs of Berber on the Nile in the second decade of the century; and Pallme listed charm-making among the duties of religious leaders in Kordofan in the 1840s. Wingate and Schweinfurth noted similar customs later in the century in the central and southwestern Anglo-Egyptian Sudan, while numerous travelers and observers reported these practices during the colonial and contemporary eras. Not only did such practices persist through time, but Fisher's work demonstrates that similar practices existed throughout Islamic Africa. See OA15.2/16.1; OA22.3; ANT, W52.36, Lt. Jean Speckel, "Monographie de la Subdivision d'Am-Dam," Am-Dam, October, 1934, 85; OA, notes on a conversation with Koussingou Albert; al-Tunisi, *Voyage au Darfour*, 290; al-Tunisi, *Voyage au Ouaday*, 633n10; Burckhardt, *Travels*, 209–10; Pallme, *Travels in Kordofan*, 185–86; Francis Reginald Wingate, *Mahdism and the Egyptian Sudan* (London, 1891), 533; Schweinfurth, *The Heart of Africa*, 2:384–85; P. M. Holt,"Holy Families and Islam in the Sudan," in his *Studies in the History of the Near East* (London, 1973), 123; Humphrey J. Fisher, "Hassebu: Islamic Healing in Black Africa," in *Northern Africa: Islam and Modernization*, Michael Brett, ed. (London, 1973), 24, 26–28, 33–36. On the relationship between prayer and charms, see Humphrey J. Fisher, "Prayer and Military Activity in the History of Muslim Africa South of the Sahara," *Journal of African History* 12:3 (1971), 391–406. For an overview of Islamic culture on the desert edge in the nineteenth century, see Escayrac de Lauture, *Le Desert*, 446–47.

72. OA2.1; OA6.2; OA14.2; OA15.2/16.l; OA 17.1; OA22.3; Grech, "Essai sur le Dar Kouti," 45–46. *Hajab* refers to a veil, screen, cover, or amulet and comes from the Arabic verb *hajaba*, whereas *warga* is derived from *waraq*, Arabic for leaf, also used for sheets of paper. See R. Derendinger,

Vocabulaire pratique du dialecte arabe centre-africain (Paris, 1923), 175.
73. OA, notes on a conversation with Issa Boukar, Ndele, 7 May 1974; OA15.1;
    OA17.2/18.1; Grech, "Essai sur le Dar Kouti," 45. Al-Hajj Mouloukou, a
    faqih residing in Ndele in 1974, was a Malian pilgrim who stopped in the city
    on his way home from the Hijaz. He lived in a house built in the western
    Sudanese style—mud bricks with elaborate points protruding from the roof,
    and topped off with an ostrich egg. He supported himself by selling charms,
    and his clientele consisted mainly of Banda, Nduka, and other non-Muslim or
    only recently Islamized peoples; northern Muslims did not consult him.
    Mouloukou married two local women and planned to spend the rest of his life
    in Ndele (OA, notes on a conversation with al-Hajj Mouloukou, Ndele, June
    1974).
74. OA, notes on a conversation with Koussingou Albert, Ndele, 12 June 1974;
    Modat, "Une tournée," 282n2. This was still true in Ndele in 1974, where
    the sultan required that parties to an accord, Muslim or non-Muslim, seal
    their agreement by swearing on a Qur'an because he believed the oath would
    assure adherence.
75. OA1.1; OA1.2; OA2.1; OA5.2/6.1; OA6.2; OA7.2/8.1; OA13.1;
    OA15.2/16.1; OA22.3, Kumm, *From Hausaland to Egypt*, 262–64;
    Works, *Pilgrims in a Strange Land*, 27–29; Birks, *Across the Savannas to
    Mecca*, 8–16; al-Naqar, *The Pilgrimage Tradition*, 104–13. The accuracy
    of this judgment is corroborated by the large numbers of Bagirmi who arrived
    in Dar al-Kuti shortly after the foundation of the new capital; this migration
    coincided with strife in Bagirmi among the ruling family, the French, and
    Rabih's forces.
76. OA15.2/16.1; OA18.2. Yadjouma Pascal (OA15.2/16.1) also suggests that
    many Hausa and Bornoans moved east following Rabih's conquest of Borno
    in 1894, the French conquest of Bagirmi, and the later French campaigns
    against Rabih in 1900.
77. OA1.2; OA2.1; OA9.2/10.1; ANF-SOM(Aix), 4(3)D21 "Rapport de l'en-
    semble, 1914," ch. 1; ANF-SOM(Aix), 4(3)D21 Baudou, "Rapport
    mensuel," Gribingui, November 1914. Froumbala offers the following
    characterization of pilgrimage traffic in the 1930s: "They went many, from
    there [Dikwa] to Ndele; Hausa, Bornoans, a hundred or two hundred, three
    hundred, four hundred people—all of them going to Mecca!"
78. OA1.2; OA18.1. Froumbala, himself a Bornoan, suggests that Bornoans
    came to Dar al-Kuti mainly to trade, and that the hajj was secondary; the
    opposite applied to the Hausa.
79. Kumm, *From Hausaland to Egypt*, 147–48, 158; Carbou, *La région*, 2:179
    (quoting Modat).
80. Birks, *Across the Savannas to Mecca*, 69–70.
81. OA4.1; OA15.2/16.1; OA18.2; ANF-SOM (Aix), 4(3)D45, Rogué,
    "Rapport trimestriel, 3ᵉ trimestre, année 1934," Ndele. Froumbala des-
    cribed himself as one of the major onion producers in Ndele in the colonial
    era; Rogué confirms his story, reporting that the Bornoan employed ten men
    in his onion fields in 1934, harvested 4,000 kilograms which he sold for a

franc per kilo, and made a profit of 2,800 francs after paying his men. Hill claims that the Hausa are also famed far and wide for onion cultivation. See Hill, *Rural Hausa*, 302.

82. OA2.1; OA5.2/6.1; OA6.2; OA7.2/8.1; OA11.2/12.1; OA13.1; OA22.3. The dress and activities of pilgrims and faqihs display a remarkable continuity from the early nineteenth century to the early years of the colonial era. Burckhardt's list of the "equipment" of western pilgrims bears close resemblance to Djian's description of faqih-pilgrims in Chad. See Burckhardt, *Travels*, 367; Djian, "Notes sur les populations musulmanes," 11.

83. OA5.2/6.1; OA13.1; OA15.2/16.1; ANF-SOM (Paris), Julien, Papiers Julien, 6P.A., "Annexe N° 4: Renseignements sur les personnages du Dar-El-Kouti"; Grech, "Essai sur le Dar Kouti," 42. Al-Hajj Muhammad, a Hausa, also enjoyed considerable influence in Ndele. Born about 1860, he went to Mecca and was among a thousand African pilgrims invited to Istanbul by the Ottoman sultan. He spent six months in the Ottoman capital as a guest of the ruler, who provided the pilgrims with transportation to Suez in 1901 at the end of their sojourn. From there he traveled south, ending up in Ndele.

84. OA3.2; OA7.1; OA9.1; OA11.1; OA15.1; Julien, "Mohamed-es-Senoussi" (1929) 64–65. In the southwestern Sudan, another zone dominated by Islam, Banda peoples have borrowed the term *karama* which they use to mean feast or festival. See Santandrea, *Languages of the Banda and Zande Groups: A Contribution to a Comparative Study* (Naples, 1965), 157.

85. OA3.2; OA11.1; OA15.1.

86. OA3.2.

87. OA, notes on a conversation with Koussingou Albert, 12 June 1974; Charles Tisserant, *Dictionnaire Banda-Français* (Paris, 1931), 317–18.

Chapter 5

Slave-Raiding, the Slave Trade, and Agricultural Production

1. See, for example, E. W. Bovill, *The Golden Trade of the Moors*, 2nd ed. rev. (London, 1968); R. Mauny, *Tableau géographique de l'ouest africain au moyen âge* (Dakar, 1961).

2. See A. G. Hopkins, *An Economic History of West Africa* (London, 1973); Hill, *Population, Prosperity, and Poverty: Rural Kano, 1900 and 1970*; Jan Hogendorn, "The Economics of Slave Use on Two 'Plantations' in the Zaria Emirate of the Sokoto Caliphate," *International Journal of African Historical Studies* 10:3 (1977), 369–83.

3. See Paul E. Lovejoy, "The Characteristics of Plantations in the Nineteenth Century Sokoto Caliphate (Islamic West Africa)," *American Historical Review* 84:5 (December 1979), 1267–92; Paul E. Lovejoy, "Polanyi's 'Ports of Trade': Salaga and Kano in the Nineteenth Century," *Canadian*

Journal of African Studies 16:2 (1982), 245–77; Steven Brock Baier, *An Economic History of Central Niger* (London, 1980); Frederick Cooper, *Plantation Slavery on the East Coast of Africa* (New Haven, 1977); Emmanuel Terray, "Long Distance Exchange and the Formation of the State: The Case of the Abron Kingdom of Gyaman," *Economy and Society* 3 (1974), 315–45; Jack Goody, *Technology, Tradition, and the State in Africa* (London, 1971); Jack Goody, *Production and Reproduction* (Cambridge, 1977).

4.   OA23.1; Kogongar, "Introduction à la vie et à l'histoire précoloniale des populations Sara du Tchad," 204–7; Dybowski, *La route du Tchad*, 268–69; P. Daigre, *Oubangui-Chari: souvenirs et témoinages, 1890–1940* (Paris, 1950), 47.

5.   OA5.1; OA21.4; OA23.1; ANF-SOM (Aix), 4(3)D9, Administrateur du Haut-Oubangui à M. le Commissaire Général du Congo-Français, "Rapport politique," Mobaye, 30 July 1902; Chevalier, *Mission*, 145–46, 158; Julien, "Mohamed-es-Senoussi" (1929), 55; Modat, "Une tournée," 233.

6.   OA18.2; ANF-SOM (Aix), 4(3)D19, "Rapport du Colonel Mordrelle, Commandant supérieur des Troupes, sur une tournée d'inspection dans le Haut-Oubangui et dans la région du Tchad," 25 July 1910; Dybowski, *La Route du Tchad*, 70; Chevalier, *Mission*, 145–46, 152–53.

7.   OA21.4; Julien, "Mohamed-es-Senoussi" (1929), 55–56. The dawn ghazzia was also a favorite tactic of Wadaian raiders, and Smith suggests that movements in darkness followed by attack at daybreak were the most commonly practiced strategies in African warfare. See Smith, *Warfare and Diplomacy in Pre-Colonial West Africa*, 162; for Wadai, see Un saharien, "La question du Ouadai," *AF* 18:8 (August 1908), 285; ANT, W53.27, Lucien, "Note sur les rezzous kirdis, miniminis, zevois, etc.," Biltine, n.d. (probably between 1911 and 1915). Finally, a Sudanese manuscript translated and annotated by Richard Hill suggests that raiding in the southern Sudan in the early nineteenth century was similar in many respects to the ghazzias conducted in Ubangi-Shari much later. See Hill, *On the Frontiers of Islam* (London, 1970), 32–43.

8.   Decorse, *Du Congo au lac Tchad*, 174.

9.   ANF-SOM (Aix), 4(3)D19, "Rapport du Colonel Mordrelle"; Gaud, *Les Mandja*, 95–96; Julien, "Mohamed-es-Senoussi" (1925), 143; (1929), 56; Chevalier, *Mission*, 280–82.

10.   Chevalier, *Mission*, 283–84, 301–3; Modat, "Une tournée," 233.

11.   Chevalier, *Mission*, 280–82, 301–3.

12.   Mario J. Azevedo, "Sara Demographic Instability as a Consequence of French Colonial Policy in Chad (1890–1940)" (doctoral dissertation, Duke University, 1976), 58.

13.   A. Mesple, "Mercuri," *Bulletin de la société de géographie d'Alger et d'Afrique du Nord* (4e trimestre, 1902), 634–36; Julien, "Mohamed-es-Senoussi," (1928), 65–66; Modat, "Une tournée," 221; Kalck, *Realités oubanguiennes*, 98.

14. OA3.2; OA4.1; OA5.2/6.1; OA7.2/8.1; OA8.2; OA12.2; OA14.2; OA15.1; OA15.2/16.1; OA21.1; OA23.1; Dybowski, *La Route du Tchad*, 268–69, 273–74; Brunache, *Le centre de l'Afrique*, 120–21, 147–48; Bruel, *La France équatoriale africaine*, 208; Santandrea, "Sanusi, Ruler of Dar Banda and Dar Kuti," 152, 155.

15. ANF-SOM (Aix), 4(3)D11, Pape (Résident de France à Ndele) à M. le Délégué permanent du Commissaire-Général dans le Territoire de l'Oubangui-Chari à Bangui, Ndele, 23 October 1904; ANF-SOM (Aix), 4(3)D13, Largeau to M. le Lt.-Gouv. de L'Oubangui-Chari-Tchad, "A/s du rattachement de N'Délé," Fort-Lamy, 30 May 1907; ANF-SOM (Aix), 4(3)D14, Lucien Fourneau, "Le rapport d'ensemble pour l'année 1908," cahier 3, sous-cahier C ("Région du Haut-Chari, Cercle de Gribingui"), 2 August 1909, 4–5; Julien, "Mohamed-es-Senoussi" (1928), 75.

16. Kumm, *From Hausaland to Egypt*, 187–88.

17. ANF-SOM (Aix), 4(3)D49, "Rapport semestriel, 2e semestre 1937," Ndele, 10 February 1938.

18. Decorse and Gaudefroy-Demombynes, *Rabah et les arabes du Chari*, 9n1. On the firearms trade in the Central Sudan in general, see Smaldone, *Warfare in the Sokoto Caliphate*, 94–109.

19. OA4.1; OA17.1; Chevalier, *Mission*, 58, 145–46; ANF-SOM (Paris), Papiers Julien, 6P.A., "Rapport du Cap^ne Julien . . . du Ba-Mingui"; Grech, "Essai sur le Dar Kouti," 51–52.

20. P. Gentil, *La conquête du Tchad*, 1:87; Julien, "Mohamed-es-Senoussi" (1929), 49; Chevalier, *Mission*, 145–46; Tisserant, *Ce que j'ai connu de l'esclavage en Oubangui-Chari*, 16–17; Carbou, *La région*, 2:158; ANF-SOM (Aix), 4(3)D17, "Rapport politique du ler trimestre 1910," Bangui, 28 April 1910.

21. Julien, "Mohamed-es-Senoussi" (1929), 49; Hill, *A Biographical Dictionary*, 272.

22. Julien, "Mohamed-es-Senoussi" (1929), 49–52. Oral traditions and other contemporary written sources confirm this general pattern of organization, as well as the names of individual banner commanders. See OA4.1; OA5.1; OA17.2/18.1; OA22.3; Chevalier, *Mission*, 146–52, 158.

23. OA3.2; OA5.2/6.1; OA15.2/16.1; Julien, "Mohamed-es-Senoussi" (1929), 50; Grech, "Essai sur le Dar Kouti," 51–52. *Mbang* is a Barma and Sara word for chief, while *ghafara* is an Arabic verb meaning "to guard" (a *ghafir* is a guard). That the sultan's personal guard would have a Barma-Arabic name is perhaps more evidence of an earlier close connection between Dar al-Kuti and Bagirmi.

24. OA3.1; OA5.1; OA11.2/12.1; Grech, "Essai sur le Dar Kouti," 51–52; Julien, "Mohamed-es-Senoussi" (1929), 49–50, 52–54.

25. Julien, "Mohamed-es-Senoussi" (1929), 52–53; AAV (Vincennes), A. E. F., L'Oubangui-Chari, série O³, ctn. 1, dossier 1, "Copie du Traité de Commerce et d'Alliance entre cheik Mohamed-es-Senoussi et la France," 24 August 1897. Modat, an exceptionally observant French resident who served

in Ndele at the end of al-Sanusi's reign, accepted the general accuracy of
Julien's estimates. See Modat, "Une tournée," 234n1.

26. Chevalier, *Mission*, 146–47; Grech, "Essai sur le Dar Kouti," 51–52.

27. Modat, "Une tournée," 234n1.; ANF-SOM (Aix), 4(3)D17, "Rapport
     politique du ler trimestre 1910."

28. Julien, "Mohamed-es-Senoussi" (1929), 54; Grech, "Essai sur le Dar
     Kouti," 51–52; ANF-SOM (Aix), 4(3)D17, "Rapport politique du ler
     trimestre 1910."

29. For a brief discussion of advances in weaponry in Europe in the nineteenth
     century and the technical differences among gun-types, see "Fusil," *La
     Grande Encyclopedie Larousse* (Paris, 1973), 5223–24.

30. OA11.2/12.1; OA15.2/16.1; OA17.2/18.1; Julien, "Mohamed-es-Senoussi"
     (1929), 52; Chevalier, *Mission*, 146–47; Grech, "Essai sur le Dar Kouti,"
     51–52; Terrier, "Snoussi d'El-Kouti," 397; ANF-SOM (Paris), Gabon-
     Congo III, dossier 13b, Dolisie, "Mission Crampel"; ANF-SOM (Aix),
     4(3)D19, Administrateur du Haut-Oubangui, "Rapport politique," Mobaye,
     30 July 1902.

31. Julien, "Mohamed-es-Senoussi" (1929), 52. Another large percentage of the
     flintlocks was taken in massacres mentioned earlier; the remainder came from
     the Congo Independent State and raids in the southeast. Once again, oral
     traditions and other contemporary sources confirm these supply patterns
     after 1900. See OA11.2/12.1; OA15.2/16.1; OA18.2; Terrier, "Snoussi
     d'El-Kouti," 397; Dampierre, *Un ancien royaume Bandia*, 467.

32. Modat came to the same conclusion when he was French resident in Ndele.
     See Modat, "Une tournée," 233, 234n1.

33. OA5.1; OA7.2/8.1; OA9.1; OA23.2.

34. Kalck, *Réalités oubanguiennes*, 81–83.

35. OA3.1; OA4.1.

36. OA5.1.

37. OA9.1; OA9.2/10.1; OA19.1/20.1; Grech, "Essai sur le Dar Kouti," 49.

38. Julien, "Mohammed-es-Senoussi" (1929), 56–57; Grech, "Essai sur le Dar
     Kouti," 49.

39. OA3.2; OA5.1; OA7.2/8.1; OA13.1; OA19.1/20.1.

40. OA19.1/20.1; OA21.4; Julien, "La situation économique du Dar-el-Kouti,"
     39.

41. Nachtigal, *Sahara und Sudan*, 1:704.

42. Ibid., 2:724.

43. Ibid.

44. OA3.2; OA11.2/12.1; OA13.1; OA19.1/20.1; OA21.4; OA23.2. On blood
     partnership, see Cordell, "Blood Partnership in Theory and Practice: The
     Expansion of Muslim Power in Dar al-Kuti," *Journal of African History*
     20:3 (1979), 379–94.

45. Fisher and Fisher, *Slavery and Muslim Society*, 87–88, 91, and throughout.

46. Yadjouma Pascal was born about 1900, and when he was very small
     al-Sanusi's men raided his village, taking him and his parents prisoner. The

raiders took them to Ndele, where his mother was sold to long distance traders. Because his father was a blacksmith, the sultan settled him in his capital. Yadjouma ended up in the sultan's compound, where he grew up doing minor household chores such as serving tea and fetching al-Sanusi's slippers. He also became a Muslim, received the name Wadai Husayn, and attended the garai with the ruler's children. After al-Sanusi's death, Yadjouma's father reclaimed him, had him initiated in the traditional Banda manner, and trained him to be a blacksmith. Ruminating over the course of his long life in 1974, Yadjouma suggested that he might have become a military commander had al-Sanusi lived: "... for other things, how do I know? Maybe he would have placed me as a big man ... or perhaps he would have put me after Wald Banda when Wald Banda died, have placed me with the drum [regiment] of Wald Banda ... I was then a bit small ... was there, he would send me, send me ... I'd open the storehouse and I brought chairs, I brought water to those visiting al-Sanusi ... but he died before me" (OA15.2/16.1). Wald Banda had been raised in al-Sanusi's household some years before Yadjouma. But Yadjouma noted, too, that the art of smithing was important in the colonial era and improved his fortunes. Despite the hardships al-Sanusi was responsible for, Yadjouma always refers to the sultan as "aba Sanusi," father Sanusi (OA3.2).

47. OA3.1 Wadaian horsemen hiding outside Sha had also kidnapped unsuspecting individuals. Khrouma Salle says that this was a minor factor in the decision to settle on the plateau at Ndele (see OA14.2). Sudanese traders in eastern Ubangi-Shari also acquired slaves by kidnapping. Tisserant wrote that in this area, the Sudanese—called Nubians or *turungu* (Banda, loanword from *turk* [Arabic]) were known as people who would take anything they wanted, including isolated individuals. The Banda labeled them *poro* (from *ayi-ke-poro*, "those who seize"). See Tisserant, *Essai sur la grammaire Banda*, 10 and 10n2.

48. On the reasons for the high demand for young women as slaves, see Claire C. Robertson and Martin A. Klein, eds., *Women and Slavery in Africa* (Madison: University of Wisconsin Press, 1983), introduction.

49. OA3.1; OA4.1.

50. Kalck, "Histoire," 3:65–66.

51. Al-Tunisi, *Voyage au Darfour*, 253; Nachtigal, *Sahara und Sudan*, 2:615, 710–11; Modat, "Une tournée," 223n1; ANF-SOM (Aix), 4(3)D49, A. E. F., Département du Dar el-Kouti, "Rapport semestriel, 2e semestre 1937," Ndele, 10 February 1938. Burton identified this general area as a major supplier of eunuchs in the late nineteenth century as well. The Middle Eastern trade in eunuchs was substantial; Burton estimated that 8,000 such slaves from all sources were imported into Egypt and Turkey annually. See PRO (London), F.O. 141/145, Richard Burton (British Consul) to Lord Granville, Trieste, 7 February 1881.

52. Modat, "Une tournée," 182.

53. Al-Tunisi, *Voyage au Ouaday*, 43n1.

54. Burckhardt, *Travels*, 290.
55. Nachtigal, *Sahara and Sudan IV*, 189; Fisher and Fisher, "Glossary," in Nachtigal, *Sahara and Sudan IV*, 415.
56. Schweinfurth, *The Heart of Africa*, 2:418–19.
57. Nachtigal, *Sahara und Sudan*, 1:692. Nachtigal's list is as follows:

Type (males)	Price (thalers)	Type (females)	Price (thalers)
old man (*kjari*)	4–5	old woman (*komorsu*)	6–10
strong adult	12–14	middle-aged woman (*schomalija*)	10–15
young adult (*gurzem*)	15–18	young girl (*surrija*)	40–100
7-span youth (*sub^cai*)	16–22		
6-span youth (*sedasi*)	20–25		
5-span youth (*chomasi*)	16–20	5-span young girl (*chomasija*)	20–25
boy eunuch (*adim*)	50–80		

58. James Richardson, *Narrative of a Mission to Central Africa* (London, 1853), 2:202–3. For a study of the slave trade in the Sokoto Caliphate (which encompassed Kano and Katsina) during this period, see David Carl Tambo, "The Sokoto Caliphate Slave Trade in the Nineteenth Century," *International Journal of African Historical Studies* 9:2 (1976), 187–217.
59. Julien, "La situation économique du Dar-el-Kouti," 38; Julien, "Mohamed-es-Senoussi" (1929), 69–70.
60. There were at least three major smallpox epidemics in precolonial Ndele between 1901 and 1906. The first occurred in late 1901 when Adam returned to the city with 2,500 captives from the southeast. One-half of the slaves died outside the city and the remainder died after arriving in the capital. The epidemic continued into early 1902, and Mercuri, the commercial agent in Ndele, wrote that there were twenty deaths each day; al-Sanusi ordered that the population be variolated for protection. Another outbreak occurred in late 1902 when one-half of a party of 2,000 new Banda Tombaggo slaves died. In 1906 French colonial authorities in Bangui reported another major outbreak of smallpox in Ndele. See Julien, "Mohamed-es-Senoussi" (1928), 65–66; Mesple, "Mercuri"; Kalck, *Réalités oubanguiennes*, 98; ANF-SOM (Aix), 4(3)D18, A. E. F., Colonie de l'Oubangui-Chari-Tchad, "Rapport annuel 1911," Bangui, 6 June 1912, 96.
61. Modat, "Une tournée," 232.
62. Kalck, "Histoire," 3:74–75.
63. Modat, "Une tournée," 232.
64. Ralph Austen has set the stage for such work with his overview of the trans-Saharan trade. See Austen, "The Trans-Saharan Slave Trade: A Tentative

Census," in *The Uncommon Market: Essays in the Economic History of the Atlantic Slave Trade*, Henry A. Gemery and Jan S. Hogendorn, eds. (New York, 1979), 23–76.

65. Kalck, "Histoire," 1:277.
66. Frederick Cooper, "The Problem of Slavery in African Studies," *JAH* 20:1 (1979), 117–19, 121–22; Cooper, *Plantation Slavery*, 1, 3–6, 18–19, 254–55, 259, 268.
67. Emile Leynaud, "Parenté et alliance chez les Banda du district de Bria, région de la Kotto, Dar-el-Kouti," *Bulletin de l'institut des études centrafricaines (Brazzaville)*, nouvelle série, 7–8 (1954), 111–12, 125, 156–57; Toque, *Essai sur le peuple et la langue Banda*, 22–23; Charles Tisserant, "Le mariage dans l'Oubangui-Chari," *Bulletin de l'institut des études centrafricaines (Brazzaville)*, nouvelle série, 2 (1951), 81; Daigre, *Oubangui-Chari*, 71, 73–74; Kalck, "Histoire," 1:xii; P. Daigre, "Les Bandas de l'Oubangui-Chari," *Anthropos* 27 (1932), 153–54.
68. OA5.2/6.1; Chevalier, *Mission*, 166, 170; Chevalier, "De l'Oubangui au lac Tchad à travers le bassin du Chari," 352; Grech, "Essai sur le Dar Kouti," 34; Modat, "Une tournée," 196.
69. One informant insisted that when an individual wanted a field, he simply cleared it. With clearing (*gata^ca*, "to cut" [Chadic Arabic]) came landholding rights (OA17.1). While this custom is common in Africa, and probably was the rule in the Ndele area following the dispersal of the population in 1911, the size of the population of the city during the heyday of al-Sanusi would, it seems to me, have precluded such a haphazard manner of land allotment. It seems more likely that cultivation areas were assigned to ethnic communities when they resettled in Ndele.
70. OA3.1; OA9.1
71. OA3.1; OA4.1; OA17.2/18.1.
72. OA3.2; OA7.2/8.1; OA8.2; OA17.2/18.1.
73. OA8.2; OA17.1; OA22.1; OA22.3; OA24.1.
74. OA4.1; OA15.2/16.1.
75. OA3.2; OA9.2/10.1; OA15.1. In this century, first the French and then the Central African Republic governments insisted that villages be located on the three or four major roads from Ndele to ease the task of tax collection and provide shelter for travelers. In many cases, villages were not near land suitable for cultivation. Today some villagers have solved this problem by building "summer" houses near their fields and living there in the growing season. They make periodic visits to their "official" residences during this time, but only permanently inhabit them in the dry season. In several instances, when interviewing informants in the 1974 rainy season, I arrived to find a village completely deserted; passers-by or people from neighboring settlements directed me through a maze of paths to informants' fields— sometimes fifteen kilometers away in the bush. Interviews with Siam Munju of Kour (OA20.3) and Ngrekoudou Ouih Fran of Ouih Fran (OA17.2/18.1) were conducted at their field houses; other informants talked to me during visits to their permanent villages (OA9.1; OA15.1; OA19.1/20.1).

76. Courtet, "Mission scientifique Chari–Lac Tchad: Le pays Snoussi," *Revue des troupes coloniales* 3 (2nd semester, 1904), 485n1.
77. Chevalier, *Mission*, 166, 168–70.
78. OA3.2; OA4.1; OA9.2/10.1; APBB, Alain Atchia, Secretaire-Générale de la Préfecture du Bamingui-Bangoran, "Liste des Villages de la Commune rurale de Mbollo-Kpata (Sous-Préfecture de Ndele)," Ndele, 29 April 1974. Today the Mbollo commune boasts a road to Ndele, a postal outlet, and a population of three thousand people—Courtet's total for all the agricultural villages in 1901–2.
79. OA3.2; OA4.1; OA5.2/6.1; OA7.2/8.1.
80. OA15.1; OA15.2/16.1; OA17.1; OA17.2/18.1; Chevalier, *Mission*, 171–73, 183–86.
81. OA15.1; OA17.2/18.1; ANF-SOM (Paris), Papiers Julien, 6P.A., "Rapport du Cap[ne] Julien sur sa reconnaissance du Ba-Mingui"; Chevalier, *Mission*, 84–85; Chevalier, "Mission scientifique au Chari et au lac Tchad," 354–55.
82. OA5.2/6.1; OA6.2; OA7.1; OA8.2; OA13.1; OA22.1; OA23.2; OA24.1; Kumm, *From Hausaland to Egypt*, 174.
83. OA5.2/6.1; OA7.2/8.1; OA13.1; OA14.2; OA21.4; OA22.1.
84. OA7.2/8.1; OA8.2; OA22.1.
85. OA, account of Souia, Nduka Doggo, Village of Manga, 1 October 1974, collected by Moussa Josef (Puskas Ricky); OA, account of Mustapha Seleman, Nduka Doggo, Village of Manga, 3 October 1974, collected by Moussa Josef (Puskas Ricky); OA, account of Zakharia Kouzoubali, Village of Manga, 30 September 1974, collected by Moussa Josef (Puskas Ricky).
86. OA, notes on two sessions with Abakar Tidjani, Runga-Nduka, Ndele, 1 June and 26 June 1974.
87. OA1.2; OA2.1; ANF-SOM (Aix), 4(3)D21, Schmoll, "Rapport de tournée, Nord-Est du Dar Kouti," Affaires politiques N° 78, Ndele, 26 March 1914 (in dossier "Dar-Kouti 1914"); Chevalier, *Mission*, 188–90.
88. OA4.1; OA13.1; OA14.1; OA17.1; OA22.3; OA24.1; Grech, "Essai sur le Dar Kouti," 20; Chevalier, *Mission*, 198–99.
89. OA5.1; OA5.2/6.1; OA6.2; OA7.1; OA7.2/8.1; OA13.1; OA14.2; OA23.1; OA23.2; OA24.1; Grech, "Essai sur le Dar Kouti," 49. For example, Awat, the son of Futur Amkur, an important landholder in Akrousoulba, became a banner leader under Sanusi. He survived the violence accompanying the sultan's assassination, and fought the French at Ouanda-Djale in 1912 (see OA6.2).
90. OA7.2/8.1; OA20.2; OA20.3; OA, account of Zakharia Kouzoubali, Nduka Doggo, Village of Manga, 30 September 1974, collected by Moussa Josef (Puskas Ricky).
91. OA7.2/8.1; OA14.1; OA20.3.
92. For descriptions of Banda agriculture, see Tisserant, "L'Agriculture dans les savanes de l'Oubangui," 212–57; P. Daigre, "Plantes alimentaires du pays Banda," *BSRC* 8 (1927), 123–34.
93. OA4.1; OA6.2; OA7.1; OA8.2; OA17.1; Kalck, "Histoire," 3:65–66;

Chevalier, *Mission*, 165. Large plantations belonging to al-Hajj Abdo were nearby.

94. OA4.1; OA6.2; OA7.2/8.1; OA8.2; OA11.1; OA13.1; OA17.1; OA17.2/18.1.
95. Chevalier,"De l'Oubangui au lac Tchad à travers le bassin du Chari," 352.
96. OA4.1; OA5.2/6.1; OA17.1.
97. OA5.2/6.1; OA7.2/8.1; OA8.2; OA11.1; OA13.1.
98. OA4.1
99. OA7.2/8.1; OA9.2/10.1; OA19.1/20.1; OA22.1; Daigre, "Les Bandas de l'Oubangui-Chari," 153.
100. Most of my information on Mouka and Ouadda comes from archival research. I was unable to collect oral data in these settlements—which still exist today—because of limitations of time and transportation.
101. ANF-SOM (Aix), 4(3)D13, Lucien Fourneau, "Rapport mensuel du mois de décembre, 1906," Bangui, 17 February 1907; CC, Cornet, "Au Coeur de l'Afrique centrale"; Modat, "Une tournée," 182; Kumm, *From Hausaland to Egypt*, 184–85.
102. ANF-SOM (Aix), 2(D)25, Bos, "Rapport," 28 April 1901, 17–18; Tisserant, *Ce que j'ai connu de l'esclavage en Oubangui-Chari*, 16–17; Modat, "Une tournée," 234.
103. ANF-SOM (Aix), 4(3)D13, Peron (Directeur, Société "La Kotto") à M. le Commandant de la Région du Haut-Oubangui, "Réponse aux lettres N°s. 353 et 356," Kassa, 11 July 1905.
104. ANF-SOM (Aix), 4(3)D45, Rogué, "Rapport trimestriel, 4e semestre, et rapport annuel, année 1934," Ndele, 30 November 1934, 3.
105. The Latin terms for these plants are cited in the following sources: Chevalier, *Mission*, 126–28; Tisserant, "L'Agriculture dans les savanes de l'Oubangui," 237, 241.
106. Julien, "Mohamed-es-Senoussi" (1929), 75; Chevalier, *Mission*, 162.
107. OA4.1; OA15.2/16.1; Chevalier, *Mission*, 221.
108. Chevalier, *Mission*, 166.
109. Recent research confirms this conclusion. See A. B. L. Stemler, J. R. Harlan, and J. M. J. deWet, "Caudatum Sorghums and Speakers of Chari-Nile Languages in Africa," *JAH* 16:2 (1975), 161–83, which gives background on sorghum cultivation in general.
110. Robert Jaulin, *La mort Sara*, 18–26 and throughout; Joseph Fortier, "Introduction," in his *Le mythe et les contes de Sou en pays Mbai-Moissala* (Paris, 1967), 26, 33–36.
111. OA9.2/10.1; Tisserant, "L'Agriculture dans les savanes de l'Oubangui," 216.
112. Gillier, "Les Bandas: notes ethnographiques," *AF-RC* 23:11 (November 1913), 391.
113. OA7.1; OA17.2/18.1; OA23.1; OA24.1. Chevalier, "Mission scientifique au Chari et au lac Tchad," 356; Chevalier, *Mission*, 217. Because nomenclature describing millet and sorghum in Africa is not at all standardized, positive

identification is difficult. Stemler and her colleagues note that "durra" and "millet" are general terms used for sorghums even in much of the academic literature. They continue: "The term 'millet' may mean *Sorghum bicolor* (great or giant millet); *Pennisetum americanum* (Linn.) K. Schum. (pearl or bulrush millet); *Eleusine coracana* (Linn.) Gaetrn. (finger millet); *Digitaria exilis* (Kippist) Stapf. (fonio acha, or hungry rice); *Digitaria ibura* Stapf. (black fonio); or *Brachiaria deflexa* (Schumach.) C. E. Hubbard ex Robyns (guinea millet)." See Stemler et al., "Caudatum Sorghum," 164n6.

114. OA, notes on a conversation with Muhammad Abakar, Ndele, 8 July 1974; OA5.1; OA7.1; OA17.2/18.2; OA23.1. The drink is used in many ritual contexts: 1) as an offering following the harvest; 2) as a libation dedicating new weapons and tools; 3) as an offering for the fertility of newly cleared and planted fields; 4) as a means of bringing good fortune to a newborn child; 5) as a blessing for a new village site; 6) as an offering by widows to their deceased mates; 7) as a general tribute during mourning; and 8) as a reward to workers engaged in group labor. Personal observation in Ndele and environs; also see Daigre, "Les Bandas de l'Oubangui-Chari," 154–55; Tisserant, "L'Agriculture dans les savanes de l'Oubangui," 211.

115. OA1.1

116. OA5.2/6.1.

117. Chevalier, *Mission*, 217.

118. ANF-SOM (Aix), 4(3)D41, Subdivision autonome de N'Délé, "Rapport trimestriel, 2ᵉ trimestre, année 1931," Ndele, 30 June 1931; ANF-SOM (Aix), 4(3)D19, "Résumé des rapports mensuels des Circonscriptions de l'Oubangui-Chari," Bangui, October 1912; APBB, District de N'Délé, "Monographe du District de N'Délé," Ndele, 1953; OA, notes on a conversation with Abakar Tidjani, Ndele, 23 June 1974; OA2.1; OA4.1; OA7.1; OA21.1; OA22.1; Santandrea, "Sanusi, Ruler of Dar Banda and Dar Kuti," 154.

119. See Christian Prioul, "Notes sur la diffusion du manioc dans la partie centrale du territoire centrafricaine," unpublished paper, Ecole Nationale d'Administration (ENA), Bangui, n.d. This brief paper provides an excellent overview of the spread of manioc in the Central African Republic. Much of this information has recently appeared in Prioul, *Entre Oubangui et Chari*.

120. Marvin P. Miracle, *Agriculture in the Congo Basin* (Madison, Wisconsin, 1967), 231–32; Reay Tannahill, *Food in History* (New York, 1973), 245–46.

121. Tisserant, "L'Agriculture dans les savanes de l'Oubangui," 217.

122. Prioul, "Notes sur la diffusion du manioc," 2–4.

123. Prioul, *Entre Oubangui et Chari*, 93–96.

124. Prioul, "Notes sur la diffusion du manioc," 3–9.

125. Tisserant, "L'Agriculture dans les savanes de l'Oubangui," 215.

126. Michel Georges, "La vie rurale chez les Banda (République centrafricaine)," *Les cahiers d'outre-mer* 16:64 (October-December 1963), 330–32; 346. Schweinfurth noted that in Mangbetu country southeast of Dar al-Kuti in

today's northeastern Zaire, manioc could be left in the ground as long as two or three years. See Schweinfurth, *The Heart of Africa*, 1:526.

127. Daigre, "Les Banda," 156; Prioul, "Notes sur la diffusion du manioc," 8–9; Tisserant, "L'Agriculture dans les savanes de l'Oubangui," 218.

128. For Dar al-Kuti this information is based on personal observation in 1974; for the Ouaka River region, see Tisserant, "L'Agriculture dans les savanes de l'Oubangui," 258.

129. Tannahill, *Food in History*, 246.

130. Hanolet, "L'exploration du commandant Hanolet vers les sources du Chari (suite)," *La Belgique coloniale*, 2ᵉ année, N° 24 (14 June 1896), 284.

131. ANT, W46.2c, Montchamp, Chef du Département du Salamat, "Au sujet de la tournée effectuée à Aboudeia du 22 septembre au 9 octobre 1937," Am Timan (Chad), 19 October 1937; ANT, W46.7, Cassamatta, Chef du Département du Salamat, "Rapport politique, ler semestre, 1940," Am Timan (Chad), 9; AMBB, No. 81 (Bangassou), "Dossiers sur les vols des acridiens," 1931–38, Bangassou.

132. ANF-SOM (Aix), 4(3)D41, Subdivision autonome de N'Délé, "Rapport trimestriel, 2ᵉ trimestre, année 1931," Ndele, 30 June 1931.

133. Decorse, *Du Congo au lac Tchad*, 60; Prins, "Voyage au Dar Rounga," 194–95; Brunache, *Le centre de l'Afrique*, 100–102, 186; Dybowski, *La Route du Tchad*, 155–58; Chapiseau, *Au pays de l'esclavage*, 102.

134. Dybowski, *La Route du Tchad*, 175–76.

135. Chevalier, "Mission scientifique au Chari et au lac Tchad," 356; Chevalier, *Mission*, 220.

136. OA1.1; OA5.1; OA5.2/6.1; OA7.1; OA9.1; OA9.2/10.1; OA15.1; OA17.2/18.1; OA19.1/20.1; OA22.1; OA23.1.

137. BENA, Dossier entitled "Rapports annuels sur la Compagnie de la Ouhame et de la Nana," document as follows: Gouvernement Général du Congo-Français, Colonie de l'Oubangui-Chari, "Rapport général sur la Société de l'Ouhame et de la Nana pour l'année 1918," Fort-Crampel, 20 August 1919. BENA holds an assortment of files dating from the early colonial period. Unfortunately, they have not yet been classified or numbered, which makes reference difficult. For a brief outline of the contents of this collection as well as a report on other archives relating to the Central African Republic and Chad, see Cordell, "Archival Report."

138. Prioul, "Notes sur la diffusion du manioc," 9–11; for sensitive accounts of the trials and tribulations of the peoples of Ubangi-Shari during the early colonial period, see the following: André Gide, *Voyage au Congo* (Paris, 1927); André Gide, *Le Retour du Tchad* (Paris, 1928); René Maran, *Batouala* (Paris, 1921 or 1938). Maran published the definitive edition of his work, which won the Prix Goncourt in 1921, in 1938.

Chapter 6

Long-Distance Commerce in Ndele

1. OA5.2/6.1; OA8.2; OA13.1; OA21.1; OA21.2; OA21.3; AAV (Vincennes), A. E. F., L'Oubangui-Chari, "Lettre N° 19 du 18 Avril 1910 du Capitaine Modat, Commandant la circonscription de N'Délé, à Monsieur le Lieutenant-Gouverneur de l'Oubangui-Chari à Bangui, "Notice ethnographique sur les populations du Dar-Kouti."

2. OA3.2; OA4.1; OA8.2; OA21.4; OA22.3. Sultan ⁶Ali Dinar of Dar Fur required merchants to carry papers giving their name and destination, which helped him to control trade and tax shipments of goods. See Alan Buchan Theobald, ⁶Ali Dinar, Last Sultan of Darfur, 1898–1916 (London, 1965), 2l6.

3. OA13.1.

4. Grech, "Essai sur le Dar Kouti," 19–54.

5. OA7.1; Rouget, L'Expansion coloniale au Congo-français, 825–26; Kumm, From Hausaland to Egypt, 185; Grech, "Essai sur le Dar Kouti," 39; Kalck, Réalités oubanguiennes, 99.

6. OA1.2; OA2.1; OA3.2; OA7.1; OA8.2; OA13.1; OA14.2; OA17.1 OA23.2; Chevalier, Mission, 153; Terrier, "Snoussi d'El-Kouti," 397–98.

7. OA1.2. In the original Chadic Arabic, the quotation is as follows: "kullu, kullu, kullu, lé askar hannahu, lé miskine hannahu, iatu . . . kullu—hu bes bantu, hu bes bantu, hu bes bantu!" See also OA19.1/20.1; OA22.3.

8. OA15.2/16.1.

9. OA3.2; OA8.2; OA17.1; OA23.1; Terrier, "Snoussi d'El-Kouti," 397–98; Al-Tunisi, Voyage au Ouaday, 275, 488; Daigre, Oubangui-Chari, 47.

10. Modat, "Une tournée," 194; Santandrea, A Tribal History, 232–33.

11. ANF-SOM (Aix), 2D25, Bos, "Rapport," 28 April 1901; Modat, "Une tournée," 182.

12. Works, Pilgrims in a Strange Land, 59; Yunes Bedis, "Tales of the Wadai Slave Trade in the Nineties," Sudan Notes and Records 23:1 (1940), 169–83.

13. OA2.1; OA4.1; OA7.1; OA15.1; OA18.2.

14. Chevalier, Mission, 153.

15. OA3.2; OA9.2/10.1; OA14.2; OA15.2/16.1; OA19.1/20.1.

16. Santandrea, "Sanusi, Ruler of Dar Banda and Dar Kuti," 155. To be sure, this attitude is partly an outgrowth of the contemporary myth of al-Sanusi common among peoples of northern and eastern Ubangi-Shari. As a great figure from the precolonial past, he is assigned attributes that he may not have had. But not all of these feelings are based on groundless sentiment; many of the informants that Santandrea encountered in the 1950s and a few of those interviewed in Ndele in 1974 were alive during the sultan's lifetime.

17. For a discussion of the landlord-broker arrangement, see Polly Hill, "Landlords and Brokers: A West African Trading System," Cahiers d'études africaines 6

(1966), 349–66; Abner Cohen, *Custom and Politics in Urban Africa: A Study of Hausa Migrants in Yoruba Towns* (Berkeley and Los Angeles, 1969), 6–9, 17–22, 38–41, 71–92, 96–103.

18. For a general presentation of the basic organization and function of a trading diaspora, see Cohen, "Cultural Strategies in the Organization of Trading Diasporas," in *The Development of Indigenous Trade and Markets in West Africa*, Claude Meillassoux, ed. (London, 1971), 266–81.

19. Schweinfurth, *The Heart of Africa*, 2:219, 228, 417; Browne, *Travels in Africa*, 285; Barth, *Travels*, 2:660; Nachtigal, *Sahara and Sudan IV*, 353–54; al-Tunisi, *Voyage au Ouaday*, 341.

20. OA3.2; OA4.1; OA8.2; OA13.1; OA15.2/16.1; OA17.1; OA23.2; ANF-SOM (Paris), Papiers Julien, 6P.A., "Annexe No. 4: Renseignements sur les personnages du Dar-El-Kouti." Even after consulting both oral and written sources, it is not always possible to distinguish the Jallaba from Fur migrants in Ndele. In his biographical notes on prominent persons in Dar al-Kuti, Julien used both terms without explaining the distinction between them. Informants in Dar al-Kuti identify both Fur and Jallaba as Jallaba, although they occasionally call some of them "Sharia." Julien suggested that "Sharia" is a local term referring to an individual of mixed Jallaba-Runga ancestry (*djellabi d'origine devenu Runga*). This definition is accurate in the case of at least one merchant mentioned here: ʿIssa Wald al-Ribb had a Jallaba father and a Runga mother.

21. OA4.1; OA5.1; OA15.2/16.1. The settled Jallaba of al-Sanusi's era fled after his assassination; others who settled in the city early in the colonial era left during a prolonged period of economic decline in the 1950s. A lone Sudanese trader-tailor lived in Ndele in 1974. He provided shelter and acted as a landlord-broker for his countrymen, who dominate the dry season truck traffic between Nyala in the southwestern Sudan and Bangui (by way of Birao and Ndele). By this time, however, the Sudanese did most of their business in Bangui—mainly exchanging cloth, Sudanese manufactured goods, and Arabic books for wood. In Ndele they sold only a few items to obtain CFA francs for the trip south.

22. OA3.2; OA4.1; OA15.2/16.1. The marriages were as follows: ʿAbd al-Rassul to ʿAzza; Rashid to ʿAjji; al-Nagar to Andaza; and Zaruk to Shamma. Fartak did not marry one of al-Sanusi's daughters, although the sultan presented him with several concubines. This information substantiates Julien's claim that Fartak was only an underling of the ruler. See ANF-SOM (Paris), Papiers Julien, 6P.A, "Annexe N° 4."

23. OA4.1.

24. OA3.1; OA3.2; OA4.1; OA14.2; OA15.2/16.1; ANF-SOM (Paris), Papiers Julien, 6P.A., "Annexe N° 4"; Grech, "Essai sur le Dar Kouti," 45, 52; Kalck, "Histoire," 3:61–62.

25. ANF-SOM (Paris), Papiers Julien, 6P.A., "Annexe N° 4."

26. OA17.1.

27. OA1.1; OA1.2; OA2.1; OA5.1; OA5.2/6.1; OA7.2/8.1; OA11.2/12.1; OA15.2/16.1; OA18.2; OA22.3; ANF-SOM (Aix), 4(3)D19, Estebe,

"Rapport d'ensemble sur la situation générale de la colonie en 1912," Bangui, October 1913; Works, *Pilgrims in a Strange Land*, 28–30. During the colonial period, Hausa and Bornoan traders played a major role in the economic life of Ubangi-Shari. The French encouraged them to settle near their administrative posts. They even installed a Hausa-Tuareg merchant named Shéffou as "chef de terre" in Fort-Crampel (today's Kaga Bandero). But the precolonial period was not forgotten; Shéffou married the daughter of al-Sanusi's son Adam. See R. P. Oliver's notes on a conversation with Shéffou in Crampel in 1966 (a copy of these notes is in the author's possession). See also ANF-SOM (Aix), 4(3)D20, "Rapport d'ensemble sur la situation générale de l'Oubangui-Chari en 1913," Bangui, 18 July 1914; BENA, Dossier entitled "Kémo-Gribingui: Rapports annuels, 1915, 1916, 1917, 1918, 1920," document as follows: Chef de la Circonscription de la Kémo-Gribingui, "Rapport annuel pour l'année 1917," 1918; BENA, Dossier entitled "Kémo-Gribingui: Rapports trimestriels, 1919, 1920, 1921," document as follows: Chef de la Circonscription, "Rapport trimestriel, année 1920, troisième trimestre," Fort-Sibut, 27 September 1920.

28. OA4.1; OA15.2/16.1. For a description of fadama agriculture near Kano in Hausaland, see Mortimore and Wilson, *Land and People in the Kano Close-Settled Zone*, 20–23. The Hausa and Bornoans introduced fadama cultivation of onions and other condiments (such as ginger, shallot, and garlic) in some of their settlements along the Logone River in southwestern Chad as well (personal communication from John A. Works, Jr., 19 August 1976). The pilgrimage route directly linked this region with Dar al-Kuti. In Ndele, the Bornoans remained major onion producers in the colonial period. Boukar Froumbala, a Bornoan informant, claims that he began growing and selling onions in Ndele in the 1930s. In 1934, the French administrator in the city estimated Boukar's onion harvest at 4,000 kilograms. See OA18.2; ANF-SOM (Aix), 4(3)D45, Rogué, "Rapport trimestriel, 3ᵉ trimestre, année 1934," Ndele.

29. OA1.2; OA2.1; OA18.2. No other sources mention ᶜAli Bimini. Of course, he may well have come to Ndele after Julien's departure in December 1902. But the fact that informants deny even having heard of him suggests that Boukar may have exaggerated his importance.

30. ANF-SOM (Paris), Papiers Julien, 6P.A., "Annexe N° 4."

31. Ibid.

32. Emile Gentil, *La chute de l'empire de Rabeh*, 58.

33. ANF-SOM (Paris), Papiers Julien, 6P.A., "Annexe N° 4." In the late nineteenth and early twentieth centuries, French colonial officials were quick to label any North African a fanatic agent of the Ottoman Porte or the Sanusiya brotherhood. Any recalcitrance towards the French was explained by reference to the Islamic menace. So writes Grech: "If, in the area of religion, the Muslim element of the country seems hostile towards you, it is assuredly due to the numerous followers of the Sanusiya who try by every means to extend their influence in this direction, and who come to carry on propaganda in favor

of their acts" (Grech, "Essai sur le Dar Kouti," 54). This phobia was not unique to the Ubangi-Shari colony, but infected the French throughout Africa. See Henri Duveyrier, *La Confrérie musulmane de Sidi Mohammed Ben Ali es-Senousi* (Paris, 1884).

34. Nachtigal, *Sahara and Sudan IV*, 202. Many North African merchants arriving in Wadai consigned merchandise to Jallaba traders at Nimro outside Abeche who then took the goods farther south.

35. OA11.2/12.1; OA17.1; OA18.2; Julien, "Mohammed-es-Senoussi" (1925), 56–57, 136–37, 142.

36. OA13.1; OA14.1; Chevalier, *Mission*, 152–53, 162. Dar Sila exported cattle, donkeys, and horses to other southern areas as well. Victor Liotard, named French Governor of Upper Ubangi in 1894, noted the activity of Sila merchants at Dem al-Zubayr and recommended that the French encourage it (although he hoped to offer exports other than slaves). See ANF-SOM (Aix), 4(3)D6, Liotard, "Résumé de la situation politique du Cercle de Dem Ziber (Août, 1897)," Dem Ziber, 10 August 1897. There is no evidence that a foreign Muslim community played an important intermediate role in the cattle industry in Ndele, as did, for example, the Hausa in Ibadan. See Cohen, *Custom and Politics*, 15–16, 74, 77–82.

37. OA5.1; OA8.2; OA21.4.

38. Hopkins, *An Economic History of West Africa*, 70. The currencies did not always perform all of these functions, but this is not a limitation peculiar to currencies in Dar al-Kuti. Curtin notes that "no currency is absolutely all-purpose in any society, simply because no society makes payments for all the purposes payments can be made." He goes on to say that for the Senegambia region "currencies were not special-purpose or general-purpose, but more-general-purpose or less-general-purpose." The same situation prevailed in northern Ubangi-Shari. See Philip D. Curtin, *Economic Change in Precolonial Africa: Senegambia in the Era of the Slave-Trade* (Madison, 1975), 233–34.

39. For a survey of cloth currencies in West and North Central Africa, and an insightful theoretical analysis of how they functioned in the economies of these regions, see Marion Johnson, "Cloth Strip Currencies," paper presented at the joint annual meeting of the African Studies Association and the Latin American Studies Association (Houston, Texas, November 1977).

40. Julien, "La situation économique du Dar-el-Kouti," 39; Grech, "Essai sur le Dar Kouti," 37.

41. OA1.1; Derendinger, *Vocabulaire pratique du dialecte arabe centre-africain*, 48. For a drawing of a roll of cloth currency, see Alison Hingston Quiggin, *A Survey of Primitive Money—The Beginning of Currency* (London, 1963), 86 (Figure 22).

42. Al-Tunisi, *Voyage au Darfour*, 318–19. Johnson makes a similar observation: "Cloth strip did sometimes circulate as a sole currency, though it was necessarily supplemented by some form of 'small change' for the smallest market transactions, since there was a lower limit beyond which fractions of a

strip ceased to be useful. Small change usually took the form of beads or grain" (Johnson, "Cloth Strip Currencies," 13).

43. Hans Wehr, *A Dictionary of Modern Written Arabic*, J. Milton Cowen, ed. (Ithaca, 1966), xiv, 777.

44. In Dar Fur, ^cAli Dinar levied a cloth tax in kind called a *tekaki* and used the material to clothe his soldiers. See Theobald, *^cAli Dinar*, 216.

45. Chevalier, *Mission*, 154.

46. Johnson, "Cloth Strip Currencies," 13. Based on his own work on the economic history of Niger, Baier also suggests that a commodity currency like cloth in Dar al-Kuti would be largely self-regulating. (Personal communication from Stephen Baier, 28 December 1976.)

47. OA9.1.

48. Tisserant submitted that the Banda terms for beads derived from Arabic: *kharaz* (Arabic) first became *krizi* in Banda, which in turn gave rise to *ke dji*, "to be round." He goes on to theorize from this evidence that the Arabic-speaking Jallaba and Khartoumer traders first introduced beads among the Banda after 1850. See Tisserant, *Essai sur la grammaire Banda*, 13.

49. OA5.1; OA6.2; OA8.2; OA11.2/12.1; OA13.1; OA21.4; OA22.3.

50. OA5.1; OA7.2/8.1; OA11.2/12.1; al-Tunisi, *Voyage au Ouaday*, 333.

51. OA4.1; OA7.2/8.1; OA9.1; OA11.2/12.1; OA17.2/18.1.

52. In part this lag was probably related to the fact that among the Banda beads were involved in customary social service payments such as bridewealth, a use of the currency that dated from well before their resettlement in Ndele.

53. The Spanish thaler was called *abu mudfa* in Arabic, "the possessor of cannons," probably because two columns resembling artillery pieces were embossed on one side. See al-Tunisi, *Voyage au Ouaday*, 163; al-Tunisi, *Voyage au Darfour*, 316; Gaston Jules Decorse, "Rapport économique et zoologique sur la région du Tchad," *AF-RC* 14:5 (May 1905), 190. The Russian thaler or *abu tera* ("the possessor of a bird") was imprinted with a large bird. See OA8.2; al-Tunisi, *Voyage au Ouaday*, 675. For a lengthy study of the thaler and its use as currency in the Muslim world, see Marcel Maurice Fischel, *Le Thaler de Marie-Thérèse* (Paris, 1912). For a study of the thaler in North Central Africa in the precolonial and colonial eras, see Raymond Gervais, "The Monetary Policy of France and Great Britain towards the M. T. Thaler in the Kanem-Bornu Region, 1880–1920" (M.A. thesis, University of Birmingham, 1979), introduction and chapter 1; Gervais, "La plus riche des colonies pauvres: la politique monétaire et fiscale de la France au Tchad, 1900–1920," *Canadian Journal of African Studies* 16:1 (1982), 5–26.

54. Grech, "Essai sur le Dar Kouti," 36.

55. OA1.1; OA8.2; OA11.2/12.1; OA15.2/16.1; OA17.2/18.1; Derendinger, *Vocabulaire pratique du dialect arabe centre-africain*, 55; Gaston Muraz, *Vocabulaire du patois arabe tchadien ou tourkou et des dialectes sara-madjingaye et sara-mbaye (S.E. du Tchad) suivi de conversations et d'un essai de classification des tribus saras* (Paris, 1926), 126.

56. Julien, "La situation économique du Dar-el-Kouti," 39; Grech, "Essai sur le

Dar Kouti," 38. These estimates check well against the quantities of ivory sold in Ndele in 1922, one of the few years in the early colonial period for which complete statistics are available. That year, buyers bought 5.5 tons in public auctions (nine months) and open market purchases (three months). Many changes occurred in Ubangi-Shari and Dar al-Kuti between 1911 and 1922, so these figures can be taken only as a very general verification of the estimates of Grech and Julien.

Ivory Purchases in Ndele, 1922

Month	Quantity (kilograms)	Price Paid	Unit Price (per kilogram)
January	1,892.3	43,248F	22F85
February	410.0	unknown, open market	unknown
March	500.0	unknown, open market	unknown
April	370.0	unknown, open market	unknown
May	745.0	11,810F	15F85
June	540.0	10,000F	18F51
July	345.4	5,627F	16F49
August	110.0	2,441F	22F19
September	148.0	2,811F	18F99
October	54.7	1,200F	21F93
November	343.0	4,800F	26F99
December	108.4	2,225F	20F52
Total	5,566.1	89,162F	16F52 (average)

57. Julien, "La situation économique du Dar-el-Kouti," 39. For details concerning the formation and activities of the concessionary companies in French Equatorial Africa during the early colonial period, see Jean Suret-Canale, *Afrique noire occidentale et centrale II: l'ère coloniale, 1900–1945* (Paris, 1964), 29–64; Catherine Coquery-Vidrovitch, *Le Congo au temps des grandes compagnies concessionaires, 1898–1930* (Paris, 1972); BENA, Jacques Serre, "Histoire économique et sociale du district de Grimari (1907–1958)." It is possible that the Belgian commercial companies in the south had begun by this time to draw ivory from the lands east of Dar al-Kuti. These operations were established well before the French Compagnie des Sultanats du Haut-Oubangui.

58. OA, notes on a conversation with Abakar Tidjani, Runga-Nduka, Ndele, 26 June 1974. Most goods (salt, sugar, etc.) came from the north well into the colonial period; only in the 1930s, when the Sudanese trader Malik and the French merchant Tours opened a truck route to Bangui, did a preponderance of imported goods come from the south. Before this time, there were "arrivages" of goods from the south to supply the outlets of ivory collection companies in the city, but generalized commerce between Ndele and Bangui was very limited.

59. Prins, "L'Islam et les musulmans," 136. Prins continued in the same vein.

"There is in this an excess of self-confidence which is understandable, coming from isolated men absorbed in a great endeavor, as the bellringer is [absorbed] by the vibrations which from his hand seem to take in all the world. But there is not one phrase from a report which should inspire greater disbelief than this: 'our voyage produced a great impression, as had been foreseen.' "

60. Kalck, *Réalités oubanguiennes*, 111. In the early colonial period, exaggerated estimates of the ivory supply led officials to demand impossibly high amounts of ivory from local authorities. The outrageous demands brought a familiar reaction: people abandoned their villages and fled into the bush.

61. Julien, "La situation économique du Dar-el-Kouti," 39. In estimating the profitability of the ivory trade in Africa during the precolonial period, it has been commonly assumed that transportation costs were low since slaves were usually used to carry the tusks. Hence the frequent association of commerce in ivory and slaves. This was not often the case in Dar al-Kuti and the Ubangi-Shari. Prins goes so far as to say that slaves never transported ivory; other sources indicate that ivory was carried by oxen or donkeys. See Pierre Prins, "Esclavage et liberté dans les sultanats du Haut-Oubangui," *Revue indigène* 12 (April 1907), 128; OA5.1; OA17.2/18.1; OA18.2; Nachtigal, *Sahara and Sudan* IV, 89; ANF-SOM (Aix), 4(3)D11, Le Délégué du Comissaire-Générale dans le territoire de l'Oubangui-Chari, "Rapport mensuel du mois de Juillet," Bangui, 20 August 1904.

62. ANF-SOM (Aix), 4(3)D9, Congo-Français, Ht-Oubangui, Poste de Rafai, "Rapport politique mensuel," May 1902.

63. Julien, "Mohammed-es-Senoussi" (1928), 74–75.

64. ANF-SOM (Aix), 4(3)D9, Sultan al-Sanusi to Bangassou, letter in Arabic with a translation by the French translator at Zemio, 22 May 1902. The French commandant in Bangassou agreed with al-Sanusi's assessment of Bangassou's culpability, reporting that in February or March 1902 the men of Tombaggo chief Badangbakia ambushed a party of Muslim merchants traveling from Ndele to Bangassou. Attacked near the Kotto River, they were bringing cattle, horses, and assorted merchandise to the Nzakara settlement. The Frenchman blamed Bangassou for the violence, noting that before the sultan killed and imprisoned the northern merchants in his capital, Muslim caravans from Ndele had always traveled in security. See ANF-SOM (Aix), 4(3)D9, Thouand (ler commandant de cercle), "Rapport du mois de Mai, 1902," Bangassou, 1 June 1902; Grech, "Essai sur le Dar Kouti," 38.

65. Julien, "La situation économique du Dar-el-Kouti," 39; Grech, "Essai sur le Dar Kouti," 37; personal communication from Stephen Baier, 28 December 1976.

66. OA7.2/8.1; OA15.1; OA17.2/18.1; OA, notes on a conversation with Souia, Nduka Doggo, Village of Manga, 1 October 1974, collected by Moussa Josef (Puskas Ricky); Gillier, "Les Bandas: notes ethnographiques," *AF-RC* 23:11 (November 1913), 386–89. The Banda traditionally hunted elephants in the dry season with a long spear called a *kukap* bearing a wide point. Individual hunters sometimes set traps for the animals, but group hunts were more

common. A village hunting party would fan out systematically, occupying the perimeter of a large tract of land known to harbor elephants. Bush fires would then be set. The animals either died in the fire or were killed by the hunters as they attempted to flee. During the early colonial period, when there was a ready market for ivory, large hunting parties killed dozens of elephants at once in this fashion. Boukar Froumbala, the Bornoan who bought ivory in Ippy for French commercial companies in the 1920s, says that sometimes a hundred elephants died in these fires (OA2.1; OA18.2). Burthe d'Annelet confirmed this practice, noting that sometimes more than fifty elephants would be killed on a single outing (*A travers l'Afrique française*, 2:1341). For a description of a Banda hunt, see Maran, *Batouala*, chapters entitled "M'Bala" (elephant [Banda]) and "Mourou" (panther [Banda]).

67. OA2.1; OA17.2/18.1; OA19.1/20.1; Chevalier, "Mission scientifique au Chari et au lac Tchad."

68. OA4.1; OA9.2/10.1; OA11.1; OA11.2/12.1. Among the Banda the chief or war leader generally had first choice of the booty taken in a military or hunting mission. But all participants had a claim to some part of the reward, including even a man who had loaned a shield to a comrade. In the case of elephants, this practice continued into the colonial period. See Toque, *Essai sur le peuple et la langue Banda*, 48; ANF-SOM (Aix), 4(3)D30, A. E. F., Colonie de l'Oubangui-Chari, Circonscription du Dar-Kouti occidental, "Rapport mensuel, année 1922, mois d'avril," Ndele.

69. OA2.1; Nachtigal, *Sahara and Sudan IV*, 81–83, including Fisher's note 1, 82; Works, *Pilgrims in a Strange Land*, 59; Kumm, *From Hausaland to Egypt*, 185; Kalck, *Réalités oubanguiennes*, 99.

70. The classifications of these plants are found in the following sources. *Fil-fil*: G. L. Lethem, *Colloquial Arabic: Shuwa Dialect of Bornu, Nigeria, and of the Region of Lake Chad* (London, 1928), 391. *Kombo*: Chevalier, *Mission*, 749; Tisserant, *Dictionnaire*, 589; Henri Carbou, *Méthode pratique pour l'étude de l'arabe parlé au Ouaday et à l'est du Tchad* (Paris, 1913), 195. *Dorot*: Lethem, *Colloquial Arabic*, 393. *Jamsinda*: L. Joly, "Essences parfumées du Haut-Oubangui français," *La parfumerie moderne* 21 (1937), 27. Joly lists the term *Kadjidji damsondok* among several for the plant.

71. Fisher, "The Eastern Maghrib and the Central Sudan," 280–82.

72. *Jamsinda* is a loan word of undetermined origin into Chadic Arabic. ᶜAbd al-Rahman Nasr of the Centre for African and Asian Studies, University of Khartoum, provided me with the word for jamsinda in Classical Arabic (personal communication, Madison, Wisconsin, 28 September 1976). Lane's *Lexicon* described the plant as "a certain kind of sweet-smelling root; it is a rhizoma, round, black, hard, like a knot," and speculated that the term was sometimes applied to a species of cyprus (*Cyperus complantus*). See Edward William Lane, *An Arabic-English Lexicon Derived from the Best and Most Copious Eastern Sources*, 8 vols. (London, 1872), 1:1361–62. The *Lexicon* was reprinted in 1956, with the original pagination (New York: Frederick Ungar).

73. OA10.2; ANT, W46.7, Cassamatta, Chef du Département du Salamat, "Rapport politique," 1er semestre, 1940, Am-Timan, 1 July 1940; Personal communication from Eric Siegel, N'Djaména (Chad), February 1974. Siegel has studied the economic history of Wadai in the nineteenth century. A reference to jamsindi as "perfume, grasses used for burning" also appears in Lethem's vocabulary of Shuwa Arabic of Borno, although local supplies of the plant probably came from the nearby Lake Chad region rather than Dar al-Kuti. See Lethem, *Colloquial Arabic*, 393.

74. OA7.1; OA10.2.

75. OA5.1; OA7.1; OA7.2/8.1; OA10.2; OA13.1; OA15.2/16.1. Nobody today recalls the exact price of the roots in precolonial Ndele, although Dingis noted that "a long time ago" a *guntar* (about fifty kilograms) of jamsinda brought two *rials* or four tukia cloth strips (the approximate price of a calf in 1901). The value of the plant increased markedly during the colonial period; Dingis' father sold it for 2½ times as much. In 1974 Dingis marketed jamsinda to Sudanese merchants from Nyala for 3,000 CFA per guntar. In the Sudan and Chad, a guntar brought four times this price. The volume of the commerce in al-Sanusi's time is also unknown, although it was not uncommon for a wealthy merchant to head north with six donkey loads. In the first half of 1974, Dingis sold thirty guntars (1,500 kilograms). See OA10.2; Julien, "La situation économique du Dar-el-Kouti," 40.

76. *Kombo* and *dorot* are also loan words of undetermined origin.

77. OA10.2; ANT, W45.2, "Rapport trimestriel du Salamat, 1er trimestre, 1926"; Carbou, *Méthode pratique*, 195; Roth-Laly, *Lexique des parlers arabes tchado-soudanais/An Arabic-English-French Lexicon of the Dialects Spoken in the Chad-Sudan Area*, 2:160; Tisserant, *Dictionnaire*, 589; Lethem, *Colloquial Arabic*, 391. In Banda, kombo is called *majindi* or *mazindi*.

78. Pallme, *Travels in Kordofan*, 49.

79. OA22.3; Julien, "Mohammed-es-Senoussi" (1929), 73; Chevalier, "Mission scientifique au Chari et au lac Tchad," 352; Chevalier, "De l'Oubangui au lac Tchad à travers le bassin du Chari," 351; Rouget, *L'expansion coloniale au Congo-français*, 826–27.

80. Julien, "La situation économique du Dar-el-Kouti," 39.

81. Chevalier, "De l'Oubangui au lac Tchad à travers le bassin du Chari," 351; Chevalier, *Mission*, 168, 222–23; Grech, "Essai sur le Dar Kouti," 44. For a drawing of the excelsa plant, see Chevalier, *Mission*, 169. Following his discovery, Chavalier sent excelsa beans to France for study. Eventually, an *excelsa* hybrid was developed and widely planted in French Indochina. In 1935 Tonkin produced 701 tons of *arabica* and 171 tons of excelsa. See Auguste Chevalier, *Le café* (Paris, 1944), 86–87, 95–96, 106; Bruel, *L'Afrique équatoriale française*, 198–99.

82. Rouget, *L'expansion coloniale au Congo-français*, 826–27; Grech, "Essai sur le Dar Kouti," 38–39; Chevalier, *Mission*, 153–54; OA7.2/8.1; OA22.3; Kalck, "Histoire," 3:64–65; Serre, "Histoire économique et sociale du district de Grimari," 60–61.

83. H. R. Palmer, Acting Resident of Kano in 1916, quoted in John Paden, *Religion and Political Culture in Kano* (Berkeley, 1973), 30–31: "At the present time, the dominant factor, as far as trade is concerned, is that Kano is the distributing centre for Manchester goods and native cloths; north, as far as Agades; east, as far as Wadai; and southeast to the region of Kuti and Darsilla, and almost to the Ubangi."

84. OA5.1; OA22.3. There were no mineral salt deposits in Dar al-Kuti or adjacent Banda lands. People traditionally acquired salt by cutting, drying, and burning several varieties of plants, and then leaching the ashes. See AMBB, N° 108 (Bangassou), Werhegge, "Salines des chefferies Bobo Daya et Gosueba," 1923; Chevalier, *Mission*, 221–22; Bruel, *L'Afrique équatoriale française*, 194; Tisserant, "L'Agriculture dans les savannes de l'Oubangui," 245.

85. ANF-SOM (Aix), 4(3)D19, Estebe, "Rapport d'ensemble sur la situation générale de la colonie en 1912," Bangui, October 1913. Estebe included a trade summary for Ndele in 1912.

86. Tisserant, "Annexe: la question de l'ondro," at end of Leynaud, "Parenté et alliance chez les Banda," 163.

87. OA18.2. Julien suggested that the sultan could at best gather ten tons of rubber. This quantity would sell for about 10,000F (4,000 magta^c), not enough to satisfy even his cloth needs. Grech estimated that a harvest of 25 tons (25,000 kilograms or about 25,000F) was within the realm of possibility, but even this quantity would not have provided adequate income. See Julien, "La situation économique du Dar-el-Kouti," 39; Grech, "Essai sur le Dar Kouti," 38.

88. Chevalier, *Mission*, 160–61.

Conclusion

1. See J. Forbes Munro, *Africa and the International Economy, 1800–1960* (Totowa, N. J.), 1976, 13–16.

2. See Cordell, "Secondary Empire and Slave-Raiding beyond the Islamic Frontier in Northern Equatorial Africa: The Case of Bandas Hakim and Sa^{c}id Baldas," 8–27.

3. For analyses of the interrelationships between long-distance trade and the domestic economy in a precolonial West African state, see Lovejoy, "Polanyi's 'Ports of Trade' "; Terray, "Long-Distance Exchange and the Formation of the State: The Case of the Abron Kingdom of Gyaman," 315–45; Emmanuel Terray, "Classes and Class Consciousness in the Abron Kingdom of Gyaman," in *Marxist Analyses and Social Anthropology*, Marc Bloch, ed. (London, 1975), 85–135.

4. To cite another example of market and non-market influence on internal exchange, the Banda of Ndele who had beads knew that beads were valued as

bridewealth. They also knew that beads were sometimes difficult to obtain, generally requiring the supply of valuable local items to Muslim traders. The merchants, in turn, established the price of beads on the basis of 1) how much they had paid for them; and 2) how much they thought the Banda wanted and needed them for important social payments. The Muslims who governed Dar al-Kuti also used state power to support the merchants and their activities.

5.   Lovejoy provides a useful statement of this intermediate position concerning another part of Africa. See "The Plantation Economy of the Sokoto Caliphate," paper presented at the annual meeting of the American Historical Association (Washington, December 1976), 46n17:

> The interaction between the market-oriented sector and that part of the economy based on redistribution needs to be explored in greater detail. The implication of the argument presented here is that neither the formalists, such as Hopkins, nor the substantivists, including Polanyi, Dalton, and others, are correct in analysing economic change purely in terms of market or non-market factors. A much more fruitful approach appears to exist through an examination of the interaction between different types of economic organization. Both Mason, in his analysis of Nupe, and Terray, in his analysis of the Gyaman province of Asante, adopt such an approach. Norman Klein, in his forthcoming study of Asante slavery, has also considered aspects of the economy from this perspective. The formalist-substantivist debate cannot be reduced to a simple dichotomy.

The published version appeared as "Plantations in the Economy of the Sokoto Caliphate," *Journal of African History* 19:3 (1978), 34–68. See also Norman A. Klein, "Inequality in Asante: A Study of the Forms and Meaning of Slavery and Social Servitude in Pre- and Early Akan-Asante Society and Culture" (Ph.D. thesis, University of Michigan, 1980).

6.   See, for example, Curtin, *The Atlantic Slave Trade: A Census* (Madison, 1969), 271.

7.   See Ralph A. Austen, "The Abolition of the Overseas Slave Trade: A Distorted Theme in West African History," *Journal of the Historical Society of Nigeria* 5:2 (1970), 257–74.

8.   Charles-André Julien, *History of North Africa from the Arab Conquest to 1830*, trans. John Petrie (New York, 1970), 1–34; Abdallah Laroui, *L'histoire du Maghreb: un essai de synthèse* (Paris, 1970), 1:73–80; John Spencer Trimingham, *Islam in the Sudan* (London, 1949), 98. A more nuanced analysis of the Arab "invasions" of North Africa is found in an article by J. Poncet, "Le mythe de la 'catastrophe' hilalienne," *Annales: Economie, Société, et Civilisation* 22:5 (1967), 1099–1120. Also see Duveyrier, *La Confrèrie musulmane de Sidi Mohammed Ben Ali es-Senousi*, throughout.

9.   Nehemia Levtzion, "Toward a Comparative Study of Islamization," in *Conversion to Islam*, 11.

10. Ibid.
11. Ibid.
12. Robert O. Collins, *Land Beyond the Rivers: The Southern Sudan, 1898–1918* (New Haven, 1971), 76–78; Collins, "Sudanese Factors in the History of the Congo and Central West Africa in the Nineteenth Century," 166–67; Bruel, *L'Afrique équatoriale française*, 181, 184; Trimingham, *Islam in the Sudan*, 103–4.

Appendix 1

The Fulani and the Islamization of Bagirmi

1. Mohammed Bello, *The Rise of the Sokoto Fulani, being a paraphrase and in some parts a translation of the Infaku'l Maisuri of Sultan Mohammed Bello*, ed. and trans. E. J. Arnett (Kano, 1922), 4–6. Nachtigal supports this suggestion (*Sahara und Sudan*, 2:699). Dede's tomb continued to be a revered monument in the colonial era in Chad. See ANT, W60.1Ab, Latruffe, Chef de la subdivision de Mangueigne, "Rapport de la tournée effectuée par M. Latruffe, commis des S.C. chef de la subdivision de Mangueigne du 6 au 10 août 1932," 1–2.

2. Mohammadou, "Kalfu," 73–75, 100–101, 103; Gaden, "Note sur le dialecte Foul, parlé par les Foulbe du Baguirmi," *Journal asiatique*, 10ᵉ série, tôme 6 January-February 1908), 5–7; Nachtigal, *Sahara und Sudan*, 2:693, 696–99; Pâques, "Origines et caractères," 183. Santerre suggests that *moodibbo* (Fulfulde) and *faqih* (Arabic) are equivalent terms, referring simply to learned Muslims. The scholarly literature, travel accounts, and my own research indicate that in the Chad basin generally, *faqih* is a broad term encompassing a great variety of scholarly and educational activities. But in northern Cameroon at least, a distinction is made between a moodibbo, a teacher versed not only in the Qur'an but in the Qur'anic sciences as well, and a mallum (Fulfulde, borrowed from the Hausa *mallum*), who is only a Qur'anic teacher. *Goni*, a Kanuri title used in Borno, is another specialized term used for a teacher who has learned the Qur'an by memory, and the Kanuri specialized in this activity. Njeuma, on the other hand, believes that the forms *mallam* and *moodibbo* are mere terms of respect for learned Muslims specifying no particular educational attainments or duties. See Santerre, *Pédagogie musulmane d'Afrique noire*, 45, 63, 171; Njeuma, "Adamawa and Mahdism," 11n11.

3. Bello, *The Rise of the Sokoto Fulani*, 4–6; Fisher, "The Eastern Maghrib and the Central Sudan," 328n1.

4. Bello, *The Rise of the Sokoto Fulani*, 4–6. Fisher notes that most accounts of Borno history place the rule of Idris Alooma at the end of the sixteenth century. ʿUmar succeeded him early in the following century. See Humphrey J. Fisher,

"The Central Sahara and Sudan," in *The Cambridge History of Africa, Volume 4, c. 1600–1790*, Richard Gray, ed. (Cambridge, 1975), 108–9. Bello's high regard for Waldid stemmed in part from one of the mallam's predictions which he took to be a reference to the coming of Usuman dan Fodio nearly two centuries later:

> . . . the time is near at hand when a certain holy man will appear in this land, he will reform the faith, he will revive religion and establish it. Whosoever among you findeth him, let him follow him. The work he shall do is a holy war. At first with his tongue, until very many people that God will prepare for him shall follow him. Then he shall make war with spears until he has conquered these countries. Of a truth he shall drive out the Sarkin Bornu from his house, just as the Sarkin Bornu drove us out of our houses. He shall conquer these countries.

Appendix 2

Genealogies of the Rulers of Precolonial Dar al-Kuti

1. Chevalier, *Mission*, 130–2.
2. Barth, Travels, 2:667; Martine, "Essai sur l'histoire du pays Salamat," 40; Santerre, *Pédagogie musulmane*, 31–33, 45, 63, 171.
3. Nachtigal, *Sahara und Sudan*, 2:693.
4. Julien suggested that Bokur ruled from 1825 to 1850, Salih from 1850 to 1870, and ᶜAqid from 1870 to 1873. Again, the even lengths of the first two reigns make Julien's data suspect. A later French administrator in south-eastern Chad attempted to put together a list of Runga sultans and concluded that between the rule of Bokur and the beginning of the colonial period, the order of rulers was impossible to determine because of conflicting data. See ANF-SOM (Paris), Papiers Julien, 6P.A., "Historique des Etats Senoussiens (Dar-el-Kouti), Annexe N° 2: Généalogie des Sultans Roungas et Senoussiens," 153; ANT, W53.4, Lt. Fouchet, "Généalogie des Sultans du Rounga et historique de la pénétration française dans ce pays," Am Timan, 5 August 1911.

Appendix 3

The Name of the New Capital

1. OA3.2; OA, notes on a conversation with Koussingou Albert, Banda Mbi, Ndele, May 1974.
2. OA15.2/16.1; Tisserant, *Essai sur la grammaire Banda*, 11.
3. OA, notes on a conversation with R. P. DeMoustier, Catholic Mission, Ndele, 5 October 1974. Pére Moustier indicated that he heard this interpretation from a Banda resident of Ndele.
4. J. Calloc'h, *Vocabulaire Français-Sango et Sango-Français, langue commerciale de l'Oubangui-Chari* (Paris, 1911), 40, 73, 77; Charles R. Taber, *A Dictionary of Sango* (Hartford, 1965), 103, 132, 261, 269.
5. OA5.2/6.1; OA9.1; OA9.2/10.1; OA11.2/12.1; OA13.1; OA17.2/18.1; OA19.1/20.1: OA, notes on a tour of the Ndele ruins with Abudullu, Banda Ngao-Marba, Ndele, 17 June 1974.
6. OA11.1; OA11.2/12.1; OA19.1/20.1.
7. OA15.2/16.1; Daigre, "Les Bandas de l'Oubangui-Chari," 690–91; Toque, *Essai sur le peuple et la langue Banda*, 38–46; Chevalier, *Mission*, 102–103. The precise meaning of the word *ndele* is lost. It does not mean "rock." Nor is any spirit in the Banda pantheon called *ndele*. Tisserant enters only the meaning "quiver" in his dictionary. See Tisserant, *Dictionnaire*, 307.

Bibliography

Oral Accounts

The people of Dar al-Kuti supplied much of the most important information about the recent history of northern Ubangi-Shari. Microfilm copies of the transcripts of interviews (transcribed in Chadic Arabic with long passages translated into English and French) conducted in Dar al-Kuti in 1974 have been deposited with the Archives of Traditional Music, Indiana University, Bloomington; and the Memorial Library, University of Wisconsin-Madison. A third copy will be deposited at the Musée Boganda in Bangui, Central African Republic, when a long-planned oral data center opens there.

The first two columns in the following list include the number of the oral account (OA) as cited in notes to this study and the number of the tape. Interview information includes the name of the informant, his ethnic identity, his age in 1974, the location of the interview, the date, and general background information. A sketch of each informant includes an assessment of his fluency in Chadic Arabic.

Account No(s).	Tape No(s).	Interviews
OA1.1	1	Boukar Froumbala, Bornoan (Kanuri), 95 years old, Quartier Borno, Ndele, 9 May 1974. Boukar speaks Chadic Arabic quite well although his conversation is sprinkled with Kanuri vocabulary. Once the head of the Bornoan community and a major property-holder in Ndele, Boukar maintained a small stall in the market in 1974.Since independence, the Bornoan community has largely disappeared.
OA1.2	1	Boukar Froumbala, Bornoan (Kanuri), 95 years old, Quartier Borno, Ndele, 11 May 1974.
OA2.1	2	Boukar Froumbala, Bornoan (Kanuri), 95 years old, Quartier Borno, Ndele, 14 May 1974.
OA3.1	3	Notes (in English) on Ndele ruins from a tour of the site with Yadjouma Pascal, Banda Mbagga, 76 years old, Quartier Artisan, Ndele, 15 May 1974. Yadjouma's Chadic Arabic is fluent and grammatically correct; he does have a heavy Banda accent. Yadjouma was taken captive by al-Sanusi's raiders as a young boy and grew up in the sultan's compound. He was present when the French

		assassinated the sultan. During the colonial period Yadjouma was a prominent Banda leader. (See chapter 5, n46.)
OA3.2	3	Yadjouma Pascal, Banda Mbagga, 76 years old, Quartier Artisan, Ndele, 16 May 1974.
OA4.1	4	Yadjouma Pascal, Banda Mbagga, 76 years old, Quartier Artisan, Ndele, 18 May 1974.
OA5.1	5	Yacoub Mahamat Dillang, Runga, 80 years old, Quartier Arabe, Ndele, 20 May 1974. Chadic Arabic is Yacoub's primary language. His parents were migrants from Dar Runga. In Dar al-Kuti they first settled at Kali-Sha and then moved to Ndele, where Yacoub was born. His mother was al-Sanusi's cousin. Although not wealthy, Yacoub's family had access to the ruling circle.
OA5.2/6.1	5 and 6	Yacoub Mahamat Dillang, Runga, 80 years old, Quartier Arabe, Ndele, 22 May 1974.
OA6.2	6	Abakar Tidjani, Runga-Nduka, 55 years old, Quartier Sultan, Ndele, 23 May 1974. Chadic Arabic is Abakar's primary language. Abakar is a grandson of al-Sanusi by Fatime, the daughter of a major Nduka earth chief. His family lived in Akrousoulba, where his father was a major landholder. Abakar worked for several European commercial houses during the colonial era and in 1974 owned a small store in the market. He also was an assistant to the mayor. A serious Muslim, he served as *imam* of the mosque, and was the *muqaddim*, or the principal official, of the Tijani lodge in Ndele.
OA7.1	7	Yacoub Mahamat Dillang, Runga, 80 years old, Quartier Arabe, Ndele, 25 May 1974.
OA7.2/8.1	7 and 8	Maarabbi Hasan and Abakar Tidjani, both Runga-Nduka, both about 55 years old, Quartier Sultan, Ndele, 28 May 1974. Maarabbi is fluent in Arabic. He is a farmer whose grandfather was Suda, the most famous earth chief of the Nduka in the Ndele region.
OA8.2	8	Assakin Mahamat Angulu, Runga-Jallaba, 76 years old, Quartier Jallaba, Ndele, 29 May 1974. Chadic Arabic is his primary language. Assakin is a farmer. His father, a Jallaba trader, settled in Sha in the 1890s, where he married a Runga woman; he received Jallaba traders on commercial visits to Ndele.
OA9.1	9	Yadri Sale (Salih), Banda Ngao, about 85 years

old, Quartier Banda Ngao-Dakpa, Ndele, 5 June 1974. Yadri's Chadic Arabic is only fair; transcribing the tape required the aid of an assistant. Yadri is a farmer and the son of a Banda Ngao chief resettled in Ndele following al-Sanusi's defeat of Ngono.

OA9.2/10.1   9 and 10   Mahamat Ngouvela Dodo, Banda Ngao-Bulu (Buru), about 55 years old, Village of Mbollo, 5 June 1974. Mahamat speaks Chadic Arabic very well, although he has a heavy Banda accent and occasionally includes Sango vocabulary items. Chief of the village and canton of Mbollo, Mahamat is the grandson of Ngono, the most prominent Banda rival of al-Sanusi. Following Ngono's death, his son (Mahamat's father), Ngouvela, became one of al-Sanusi's soldiers.

OA10.2   10   Yusuf Dingis, Arab Salami, about 45 years old, Quartier Arabe, Ndele, 8 June 1974. Yusuf speaks Sudanese Arabic. An Arab from the Salamat, Yusuf settled in Haraze in Dar Runga, where he married a Runga woman. He spent several years in the Sudan and then settled in Ndele, where he was the major producer of jamsinda in 1974.

OA11.1   11   Abudullu Yiala Mende, Banda Ngao-Banda Marba-Kresh, about 70 years old, Quartier Artisan, Ndele, 10 June 1974. Abudullu is fluent in Chadic Arabic but has a pronounced Banda accent. A leatherworker and farmer, Abudullu also had a Banda name—Yiala. His father was a Banda Marba originally taken captive by Rabih. He later escaped and joined the ranks of Ngono's fighters. Following Ngono's death he became a bazingir of al-Sanusi. Abudullu's mother was a Kresh woman captured by al-Sanusi.

OA11.2/12.1   11 and 12   Abudullu Yiala Mende, Banda Ngao–Banda Marba-Kresh, about 70 years old, Quartier Artisan, Ndele, 12 June 1974.

OA12.2   12   Nguengue, Sara Mbai, about 80 years old, Quartier Sarazoignons, Ndele, 13 June 1974. Nguengue's Arabic is fair. A farmer whose parents were also cultivators, Nguengue came to Ndele in 1918, where he cared for the horses of a French ivory dealer.

OA13.1   13   Khrouma Sale (Salih), Runga Bagrim, about 80 years old, Village of Koundi, 19 June 1974.

Chadic Arabic is his primary language. In 1974 Khrouma was the chief of the village of Koundi, which is inhabited by descendants of Kobur. Khrouma's grandfather was the brother of Abakar, al-Sanusi's father; his father was a close advisor to al-Sanusi and fought in the sultan's armed forces.

OA14.1   14   Abdel-Banat Otman, Dajo, about 85 years old, Village of Koundi, 20 June 1974. Abdel-Banat speaks Chadic Arabic well. A farmer, Abdel-Banat was born in Dar Sila. His family settled in Dar al-Kuti after fleeing Dar Sila at the time of the French conquest in 1916.

OA14.2   14   Khrouma Sale (Salih), Runga Bagrim, about 80 years old, Village of Koundi, 21 June 1974.

OA15.1   15   Mittendumu Albert, Banda Mbatta-Banda Mbagga, about 70 years old, Quartier Tipoyeur, Ndele, 25 June 1974. Mittendumu's Chadic Arabic is marginal. This interview was conducted in Sango with the aid of an interpreter. A farmer, Mittendumu is the son of a Banda Mbagga whom al-Sanusi re-settled in Ndele. His mother was a Banda Mbatta from a family that included several ritual leaders.

OA15.2/16.1   15 and 16   Yadjouma Pascal, Banda Mbagga, 76 years old, Quartier Artisan, Ndele, 30 June 1974.

OA17.1   17   Assakin Mahamat Angulu, Runga-Jallaba, 76 years old, Quartier Jallaba, Ndele, 5 July 1974.

OA17.2/18   17 and 18   Ngrekoudou Ouih Fran, Banda Toulou, about 80 years old, Village of Ouih Fran, 7 July 1974. Ngrekoudou's Chadic Arabic is fair. He lapses into Banda on occasion; an interpreter helped guide this interview. Ngrekoudou is chief of the village of Ouih Fran and a farmer. His paternal uncle was Rufuko, the leader of the Banda Toulou in al-Sanusi's time. His mother was a Lutos, taken captive in a raid southwest of Ndele.

OA18.2   18   Boukar Froumbala, Bornoan (Kanuri), 95 years old, Quartier Borno, Ndele, 9 July 1974.

OA19.1/20.1   19 and 20   Balingonvo Jean, Banda Ngonvo, about 80 years old, Quartier Artisan, Ndele, 15 July 1974. This interview was conducted in Banda with the aid of an interpreter. Balingonvo is a farmer whose grandfather occasionally served as spokesperson for the Banda Ngonvo in their dealings with al-Sanusi.

OA20.2   20   Kiti Gouya, Nduka Gollo, about 75 years old, Village of Yangoundarsa, 12 August 1974. Kiti's

Chadic Arabic is fairly good. A farmer, Kiti was born in Ndele shortly before al-Sanusi's assassination.

OA20.3   20   Siam Munju, Nduka Gollo, about 70 years old, Village of Kour, 23 August 1974. Siam speaks Chadic Arabic fairly well, although he has a heavy Nduka accent. He is a farmer whose parents lived in Yangoundarsa, a village five kilometers west of Ndele, at the time of al-Sanusi's death. Siam worked for early French administrators.

OA21.1   21   al-Hajj Abakar Zacharia, Runga, about 80 years old, Village of Mbangbali, 29 August 1974. Chadic Arabic is his primary language. Born in Ndele, al-Hajj Abakar was chief of the village of Mbangbali in 1974. His father's family was from Dar Runga and his father migrated to Dar al-Kuti while al-Sanusi was still at Sha. His mother was a Banda Linda, taken in raiding south of Ndele. Al-Hajj is a very prominent member of the Runga community outside Ndele; he enjoys particular renown because he is one of the few Runga to have made the pilgrimage.

OA21.2   21   Ahmed Issa, Runga, about 75 years old, Village of Mbangbali, 30 August 1974. Chadic Arabic is his primary language. Ahmed is a farmer whose parents and paternal grandfather migrated to Ndele in the time of al-Sanusi. Ahmed was born in the city. Following the sultan's death, Ahmed's brother fled with Allah Jabu to Ouanda-Djale and continued on to the Salamat, only returning to Dar al-Kuti in the late 1910s.

OA21.3   21   Hanno Shargan, Runga Mangale, about 80 years old, Village of Mbangbali, 29 September 1974. He speaks Chadic Arabic very well. Hanno is a farmer whose parents migrated from Dar Runga. After al-Sanusi's death they fled to the Salamat, returning to Dar al-Kuti in 1914.

OA21.4   21   al-Hajj Abakar Zacharia, Runga, about 80 years old, Village of Mbangbali, 29 September 1974.

OA22.1   22   Adoum Oumar, Runga, about 50 years old, Village of Manga, 29 September 1974. Chadic Arabic is his primary language. Chief of the village of Manga in 1974, Adoum's father was a Runga who served as chief in the 1950s. His grandfather led the community of Runga Issa-Tinia in Ndele under al-Sanusi.

OA22.2	22	Abi Sara, Nduka Doggo, about 75 years old, Village of Manga, 30 September 1974. Abi is a farmer who speaks Chadic Arabic fairly well, although with a Nduka accent. He provided very little autobiographical information.
OA22.3	22	Yahya Issa-Din, Runga Tunjur, about 75 years old, Village of Birbatouma, 30 September 1974. Yahya is fluent in Chadic Arabic. He is a farmer whose parents were born in Dar Runga. His paternal grandfather migrated from Runga to Dar al-Kuti, where he traded in cloth, kombo, and coffee.
OA23.1	23	Abdoulaye Oumbra, Sara Dinjo-Banda Linda, about 80 years old, Village of Djamssinda, 1 October 1974. Abdoulaye's Chadic Arabic is not fluent but quite good nonetheless. He is a farmer whose father migrated to the Ndele area following the French conquest where he met his mother.
OA23.2	23	Khrouma Sale (Salih), Runga Bagrim, about 80 years old, Village of Koundi, 10 October 1974.
OA24.1	24	Yacoub Soudour Tekai, Runga Bua, about 85 years old, Village of Akrousoulba-Dil, 12 October 1974. Chadic Arabic is his primary language. Yacoub is a former chief of the Runga village of Dil whose parents migrated to Dar al-Kuti from Dar Runga, attracted by the prosperity of al-Sanusi's territories.

Archival Material

Central African Republic

AMBB, Archives du Musée Boganda, Bangui.
   The Musée Boganda holds documents from Bossangoa (circonscription de l'Ouham) and Bangassou (circonscription du Mbomou), along with scattered reports from other regions of Ubangi-Shari.

BENA, Bibliothèque de l'Ecole Nationale d'Administration, Bangui.
   The library of L'Ecole Nationale d'Administration holds items from the Kémo-Gribingui regional archives. They are not classed or organized, and the labels on the files do not always correspond to the contents.

APBB, Archives de la Préfecture du Bamingui-Bangoran, Ndele.
   The prefectural archives hold very few documents from the early colonial period. There are a few reports dating from the 1950s, however, that give the background to disputes concerning land, chiefship, and settlement. There is a lengthy accounting of tusks sold in the region in the 1940s.

ASPN, Archives de la Sous-Préfecture de Ndele, Ndele.
Administrative, financial, and local policy reports dating primarily from the 1950s.

Chad

ANT, Archives Nationales du Tchad, N'Djaména.
Série W. Political reports for all parts of Chad, 1905–1961.

France

ANF-SOM (Paris). Archives Nationales de France, Section d'Outre-Mer, Paris.
Afrique III, IV. Exploration and expeditions, 1852–1913; Tunisia, Tripolitania, the Sahara, Egypt, the Upper Nile, Chad, Wadai, Wadai and Ndele, Muslim policy in general.
Afrique Equatoriale Française, IV, XV, XVI, XIX. Territorial expansion and local policy; concessionary companies, 1897–1913; military affairs, 1902–15; transportation and inspection.
Tchad I, III. Early expeditions (Crampel, Dybowski, Maistre), Rabih, Mercuri in Ndele, Prins in the Haut-Oubangui, Destenave; expeditions, 1906–18; Mission Bonnel de Mezières.
Gabon-Congo I, II, III, IV. Haut-Oubangui, 1890s; exploration and expeditions (Fourneau, Crampel, Dybowski, Brazza, Decazes, Clozel, Grech, Julien); memoires and publications on Ubangi area by Grech, Bruel, Destenave, Largeau, Lamothe; territorial expansion and local policy: Ubangi, Upper Nile, Bahr al-Ghazal, Chad.
Gabon-Congo VII, IX, X, XII, XIII, XIV, XV, XVI. Slave trade, labor, Compagnie des Sultanats du Haut-Oubangui, S.A. "La Kotto," military affairs.
Papiers d'Agents, 6P.A., Papiers Juliens.
ANF-AE (Paris). Archives Nationales de France, Ministère des Affaires Etrangères, Paris.
Fonds Mémoires et Documents, Afrique 74, 94, 113, 132, 133, 139 (Congo et Gabon).
Série: Correspondance consulaire et commerciale, 1793–1901. Le Caire, Benghazi, Tripolie de Barbarie.
Fonds correspondance politique des consuls, 1871–1896. Egypte (avec le Soudan), Turquie: Tripolie de Barbarie.
Nouvelle série (NS): Correspondance politique et consulaire, 1897–1918. Afrique Equatoriale Française (Oubangui), Egypte, Turquie: Libye, Tripolitaine, Cyrenaique.
AAV (Vincennes). Archives Nationales de France, Ministère d'Etat chargé de la Défense Nationale, Service historique de l'Armée, Château de Vincennes.
Section Outre-Mer. Série O³, Afrique Equatoriale Française. Généralités, Oubangui-Chari, Tchad. Correspondance concerning Wadai, Modat's reports on Ndele and Kafiakinji, information on Dar Runga and Dar Massalit, 1902–13.

ANF-SOM (Aix-en-Provence). Archives Nationales de France, Section d'Outre-Mer, Depôt à Aix-en-Provence.
    A. E. F., Série B, S/série 2B, La correspondance générale du Commissaire général dans le Congo-Français, 1886–1909.
    A. E. F., Série D, S/série 2D, Politique et administration générale: Négociations internationales de délimitation de frontière, et Missions d'exploration.
    A. E. F., Série D, S/série 4D, Rapports politiques, 1889–1940: classement 4(3)D, Oubangui-Chari (1889–1940s); classement 4(4)D, Tchad (1901–1920).
    A. E. F., Série D, S/série 5D, Correspondance et rapports divers des Affaires politiques et de l'Administration générale (1907–1920).

Great Britain

PRO (London), Public Record Office, London.
    Foreign Office 2 series. Correspondence and reports:
    Tripoli, Benghazi, information on Rabih collected from trans-Saharan merchants.
    Foreign Office 101 series. Correspondence and reports from the Tripoli consuls.
    Foreign Office 141 series. The Sudan, the slave trade, mapping of the Wadai-Dar Fur frontier.
    Foreign Office 160 series. Embassy and consular archives, Tripoli (Libya), 1870–1906.
    Foreign Office 407 series. Egypt and Sudan.
    Foreign Office 867 series. Anglo-Egyptian Sudan.
    Foreign Office 881 series. Confidential prints: slave trade on the Red Sea, intelligence reports on the Sudanese Mahdiya, caravan routes in the eastern Sahara and Nile regions, events on the Upper Nile (1890–97).

Published Material, Unpublished Papers, Theses, and Notes

Abun-Nasr, Jamil M. *The Tijaniyya: A Sufi Order in the Modern World.* London: Oxford University Press, 1965.
Adeleye, R. A. "Rabih b. Fadlallah, 1879–1893: Exploits and Impact on Political Relations in Central Sudan." *Journal of the Historical Society of Nigeria* 5:2 (June 1970), 223–42.
Alis, Harry. "L'Expédition Crampel." *Afrique Française* 1:9 (September 1891), 2–5.
Alis, Harry. "La Mission Paul Crampel." *Afrique Française* 1:3 (March 1891), 3–6.
Arkell, A. J. *A History of the Sudan: From the Earliest Times to 1821.* 2nd ed. London: Athlone, 1961.
Assemblées chrétiennes du Tchad. *Dictionnaire français-arabe (dialecte du Tchad).* Doba, Tchad: n.d.

Austen, Ralph A. "The Abolition of the Overseas Slave Trade: A Distorted Theme in West African History." *Journal of the Historical Society of Nigeria* 5:2 (1970), 257–74.

Austen, Ralph A. "The Trans-Saharan Slave Trade: A Tentative Census." In *The Uncommon Market: Essays in the Economic History of the Atlantic Slave Trade*, Henry A. Gemery and Jan S. Hogendorn, eds. New York: Academic Press, 1979.

Azevedo, Mario J. "Sara Demographic Instability as a Consequence of French Colonial Policy in Chad (1890–1940)." Ph.D. dissertation, Duke University, 1976.

Babikir, Arbab Djama. *L'Empire de Rabeh.* Paris: Dervy, 1950.

Baier, Stephen Brock. *An Economic History of Central Niger.* London: Oxford University Press, 1980.

Barth, Heinrich. "Account of Two Expeditions in Central Africa by the Furanys." *Journal of the Royal Geographical Society of London* 23 (1853), 120–22.

Barth, Heinrich. *Travels and Discoveries in North and Central Africa.* 3 vols. 1857–59; London: Frank Cass, 1965.

Bayle des Hermens, Roger de. *Recherches préhistoriques en République Centrafricaine.* Paris: Librairie C. Klincksieck, 1975.

Bedis, Yunes. "Tales of the Wadai Slave Trade in the Nineties." *Sudan Notes and Records*, 23:1 (1940), 169–83.

Bello, Mohammed. *The Rise of the Sokoto Fulani, being a paraphrase and in some parts a translation of the Infaku'l Maisuri of Sultan Mohammed Bello.* E. J. Arnett, ed. and trans. Kano: 1922.

Birks, J. S. *Across the Savannas to Mecca: The Overland Pilgrimage from West Africa.* London: C. Hurst, 1978.

Bloch, Marc, ed. *Marxist Analyses and Social Anthropology.* London: Malaby Press, 1975.

Bohannan, Paul, and Philip Curtin. *Africa and Africans.* Rev. ed. Garden City, N.Y.: American Museum of Natural History, 1971.

Boucher (L'Administrateur des colonies, Chef de la Circonscription du Dar-Kouti oriental). "Monographie du Dar-Kouti oriental." Birao: typed manuscript, 1934. Included in both the Archives du Musée Boganda, Bangui (AMBB), and the Collection Cabaille, Bangui (CC).

Bovill, E. W. *The Golden Trade of the Moors.* 2nd ed. rev. London: Oxford University Press, 1968.

Brenner, Louis. *The Shehus of Kukawa: A History of the Al-Kanemi Dynasty of Bornu.* London: Oxford University Press, 1973.

Brown, Roger Glenn. *Fashoda Reconsidered: The Impact of Domestic Politics on French Policy in Africa, 1893–1898.* Baltimore: The Johns Hopkins University Press, 1970.

Browne, William George B. *Travels in Africa, Egypt, and Syria from the Year 1792 to 1798.* London: T. Cadwell, 1806.

Bruel, Georges. *L'Afrique équatoriale française.* Paris: E. Larose, 1930.

Bruel, Georges. *La France équatoriale africaine: le pays, les habitants, la colonisation, les pouvoirs publics.* Paris: E. Larose, 1935.

Bruel, Georges. "Mohamed-es-Senoussi et ses états (Lettre de rectification)." *Bulletin de la société des recherches congolaises* 11 (1930), 93–101.

Brunache, Paul. *Le centre de l'Afrique—autour du Tchad.* Paris: Ancienne Librairie Germer Ballière, 1894.

Burckhardt, John Lewis. *Travels in Nubia.* London: John Murray, 1822.

Burthe d'Annelet. *A travers l'Afrique française du Sénégal au Cameroun par les confins libyens . . . et du Maroc par les confins sahariens (octobre 1932-juin 1935).* 2 vols. Paris: Didot, 1939.

Cabaille Collection. A collection of typed manuscripts, mimeographed reports, and printed pamphlets from the early colonial period in Chad and Ubangi-Shari. Cabaille was the director of the Service de Chasse in Ubangi-Shari during the colonial and early independence periods, and spent many years in the northern part of the colony setting up game parks. His documents include those by Boucher and Cornet.

Cadalvene, Edmond de, and J. de Breuvery. *L'Egypte et la Turquie de 1829 à 1836.* 2 vols. Paris: Arthur Bertrand, 1836.

Calloc'h, J. *Vocabulaire Français-Sango et Sango-Français, langue commerciale de l'Oubangui-Chari.* Paris: Librairie Paul Geuthner, 1911.

Calonne-Beaufaict, Adolphe de. *Azande: Introduction à une ethnographie générale des bassins de l'Ubangi-Uélé et de l'Aruwimi.* Brussels: Maurice Lamertin, 1921.

The Cambridge History of Africa, Volume 3, c. 1050-c. 1600. Roland Oliver, ed. Cambridge: Cambridge University Press, 1977.

The Cambridge History of Africa, Volume 4, c. 1600-1790. Richard Gray, ed. Cambridge: Cambridge University Press, 1975.

The Cambridge History of Africa, Volume 5, c. 1790-c. 1870. John E. Flint, ed. Cambridge: Cambridge University Press, 1976.

Caprile, J. P., and J. Fédry. *Le Groupe des langues "sara" (République du Tchad).* Lyon: Afrique et Langage, 1969.

Carbou, Henri. *Méthode pratique pour l'étude de l'arabe parlé au Ouaday et à l'est du Tchad.* Paris: Paul Geuthner, 1913.

Carbou, Henri. *La région du Tchad et du Ouadai.* 2 vols. Paris: Leroux, 1912.

Chad. Direction générale de l'information. *Annuaire officiel du Tchad.* Paris: Diloutremer, 1972.

Chapiseau, Félix. *Au pays de l'esclavage: moeurs et coutumes de l'Afrique centrale, d'après les notes recueillies par Béhagle.* Paris: Maisonneuve, 1900.

Chevalier, Auguste. *Le café.* Paris: Presses Universitaires de France, 1944.

Chevalier, Auguste. "De l'Oubangui au lac Tchad à travers le bassin du Chari." *La Géographie* 9 (1904), 343–68.

Chevalier, Auguste. "Exploration scientifique dans les états de Snoussi, sultan du Dar-el-Kouti." *La Géographie* 8 (1903), 89–95.

Chevalier, Auguste. *Mission Chari-lac Tchad, 1902–1904: l'Afrique Centrale Française, récit du voyage de la mission.* Paris: Challamel, 1907.

Chevalier, Auguste. "Mission scientifique au Chari et au lac Tchad." *La Géographie* 7 (1903), 354–61.

Ciocardel, R., Birlea, and Gbakpoma. *Eléments pour la géologie de l'Afrique*. 3 vols. Bangui: Université Jean-Bedel Bokassa, Institut Universitaire Technologique de Mines et Géologie, 1974.

Cohen, Abner. "Cultural Strategies in the Organization of Trading Diasporas." In *The Development of Indigenous Trade and Markets in West Africa*, Claude Meillassoux, ed. London: International Africa Institute, 1971.

Cohen, Abner. *Custom and Politics in Urban Africa: A Study of Hausa Migrants in Yoruba Towns*. Berkeley and Los Angeles: University of California Press, 1969.

Collins, Robert O. *King Leopold, England, and the Upper Nile, 1899–1909*. New Haven: Yale University Press, 1968.

Collins, Robert O. *Land Beyond the Rivers: The Southern Sudan, 1898–1918*. New Haven: Yale University Press, 1971.

Collins, Robert O. *The Southern Sudan, 1883–1898: A Struggle for Control*. New Haven: Yale University Press, 1962.

Collins, Robert O. "Sudanese Factors in the History of the Congo and Central West Africa in the Nineteenth Century." In *Sudan in Africa*, Yusuf Fadl Hasan, ed. Khartoum: Khartoum University Press, 1971.

Comyn, D. C. E. *Service and Sport in the Sudan*. London: John Lane, 1911.

Cooper, Frederick. *Plantation Slavery on the East Coast of Africa*. New Haven and London: Yale University Press, 1977.

Cooper, Frederick. "The Problem of Slavery in African Studies." *Journal of African History* 20, 1 (1979), 103–25.

Coquery-Vidrovitch, Catherine. *Le Congo au temps des grandes compagnies concessionaires, 1898–1930*. Paris: Mouton, 1972.

Cordell, Dennis D. "Archival Report: Research Resources in Chad and the Central African Republic." *History in Africa*, 2 (1975), 217–20.

Cordell, Dennis D. "Blood Partnership in Theory and Practice: The Expansion of Muslim Power in Dar al-Kuti." *Journal of African History* 20:3 (1979), 379–94.

Cordell, Dennis D. "Dar al-Kuti: A History of the Slave Trade and State Formation on the Islamic Frontier in Northern Equatorial Africa (Central African Republic and Chad) in the Nineteenth and Early Twentieth Centuries." Ph.D. dissertation, University of Wisconsin-Madison, 1977.

Cordell, Dennis D. "Eastern Libya, Wadai, and the Sanusiya: A Tariqa and a Trade Route." *Journal of African History* 18:1 (1977), 21–36.

Cordell, Dennis D. "Review of Nehemia Levtzion, ed., *Conversion to Islam*." *Canadian Journal of African Studies* 16:2 (1982), 419–22.

Cordell, Dennis D. "The Savanna Belt of North Central Africa." In vol. 1, *History of Central Africa*, David Birmingham and Phyllis Martin, eds. London: Longman, 1983.

Cordell, Dennis D. "Secondary Empire and Slave-Raiding beyond the Islamic Frontier in Northern Equatorial Africa: The Case of Bandas Hakim and Saʿid Baldas." Paper presented at the Ninety-Second Annual Conference, American Historical Association, Dallas, Texas, 1977.

Cornet. "Au Coeur de L'Afrique Centrale." Printed pamphlet. N.p.: 12 August 1916. Included in the Cabaille Collection (CC).

Courtet, H. "Mission scientifique Chari-lac Tchad: Le pays Snoussi." *Revue des troupes coloniales* 3 (1904), 483–86.

Courtet, H. "La mouche tsé-tsé." Appended to Auguste Chevalier, *Mission Chari-lac Tchad, 1902–1904: l'Afrique Centrale Française, récit du voyage de la mission.* Paris: Challamel, 1907.

Cuoq, Joseph M., ed. and trans. *Recueil des sources arabes concernant l'Afrique occidentale du VIIIᵉ au XVIᵉ siècle (Bilad al-Sudan).* Paris: Editions du Centre national de la recherche scientifique, 1975.

Cureau, Adolphe Louis. *Les sociétés primitives de l'Afrique équatoriale.* Paris: A. Colin, 1912.

Curtin, Philip D. *The Atlantic Slave Trade: A Census.* Madison: University of Wisconsin Press, 1969.

Curtin, Philip D. *Economic Change in Precolonial Africa: Senegambia in the Era of the Slave Trade.* Madison: University of Wisconsin Press, 1975.

Daigre, P. "Les Bandas de l'Oubangui-Chari." *Anthropos* 26 (1931), 647–95; 27 (1932), 153–81.

Daigre, P. *Oubangui-Chari: souvenirs et témoinages, 1890–1940.* Paris: Maison Provinciale des Pères du Saint-Esprit, 1950.

Daigre, P. "Plantes alimentaires du pays Banda." *Bulletin de la société des recherches congolaises* 8 (1927), 123–34.

Dampierre, Eric de. *Un ancien royaume Bandia du Haut-Oubangui.* Paris: Plon, 1967.

Dampierre, Eric de. *Des ennemis, des Arabes, des histoires . . .* Paris: Société d'ethnographie, 1983.

Davies, R. "The Masalit Sultanate." *Sudan Notes and Records* 7:2 (1924), 49–62.

Decorse, Gaston Jules. *Du Congo au lac Tchad: la brousse telle qu'elle est, et les gens tels qu'ils sont (Misson Chari-lac Tchad, 1902–1904).* Paris: Challamel, 1906.

Decorse, Gaston Jules. "Rapport économique et zoologique sur la région du Tchad." *Afrique Française: renseignements coloniaux* 14:5 (May 1905), 189–97; 14:6 (June 1905), 221–27; 14:7 (July 1905), 268–75.

Decorse, Gaston Jules, and Maurice Gaudefroy-Demombynes. *Rabah et les arabes du Chari: documents arabes et vocabulaire.* Paris: Librairie Orientale et Américaine, 1906.

Delafosse, Maurice. *Enquête coloniale dans l'Afrique française.* Paris: Société d'éditions géographiques, maritimes, et coloniales, 1930.

Derendinger, R. *Vocabulaire pratique du dialecte arabe centre-africain.* Paris: Imprimerie André Tournon, 1923.

"Les derniers événements des territoires du Tchad." *Afrique Française* 21:2 (February 1911), 53–56.

Deschamps, Hubert, ed. *Histoire générale de l'Afrique noire.* 2 vols. Paris: Presses Universitaires de France, 1970 and 1971.

Devallée. "Le Baghirmi." *Bulletin de la société des recherches congolaises* 7 (1925), 3–76.

Djian. "Notes sur les populations musulmanes du territoire du Tchad au point de vue politico-réligieux." *Bulletin de la société des recherches congolaises,* 6 (1924).

Duveyrier, Henri. *La Confrérie musulmane de Sidi Mohammed Ben Ali es-Senousi*. Paris: Société de Géographie, 1884.

Dybowski, Jean. *La Route du Tchad du Loango au Chari*. Paris: Librairie Firmin-Didot, 1893.

Ehret, Christopher, and Merrick Posnansky, eds. *The Archaeological and Linguistic Reconstruction of African History*. Berkeley and Los Angeles: University of California Press, 1982.

Elles, R. J. "The Kingdom of Tegali." *Sudan Notes and Records* 18:1 (1935), 1–35.

Ensor, F. Sidney. *Incidents on a Journey through Nubia to Darfoor*. London: W. H. Allen, 1881.

Escayrac de Lauture, P. H. Stanislas d'. *Le Désert et le Soudan*. Paris: J. Dumaine, 1853.

Escayrac de Lauture, P. H. Stanislas d'. *Mémoire sur le Soudan, géographie naturelle et politique,histoire et ethnographie, moeurs et institutions de l'empire des Fellatas, du Bornou, du Baguirmi, du Waday, du Dar-Four*. Paris: A. Bertrand, J. Dumaine, F. Klincksieck, 1855–56.

"L'Expédition Crampel." *Afrique Française* 1:1 (January 1891), 2–5.

Ferrandi, Jean. "Abéché, capitale du Ouadai." *Afrique Française: renseignements coloniaux* 22:10 (October 1912), 349–70.

Ferrandi, Jean, and Capitaine Lame. "Fort-Lamy, chef-lieu du territoire du Tchad." *Afrique Française: renseignements coloniaux* 22:3 (March 1912), 101–11.

Fischel, Marcel Maurice. *Le Thaler de Marie-Therése*. Paris: Giard et Brière, 1912.

Fisher, Allan G. B., and Humphrey J. Fisher. *Slavery and Muslim Society in Africa*. New York: Doubleday, 1971.

Fisher, Humphrey J. "The Central Sahara and Sudan." In *The Cambridge History of Africa, Volume 4, c. 1600–1790*, Richard Gray, ed. Cambridge: Cambridge University Press, 1975.

Fisher, Humphrey J. "Conversion Reconsidered: Some Historical Aspects of Religious Conversion in Black Africa." *Africa* 43:1 (1973), 27–40.

Fisher, Humphrey J. "The Eastern Maghrib and the Central Sudan." In *The Cambridge History of Africa, Volume 3, c. 1050-c. 1600*, Roland Oliver, ed. Cambridge: Cambridge University Press, 1977.

Fisher, Humphrey J. "Hassebu: Islamic Healing in Black Africa." In *Northern Africa: Islam and Modernization*, Michael Brett, ed. London: F. Cass, 1973.

Fisher, Humphrey J. " 'He Swalloweth the Ground with Fierceness and Rage': The Horse in the Central Sudan. I. Its Introduction." *Journal of African History* 13:3 (1972), 367–88.

Fisher, Humphrey J. " 'He Swalloweth the Ground with Fierceness and Rage': The Horse in the Central Sudan. II. Its Use." *Journal of African History* 14:3 (1973), 355–79.

Fisher, Humphrey J. "Prayer and Military Activity in the History of Muslim Africa South of the Sahara." *Journal of African History* 12:3 (1971), 391–406.

Fortier, Joseph, ed. *Le Mythe et les contes du Sou en pays Mbai-Moissala*. Paris: Julliard, 1967.

Fresnel, Fulgence. "Mémoire sur le Waday: notice historique et geographique sur le Waday et les relations de cet empire avec la côte septentrionale de l'Afrique." *Bulletin de la société de géographie de Paris*, série 3, 9 (1848), 245–54; 11 (1849), 5–75; 13 (1850), 82–116, 341–59; 14 (1850), 153–92.

"Fusil." In *La Grande Encyclopédie Larousse*. Vol. 25. Paris: Librairie Larousse, 1973.

Gaden, Henri. *Essai de grammaire de la langue baguirmienne, suivi de textes et de vocabulaires baguirmien-français et français-baguirmien*. Paris: E. Leroux, 1909.

Gaden, Henri. "Les états musulmans de l'Afrique centrale et leurs rapports avec La Mecque et Constantinople." *Questions diplomatiques et coloniales*, t. 24 (1907), 436–47.

Gaden, Henri. *Manuel de la langue baguirmienne*. Paris: n.p., 1908.

Gaden, Henri. "Note sur le dialecte Foul, parlé par les Foulbe du Baguirmi." *Journal asiatique*, 10è série, tôme 6 (January-February 1908), 5–70.

Gaud, Fernand. *Les Mandja (Congo-Français)*. Brussels: deWit, 1911.

Gaudefroy-Demombynes, Maurice. *Documents sur les langues de l'Oubangui-Chari*. Paris: Leroux, 1906.

Gemery, Henry A., and Jan S. Hogendorn, eds. *The Uncommon Market: Essays in the Economic History of the Atlantic Slave Trade*. New York: Academic Press, 1979.

Gentil, Emile. *La chute de l'empire de Rabah*. Paris: Hachette, 1902.

Gentil, Pierre. *La conquête du Tchad (1894–1916)*. 2 vols. Vincennes: Service historique, Etat-Major de l'Armée de Terre, Ministère d'Etat chargé de la Défense Nationale, 1971.

Georges, Michel. "La vie rurale chez les Banda (République centrafricaine)." *Les cahiers d'outre-mer* 16:64 (October-December 1963), 321–59.

Gervais, Raymond. "The Monetary Policy of France and Great Britain towards the M. T. Thaler in the Kanem-Bornu Region, 1880–1920." M.A. thesis, University of Birmingham, 1979.

Gervais, Raymond. "La plus riche des colonies pauvres: la politique monétaire et fiscale de la France au Tchad, 1900–1920." *Canadian Journal of African Studies* 16:1 (1982), 93–112.

Gessi, Romolo. *Seven Years in the Soudan: Being a Record of Explorations, Adventures, and Campaigns against the Arab Slave Hunters*. London: Sampson Low, Marston, 1892.

Gide, André. *Le Retour du Tchad*. Paris: Librairie Gallimard, 1928.

Gide, André. *Voyage au Congo*. Paris: Librairie Gallimard, 1927.

Gillier. "Les Bandas: notes ethnographiques." *Afrique Française: renseignements coloniaux* 23:10 (October 1913), 346–55; 23:11 (November 1913), 386–96.

Goody, Jack. *Production and Reproduction*. Cambridge: Cambridge University Press, 1977.

Goody, Jack. *Technology, Tradition, and the State in Africa*. London: Oxford University Press, 1971.

Gosselin, Gabriel. *Travail et changement social en pays Gbeya (R.C.A.)*. Paris: Librairie C. Klincksieck, 1972.

Gray, Richard. *History of the Southern Sudan, 1839–1889.* London: Oxford University Press, 1961.

Grech. "Essai sur le Dar Kouti au temps de Snoussi." *Bulletin de la société des recherches congolaises* 4 (1924), 19–54.

Greenberg, Joseph H. *The Languages of Africa.* Bloomington, Ind.: Research Center for the Language Sciences, 1966.

Grellet, Gérard, Monique Mainguet, and Pierre Soumille. *La République centrafricaine.* Paris: Presses Universitaires de France, 1982.

Hallam, W. K. R. "The Itinerary of Rabih Fadl Allah, 1879–1893." *Bulletin de l'Institut Fondamental de l'Afrique noire*, série B, N° 1, t. 30 (1968), 165–81.

Hallam, W. K. R. *Life and Times of Rabih Fadl Allah.* Devon: Arthur H. Stockwell, 1977.

Hanolet, Léon. "L'Exploration du commandant Hanolet vers les sources du Chari." *La Belgique coloniale* 2:23 (7 June 1896), 268–72; 2:24 (14 June 1896), 281–84.

al-Hasan, Musa al-Mubarak. *Tarikh Darfur al-siyasi, 1882–1898.* Khartoum: Khartoum University Press, n.d. (c. 1970).

Hasan, Yusuf Fadl. "The Penetration of Islam in the Eastern Sudan." In *Islam in Tropical Africa*, I. M. Lewis, ed. London: Oxford University Press for the International African Institute, 1966.

Hasan, Yusuf Fadl, ed. *Sudan in Africa.* Khartoum: Khartoum University Press, 1971.

Hayer, Jeffrey Edward. "A Political History of the Maba Sultanate of Wadai: 1635–1912." M.A. thesis, University of Wisconsin, Madison, 1975.

Headrick, Daniel R. *The Tools of Empire: Technology and European Imperialism in the Nineteenth Century.* New York: Oxford University Press, 1981.

Henige, David P. *The Chronology of Oral Tradition: Quest for a Chimera.* Oxford: Clarendon Press, 1974.

Hilaire. "L'Occupation du Dar-Sila: rapport du Colonel Hilaire sur les opérations du 13 au 17 mai 1916 et la ré-occupation de Goz-Beida." *Afrique Française: renseignements coloniaux* 27:5–6 (May-June 1917), 105–18.

Hill, Polly. "Landlords and Brokers: A West African Trading System." *Cahiers d'études africaines* 6 (1966), 349–66.

Hill, Polly. *Population, Prosperity and Poverty: Rural Kano, 1900 and 1970.* Cambridge: Cambridge University Press, 1977.

Hill, Polly. *Rural Hausa: A Village and a Setting.* Cambridge: Cambridge University Press, 1972.

Hill, Richard. *A Biographical Dictionary of the Anglo-Egyptian Sudan.* London: Oxford University Press, 1951.

Hill, Richard. *On the Frontiers of Islam.* London: Oxford University Press, 1970.

Hillelson, S. *Sudan Arabic: An English-Arabic Vocabulary.* London: Sudan Government, 1930.

Hogendorn, Jan S. "The Economics of Slave Use on Two 'Plantations' in the Zaria Emirate of the Sokoto Caliphate." *International Journal of African Historical Studies* 10:3 (1977), 369–83.

Holt, P. M. "Egypt and the Nile Valley." In *The Cambridge History of Africa, Volume 5, c. 1790–c. 1870,* John E. Flint, ed. Cambridge: Cambridge University Press, 1976.

Holt, P. M. "Holy Families and Islam in the Sudan." In *Studies in the History of the Near East*, P. M. Holt, ed. London: F. Cass, 1973.

Holt, P. M. *A Modern History of the Sudan.* New York: Praeger 1981.

Holt, P. M. *Studies in the History of the Near East.* London: Frank Cass, 1973.

Hopkins, A. G. *An Economic History of West Africa.* London: Longman, 1973.

Horton, Robin. "African Conversion." *Africa* 41:2 (1971), 85–108.

Horton, Robin. "On the Rationality of Conversion, Part I." *Africa* 45:3 (1975), 219–35.

Horton, Robin. "On the Rationality of Conversion, Part II." *Africa* 45:4(1975), 373–99.

Jaulin, Robert. *La mort Sara.* Paris: Plon, 1967.

Johnson, Marion. "Calico Caravans: The Tripoli-Kano Trade after 1880." *Journal of African History* 17:1 (1976), 95–118.

Johnson, Marion. "Cloth Strip Currencies." Paper presented at the joint annual meetings of the African Studies Association and the Latin American Studies Association, Houston, Texas, 1977.

Joly, L. "Essences parfumées du Haut-Oubangui française." *La parfumerie moderne* 21 (1937), 25–33, 191–205.

Jomard, M. "Préface." In Mohammed ibn-Omar El-Tounsy (Muhammad ibn ᶜUmar al-Tunisi), *Voyage au Darfour.* S. Perron, trans. Paris: Duprat, 1845.

Julien, Charles-André. *History of North Africa from the Arab Conquest to 1830.* John Petrie, trans. New York: Praeger, 1970.

Julien, Emile, "Le Dar Ouadai." *Afrique Française: renseignements coloniaux* 14:2 (February 1904), 51–62; 14:3 (March 1904), 87–92; 14:4 (April 1904), 108–10; 14:5 (May 1904), 138–43.

Julien, Emile. "Mohamed-es-Senoussi et ses états." *Bulletin de la société des recherches congolaises* 7 (1925), 104–77; 8 (1927), 55–122; 9 (1928), 49–96; 10 (1929), 45–88.

Julien, Emile. "La situation économique du Dar-el-Kouti." *Afrique Française: renseignements coloniaux* 14:1 (January 1904), 38–40.

Kalck, Pierre. *Central African Republic: A Failure in de-Colonisation.* Barbara Thompson, trans. London: Pall Mall Press, 1971.

Kalck, Pierre. "Histoire de la République Centrafricaine des origines à nos jours." 4 vols. Thèse du doctorat d'ètat, Université de Paris, Sorbonne, 1970.

Kalck, Pierre. *Histoire de la République Centrafricaine des origines préhistoriques à nos jours.* Paris: Berger-Levrault, 1974.

Kalck, Pierre. "Paul Crampel, le centrafricain." *L'Afrique littéraire et artistique* 2 (1968), 60–63.

Kalck, Pierre. *Réalités oubanguiennes.* Paris: Berger-Levrault, 1959.

Kalck, Pierre. "Les savanes centrafricaines." In vol. 2, *Histoire générale de l'Afrique noire*, Hubert Deschamps, ed. Paris: Presses Universitaires de France, 1971.

Kapteijns, Ludwien. "Dar Sila: The Sultanate in Precolonial Times, 1870–1916." *Cahiers d'études africaines*, in press.

Kapteijns, Ludwien. "Mahdist Faith and Sudanic Tradition: History of Dar Masalit, 1870–1930." Doctoral dissertation, Universiteit van Amsterdam, 1982.

Kieffer, Louis Jules Fredéric. "Le Kouti: le massacre de la mission Crampel." *Bulletin de la société de géographie d'Alger et d'Afrique du Nord* (1905), 290–303.

Klein, Norman A. "Inequality in Asante: A Study of the Forms and Meaning of Slavery and Social Servitude in Pre- and Early Akan-Asante Society and Culture." Ph.D. thesis, University of Michigan, 1980.

Kogongar, Gaya J. "Introduction à la vie et à l'histoire pré-coloniale des populations Sara du Tchad." Thèse du doctorat du 3ᵉ cycle, Université de Paris, Sorbonne, 1971.

Kumm, Karl. *From Hausaland to Egypt, through the Sudan.* London: Constable, 1910.

Lamar, Howard, and Leonard Thompson, eds. *The Frontier in History: North America and Southern Africa Compared.* New Haven: Yale University Press, 1981.

Lane, Edward William. *An Arabic-English Lexicon Derived from the Best and Most Copius Eastern Sources.* 8 vols. 1872; New York: Frederick Ungar, 1955.

Lanier, H. "L'ancien royaume du Baguirmi." *Afrique Française: renseignements coloniaux* 35:10 (October 1925), 457–74.

Laroui, Abdallah. *L'histoire du Maghreb: un essai de synthèse.* 2 vols. Paris: Maspero, 1970.

Lebeuf, Annie M. D. "Boum Massenia: capitale de l'ancien royaume de Baguirmi." *Journal de la société des africanistes*, 37 (1967), 214–44.

Lebeuf, Annie M. D. *Les populations du Tchad au nord du dixième parallèle.* Paris: Presses Universitaires de France, 1959.

Lebeuf, Annie M. D. *Les principautés kotoko.* Paris: Presses Universitaires de France, 1969.

LeCornec, Jacques. *Histoire politique du Tchad de 1900 à 1962.* Paris: Librairie générale de droit et de jurisprudence, 1963.

Lethem, G. L. *Colloquial Arabic: Shuwa Dialect of Bornu, Nigeria, and of the Region of Lake Chad.* London: Crown Agents for the Colonies, 1928.

Levtzion, Nehemia, ed. *Conversion to Islam.* New York: Holmes and Meier, 1979.

Levtzion, Nehemia. "Toward a Comparative Study of Islamization." In *Conversion to Islam*, Nehemia Levtzion, ed. New York: Holmes and Meier 1979.

Levtzion, Nehemia, and J. F. P. Hopkins, eds. *Corpus of Arabic Sources for West African History.* Cambridge: Cambridge University Press, 1980.

Lewicki, Tadeusz. *Arabic External Sources for the History of Africa to the South of Sahara.* London: Curzon Press, 1974.

Lewis, I. M., ed. *Islam in Tropical Africa.* London: Oxford University Press for the International African Institute, 1966.

Leynaud, Emile. "Parenté et alliance chez les Banda du district de Bria, région de la Kotto, Dar-el-Kouti." *Bulletin de l'institut d'études centrafricaines (Brazzaville)*, nouvelle série, 7–8 (1954), 109–64.

Lovejoy, Paul E. "The Characteristics of Plantations in the Nineteenth Century Sokoto Caliphate (Islamic West Africa)." *American Historical Review* 84:5 (December 1979), 1267–92.

Lovejoy, Paul E. "Indigenous African Slavery." *Historical Reflections/ Reflexions historiques* 45:2 (1979), 19–83.

Lovejoy, Paul E. "The Plantation Economy of the Sokoto Caliphate." Paper presented at the Ninety-First Annual Conference, American Historical Association, Washington, D.C., 1976.

Lovejoy, Paul E. "Plantations in the Economy of the Sokoto Caliphate." *Journal of African History* 19:3 (1978), 341–68.

Lovejoy, Paul E. "Polanyi's 'Ports of Trade': Salaga and Kano in the Nineteenth Century." *Canadian Journal of African Studies* 16:2 (1982), 245–77.

Mack, John, and Peter Robertshaw, eds. *Culture History in the Southern Sudan: Archaeology, Linguistics and Ethnohistory.* Nairobi: British Institute of Eastern Africa, 1982.

Madina, Maan Z., comp. *Arabic-English Dictionary of the Modern Literary Language.* New York: Pocket Books, 1973.

Maistre, Casimir Léon. "Rapport de la Mission Maistre." *Afrique Française* 3:6 (June 1893), 2–11.

Maistre, Casimir Léon. *A travers l'Afrique centrale du Congo au Niger, 1892–1893.* Paris: Hachette, 1895.

Malval, Jean. *Essai de chronologie tchadienne (1707–1940).* Paris: CNRS, 1974.

Maran, Réné. *Batouala.* Paris: Editions Albin-Michel, 1921. The definitive edition was published in 1938.

Martine, F. "Essai sur l'histoire du pays Salamat et les moeurs et coutumes de ses habitants." *Bulletin de la société des recherches congolaises* 5 (1924), 19–88.

Mauny, Raymond. *Tableau géographique de l'ouest africain au moyen-âge.* Dakar: IFAN, 1961.

McCall, Daniel F., and Norman R. Bennett, eds. *Aspects of West African Islam: Boston University Papers on Africa V.* Boston: Boston University Press, 1971.

Meillassoux, Claude, ed. *The Development of Indigenous Trade and Markets in West Africa.* London: Oxford University Press for the International African Institute, 1971.

Mesple, A. "Mercuri." *Bulletin de la société de géographie d'Alger et d'Afrique du Nord* (4e trimestre, 1902), 634–36.

Michel, Marc. *La mission Marchand, 1895–1899.* Paris: Mouton, 1972.

Miracle, Marvin. *Agriculture in the Congo Basin.* Madison: University of Wisconsin Press, 1967.

Modat. "Une tournée en pays Fertyt." *Afrique Française: renseignements coloniaux* 22:5 (May 1912), 177–98; 22:6 (June 1912), 218–37; 22:7 (July 1912), 270–89.

Mohammadou Eldridge. "Kalfu ou l'Emirat Peul de Baguirmi et les toorobbe Sokkoto." *Afrika Zamani: revue d'histoire africaine/Review of African History* 4 (1975), 67–114.

Mortimore, M. J., and J. Wilson. *Land and People in the Kano Close-Settled Zone.* Zaria: Ahmadu Bello University, Department of Geography, 1965.

Munro, J. Forbes. *Africa and the International Economy, 1800–1960*. Totowa,
    N.J.: Rowman and Littlefield, 1976.
Muraz, Gaston. *Vocabulaire du patois arabe tchadien ou tourkou et des dialectes
    sara-madjingaye et sara-mbaye (S.E. du Tchad) suivi de conversations et d'un
    essai de classification des tribus saras*. Paris and Limoges: Charles Lavauzelle,
    1926.
Murdock, George. *Africa: Its Peoples and Their Culture History*. New York:
    McGraw-Hill, 1959.
Nachtigal, Gustav. *Sahara and Sudan I: Tripoli, the Fezzan and Tibesti*. Allan G.
    B. Fisher and Humphrey J. Fisher, trans. London: C. Hurst, 1974.
Nachtigal, Gustav. *Sahara and Sudan II: Kawar, Bornu, Kanem, Borku,
    Ennedi*. Allan G. B. Fisher and Humphrey J. Fisher, trans. London: C. Hurst,
    1980.
Nachtigal, Gustav. *Sahara and Sudan IV: Wadai and Darfur*. Allan G. B. Fisher
    and Humphrey J. Fisher, trans. London: C. Hurst, 1971. .
Nachtigal, Gustav. *Sahara und Sudan: Ergebnisse Sechsjähriger Reisen in Afrika*.
    3 vols. 1879–89; Graz: Akademische Druck-ü. Verlagsanstalt, 1967.
al-Naqar, ᶜUmar. *The Pilgrimage Tradition in West Africa*. Khartoum: Khartoum
    University Press, 1972.
Nebout, Albert. "La Mission Crampel." *Bulletin de la société normande de
    géographie* 14 (1892), 217–47.
Nebout, Albert. "La Mission Crampel." *Tour de Monde* 64 (1892), 1–65.
Nelson, Harold D., et al. *Area Handbook for Chad*. Washington: U.S. Govern-
    ment Printing Office, 1972.
Niane, D. T. *Sundiata: An Epic of Old Mali*. G. D. Picket, trans. London:
    Longman, Green, 1965.
Njeuma, Martin Z. "Adamawa and Mahdism: The Career of Hayatu ibn Saᶜid
    in Adamawa, 1878–1898." *Journal of African History* 12:1 (1971), 61–77.
Nock, Arthur Darby. *Conversion: The Old and the New in Religion from Alexander
    the Great to Augustine of Hippo*. London and New York: Oxford University
    Press, 1933.
"Une nouvelle version du combat de N'Délé." *Revue indigène* 6:65 (September
    1911), 521–23.
O'Fahey, Rex S. "Fur and Fartit: The History of a Frontier." In *Culture History
    in the Southern Sudan: Archaeology, Linguistics and Ethnohistory*, John
    Mack and Peter Robertshaw, eds. Nairobi: British Institute in Eastern Africa,
    1982.
O'Fahey, Rex S. "Slavery and the Slave Trade in Dar Fur." *Journal of African
    History* 14:1 (1973), 29–43.
O'Fahey, Rex S., and J. L. Spaulding. *Kingdoms of the Sudan*. London: Methuen,
    1974.
Olivier, Pierre (R.P.). "Notes on a conversation with Shéffou, famous Hausa chief
    of Fort-Crampel." Handwritten notes taken shortly before Shéffou's death,
    Crampel (Kaga Bandero), Central African Republic, 1966.
Oppenheim, Max Adrian Simon (freiherr von). *Rabeh und das Tschadseegebiet*.
    Berlin: D. Reimer (E. Vohsen), 1902.

Oppenheim, Max Adrian Simon (freiherr von). "Rapports sur le Ouadai, le Dar el-Kouti, et le Senoussia." *Etudes et documents tchadiens*, série B, N° 1 (1968). Fort-Lamy (N'Djaména): Institut tchadien des sciences humaines, 1968.

Paden, John. *Religion and Political Culture in Kano*. Berkeley: University of California Press, 1973.

Pallme, Ignatius. *Travels in Kordofan*. London: J. Madden, 1844.

Pannenberg, Wolfhart. *Basic Questions in Theology*. Vol. 2. London: S.C.M. Press, 1971.

Pâques, Viviana. "Origine et caractères du pouvoir royale au Baguirmi." *Journal de la société des africanistes* 37:2 (1967), 183–216.Petherick, John. *Egypt, the Soudan, and Central Africa*. London: W. Blackwood and Sons, 1861.

Poncet, J. "Le mythe de la 'catastrophe' hilalienne." *Annales: Economie, Société, et Civilisation* 22:5 (1967), 1099–1120.

Prins, Pierre. "Esclavage et liberté dans les sultanats du Haut-Oubangui." *Revue indigène* 12 (April 1907), 126–36.

Prins, Pierre. "L'Islam et les musulmans dans les sultanats du Haut- Oubangui." *Afrique Française: reseignements coloniaux* 17:6 (June 1907), 136–42; 17:7 (July 1907), 163–73.

Prins, Pierre. "Les troglodytes du Dar Banda et du Djebel Méla." *Bulletin de géographie historique et descriptive* (1909), 11–26.

Prins, Pierre. "Voyage au Dar Rounga: résultats scientifiques." *La Géographie* 1:3 (1900), 193–96.

Prioul, Christian. *Entre Oubangui et Chari vers 1890*. Paris: Laboratoire d'ethnologie et de sociologie comparative, Université de Paris X (Nanterre), 1981.

Prioul, Christian. "Notes sur la diffusion du manioc dans la partie centrale du territoire centrafricaine." Bangui: L'Ecole Nationale d'Administration, mimeographed, n.d.

Prioul, Christian. "Le Velad-el-Kouti et le seuil Oubangui-Chari, 1830–1892." Bangui: L'Ecole Nationale d'Administration, mimeographed, n.d.

Quiggin, Alison Hingston. *A Survey of Primitive Money: The Beginning of Currency*. London: Methuen, 1963.

Ramm, François. "Le peuplement des savanes de l'Afrique centrale: essai historique." Transcript of a lecture delivered at the Centre Protestant pour la Jeunesse, and distributed in the *Cahiers du Centre Protestant pour la Jeunesse*. Bangui: Centre Protestant pour la Jeunesse, mimeographed, 13 December 1972.

Reyna, Steven Perry. "The Costs of Marriage: A Study of Some Factors Affecting Northwest Barma Fertility." Ph.D. dissertation, Columbia University, 1972.

Richardson, James. *Narrative of a Mission to Central Africa, Performed in the Years 1850 and 1851*. 2 vols. London: Chapman and Hall, 1853.

Robertson, Claire C., and Martin A. Klein, eds. *Women and Slavery in Africa*. Madison: The University of Wisconsin Press, 1983.

Robinson, Ronald, and John Gallagher with Alice Denny. *Africa and the Victorians: The Climax of Imperialism in the Dark Continent*. New York: St. Martin's Press, 1961.

Roth-Laly, Arlette, comp. *Lexique des parlers arabes tchado-soudanais/An Arabic-English-French Lexicon of the Dialects Spoken in the Chad-Sudan Area*. 4 vols. Paris: CNRS, 1969, 1971, 1972.

Rouget, Fernand. *L'expansion coloniale au Congo-franç*ais. Paris: Emile Larose, 1906.

Un saharien. "La question du Ouadai." *Afrique Franç*aise 18:8 (August 1908), 282–87.

Santandrea, Stefano. *Ethno-Geography of the Bahr el Ghazal (Sudan)*. Bologna: Editrice Missionaria Italiana, 1981.

Santandrea, Stefano. *Languages of the Banda and Zande Groups: A Contribution to a Comparative Study*. Naples: Instituto Universitario Orientale, 1965.

Santandrea, Stefano. "Sanusi, Ruler of Dar Banda and Dar Kuti in the History of the Bahr al-Ghazal." *Sudan Notes and Records* 38 (1957), 151–55.

Santandrea, Stefano. *A Tribal History of the Western Bahr el-Ghazal*. Bologna: Centro librario dei Missionari Comboniani, 1964.

Santerre, Renaud. *Pédagogie musulmane d'Afrique noire*. Montréal: Les Presses de l'Université de Montréal, 1973.

Saxon, Douglas E. "Linguistic Evidence for the Eastward Spread of Ubangian Peoples." In *The Archaeological and Linguistic Reconstruction of African History*, Christopher Ehret and Merrick Posnansky, eds. Berkeley and Los Angeles: University of California Press, 1982.

Schweinfurth, Georg. *The Heart of Africa: Three Years' Travels and Adventures in the Unexplored Regions of Central Africa, 1868–1871*. 2 vols. Ellen Frewer, trans. New York: Harper and Brothers, 1874.

Seetzen, M. U. J. "Nouveaux renseignements sur l'intérieur de l'Afrique." *Annales des voyages, de la géographie, et de l'histoire* 21 (1813), 145–79.

Seetzen, M. U. J. "Nouvelles recherches sur l'intérieur de l'Afrique," *Annales des voyages, de la géographie, et de l'histoire* 19 (1812), 164–84.

"Es-Senoussi." *Afrique Française* 21:3 (March 1911), 94.

Serre, Jacques. "Histoire économique et sociale du district de Grimari (1907–1958)." 2 vols. Bangui: L'Ecole Nationale d'Administration, Salle de documentation, document no. 82, mimeographed, 1960.

Shaw, W. B. K. "Darb al-Arba^c in: The Forty Days' Road." *Sudan Notes and Records* 12:1 (1929), 63–71.

Shuqayr, Na^{c}um. *Tarikh al-Sudan wa Jughrafiya*. Beirut: Dar al-Thaqafiya, 1967.

Sillans, Roger. *Les savanes de l'Afrique centrale*. Paris: Le Chevalier, 1958.

Smaldone, Joseph. "The Firearms Trade in the Central Sudan in the Nineteenth Century." In *Aspects of West African Islam: Boston University Papers on Africa V*, Daniel F. McCall and Norman R. Bennett, eds. Boston: Boston University Press, 1971.

Smaldone, Joseph. *Warfare in the Sokoto Caliphate: Historical and Sociological Perspectives*. Cambridge: Cambridge University Press, 1977.

Smith, Robert S. *Warfare and Diplomacy in Pre-Colonial West Africa*. London: Methuen, 1976.

Stemler, A. B. L., J. R. Harlan, and J. M. J. deWet. "Caudatum Sorghums and Speakers of Chari-Nile Languages in Africa." *Journal of African History* 16:2 (1975), 161–83.

Stevenson, R. C. "Some Aspects of the Spread of Islam in the Nuba Mountains (Kordofan Province, Republic of the Sudan)." In *Islam in Tropical Africa*, I. M. Lewis, ed. London: Oxford University Press for the International African Institute, 1966.

Suret-Canale, Jean. *Afrique noire occidentale et centrale II: l'ère coloniale (1900–1945)*. Paris: Editions sociales, 1964.

Taber, Charles R. *A Dictionary of Sango*. Hartford: Hartford Seminary Foundation, 1965.

Tambo, David Carl. "The Sokoto Caliphate Slave Trade in the Nineteenth Century." *International Journal of African Historical Studies* 9:2 (1976), 187–217.

Tannahill, Reay. *Food in History*. New York: Stein and Day, 1973.

Terray, Emmanuel. "Classes and Class Consciousness in the Abron Kingdom of Gyaman." In *Marxist Analyses and Social Anthropology*, Marc Bloch, ed. London: Malaby Press, 1975.

Terray, Emmanuel. "Long-Distance Exchange and the Formation of the State: The Case of the Abron Kingdom of Gyaman." *Economy and Society* 3 (1974), 315–45.

Terrier, Auguste. "Snoussi d'El-Kouti." *Afrique Française* 13:12 (December 1903), 393–98.

Theobald, Alan Buchan. *ᶜAli Dinar, Last Sultan of Darfur*, 1898–1916. London: Longman, 1965.

Thompson, Leonard, and Howard Lamar. "Comparative Frontier History." In *The Frontier in History: North America and Southern Africa Compared*, Howard Lamar and Leonard Thompson, eds. New Haven: Yale University Press, 1981.

Tisserant, Charles. "L'Agriculture dans les savanes de l'Oubangui." *Bulletin de l'institut des études centrafricaines (Brazzaville)*, nouvelle série, N° 6 (1953), 209–74.

Tisserant, Charles. *Ce que j'ai connu de l'esclavage en Oubangui-Chari*. Paris: Plon, 1955.

Tisserant, Charles. *Dictionnaire Banda-Français*. Paris: Institut d'ethnologie, 1931.

Tisserant, Charles. *Essai sur la grammaire Banda*. Paris: Institut d'ethnologie, 1930.

Tisserant, Charles. "Le mariage dans l'Oubangui-Chari." *Bulletin de l'institut des études centrafricaines (Brazzaville)*, nouvelle série, N° 2 (1951), 73–102.

Toque, Georges. *Essai sur le peuple et la langue Banda*. Paris: André, 1904.

Trimingham, John Spencer. *Islam in the Sudan*. London: Oxford University Press, 1949.

Trimingham, John Spencer. *Islam in West Africa*. London: Oxford University Press, 1959.

El-Tounsy, Mohammed ibn-Omar (Muhammad ibn ᶜUmar al-Tunisi). *Voyage au Darfour*. S. Perron, trans. Paris: Duprat, 1845.

El-Tounsy, Mohammed ibn-Omar (Muhammad ibn ᶜUmar al-Tunisi). *Voyage au Ouaday*. S. Perron, trans. Paris: Duprat, 1851.

Tubiana, Marie-José. "Un document inédit sur les sultans du Wadday." *Cahiers d'études africaines* 2 (1960), 49–112.

Tubiana, Marie-José. *Survivances préislamiques en pays Zaghawa*. Paris: Institut d'ethnologie, 1964.

Tucker, A. N. *The Eastern Sudanic Languages*. London: Oxford University Press for the International African Institute, 1940.

Vergiat, A. M. *Moeurs et coutumes des Mandja*. Paris: Payot, 1937.

von Grunebaum, Gustav. "The Problem: Unity in Diversity." In *Unity and Variety in Muslim Civilization*. Gustav von Grunebaum, ed. Chicago: University of Chicago Press, 1955.

Wallerstein, Immanuel. *The Modern World-System I: Capitalist Agriculture and the Origins of the European World Economy in the Sixteenth Century*. New York: Academic Press, 1974.

Walz, Terence. *Trade between Egypt and Bilad as-Sudan, 1700–1820*. Paris and Cairo: Institut français d'archéologie orientale du Caire, 1978.

Wehr, Hans. *A Dictionary of Modern Written Arabic*. J. Milton Cowen, ed. Ithaca: Cornell University Press, 1966.

West, Richard. *Congo*. New York: Holt, Rinehart, and Winston, 1972.

Wilson, C. T., and R. W. Felkin. *Uganda and the Egyptian Sudan*. 2 vols. London: Sampson Low, 1882.

Wingate, Francis Reginald. *Mahdism and the Egyptian Sudan*. London: Macmillan, 1891.

Works, John A., Jr. *Pilgrims in a Strange Land: Hausa Communities in Chad*. New York: Columbia University Press, 1976.

El-Zubeir Pasha. *Black Ivory, or the Story of El-Zubeir Pasha, Slaver and Sultan, as Told by Himself*. H. C. Jackson, trans. New York: Negro Universities Press, 1970.

INDEX

^cAbd al-Mintalib, Kobur's son, 166

Abdo, al-Hajj, advisor to al-Sanusi: biographical sketch, 63–64; house in Ndele, 91; as pilgrim, 101; one of few Hausa advisors, 142

Abeche: arrival of slaves in, 22; population of, 85; Dar al-Kuti students in, 98; taxes paid in cloth, 181

AbuBakr, al-Sanusi's father, 60

AbuGhern, Islamic center, 41

Adam, al-Sanusi's son: slave-raiding of, 72; assassination, 74, 96; house in Ndele, 87, 89; as military leader, 112; personal plantations of, 127–28

Advisors, Muslim: to al-Sanusi, 62–64

Agriculture: overview, 10; among Runga, 36; around Ndele, 83, 103; labor force in Ndele, 110; production in Dar al-Kuti, 122–35; in Banda lands near Ndele, 125; among Banda, 128; in secondary centers, 129–30; following French conquest, 131; articulated with trade, 137; fadama or marshland, in Ndele, 142, 234*n28*

Akrousoulba, Runga village: fishing and fish trade in, 38, 126

^cAli, sultan of Wadai: identified, 21; wars with Bagirmi, 40

Allah Jabu, leader of al-Sanusi's forces: and Wadaian attack at Kali-Sha, 65; at Ouanda-Djale, 74–75; house in Ndele, 87; as military leader, 112–13

Ammunition: contraband in, 139

Amulets: Islamic in Ndele, 99. *See* Charms, Islamic; Islam

Ancestor spirits: among Runga, 36. *See* Religions, classical African

Aouk River: flood plain, 31; source of, 32; source of fish for Ndele, 127; jamsinda production along, 152

Aphrodisiacs: Muslim imports of, 151

^caqid, governor of Dar al-Kuti, 44

^caqid, governor of Salamat, 21–22

^caqid, Runga sultan: marriage alliance with al-Sanusi, 60

Ara, Banda Ngao chief, 67

Ara, settlement: visited by Pierre Prins, 69; al-Sanusi's sojourn in, 80

Arabic: use of in Ndele, 96; spread of names, 162; survey of sources on Africa in, 189*n17*

Arabic, Chadic, 3, 173

Arabs, Rizayqat: relations with Dar Fur, 18; with al-Zubayr, 28. *See* al-Zubayr

Archives: survey of in Ndjaména and Bangui, 195*n71*

Armaments *See* Firearms

Army, Dar al-Kuti. *See* Military; Slave-raiding

Assassination: of al-Sanusi, 75. *See* al-Sanusi; Adam

Azande: and "Gnum Gnum," 16; raids by Rabih among, 28

Azande states: trade with north, 68; slave-raiding bands from, 111

al-Azhar, university: and students from Dar al-Kuti, 98

Baadjia: source of slaves, 16

Bagirmi: location of, 11; sphere of influence in south, 15; Wadaian invasion, 20; historical research on, 39; emigrants and emigration, 39–40; crafts center, 40; low birthrate, 40; eunuch exports, 40, 119; Islamic center, 40–44, 165; Sara clients of, 41; royal exiles from, 45; origin of name Jugultum, 45–46; mythical founders of, 46; Rabih's conquest, 59–60; and pilgrimage, 99; selection of slaves in, 116; use of letters of introduction in, 137; French campaigns in, 141; marriage with non-Muslims in Dar Fur, 185; captives taken to Wadai, 192*n46*; term Barma, 200*n35*; and Shari River, 200*n35*. *See* Bagirmi, in

269

Index

history of, 17; and Mahdiya, 19; and al-Zubayr, 19; and Turko-Egyptian regime, 19, 56; relations with Wadai, 20; dependence on trans-Saharan network, 30, 143; and copper from Hufrat al-Nuhas, 38; Bagirmi villages in, 40; bazingers from, 46; Dar al-Kuti students in, 98; horses in, 104; letters of introduction in, 137; cloth strips in, 146–47, 236n44; ivory trade in, 151; and integration of North Central Africa into international economy, 158; concept of stateless societies applied to, 189n8; early expeditions to far south, 190n21, 190–91n26
Dar Goula, 16. *See* Goula
Dar Jenakherah, 15
Dar Kulla. *See* Dar Goula
Dar Massalit: location of, 11; studies of, 188n6
Dar Runga: relations with Wadai, 2, 20, 21, 44; location of, 11; slave-raiding in, 15, 53, 60; Muslim perceptions of, 16; links with Dar al-Kuti, 31; as Runga homeland, 35; and Runga in south, 36, 38, 136; political history of, 37; historical research on, 39; depopulation of, 58; al-Sanusi's relations with, 60, 65; ironworking in, 91; eunuch "production" in, 119; letters of introduction in, 137; cloth in, 144, 146–47; ivory trade in, 151; jamsinda in, 152; studies of, 188n6; fish trade in, 199–200n31. *See* Runga
Dar Sila: location of, 11; slave-raiding in, 15; Wadaian invasion of, 20; bonds by marriage with al-Sanusi, 64; emigrants in Ndele, 93; slave-raiding bands from, 111; use of letters of introduction in, 137; cloth strip exports from, 146–47; studies of, 188n6; cattle exports from, 235n36. *See* Dajo
Dar Tama: location of, 11; Wadaian invasion of, 20; language of, 35
Death rates: effect on estimating Ndele population, 121
Dem Genawi: settlement similar to Ndele, 2
Dem Idris: settlement similar to Ndele, 2
Demography: Bagirmi population threatened by Islamic reform, 42; impact of

Rabih's campaigns on Dar Runga, 58; impact of slave trade, 160. *See* Depopulation; Ndele, demography; Population
Depopulation: and Muslim/non-Muslim contact, 16; and slave-raiding, 30, 111, 160; and Islamic revivalism, 42, 43; of Dar Runga, 58, 65; around Ndele, 83; between Ndele and Kafiakingi, 122. *See* Demography; Ndele, demography; Population
Dem Zubayr: settlement similar to Ndele, 2; importance of, 67
Diaspora trading communities: characteristics of, 139–40
Djougoultoum. *See* Jugultum, ᶜUmar
Djougueldou. *See* Jugeldu
Domestic group: as labor force, 123. *See* Kinship
Dorot: uses of in Sahel, 152–53
Drought: and Bagirmi emigration, 38, 43; rare in Dar al-Kuti, 131; and Wadaian emigration, 202n55
Dybowski, Jean, French expedition of: in Dar al-Kuti, 69

Earth chiefs: alliances with Muslim traders, 13; among Nduka, 13, 33, 35, 126; relations with al-Sanusi, 82, 129, 150–51; possessed slaves, 127; ivory offered to, 150–51
Eastern Sudanic languages: and Runga, 36
Ecological gradient: implications of, along Ubangi, 10; as basis for regional trade, 38
Economy, international: Islamic world as periphery of, 1, 10; integration of North Central Africa, 1, 94, 143, 158, 159. *See* Trade
Education: Islamic, in Ndele, 98
Egypt: use of slave soldiers, 17; and slave trade, 28; conquests of, 57; impact of modernization of, in Central Africa, 57, 159, 191n29; as example of secondary empire, 61; influence in Sudan, 158
Elephant hunting: in Dar al-Kuti, 37; by Banda, 238–39n66
Emigration: from Bagirmi, 38, 40, 43. *See* Bagirmi; Migrants; Migration
Epidemics: smallpox, in Ndele, 226n60
Ethnicity: role in military organization, 57,

47; on founding of Ndele, 80–81; express
nostalgia for al-Sanusi, 139; on Wadaian
conquests, 191–92n37; and chronology,
203n60; on Jagara, 211n47
Ottoman Porte, 234–35n33
Ouadda: Mahammadi governs, 89; secondary settlement, 112, 129, 159; "production" of eunuchs in, 119; sends tribute
to al-Sanusi, 129; clandestine trade from,
138; kombo purchases in, 153
Ouaka River, 72
Ouaham River, 17
Ouanda-Djale: copper in, 38; possible refuge
for al-Sanusi, 74; site of resistance to
French, 75; Kamun's flight to, 90; independent trading from, 138; kombo
purchases in, 153. See Yulu
Ouih, Banda Toulu village: agricultural
production in, 124

Pepper, Ethiopian. See Kombo
Pilgrimage: and Islamization, 42; routes, 42,
80; opportunity to learn about world, 63;
duration of, 100; in Ndele, 142, 220n77;
impact along Islamic frontier, 162; and
Islamization in Bagirmi, 165.
See Pilgrims
Pilgrims: from Chad in Cairo, 15; Hausa in
Wadai, 22; numbers, 43; earliest ᶜaqid of
Dar al-Kuti, 44; marriage alliances with
rulers, 45; knowledge of outer world, 64,
101; in Ndele, 85, 93, 98–101, 142,
221n83; dress of, 221n82. See Pilgrimage
Plantations: around Ndele, 83; of Adam, 92,
127–28; of al-Sanusi, 92, 127–28; in East
Africa, 123; in the Americas, 123; failure
of system around Ndele, 123–24; group
labor on, 128; slave labor used on, in
Ndele, 159. See Agriculture; Labor;
Slaves
Planting rituals: among Nduka, 35; syncretic
nature of, in Ndele, 128
Plants: odiferous, exported from Dar
al-Kuti, 136, 151–54, 239n70;
in Ndele, 141–42
Population: redistribution in Dar al-Kuti, 3;
role of violence, 10, 13, 26, 161; resettlement in Ndele, 50–51, 82, 92; of Mbele,
66, 210–11n45; of Muslims in Dar
al-Kuti, 67; in Ndele, 89, 122, 131;

density in Ubangi-Shari and Mobaye,
194n65. See Demography; Depopulation;
Ndele, demography
Porters: supplied to French, 71, 157
Potatoes, sweet, 134
Potsherds: indicate population density, 89,
91; among Ndele ruins, 187n4
Pottery: produced by Nduka, Sara, Runga,
37
Prins, Pierre, French explorer: meets
al-Sanusi, 69
Production: agricultural, 122–35, 158;
cloth, 145–46; domestic, and long-
distance trade, 159

Qadiriya, Islamic brotherhood: in Dar
al-Kuti, 98
Qatrun, 142
Qur'an, 97–99. See Islam

Rabih b. Fadlallah: identified, 21; slave-
raiding of, 28, 29, 48, 53, 59; leaves
Sudan, 29, 53, 56, 57; resettlement of
slaves, 40; in Dar Runga, 46, 53, 58–59;
conflict with Wadai, 53, 58–59; army of
53, 57, 58, 158; among Sara, 53, 58, 59,
65; and Mahdiya, 56, 60; military career
of, 57; firearms of, 57, 59; slave recruitment of, 57, 58, 123; and French 58, 68;
strategies of, 59; conquers Bagirmi, 59,
65; conquers Borno, 60, 141; impact on
pilgrimage, 99; and Islamization, 162;
itineraries of, 206n3. See Rabih b.
Fadlallah, in Dar al-Kuti
Rabih b. Fadlallah, in Dar al-Kuti: relations
with al-Sanusi, 29, 60, 61, 65; raids, 46,
48, 59; and Kobur, 47, 59, 61; perceptions
of, 53, 56; departure, 58, 60, 61, 65; and
Mission Crampel, 61, 65; growth of army
in, 112, 114–15; chronology of, 208n27.
See Rabih b. Fadlallah
Rafai: similar to Ndele, 3; trade with Wadai,
22; Belgian arrival in, 64; traders from
Mbele in, 66; relations with Saᶜid Baldas,
68. See Mbomu states
"Regroupement": during colonial and
independence eras, 227n75. See
Resettlement
Relations of production: in Dar al-Kuti,
159, 161

124; reconstituted at Sokoumba, 205–6n79

Shala: as source of slaves, 16; as Binga homeland, 23

Shallots: introduced in Dar al-Kuti, 130

Shari River: sources, 9, 32; and Sara migrations, 25; links Bagirmi and Kuti, 38; importance to Bagirmi, 200n35

al-Sharif, Muhammad, Wadai sultan: southern campaigns of, 20

Sharif al-Din, Faqih, 42–43

Shendi: slave categories in, 121

Slave-gun cycle: in Dar al-Kuti, 103

Slave-raiding: and Dar al-Kuti economy, 2, 73, 157; centers, 3; kagas offer refuge from, 9; non-Muslim participation in, 13, 57; frontier of, 15; overview of, 15, 17, 26, 31, 37, 46, 52, 56; results in non-Muslim migration, 23, 33, 82–83, 111, 122; from Wadai and Dar Fur, 26, 33, 66, 67, 204n69, 222n7; among Banda, 26, 40, 74; by al-Sanusi, 29, 40, 50, 53, 65, 73, 103–11, 126, 157; by Rabih, 40, 53; and Nduka, 50, 66, 126; and Islamization, 53, 99, 162; among Runga, 58, 66; French attempts to limit, 70, 71, 72; by Adam, 72; in Ouaka and Kotto Rivers region, 72; as way of mobilizing labor, 79; and resettlement of captives, 82–83, 122; causes depopulation, 83, 111; organization and tactics of, 94, 104, 109; resistance to, 109; in Gribingui River area, 111; mortality rates during, 109–10, 121; encourages manioc diffusion, 132; described by al-Tunisi, 199n29; kidnapping, 225n46. See Captives; Slavery, Muslim; Slaves; Slave trade

Slavery, Muslim, 123. See Captives, Slaveraiding; Slaves; Slave trade

Slaves: exchanged for northern imports, 2, 10; sources of, 16; as soldiers and raiders, 17, 18, 57; numbers arriving in Wadai, 22; from Salamat, 22, 48; demand for, 29–30; acquiescence of, 30, 125; integration into harems, 57; and al-Sanusi, 73, 74, 85, 115–22, 215n19; resettled, 85, 92, 110, 115–22; evacuation from Ndele, 90; provided to faqihs, 98; selection of, 110, 115, 116; punishment of, 116; prices of, 117–21, 145, 147; preference for women,

117, 118, 121, 225n48; categories of, 117–21; export totals from Ndele, 121–22; as labor force, 122, 124, 125, 157; escape, 125; among Nduka, 127; in Runga villages, 127; exchanged for cattle, 157; as both producers and commodities, 159–60; exchanged for cloth, 179; Banda slave biography, 224–25n46; and ivory transport, 238n61. See Captives; Slaveraiding; Slavery, Muslim; Slave trade

Slave trade: in Dar al-Kuti economy, 2, 136, 157; in Nile basin, 11, 18, 28; in Kobur's time, 47–48; expansion of, in Dar al-Kuti, 52; from Mbele, 67; and French in Ndele, 73, 94; volume in Ndele, 121–22; al-Sanusi as agent for Banda, 138; limited among Hausa and Bornoans, 141; demographic impact of, 160; danger of sale into trans-Saharan, 215n19. See Captives; Slave-raiding; Slavery, Muslim; Slaves

Sleeping sickness: among horses in Ndele, 104. See Tse-tse flies

Smallpox: among raiders and slaves, 110; in Ndele, 226n60

Société "La Kotto": factory in Ndele, 89; al-Sanusi's monopoly, 129–30

Sokoto Caliphate: sultan cAliya of, 22; and Usuman dan Fodio, 41; and Bagirmi jihad, 43. See Bello, Muhammad; dan Fodio, Usuman

Sorghum: on al-Sanusi's plantations, 127–28; uses and features of, 130–34; imprecise terminology for, 229–30n113. See Millet

Spheres of exchange: in Dar al-Kuti, 144, 147

Stateless societies: in North Central Africa, 10; concept applied to Fur, 189n8

States: in North Central Africa, 10, 12

Sudan: Egyptian conquest of, 56; refuge in, 90; al-Sanusi's raiding reaches, 104; slave-raiding from, 111; provides military expertise, 113; exports cloth, 146–47; imports odorific plants, 151; truck traffic to, 233n21

Sugar: imports in Ndele, 155–56

Sultan: term indicates new era, 32; compared with faqih, 47

Sultanates, 11, 188n6